REGIONAL INTEGRATION IN LATIN AMERICA AND THE CARIBBEAN: THE POLITICAL ECONOMY OF OPEN REGIONALISM

Regional Integration in Latin America and the Caribbean: The Political Economy of Open Regionalism

Edited by
Victor Bulmer-Thomas

Institute of Latin American Studies
31 Tavistock Square, London WC1H 9HA
http://www.sas.ac.uk/ilas/publicat.htm

This book has been produced with the financial assistance of the European Community. The views expressed herein are those of the authors and can therefore in no way be taken to reflect the official opinion of the European Community.

Institute of Latin American Studies
School of Advanced Study
University of London

British Library Cataloguing-in-Publication Data

A catalogue record for this book is available
from the British Library
ISBN 1 900039 42 7

Contents

Notes on Contributors

Ann Bartholomew is a Research Fellow, Centre for Brazilian Studies, University of Oxford and Lecturer in Economics, ILAS. Her research interests include trade liberalisation and regional integration in Latin America, particularly MERCOSUR and the effects on trade and foreign investment flows of trade integration between Argentina and Brazil.

Earl Boodoo was previously Graduate Research Assistant at the University of the West Indies, St Augustine Campus, Trinidad & Tobago. He is now a doctoral student in the School of Economics, University of Nottingham, and is engaged in research on trade policy, poverty and applied general equilibrium modelling.

Roberto Bouzas is an Argentine economist with degrees from the University of Buenos Aires and Cambridge University. He is a Senior Research Fellow at the Latin American School of Social Sciences and an Independent Research Fellow at the National Council for Scientific and Technical Research. Roberto Bouzas teaches at the Universidad de Buenos Aires, Universidad Torcuato Di Tella and Universidad de San Andrés. His latest book (co-authored with José María Fanelli) is *MERCOSUR. Integración y Crecimiento* (Buenos Aires, 2001).

Victor Bulmer-Thomas is Director of the Royal Institute of International Affairs and Honorary Research Fellow at the Institute of Latin American Studies (ILAS), University of London. From 1992 to 1998 he was Director and from 1998 to 2001 Senior Research Fellow of ILAS. His research interests include income distribution and poverty, the economic history of Latin America and the long-run development of the wider Caribbean.

Philip Colthrust is an economist in the Quantitative Methods Section, Research Department, Central Bank of Trinidad & Tobago. His responsibilities include providing policy support to the Central Bank in the areas of Monetary Union in CARICOM; the CARICOM Single Market and Economy; International Competitiveness; and E-commerce. He currently serves as one of the representatives of the Central Bank of Trinidad & Tobago on the Technical Team attached to the Council of CARICOM Central Bank Governors. This team is in the process of re-assessing Monetary Union in CARICOM.

vii

Robert Devlin has been an economist at the Inter-American Development Bank in Washington, DC, since 1994 and is currently Deputy Manager of the Integration and Regional Programs Department. He had previously worked with the United Nations Economic Commission for Latin America and the Caribbean, in Santiago de Chile. He has published widely in the area of international economics and economic development. He is on the Advisory Board of the North American Economics and Finance Association (NAEFA) and the Latin American Trade Network (LATN).

Antoni Estevadeordal is a Senior Trade Economist with the Integration, Trade and Hemispheric Issues Division within the Integration and Regional Programs Department of the Inter-American Development Bank. Prior to joining the IDB, Dr Estevadeordal taught at Harvard University and the University of Barcelona. His fields of expertise include trade, investment, regional economic integration and comparative economic history. He has published widely in major journals and contributed as author or editor in several books.

Valpy FitzGerald is Reader in International Economics and Finance at Oxford University and a Professorial Fellow at St Antony's College, Oxford. His current research concerns access of developing counties to global markets and he is working with the British Government, UNCTAD and the Ford Foundation on projects in this field.

Andrew Hurrell is University Lecturer in International Relations at Oxford University and Fellow of Nuffield College. His major interests include international relations theory with particular reference to international law and institutions and the international relations of Latin America, with particular reference to Brazil. Recent publications include: (co-editor with Louise Fawcett), *Regionalism in World Politics* (Oxford, 1995), (co-editor with Ngaire Woods), *Inequality, Globalization and World Politics* (Oxford, 1999); and *Hedley Bull on International Society* (Basingstoke, 2000).

Helen McBain is Economic Affairs Officer at UN ECLAC in Port-Of-Spain, Trinidad. Prior to that she was Research Fellow and Deputy Director — Issues in Caribbean International Economic Relations Project — at the Institute of Social and Economic Research of the University of the West Indies in Jamaica. She also taught international economics and public policy at the Consortium Graduate School of Social Sciences of the University. Her research and writings are in the areas of economic development and international trade and financial issues.

Shelton Nicholls is Lecturer in the Department of Economics, University of the West Indies, St. Augustine Campus and Visiting Commonwealth Research Fellow at the School of Economics, University of Nottingham (2000–2001). He has also held research fellowships/associateships with the Institute of Latin American Studies (ILAS), University of London and the Caribbean Centre for Monetary Studies (CCMS), University of the West Indies, St Augustine Campus. His current research interests centre on economic integration and trading blocs in Latin America and the Caribbean; emerging financial markets in the Caribbean; trade in services; and the WTO.

Sheila Page is Research Fellow at the Overseas Development Institute, London, having previously worked at Queen Elizabeth House, Oxford, and the National Institute of Economic and Social Research. Her publications include *Regions and Developing Countries* (Basingstoke, 2000), *How Developing Countries Trade* (London, 1994) and *Monetary Policy in Developing Countries* (London, 1993). Current research interests focus on regional groups among developing countries and between developing and developed countries, tourism in developing countries and how and why developing countries participate in international negotiations.

Pablo Rodas-Martini is the Director of Central America in the World Economy of the twenty-first century project financed by IDRC. He also works as external consultant of ASIES. He writes twice a week for *El Periódico* in Guatemala on economic and political issues. He has published academic papers on macroeconomics and fiscal policy, as well as on trade and globalisation, and income distribution and human development.

Riordan Roett is the Sarita and Don Johnston Professor of Political Science and Director of the Western Hemisphere Program at the Johns Hopkins Paul H. Nitze School of Advanced International Studies (SAIS) in Washington, DC. From 1983 to 1995, he served as a consultant to the Chase Manhattan Bank in various capacities; in 1994–1995 he was the Senior Political Analyst in the Emerging Markets division of the bank's International Capital Markets group. From 1989 to 1997, he served as a Faculty Fellow of the World Economic Forum at the annual meeting in Davos, Switzerland.

Garnett Samuel is an economist in the Trade and International Developments section, Research Department, Central Bank of Trinidad & Tobago. He has provided technical support to the Central Bank on issues related to negotiations in the World Trade Organisation,

CARICOM Single Market and Economy and the Free Trade Area of the Americas. Most recently, he has served in an advisory capacity to the chairman of the Negotiating Group on Investment under the Free Trade Area of the Americas (FTAA).

Ben Ross Schneider teaches politics at Northwestern University. He is the author of 'Why is Mexican Business so Organized?' forthcoming in the *Latin American Research Review*, and co-editor of *Reinventing Leviathan: The Politics of Administrative Reform in Developing Countries*, forthcoming with the North-South Press. His previous books include *Business and the State in Developing Countries* (Ithaca, 1997) and *Politics within the State: Elite Bureaucrats and Industrial Policy in Authoritarian Brazil* (Pittsburgh, 1991).

Hernán Soltz is Assistant Professor of International Economics at the University of Buenos Aires and is Associate Research Fellow at the Latin American School of Social Sciences/Sede Argentina and a grantee of the National Council for Scientific and Technical Research (CONICET).

List of Tables

List of Figures

Introduction

Victor Bulmer-Thomas

Regional integration has a long history in Latin America and the Caribbean — as in Europe. Unlike the European Union (EU), however, there is no seamless web leading from the first steps towards regionalism in the late 1950s to the latest developments. On the contrary, regionalism in Latin America and the Caribbean (LAC) can be divided into two very different phases with a structural break in the middle.

The first phase, now known as 'old' regionalism, can best be understood as an attempt to carry out import-substituting industrialisation (ISI) at the regional level. That is why intra-regional trade liberalisation under the first schemes was limited to the manufacturing sector and tariffs on trade with third countries remained very high. Regionalism was seen primarily as a way of reviving the dynamism of the industrial sector in countries where domestic output was limited by the size of the national market and as a means to promote modern manufacturing in countries where economies of scale were impossible at the national level.

Old regionalism was not without its successes, but domestic firms remained high cost and incapable in most cases of exporting to the rest of the world. When the debt crisis struck the region at the beginning of the 1980s, all countries were faced with the need to generate trade surpluses quickly in order to service their debts. Imports — both extra- and intra-regional — were cut and regional integration schemes suffered accordingly. By the middle of the 1980s there were few voices raised in favour of regionalism and the major international financial institutions (IFIs) were strongly opposed.

The revival of regionalism after the debt crisis was at first greeted with scepticism. 'New' regionalism, however, is not designed to promote ISI nor does it require high tariffs on trade with the rest of the world. It is not limited to the manufacturing sector nor does it discriminate against extra-regional exports. Instead, new regionalism includes in its agenda a whole range of novel issues designed to prepare LAC countries for the challenge of globalisation and to encourage integration of the LAC economies into the world system of trade and payments.

Almost a decade ago, the Economic Commission for Latin America and the Caribbean (ECLAC) coined the phrase 'open regionalism' to describe the process under which LAC countries were pursuing regionalism while at the same time dismantling the barriers on trade with third countries and opening their markets to foreign investment.[1] Whether we describe regionalism as 'new' or 'open', there is clearly a sense in which it is different from old regionalism (see Chapter 1).

There is now a broad consensus among LAC countries that regional integration can help them adjust to the new world order, but there is much less agreement on how to achieve it and what reforms are needed to bring it about. Part of the problem is a confusion over the nature of globalisation as well as legitimate concerns over the relationship between regionalism on the one hand and the multilateral system on the other.

Globalisation has eight key dimensions, one of which is not new and two of which have barely begun. The 'traditional' dimension is trade liberalisation in goods, which began with the creation of the General Agreement on Tariffs and Trade (GATT) in 1947 and has been vigorously pursued through a series of trade rounds. The last of these was the Uruguay Round, begun in 1986 and completed in 1993, which paved the way for the replacement of GATT by the World Trade Organisation (WTO) and which included trade in agricultural products for the first time. GATT and the WTO have overseen a process under which trade in goods has grown more rapidly than global production in all but two of the last 50 years, leading to a much increased share of trade in world GDP.

The second dimension of globalisation is trade in services. Previously regarded as 'non-traded', services now account for 20 per cent of world trade and the proportion is expected to rise in the future. The General Agreement on Trade in Services (GATS) provides the basic legal framework within the WTO, but this is an area where future multilateral agreements can be expected covering activities that are either excluded (e.g. construction) or where previous agreements are still limited in scope (e.g. financial services).

The third dimension is the liberalisation of capital flows. In some respects, this has been going on for almost as long as trade liberalisation in goods, but there was a qualitative leap in the scale of liberalisation in the 1980s resulting in a huge jump in the annual inflows and outflows to and from almost all countries. Unlike with trade, there is no single international institution responsible for liberalisation of capital flows, but the International Monetary Fund (IMF), the World Bank and the Bank for International Settlements (BIS) have all played an important role in promoting capital flows between countries.

The fourth dimension is direct foreign investment (DFI) by multinational companies (MNCs). This has also experienced a qualitative leap and MNCs now account for over half of all world trade with intra-firm trade between different subsidiaries accounting for roughly a third

---

[1] See ECLAC (1994).

of total trade. Attempts in the late 1990s to create a multilateral framework for the governance of MNCs failed, but this has not prevented DFI from surging ahead with flows to certain LAC countries breaking all records in recent years (see Chapter 2).

The fifth dimension is the adoption by the WTO of a rules-based system for trade in goods and services that provides for the resolution of conflicts and a binding system of arbitration. Trade practices that were once commonplace (e.g. quotas) have now been outlawed except in a few rare cases and the circumstances under which exports can be promoted through public policy have been narrowly circumscribed. Despite these restrictions, membership in the WTO has been growing fast and the organisation can expect to reach a membership of 150 countries in the next few years.[2]

The rules-based system has been grappling with the problem of how to link labour and environmental standards to trade.[3] There has been no multilateral agreement so far, but the desire of most developed countries to ensure that certain minimum standards are imposed on all members of the WTO makes it likely that a link will be created in the not-so-distant future. Indeed, the link is likely to form a major part of any new trade round launched under the auspices of the WTO.

The sixth dimension of globalisation concerns the rules for patents and intellectual property. In a knowledge-based economy, such rules are increasingly important and explain the creation of the World Intellectual Property Organisation (WIPO) with its headquarters in Geneva. There is considerable unhappiness among developing countries at the rules governing intellectual property, although these were negotiated under the Uruguay Round. The problem has been the intense pressure from developed economies that developing countries face when reforming domestic legislation to comply with international obligations.

The next two dimensions of globalisation have barely begun. The first concerns the free movement of labour. In the last great wave of globalisation before the First World War, labour migration was a crucial part of the story. A globalisation process in which one factor of production (capital) is free, but not the other (labour) is like Hamlet without the prince. It is a distorted globalisation that has no justification in economic theory and which can be very damaging to world welfare by privileging capital at the expense of labour. The freer movement of labour, however, will be required by globalisation both as a complement to trade in services and to serve as a means for transferring workers to markets in which there is a shortage of labour.

---

[2] At the beginning of 2001, membership was 142. It is worth recalling that GATT began life with only 23 members.

[3] On the link with the environment, see Nordström and Vaughan (1999).

The final dimension concerns the environment. Global warming, the hole in the ozone layer and other environmental hazards impose a responsibility on states to co-operate at the world level. The modest steps taken so far show that co-operation is both possible and necessary. A reduction in global emissions of greenhouse and other gases, however, may only be possible if countries are able to trade in pollution, purchasing permits in the case of states that need to reduce emissions and selling them in the case of countries that are below their targets. This dimension of globalisation is set to become much more important in the future with or without the ratification of the Kyoto Protocol.[4]

These different dimensions of globalisation represent a challenge — perhaps even a threat — for LAC countries. Yet greater integration into the world economy through increased flows of goods, services, and factors of production need not necessarily require a regional response. In theory, each nation could frame its response through a multilateral framework without any need for regionalism. Indeed, in some cases (e.g. the threat of global warming), multilateralism is the only response that makes any sense.

It is surely no accident, however, that almost every country in the world has chosen to meet the challenge of globalisation in part through a regional response. The United States has added a regional weapon to its armoury in the last decade. Even Japan, the most isolationist of the developed countries, has begun to participate in regional fora and negotiate free trade agreements with neighbouring countries. Every one of the 33 LAC countries participates in at least one regional scheme and some have joined several.

The reasons why countries add a regional dimension to their response to globalisation are varied, although there are certain common threads. The motivation for the European Union, for example, is not the same as for the United States. LAC countries also differ among themselves in the way they approach regionalism. Small countries are unlikely to see the problem in the same way as large countries, while poorer states will pursue different policies from richer nations. This creates multiple objectives that not all countries share and which can cause confusion and misunderstandings among states.

The US interest in regionalism began at the end of the 1980s with the signing of the free trade agreement with Canada (CUFTA). Previously, the USA had been the most vocal and committed supporter of multilateralism, eschewing regionalism for itself and being either hostile or indifferent towards regional integration in the rest of the Americas. The North American Free Trade Agreement (NAFTA), which replaced

---

[4] The Kyoto Protocol, committing developed countries to reduce their emissions of greenhouse and other gases below their 1990 levels, was signed in 1997. It has not yet been ratified by enough states to bring it into force.

CUFTA at the start of 1994 and included Mexico, marked a further step in the USA's conversion to regionalism. This was followed by the launch of negotiations for a free trade area of the Americas (FTAA) in 1998 and two years later an agreement to negotiate a free trade pact with Chile. In addition, the USA has participated fully in the Asia Pacific Economic Cooperation (APEC) process and signed a free trade agreement with Jordan.

There are two main reasons for the US interest in regionalism after years of indifference. First, it is much easier for the USA to control the agenda if it is negotiated regionally rather than multilaterally. The USA may be the only military superpower, but it is not the only economic one and must share the stage with the EU and — to a lesser extent — Japan. The difficulties in bringing the Uruguay Round to a successful conclusion (it took seven years and came close to defeat) were in large part caused by the trade frictions between the USA and the EU, frictions that also undermined the attempts to launch a new trade round under the auspices of the WTO in Seattle in 1999.

Secondly, regionalism allows the USA to pursue an agenda that goes beyond what can be achieved at the multilateral level. The clearest example is the US interest in labour and environmental standards as an adjunct of trade policy. While progress on this link has so far proved impossible at the multilateral level, the USA was able to include labour and environmental standards — albeit as side agreements — in NAFTA. They were then included in the full text of the free trade agreement (FTA) with Jordan and will form an integral part of any FTA with Chile. It is likely that any FTAA that includes the United States will establish some link between trade policy and labour and environmental standards (see Chapter 9).

For European countries, both those inside the EU and the 12 applicants, the rationale for regionalism is quite different. These countries do most of their trade with each other so that Europe has become a single economic space. Even before the Treaty of Rome was signed in 1957, the six countries that would form the European Economic Community (EEC) did one-third of their trade with each other and this figure is now close to two-thirds for the 15 countries of the EU. The applicant countries, such as Poland, already send more than 50 per cent of their exports to the EU and this proportion is expected to increase after accession.

None of these arguments is of much relevance for LAC countries, who do not have any hope of controlling the multilateral agenda. Thus, regionalism in Latin America needs a different set of objectives if it is to justify the efforts put into its promotion. Finding those goals has always been problematic in the region and helps to account for the widespread confusion about the costs and benefits of regionalism as well as the rationale of the whole process.

The logical starting point is free trade in goods through the elimination of tariffs on intra-regional trade. This in practice is how most integration schemes in LAC countries have operated and it leads either to a free trade area (FTA) or a customs union (CU) depending on whether tariffs on third countries are set nationally (a FTA) or regionally (a CU). Zero tariffs on trade in manufactured goods was the main objective of old regionalism, while zero tariffs on all goods (including agricultural products) is an important part of the new regionalism story.

There are two main problems with this. First, it addresses only one of the challenges of globalisation outlined above, i.e. liberalisation of trade in goods. It does nothing to prepare countries for the other dimensions of globalisation and it does not tackle the non-tariff barriers that in practice are often a more important obstacle to free trade in goods than tariffs.

Secondly, intra-regional trade in goods in most LAC schemes represents only a minority of total trade. The highest share is found in MERCOSUR where it has stabilised in recent years at approximately 20 per cent. In the Central American Common Market (CACM) it does not exceed 15 per cent. In the Andean Community it is closer to ten per cent and in the Caribbean Community (CARICOM) it is little more than five per cent. Only in NAFTA is the share of intra-regional trade in total trade high, exceeding 40 per cent for the three members as a whole, although it is much higher (greater than 80 per cent) for Mexico and Canada.[5]

Optimists sometimes argue that the vigorous pursuit of regionalism in LAC countries could increase this share significantly. They point to the success of the EU in raising the share to nearly two-thirds. However, as pointed out above, this is not an appropriate point of comparison. The schemes currently in operation in Latin America and the Caribbean (excluding NAFTA) will not be able to raise the share of intra-regional to total trade by much. Thus, extra-regional trade will remain far more important for most of the LAC countries and this means that there are limits to what can be achieved by regionalism in the pursuit of liberalisation of trade in goods.

This conclusion — that regionalism in LAC countries cannot be justified only or mainly by trade in goods — has one important implication. It means that the traditional standard by which integration has been judged (trade creation versus trade diversion) is not particularly relevant. Trade creation (TC) measures the replacement of high cost domestic production by cheaper imports from a partner, while trade diversion (TD) measures the replacement of cheaper imports from

---

[5] See the Statistical Appendix for the share of intra-regional trade in total trade for the different schemes in recent years.

the rest of the world by more expensive imports from a partner. Welfare is then said to increase if TC exceeds TD and to fall if TD exceeds TC.

The measurement of TC and TD for all integration schemes has been a major priority for economists. Yet the assumptions on which the welfare conclusions are based (e.g. full employment) are not very appropriate for LAC countries. Where intra-regional trade is a major part of total trade (as in the European Union) or where the countries play a significant role in total world trade (e.g. NAFTA), there is perhaps a justification for the emphasis on TC and TD. However, this is not the case in most LAC schemes and the reduction in the level of the external tariffs means that TD is likely to be much less important in new regionalism than in the old version. The intense debate about net trade diversion in MERCOSUR (see Chapter 10) has been out of proportion to the scale of the problem.

Free trade in goods, therefore, is not in general a sufficient justification for regionalism in LAC countries. However, there is one exception. Where the integration scheme under consideration is broadened to include all the Americas the share of intra-regional to total trade would rise above 50 per cent for almost all LAC countries. This reflects the importance of the United States as a trade partner for most LAC countries. Indeed, for countries outside MERCOSUR the combination of trade with their neighbours and trade with the United States represents on average two-thirds of total trade — a figure that is as high as intra-regional trade in the European Union.

For MERCOSUR countries trade with the United States is much less important than for the rest of Latin America.[6] However, Paraguay and Uruguay already do most of their trade with their MERCOSUR partners and for MERCOSUR as a whole the EU is a more important trade partner than the United States. A free trade agreement between MERCOSUR and the EU, currently under negotiation, would raise the share of intra-regional to total trade to nearly 50 per cent for MERCOSUR, while the successful completion of the FTAA would raise it close to 70 per cent.

The objective of hemispheric free trade, coupled perhaps with a free trade agreement with the EU,[7] is therefore a rational strategy for LAC countries. The liberalisation of intra-regional trade, when the 'region' accounts for some two-thirds of total trade, is an approximation to full liberalisation of trade in goods under the multilateral system. Nor is this a distant dream, as the deadline for the start of the FTAA has been set at 2005, while the MERCOSUR negotiations with the EU have a similar (if unofficial) date for conclusion. For those Latin American countries that are members of APEC (Chile, Mexico and Peru), there is the additional

---

[6] See Bulmer-Thomas and Page (1999), p. 90, Figure 4.1.

[7] Mexico already has such an agreement, which went into force in 2000.

incentive of free trade in goods with Asia starting in 2010. To achieve the same objective under the auspices of the WTO is likely to be both more difficult and more time-consuming.

The second justification for regionalism in LAC countries concerns free trade in services. The importance of primary products in international trade continues to decline, leaving a question mark over the prospects for developing country exports. LAC countries suffer from discrimination against their traditional primary product exports, weak commodity prices in many years and declining net barter terms of trade. Services offer an attractive alternative and regional integration a suitable platform from which to launch service exports.

It has often been claimed that developing countries are acquiring a comparative advantage in manufacturing while developed countries are shifting to service exports so that in future the division of international labour will be based on the exchange of manufactured goods from the south for services from the north. This is very misleading. Services are very heterogeneous and include activities in which developing countries can be very competitive (e.g. transport, construction, software, medical treatment). Many of these activities remain outside the auspices of the GATS and the WTO, so that it is difficult for developing countries to exploit their cost advantages over developed nations. Regionalism provides an opportunity to promote trade in services over and above what is possible under a multilateral system. Mexico is making full use of this facility under NAFTA, which covers almost all services, while the other LAC schemes have begun to take the first steps in this direction. As with trade in goods, intra-regional trade in services can serve as a useful apprenticeship before exporting services to the rest of the world.

The third justification for regionalism in LAC countries is to increase the rate of investment. This can happen for several reasons. Regional integration will create new opportunities for investment (e.g. in infrastructure improvements) as well as providing scope for special treatment of foreign investment by nationals of member states. Regionalism also allows countries to offer more rigorous protection of contracts reached by nationals of member states as well as faster and more efficient mechanisms for resolving conflicts. All these issues are explored by Sheila Page in Chapter 2 in her analysis of the link between regional integration and investment in LAC countries.

The fourth justification for regionalism in LAC countries is the possibility of increasing bargaining power in multilateral negotiations. No single LAC country, with the exception of Brazil, has much of a chance of influencing the multilateral agenda. A group of LAC countries, however, acting together and speaking with one voice, has much more of an opportunity to be heard. The best example of this is the Caribbean Regional Negotiating Machinery (RNM), which allows CARICOM to 'punch above its weight' not only at the WTO and other multilateral fora, but also in the negotiations for the FTAA and other hemispheric initiatives. This theme is explored by Shelton Nicholls et al. in Chapter 6.

For some of the smaller countries, particularly in Central America, regionalism offers a further opportunity. Not only are these countries unable to influence the international agenda, they are also often unaware of the issues. Their staff in Geneva and Washington, DC, are not able to keep abreast of the new developments in international negotiations and their officials and ministers have to participate in a constant round of meetings with little hope of influencing the outcome. Regionalism can provide a modest improvement through the pooling of staff, the sharing of knowledge and the circulation of reports.

It is not hard, therefore, to justify the pursuit of regionalism in LAC countries. Theory and practice, however, are not the same thing. There is still a great deal of confusion about the way in which regionalism should operate in Latin America and the Caribbean and this is not altogether surprising. Each of the justifications given above for regionalism has different implications for the most efficient institutions, the appropriate number of members and the rules to be applied.

Consider first the case of membership. If the main objective is trade in goods, most countries — and certainly all South American countries — would want to be associated with Brazil, the largest LAC country by far in terms of population and GDP. If, however, the objective is an increase in bargaining power, it is not so clear that participating with Brazil in an integration scheme is desirable, since a small country is unlikely to be able to persuade Brazil to change its negotiating position in international fora. This helps to explain the ambivalence and inconsistency Chile has shown towards MERCOSUR in the last few years.[8]

Consider also the question of services. One of the most important ways in which service trade can be promoted between regional partners is through an increase in transparency allowing consumers to compare prices offered by the different service providers. The desire to promote trade in services through integration therefore leads very naturally to the idea of a common currency.

A common currency, however, can be either a foreign asset (i.e. the US dollar) or a regional unit of account (e.g. the Eastern Caribbean

---

[8] In the first half of the 1990s, Chile's preference was membership of NAFTA. In the second half, as the prospect of NAFTA entry receded, Chile joined MERCOSUR as an associate member before stating its interest in becoming a full member. At the end of 2000, however, Chile began negotiations for a FTA with the USA, making full membership of MERCOSUR very difficult, if not impossible.

dollar).[9] Yet this choice has very different implications. Dollarisation should bring with it an increase in credibility and a fall in real interest rates. A regional currency preserves seigniorage (through control of the note issue and the monetary base) and the possibility of an active exchange rate policy. It is not surprising therefore that LAC countries, while inching towards common currencies, differ sharply among themselves as to the merits of the two strategies.

Clarity with regard to the different objectives of regionalism is therefore the first step. Only then will it be possible to fashion an integration scheme that has a realistic prospect of delivering the benefits. This problem is not unique to LAC countries, as the European experience shows all too clearly, but it is perhaps particularly acute in Latin America. Canada and the United States seem fairly clear about what they expect from regional integration and each country has prepared a road map to guide them towards their chosen destination. LAC countries need their own road maps and there are likely to be many different versions. This means that there will continue to be a place for sub-regional schemes within a broader effort to achieve hemispheric integration.

This book examines regionalism in Latin America and the Caribbean from four perspectives: economic, institutional, political and the relation to the rest of the world. The purpose is to seek answers to the questions raised by LAC countries' efforts to use regionalism to address the challenges of globalisation and, in particular, to explore the nature and meaning of open regionalism. This thematic treatment draws on the experience of the different schemes currently in place in the region: NAFTA, CACM, CARICOM, the Andean Community and MERCOSUR. These schemes are therefore used to illustrate the broader issues raised by regionalism.

The first section on the economic dimension begins with a study of new regionalism by Robert Devlin and Antoni Estevadeordal (Chapter 1). This examines the difference in both theory and practice between old and new regionalism and asks to what extent the two are really different. Despite some blurring at the edges, the authors conclude that the differences are both substantial and significant.

This is followed, in Chapter 2, by Sheila Page's study of the relationship between regional integration and investment in LAC countries. The impact of regionalism on investment flows is one of the justifications for integration schemes in LAC countries (see above) and yet there have been very few studies of the relationship. Page's chapter makes clear that there are ways in which investment can be promoted

---

[9] The Eastern Caribbean dollar is the currency shared by the members of the Organisation of Eastern Caribbean States. The members share a central bank. See Van Beek et al. (2000).

even if most LAC schemes have failed to take advantage of these degrees of freedom. She emphasises the difficulties placed in the way of analysis by the absence of data on cross-border investment flows.

Trade liberalisation, whether at the regional or multilateral level, implies a reallocation of resources. The cost of adjustment is widely assumed to be lower when a high proportion of trade between regional partners is in the same products or product groups. Intra-industry trade (IIT), as it is usually called, may enable firms to shift from one product line to another within the same activity without the need to close down. This phenomenon, of huge importance in trade between developed countries, has been much less studied in LAC countries on the grounds that trade is mainly with developed countries and can be explained in terms of traditional inter-industry specialisation.

In Chapter 3, Victor Bulmer-Thomas examines the nature and extent of IIT in LAC countries. He finds that it has been growing in importance and is also more important in trade between partners in integration schemes than in trade with the rest of the world. However, he questions whether IIT in general implies lower costs of adjustment for LAC countries since most IIT is 'vertical' rather than 'horizontal', which implies that the quality of the goods being traded in the same product group is very different.[10] When IIT is vertical (e.g. the trade in clothing between the United States and Haiti), the costs of adjustment from a loss of competitiveness may be as high as in the case of inter-industry trade.

The second part of the book is devoted to institutions. Chapter 4 examines the institutions of MERCOSUR. The authors recognise the progress made in the early years of MERCOSUR when institutions were weak, but political commitment was strong. However, they question whether this combination will work in the future and explore the areas in which institutions will need to be strengthened.

In Chapter 5, Valpy FitzGerald considers the monetary and financial framework for NAFTA. While noting the extraordinary increase in trade flows in the last decade between Mexico and its northern partners, FitzGerald argues that the financial arrangements are unsustainable with the current institutions. He argues in favour of an institutional reform that will give Mexico some influence over the conduct of monetary policy in the USA rather than leaving her at the mercy of unilateral changes.

Part 2 of the book concludes with a chapter by Shelton Nicholls et al., which looks at the institutional arrangements in the three other schemes: CACM, CARICOM and the Andean Community. All three schemes are

---

[10] IIT is said to be vertical when the unit price of exports and imports differ by more than 15 per cent (or some other arbitrary figure). IIT is then said to be horizontal when the prices differ by less than 15 per cent.

marked by a proliferation of institutions, although many of these do not function effectively and in some cases do not function at all. The authors explore the logic of the institutional arrangements in all three schemes and ask which institutions are working effectively and why. They find that funding is an obstacle in all three cases, although they are reluctant to assume that additional funds would necessarily resolve all the problems.

The third part of the book addresses the politics of regionalism. It begins with a chapter by Ben Ross Schneider that looks at the relation between business and the public sector. The author finds major differences in the way this relationship works in several Latin American countries and he then asks how this has affected the dynamics of the integration process in the region.

Chapter 8 by Andrew Hurrell pursues the same theme, but this time limited to the case of MERCOSUR. He notes that the politics of regionalism acquired new salience with the difficulties faced by the integration scheme since 1997 when intra-regional trade has lost its dynamism. Hurrell explores the different interest groups and institutions as well as power and state interests that combine to make the integration process work. He concludes in a broadly optimistic vein, arguing that MERCOSUR has now become too important — at least for Argentina and Brazil — to fail.

Part 3 concludes with an examination by Riordan Roett of the US role in hemispheric integration. The adoption of a more sympathetic attitude to regionalism by the US administration has undoubtedly helped LAC countries to move towards new regionalism. Roett charts this change in US policy while exploring what the United States hopes to achieve from regionalism. Finally, Roett considers what impact the Bush presidency (2001–) will have on the negotiations for a Free Trade Area of the Americas.

The final part of the book is devoted to the relationship between regionalism and the rest of the world. This in many respects is the core of open regionalism, since the degree to which regionalism and multilateralism are compatible is ultimately an empirical question.

In Chapter 10 Ann Bartholomew finds that MERCOSUR has been very successful in promoting both intra- and extra-regional imports, although it has not been so successful in promoting intra- and extra-regional exports. Thus, MERCOSUR has not been guilty of high levels of trade diversion, but at the same time has done little to help the member states forge closer links with the world economy through an expansion of exports to the rest of the world.

In Chapter 11, Pablo Rodas-Martini contrasts the lack of progress towards open regionalism in Central America at the 'macro' level with the results from a sample of businesses suggesting that at the 'micro' level regional integration is seen as an important component of industrial expansion. It is a good example of how integration can proceed at the 'grassroots' level even when governments fail to deliver on their promises and institutions are weak.

The book concludes with a study of open regionalism in the Caribbean by Helen McBain (Chapter 12). CARICOM members have devoted considerable attention to the issue of intra-regional trade despite the low levels of exports and imports between the countries of the Caribbean. However, the architects of CARICOM have been conscious of the need to pursue open regionalism and the framework for promoting intra-regional trade has not in general impeded either extra-regional exports or imports.

These results lead to a sober assessment of the state of regional integration in Latin America and the Caribbean. Although new regionalism is clearly different from the old variety, it has not been able to escape from many of the same weaknesses: commitments are made, but not honoured; intra-regional trade is vulnerable to external shocks and is pro-cyclical rather than anti-cyclical; institutions are weak and inadequately financed.

These deficiencies must be put in perspective. Regionalism has given LAC countries opportunities that would not otherwise exist. A large number of firms now depend on sales to partner countries, creating an important interest group in favour of the integration process, and cross-border investment flows are growing in importance. Regionalism is never easy (witness the European experience) and progress is often frustratingly slow. The costs of new regionalism — financial, economic and political — have been very modest and the potential benefits remain significant. Finally, all LAC countries remain committed to the multilateral process and regionalism remains a complement to multilateralism rather than a threat. No country therefore sees any reason to discard regionalism in their pursuit of greater competitiveness and efficiency. As these chapters show, it is a useful adjunct even if it will never be a panacea.

PART 1:
ECONOMICS

CHAPTER 1

What's New in the New Regionalism in the Americas?

Robert Devlin and Antoni Estevadeordal

The centrifugal forces of increasing economic globalisation in the 1990s were matched by the centripetal forces of regionalisation. While seemingly pulling in opposite directions, the two forces reflected complementary dimensions of dynamic capitalist market development.[1] The completion of the Uruguay Round and increased membership in the World Trade Organisation (WTO) were accompanied by a situation in which regional integration schemes became commonplace; indeed, practically all WTO members are now party to one or more regional accords.[2]

Latin America is a good example of these dual forces. Between the mid-1980s and 1990s the region unilaterally reduced its average external tariff from over 40 per cent to 12 per cent. The region also actively participated in the Uruguay Round and by the end of the decade all Latin American and Caribbean (LAC) countries (except the Bahamas) were members of the WTO. Meanwhile, there was a parallel wave of new reciprocal free trade and integration agreements, more than 20 in total (see Table A.1 in the Statistical Appendix). These trends were accompanied by a strong average growth of international trade in the 1990s (especially on the import side, the value of which expanded by 18 per cent per year until the Asian crisis), and a marked increase in intra-regional trade (intra-regional exports rose from 13 per cent of the total in 1990 to 20 per cent towards the end of the decade).

Regional integration schemes in Latin America are not new. Originally, these were motivated largely by political objectives.[3] However, in the post-war era economic development became the central goal. In the 1950s there was much discussion of creation of a Latin American Common Market. Following a decade of negotiations and debate, the Latin American Free Trade Association (LAFTA), comprising the South American countries and Mexico, and the Central American Common Market (CACM) were officially launched in 1960. Later the Andean Group (AG) was founded in 1969. While the agreements experienced some success (especially the CACM), they were short lived.

---

[1] Oman (1998).
[2] WTO (1995).
[3] Townsend (1988).

By the second half of the 1970s all of them were in difficulty, falling into open crisis in the 1980s.[4]

Some of the stylised facts about the old post-war economic integration initiatives are:[5]

- The central objective of the agreements was to support the prevailing state-led import substitution industrialisation (ISI) model of development. The model was expressive of export pessimism, scepticism regarding private markets and great concern about the presence of, and dependence on, foreign firms. The goal was to industrialise by substituting imports behind high levels of national protection (effective protection could be 150–200 per cent) together with state planning and direct public sector intervention in markets. The model prospered for a number of decades, but began to falter in the 1950s. The prevailing opinion in the region was that this was due to the small size of domestic markets.

- Given the overall policy objective, the logic of regional integration was to overcome the stated limitations through the creation of a regional market. The approach was to eliminate internal barriers to trade, maintain — or even increase — external protection and expand industrial planning to the regional level. The explicit goal was to divert third party imports to intra-regional production and eventually exports to the rest of the world. The sustainability of the initiatives depended on successful opening of national markets to intra-regional trade.

- The basic development model of the region was inward-looking and hence so too was regional integration. The effects of integration on commercial links with the industrialised countries' markets and the multilateral system were not a central policy issue in view of the export pessimism of the times and the 'virtues' of protection. In the first episode of integration only a handful of LAC countries were even active members of the GATT. Moreover, ideological concerns about foreign dependence created ambivalence, or outright restrictions, regarding foreign direct investment's (FDI) participation in regional schemes.

- Reflecting the primacy of national protection, the old integration's liberalisation mechanisms tended to be based on multiple positive lists, the full definition of which typically emerged only after protracted step-by step negotiations (the exception was the CACM). Consequently, schemes had an extremely high degree of selectivity, further complicated by complex arrangements for special and differential treatment for the lesser developed members. This,

---

[4] Orego Vicuña (1977).

[5] For a detailed analysis of the period see Devlin, Estevadeordal and Katona (2001).

coupled with the creation of costly bureaucratic architecture inspired by the European experience (LAFTA was the exception) together with sectoral industrial programming, eroded credibility with the private sector.

- In terms of liberalisation and trade, the old schemes generally did not succeed in meeting their most basic objectives. Negotiations and liberalisation schedules bogged down quickly. Hence, effective liberalisation was limited and growth of intra-regional trade modest (Central America was again the exception). Other disciplines often did not go beyond paper accords. The primacy of national protection in the ISI model, authoritarian regimes, inefficient bureaucratic interventions, perceptions of asymmetric gains among partners, and economic and political instability all contributed to the old integration's failure to take off, or its tendency to stall relatively quickly.

- Of the three initiatives, only Central America achieved substantial liberalisation: 95 per cent of all tariff lines were fully liberalised for several years. A common external tariff (adjusting rates upward) was established. Regional exports grew significantly, to peak at 26 per cent of the total exports, until serious political problems emerged in the CACM in the late 1960s.

Many trade theorists, following the Vinerian framework on the welfare effects of preferential trade arrangements, viewed these early post-war initiatives with scepticism. To evaluate welfare, the Vinerian perspective was quite appropriate given the inward-looking nature of the integration processes and the immediate explicit objective of diverting trade for ISI through high levels of external protection. Moreover, there was sufficient cause for scepticism about the creation of so-called 'dynamic effects' given the relatively closed national markets and restraints on competition and foreign investment.

Some of this same scepticism has re-emerged during the current wave of New Regionalism. Major concerns are about trade diversion and the undermining of the multilateral system. Other analysts, however, have argued that the New Regionalism is **really** new and demands a much broader framework of evaluation than the static trade creation/diversion analysis of Viner.[6] This chapter argues that Latin America's recent wave of regional integration is indeed a New Regionalism, quite different from the old, and hence merits a more comprehensive perspective than in the past.

Section 1 analyses the New Regionalism, contrasting it with the old schemes in some of the key features of regional integration and development policy. Section 2 evaluates some of the results of the New

---

[6] Ethier (1998).

Regionalism and then in Section 3 we outline some lingering 'old' features of the New Regionalism. The last section contains conclusions.

The New Regionalism

The Resurgence of Regionalism in the 1990s

The debt crisis of the 1980s and consequent balance of payments problems induced a deep recession in the LAC regions and with that a severe contraction of imports. Since intra-regional imports are the other side of intra-regional exports, the collapse in the Latin American economy also induced a collapse of intra-regional trade and open crisis in the already flagging formal integration agreements. The general economic paralysis in the region, coupled with the emergence of a new development strategy based on market opening, undistorted relative prices and privatisation/deregulation seemed to some to be the final deathblow for regional integration. However, to the surprise of many observers, new regional initiatives began to appear in the second half of the 1980s and a true resurgence materialised in the decade of the 1990s.

While the earliest agreements in this new wave were relatively unsophisticated and very limited in scope, the later accords of the 1990s were comprehensive, with some at the technological edge of regional integration.

The initial arrangements were negotiated as Economic Complementary Agreements (ACE in the Spanish acronym) under the framework of the Latin American Integration Association (ALADI in Spanish), which was created in 1980 as the successor to LAFTA. ALADI eschewed the grand objectives of the 1960s in favour of limited agreements confined to market access via the exchange of partial or full preferences on trade in specific products with accompanying rules for use of safeguards, rules of origin, etc.

The limited scope ACE agreements in the Southern Cone evolved into the birth of MERCOSUR (Argentina, Brazil, Paraguay and Uruguay) in 1991. The MERCOSUR customs union agreement is progressively evolving towards greater levels of integration, with the goal of becoming a common market. It also incorporated Bolivia and Chile as associate free trade area members in 1996. Meanwhile, a presidential initiative in the Andean Group induced the member countries to free trade in the early 1990s and form a customs union among three of them (Colombia, Venezuela and Ecuador). The agreement changed its name to the Andean Community in 1995 and set out the objective of a common market by 2005. A similar initiative relaunched integration in the Central American Common Market in 1990.

While the first ACE agreements in ALADI were being negotiated, Canada and the United States launched free trade negotiations in 1986 that would radically transform the landscape of international trade negotiations. The agenda was vast and introduced pioneering issues vis-à-vis the multilateral trading system. For at least ten years, the USA had been pushing with little success to expand the GATT agenda to include trade in services, investment, government procurement and other 'new issues'. Lacking consensus at the multilateral level, the USA opted to pursue bilateral trade agreements in which disciplines in these areas could become a reality and influence the conduct of multilateral negotiations. Not only did the Canada–USA negotiations establish model disciplines in a whole range of areas, but also new approaches to older issues such as rules of origin and dispute settlement. On a larger level, what made the Canada–USA free trade area such a watershed was that negotiations moved beyond market access barriers at the border to traditionally sovereign policy areas related to how societies regulate their domestic economies.

The subsequent NAFTA negotiations that included Mexico were built on the innovations of the Canada–USA accord. NAFTA, launched in 1994, was historic because it represented the first time a Latin American country would link up with an industrialised partner. Moreover, it became a prototype for other new initiatives in the Americas during the decade. A series of new Mexican bilateral free trade areas (FTAs) throughout the region, as well as one between Chile and Canada, followed the NAFTA model.

Other bilateral FTAs were promoted by Chile; they first followed a more traditional market access in goods approach, but later increasingly adopted many NAFTA-like characteristics. Meanwhile, the major subregions pursued 'deep' integration involving larger commitments in terms of loss of sovereignty than one finds in a FTA.

This renewed activity continues today. MERCOSUR has been negotiating with the Andean Community to create a free trade area in South America and with the European Union (EU) for a transatlantic FTA. Mexico launched in 2000 a free trade area with the EU and is, along with Chile and Peru, a member of the Asia Pacific Economic Cooperation (APEC) forum. Chile is negotiating as well with South Korea and the EU. Finally, 34 countries of the hemisphere (all except Cuba) are quite advanced in negotiating a Free Trade Area of the Americas (FTAA) agreement, which is scheduled to emerge in 2005.

The Objective

In line with its instrumental role, the objective of regional integration in Latin America has shifted with the region's new overall strategy for development. In essence, the New Regionalism of the 1990s is an integral part of the broad-based structural reforms that have been underway in Latin America since the mid-1980s. The central features of today's strategy include an opening to world markets, promotion of the private sector and withdrawal of the state from direct economic activity.

The New Regionalism's link to the structural reform process is most clearly observed in trade liberalisation. In effect, regional integration is the third tier of a three-tiered process. As mentioned above, Latin America's average external tariff was radically reduced between 1985 and 1995. The average maximum tariffs in the region fell from more than 80 per cent to 40 per cent with only two countries presently applying maximum tariffs of up to 100 per cent on a small number of products. Average tariff dispersion has declined from 30 per cent in the mid-1980s to a low of nine per cent today. The highest dispersion rate, as measured by the standard deviation, is currently under 15 per cent.[7]

The second tier is at the multilateral level. A decade of multilateral Uruguay Round negotiations ended in April 1994 with the signature in Marrakesh of the Final Act. That round was concerned with two basic issues regarding market access: (i) reducing obstacles to trade in goods and services and (ii) making the new levels of market access legally binding under tougher WTO regulations and procedures. In the area of tariff liberalisation, this last round of the GATT negotiations implied a very substantial commitment on the part of Latin America to dismantle import barriers and adopt new disciplines. The central obligation with respect to tariffs requires countries to 'bind' them to a specified maximum. The latest round resulted in a significant increase in this commitment. In the case of developed countries, the increase went from 22 to 72 per cent; and in the case of countries in transition, it went from 78 to 98 per cent. Latin America as a whole agreed to bind practically *all* tariff lines (albeit, above applied rates).

Liberalisation at the unilateral and multilateral levels has helped to incorporate LAC countries into the world economy. In the 1990s, extra-regional imports grew at a relatively high average rate of 18 per cent per year, more than tripling to US$280 billion. This was 50 per cent faster than the growth of extra-regional exports. The region's extra-regional import coefficient (with respect to GDP) rose from one fifth in the late 1980s, to one third in the late 1990s.

For a region with a modern history of closed economies, this two-level opening was clearly dramatic. While bringing benefits of more competition, lower input costs and enhanced consumption possibilities, the opening also introduced new difficulties. These included fiscal burdens, real resource costs from capital and labour made newly redundant, as well as political costs due to shifting domestic economic coalitions and the real or perceived threats of globalisation. The large

---

[7] There are still, however, some important peak tariffs. On average, approximately 22 per cent of tariff lines are subject to rates above 20 per cent. Moreover, there are still some countries with maximum tariffs above 70 per cent.

and rapid external liberalisation at the start of the 1990s could lean on considerable 'water' in national tariff schedules, while needed fiscal adjustments were quite straightforward. When tariffs moved closer to differential margins of competitiveness between home and abroad and fiscal options narrowed during the course of the 1990s, the political economy of trade liberalisation became considerably more challenging (during the course of the 1990s).

Governments have used support for regional integration as a signal of their continued commitment to liberalisation even when political or economic conditions for further unilateral opening are difficult and when reciprocal multilateral initiatives are in a transitional phase, as has been the case since the end of the Uruguay Round. In this context, regional integration has become a vital third tier of liberalisation that has helped ensure continued momentum in the process. The fiscal implications of preferential liberalisation among Latin American neighbours are less burdensome because typically levels of trade are initially small due to history as well as the legacy of protection. Political resistance to regional integration also can be less entrenched. It takes place within a delimited and familiar market space which reflects more symmetric competition than is found in the international arena. Moreover, there is a compensatory element of reciprocal exports in tandem with reciprocal imports, making for a potentially more balanced fallout of short-term costs and benefits. Regional opening can even be politically popular due to domestic receptiveness to 'getting together' with certain neighbours.[8]

Regional integration is therefore being used today as an effective policy tool to deepen liberalisation, further reduce average levels of protection and reinforce the winds of competition. Figure 1.1 illustrates for the MERCOSUR partners, Argentina and Brazil, how regional commitments are working with unilateral and multilateral processes to create more open economies.

Regional based rules and peer pressure are also useful to 'lock-in' liberalisation commitments that under unilateral policy alone might be reversed. It is true that some countries, largely in response to severe fiscal or balance of payments shocks, temporarily increased protection during the late 1990s. However, such measures have usually exempted regional integration partners, due to trade treaty obligations. Customs unions such as MERCOSUR can make it difficult for any member country to raise tariffs on third parties since a plurilateral consensus must be reached.[9] The lock-in effects of regional schemes (in

---

[8] This can be because you love your neighbour, or because you are tired of conflicts with your neighbour and hope trade will support a broader political initiative for peace. Devlin and Ffrench-Davis (1999).

[9] Mexico has exempted NAFTA partners from some recent increases in protection. In

combination with WTO bindings) have contributed to anchoring the trade liberalisation process and retard back-pedalling.

Figure 1.1: Evolution of External and Internal Tariffs in Selected MERCOSUR Countries

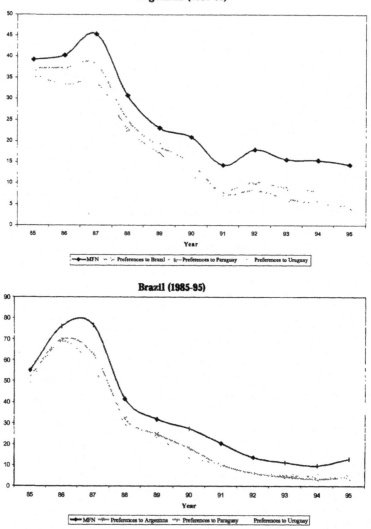

Source: Estevadeordal, A., Goto, J., and Saez, R. (2000).

From the above it is clear that the instrumental role of the new regional integration is dramatically different from that of the old schemes.

MERCOSUR, community obligations have made it more difficult to extend protection to their partners and third parties.

However, the New Regionalism contrasts with the old in other dimensions as well.

- Attracting foreign direct investment (FDI). The old fears of dependence on FDI have evolved into an appreciation of FDI's contribution to enhanced international competitiveness and access to export markets. In an era of globalisation there is an intensive worldwide competition for this type of capital. Today the creation of a regional market like MERCOSUR is being deployed not as a way to restrict FDI as in the past, but rather as a way to distinguish countries from the world pack and attract FDI.[10] Agreements which have successfully created a regional trademark, such as NAFTA and MERCOSUR, have become successful beacons for attracting this type of capital.[11] Chapter 2 of this book explains this in more detail.

- Intra-regional trade. The creation of a regional market has promoted trade and investment activity that is generating dynamic transformation effects in productive sectors. This is something that the old integration sought, but largely did not achieve, due to domestic price and regulatory distortions and the inability to open the regional market. With respect to international markets, the strong growth of intra-regional exports reflects a more diversified product mix, a greater participation of differentiated, knowledge-based manufactured goods, and expanding specialisation and scale economies through intra-industry trade (see Chapter 3).[12] Firms have reoriented their marketing, investment and strategic alliances to exploit the regional market. Moreover, trade in some sectors, such as dairy products and textiles, is a welcome outlet given severe protection in international markets. These dynamic transformation effects are contributing to more competitive economies which can face the challenges of globalisation.[13]

- Geopolitics. The outward orientation of LAC countries has raised demand for more active and strategic participation in hemispheric and world forums. Regional integration has allowed countries to co-operate and be more effective global players. In the Free Trade Area of the Americas process, for example, MERCOSUR, the Andean and CARICOM countries now each negotiate as a bloc, giving them more impact in the negotiations than if each country had acted alone.

---

[10] Ethier (1998).

[11] CEPAL (2000).

[12] The share of manufactured exports in intra-bloc trade was considerably higher than their share in total trade in the mid-1990s: CACM (70 per cent vs 30 per cent); Andean Community (63 per cent vs 21 per cent) and MERCOSUR (61 per cent vs 48 per cent) (IDB, 1999a).

[13] For analysis that captures some of the dynamic sectoral effects of regional integration in Latin America see Hasenclever et al. (1999); Nofal and Wilkinson (1999); Echavarría (1998); and Gereffi and Martínez (1999).

Regional integration and trade has also helped democratic countries seal hard won peace on frontiers with a tradition of military conflict. It moreover has set up a solidarity network (through democratic clauses) to protect the region's still young democracies. MERCOSUR's experience is a good example on both accounts: its formerly conflictive borders are now the most pacified and heavily trafficked in Latin America. The old integration was not able to achieve this because the primacy of protection blocked growth of commercial trade between neighbours, while many of the sponsors of the initiatives were often nationalistic authoritarian regimes with a vested interest in restricted borders, territorial disputes and non-democratic institutions.

Finally, the new face of regionalism is well exhibited by a phenomenon that would have been inconceivable just ten years ago: Latin America linking up in reciprocal trade agreements with the USA and other industrialised nations. These 'big market' agreements have more formidable costs and challenges than intra-Latin American agreements. The liberalisation is sharply asymmetric because the industrialised economy is already very open. Given that the more developed country is already a major trading partner, the loss of tariff revenue for the LAC country is important. The ensuing competition moreover is world class. Why do it? Because an agreement with a credible industrialised country provides a powerful anchor that greatly magnifies many of the aforementioned positive effects of integration on structural reform, such as lock-in and signalling, attraction of FDI, productive transformation, protection of democracy, etc. The agreement is also a way to eliminate peak protection in sensitive sectors of the industrialised partner and create binding legal mechanisms for access to the industrialised market and dispute settlement. In sum, these types of agreements are seen as an especially powerful tool of economic and political transformation.

Modalities

This section will outline some of the most relevant features of the structure of the liberalisation process emerging from the agreements of the 1990s. Given the very large number and diversity of agreements during this period, a core group of representative accords has been selected in order to derive from them some general stylised features of the New Regionalism. The analysis will focus more on the intra-regional liberalisation of selected agreements than on the formation of common external trade policies.

The new generation agreements, following in many respects the NAFTA model, moved towards tariff phase-out programmes based on pre-programmed schedules at the outset, which are relatively quick, automatic, and nearly universal. This contrasts quite sharply with the laborious step by step development of positive lists that characterised most of the old regionalism.

In the new integration agreements a high percentage of products was liberalised immediately, while for products regarded as 'sensitive' special phase-out periods were agreed to or lists of exceptions established.[14] The negotiations usually started with an agreement on a base rate or base level from which phase-out schedules are applied. Those base rates usually coincide with the most favoured nation (MFN) applied rates to third parties at the time of negotiations. This has been the case, for instance, of NAFTA after initial discussions about using GATT bound rates were rejected. In other cases, such as the G3 (Mexico–Colombia–Venezuela) negotiations, it was necessary to take into account previous preferences negotiated under other agreements in order to establish the initial base rate. These rates also could be negotiated so that phase-out schedules would begin from lower rates. In a second stage, parties defined several tariff elimination programmes or phase-out schedules to bring base rates to zero in a specified time period.

There has been very little empirical analysis of the depth and the effects of this new preferential liberalisation. The degree of liberalisation achieved to date can be illustrated in Figure 1.2. It shows the average level and dispersion of the preferential margins, by sector, resulting from bilateral preferential negotiations between LAC countries in two benchmark years: before the new regionalism started and for the year 1995.[15]

In 1985 most of the region still had relatively high MFN tariffs. This is because the process of unilateral liberalisation had not yet begun and the multilateral negotiations of the Uruguay Round had not yet been completed. At the same time, most traditional preferences negotiated under the ALADI framework and other subregional agreements had eroded over time and had not been renegotiated, partly due to the trauma of the debt crisis. As a result, the degree of preferential liberalisation among countries was quite low, with the average values of margins of preference being below five per cent.

---

[14] It is interesting to note that some of these elements were present in the old integration schemes as well, e.g., pre-programmed tariff phase-out in the AG (albeit on a much smaller portion (50 per cent) of total trade), or the near-universal internal liberalisation of the CACM. None of the earlier groups, however, were based on the principle of openness to third parties.

[15] For each product category, defined at the International Standard Industrial Classification (ISIC) 5-digit level of disaggregation, the margin of preference (MP) is computed for a selected number of the bilateral preferential relations among countries in the region. Then, for each product the maximum, the minimum and the average MP levels in all those bilateral relations are selected. Finally, the distribution of these maximum, minimum and average values across agreements are plotted for an aggregated sector defined at the ISIC 2-digit level.

Figure 1.2: Preferential Margins (PM) in Latin American Agreements: Distribution of Maximum, Minimum and Average Levels

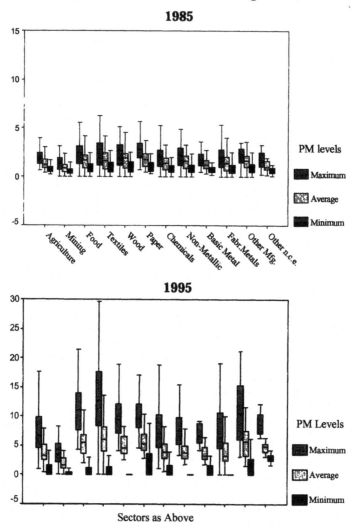

Note: As a measure of relative dispersion we use boxplots representing the interquartile ranges. The line in the middle of the box represents the median or 50th percentile of the data. The box extends from the 25th percentile ($x_{[25]}$) to the 75th percentile ($x_{[75]}$), the so-called interquartile range (IQR). The lines emerging from the box are called the whiskers and they extend to the upper and lower adjacent values. The upper adjacent value is defined as the largest data point less than or equal to $x_{[75]} + 1.5$ IQR. The lower adjacent value is defined as the smallest data point greater than or equal to $x_{[25]} + 1.5$ IQR. Observed points more extreme than the adjacent values are individually plotted.

The picture changes dramatically ten years later (see Figure 1.2). The MFN tariffs had already been reduced through unilateral and multilateral policies. However, parallel to this most preferential relations had been renegotiated under the new agreements, lowering preferential tariffs even more than the substantial drop in tariffs to third parties. This resulted in average levels higher than before, at around five per cent. However, the most important difference is the higher dispersion for maximum values, meaning that there is more variance in the discriminatory policies pursued by countries for at least selected sectors.

Table 1.1 presents the degree of trade liberalisation achieved by 1995 for a number of agreements as well as an estimate (assuming zero elasticity of imports to tariff liberalisation) of the percentage of imports by product in 2006 when full liberalisation is reached. First, it is important to note that the table confirms what was stated earlier, i.e., in many cases the levels of bilateral imports subject to liberalisation were a relatively small share of total imports. Although most programmes will eliminate internal tariffs for almost all products by 2006, the internal structure of the phase-out programmes varies widely across agreements. Meanwhile, the average percentage of exceptions is low, around five per cent, which contrasts favourably with most of the old agreements.

Figure 1.3 normalises the phase-in of internal liberalisation of all agreements (for which the authors have data) as if all had started on the same date. It then presents the percentage of items and bilateral trade that will be subject to dismantling of tariffs over a ten-year time period, the usual GATT consistent framework for creation of a free trade area.[16] What is evident from the figures is the different built-in speeds of each agreement. For some agreements, more than 50 per cent of the products become free of tariffs during the first year of implementation of the agreement. For others, those percentages will not be reached until the fifth year or later. Four patterns are observed. First, there are the US and Canadian sides of NAFTA vis-à-vis Mexico, the Mexico–Costa Rica FTA and the Mexican side of its FTA with Bolivia, all of which liberalise a high percentage of trade in the first year. Then there are the Chilean bilaterals and the Bolivian side of its Mexican FTA, which achieve high levels of liberalisation by year five. A third pattern is the Mexican side of NAFTA, which undertakes the bulk of its opening between years five and ten. Finally, the G-3 did not undertake much liberalisation at all until after year five. The figure also displays a relatively high degree of reciprocity in liberalisation schedules with the notable exception of NAFTA and the Mexico–Bolivia FTA.

---

[16] In reality, of course, the phase in programmes are discrete in time rather than continuous. However, for visual purposes the figures even out the discrete phases with a continuous fitting line.

Table 1.1: New Regionalism: Selected Trade Liberalisation Programmes in the Americas

Agreement	% Bilateral Imports to Western Hemisphere Imports 1995	% Bilateral Imports to Total Imports 1995	% Liberalised Items 1996	2006
CHILE–MEXICO (1992)				
Chile–Mexico	7.3	3.9	95.5	98.4
Mexico–Chile	0.9	0.7	95.0	98.2
CHILE–VENEZUELA (1993)				
Chile–Venezuela	2.7	1.5	0.7	96.6
Venezuela–Chile	1.7	1.2	0.7	95.7
CHILE–COLOMBIA (1994)				
Chile–Colombia	1.7	0.9	4.1	91.3
Colombia–Chile	2.1	1.4	5.3	91.3
CHILE–ECUADOR (1995)				
Chile–Ecuador	2.5	1.4	3.9	96.4
Ecuador–Chile	4.1	2.7	5.1	96.1
G–3 (1995)				
Mexico–Colombia	0.2	0.1	7.6	90.9
Colombia–Mexico	4.9	3.3	4.1	90.8
Mexico–Venezuela	0.4	0.3	2.4	76.4
Venezuela–Mexico	4.8	3.4	0.4	76.8
MEXICO–COSTA RICA (1995)				
Mexico–Costa Rica	0.0	0.0	86.4	99.3
Costa Rica–Mexico	5.3	4.0	73.2	97.8
MEXICO–BOLIVIA (1995)				
Mexico–Bolivia	0.0	0.0	61.8	96.5
Bolivia–Mexico	2.2	1.4	59.2	96.4
MERCOSUR (1995)				
Argentina–MERCOSUR	44.1	22.7	96.6	99.9
Brazil–Argentina	31.3	13.8	99.4	99.9
Paraguay–MERCOSUR	71.1	40.4	92.8	99.9
Uruguay–MERCOSUR	73.6	46.1	86.3	99.9
MERCOSUR–CHILE (1996)				
Argentina–Chile	5.0	2.6	4.4	94.7
Chile–Argentina	16.8	8.9	4.4	95.0
Brazil–MERCOSUR	5.0	2.2	4.4	94.7
Chile–Brazil	14.5	7.7	4.4	97.6
Uruguay–Chile	2.7	1.7	4.4	94.8
Chile–Uruguay	0.5	0.3	4.4	95.4
Paraguay–Chile	4.6	2.6	4.4	95.0
Chile–Paraguay	0.7	0.4	4.4	93.5
MERCOSUR–BOLIVIA (1997)				
Argentina–Bolivia	0.5	0.3	5.4	97.1
Bolivia–Argentina	14.1	8.8	7.3	92.2
Brazil–Bolivia	0.1	0.1	5.6	97.1
Bolivia–Brazil	19.5	12.1	7.3	92.2
Uruguay–Bolivia	0.1	0.1	4.8	97.1
Bolivia–Uruguay	0.5	0.3	7.3	92.2
Paraguay–Bolivia	0.1	0.1	5.0	97.1
Bolivia–Paraguay	0.1	0.1	8.7	92.3

Source: Integration, Trade and Hemispheric Issues Division, Integration and Regional Programs Department, IDB.

Figure 1.3: New Regionalism: Speed of Intra-Regional Tariff Liberalisation

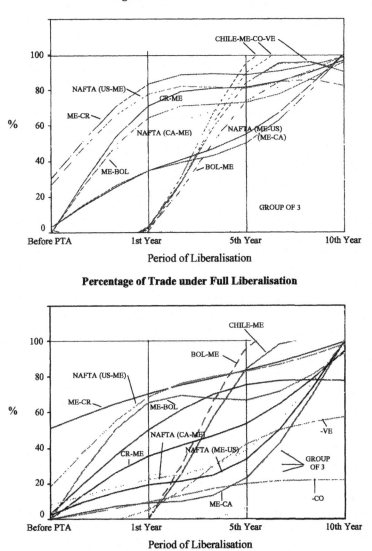

Percentage of Items under Full Liberalisation

Percentage of Trade under Full Liberalisation

The picture changes when considering how much of bilateral trade will be affected by the elimination programme. Even with the caveat that the projections are based on the import structure of the initial period and therefore assume an unrealistic null elasticity of imports vis-à-vis tariff elimination, the data in the bottom half of Figure 1.3 reflect a much higher degree of variance and no discernible pattern regarding the speed of the programmes and the levels of reciprocity. When the examination of the same agreements is done sectorally (not shown), one observes that the intra-sectoral dispersion among the agreements is quite marked and that agricultural products generally have the most gradual liberalisation schedules. Finally, with few exceptions, most of the bilateral trade in the selected agreements becomes fully liberalised in a ten-year period.

It is important to note that tariffs are only part of the story. Because of its discriminatory nature, a preferential free trade agreement must distinguish 'non-member originating' from 'member originating' products in order for a good to be granted the preferential access. The importance of this rises when there are multiple preferential agreements with several partners. Indeed, the growth of international trade in goods that are not manufactured in a single country has raised the issue of the rules for determining the 'origin' of traded goods into one of the most important and complex areas of preferential market access negotiations. The economic analysis of rules of origin (ROO) has been relatively limited in both formal modelling as well as empirical testing. It has been argued, from an analytical point of view, that the way in which ROO are defined and applied within modern preferential agreements plays an important role in determining the degree of protection they confer and the level of distortionary trade they produce.[17]

One of the key features of the New Regionalism, which contrasts with the old processes, is the very general application of automaticity and universalism in the tariff elimination programmes. It has also introduced an extremely selective procedure through the discretionary application of ROO. In the old agreements, mostly under the ALADI framework, there was a general rule applied across-the-board based on a change in tariff classification at the heading level or, alternatively, a regional value-added rule of at least 50 per cent of the f.o.b. export value.[18] In the New Regionalism, mostly attributable to agreements that follow the NAFTA model of ROO, one finds a system of general rules plus additional product-specific rules negotiated at the six-digit level of the Harmonised System (HS).

There are two basic criteria to determine origin. The criterion of 'wholly produced', where only one country enters into the consideration of origin, and the criterion of 'substantial transformation', where two or more countries have taken part in the production process. The first criterion applies mainly to natural resources which have been entirely extracted from the soil or harvested within the country, or manufactured there from any of these products. Such products acquire origin by virtue of the total absence of the use of any second country's

---

[17] For some of the more analytical work in this area, see Garay and Quintero (1999); Garay and Estevadeordal (1996); and Córdoba (1996).

[18] However, the old ALADI framework was only loosely enforced.

components or materials. Even a minimal content of imported components will imply losing its status of 'wholly produced'.

Table 1.2: New Regionalism: Structure of Rules of Origin in Selected Agreements

		FTA US-CA	NAFTA	G-3	Mexico-Costa Rica	Mexico-Bolivia	Canada-Chile	Mercosur-Chile	Mercosur-Bolivia
RULES OF ORIGIN BASED ON CHANGE OF CHAPTER	CC	16.7	27.0	20.0	27.8	20.9	26.5		
	CC/E		5.8	6 0	5.8	6.7	5 3		
	CC/OR	8.4		5.5		6.3			
	CC/E/OR		5.7	6.7	5.8	6.2	7.9		
	CC/RC/OR			2.7		1.2			
	CC or CH/RC				1.0				
	CC or CH/E/RC		1.3				2 0		
	CC or CS/RC	12.8							
	CC or CS/E/RC		1.1				1.0		
	CC/E or CH/E	16.2							
	CC/E or CH/RC	2 5							
	CC/E or CS/E/RC		11 2						
	Subtotal	56 6	52.1	40 9	40.4	41.3	42 7	0.0	0.0
RULES OF ORIGIN BASED ON CHANGE OF HEADING	CH	21.1	7.9	14.8	14.9	15.2	8.9		
	CH/E	6.3	14.2	13 2	16 3	13.9	14 6		
	CH/RC	5 8	3.1	2 0	2 6	2.2	3 4	10.0	11.9
	CH/OR			1 0				20 0	21.2
	CH/E/OR	5.8				1.7			
	CH/RC/OR			8.1		10.0		24.0	22 3
	CH/E/RC/OR			4.9					
	CH or RC				1.0			46.0	44.6
	CH or CH/RC								
	CH or CS/RC		6 9	1.0	1.1				
	CH or CS/E/RC				7.4		7.5		
	CH/E or CS/E/RC						1 1		
	CH/E or CH/RC								
	CH/E or CH/E/RC		1.9		2.6		2.5		
	Subtotal	39.0	34.0	45.0	45.9	43 0	38.0	100 0	100 0
RULES OF ORIGIN BASED ON CHANGE OF SUB-HEADING	CS	1.1	1.3	1.0	1.6	1.7	11.0		
	CS/E				1 3	1 3	1.6		
	CS/RC			4.6	4.2	4.2			
	CS/E/OR								
	CS or RC				1 3	1 3			
	CS or CS/RC								
	CS/E or CS/RC								
	Subtotal	1.1	1.3	5.6	8 4	8 5	12.6	0.0	0 0
	Total	96.7	87.4	91.5	94.7	92 8	93.3	100.0	100.0

Notes Only percentages above 1% of the total are reported. The following abbreviations are used (see text): CC - Change of Chapter; CH - Change of Heading, CS - Change of Subheading; CI - Change of Item; E - Change of Tariff Classification including Exceptions; OR - Other Technical Requirements; RC - Regional Value Content Criteria.
Source Author's calculations

The 'substantial transformation criterion' has been more vague, leaving discretion in its application to national customs authorities. The negotiations under NAFTA were mostly concerned with giving more precision to ROO through the use of three methodologies: (i) a change in tariff classification, requiring the product to change its tariff heading (chapter, heading, sub-heading or item) under the HS in the originating country; (ii) a domestic content rule, requiring a minimum percentage of local value added in the originating country (or setting the maximum percentage of value originating in non-member countries); and (iii) a technical requirement, prescribing that the product must undergo specific manufacturing processing operations in the originating country.

Table 1.2 measures the degree of specificity provided in ROO, computing the percentage of tariff lines that use a specific pattern. It is important to note that there are significant differences among the rules when patterns of ROO are compared across agreements. The FTA agreement between the United States and Canada had already an important degree of specificity. However, NAFTA rules are even more complex when one considers the degree of exceptions introduced at different changes in tariff classification. Also, and this is not reported in the table, the specificity introduced in NAFTA is much greater when one takes into account the methods of computing regional value content, or other administrative provisions in implementing the system. The NAFTA model was exported to the G-3 agreement, Mexico's bilaterals with Costa Rica, Nicaragua and Bolivia, as well as Chile's recent bilaterals with Mexico and Canada. Meanwhile, rules introduced under MERCOSUR and the MERCOSUR bilaterals with its associate members (Chile and Bolivia), as well as the Central America Common Market's rules of origin, can be considered intermediate models between the two extremes of ALADI and NAFTA.

From one angle the New Regionalism's deployment of ROO is a step backwards from the simpler arrangements in the old regional agreements. The growing use of complex rules of origin highlights the fact that modest specificity in the tariff phase-out programmes of the New Regionalism has been at least partially offset by a built-in selective instrument through product specific rules of origin. In NAFTA there is empirical evidence of selective protection through the agreement's rules of origin.[19] If the protectionist and investment diverting effects of rules of origin are serious, one could indeed face effects equivalent to the very distortionary tariff-based instruments under the old regionalism. The spread of rules of origin also raises the issue of transparency and transaction costs. On the other hand, as we have noted, the New Regionalism is much more than trade as such. To the extent that agreements are supportive of overall structural reform, ROO could be considered endogenous protection that guarantees both the achievement and sustainability of an agreement. In any event, to draw firm conclusions in this area one must undertake difficult empirical evaluations of the degree of 'bite' in the region's ROO systems and weigh that cost against other benefits derived from the agreement.[20]

---

[19] Estevadeordal (1999).

[20] Garay and Quintero (1999); and Córdoba (1996) have made advances in this area.

Aside from the generally more rapid and universal nature of liberalisation, coupled with use of more specific ROO, there are several other distinguishing features of the New Regionalism vis-à-vis the old.

- Market driven. The expansion of the regional market is being driven primarily by the private sector and market-based decisions on intra-regional export and investment. Any transformation effects derived from regional integration are being achieved without the state planning and programming that characterised earlier initiatives.
- Special and Differential Treatment (S&D). In the agreements of the 1990s there has been relatively little attention to S&D for the least developed countries. Arrangements are modest, if they exist at all. The most typical arrangement is a more extended phase-in of one or more disciplines. For example, in MERCOSUR, Paraguay and Uruguay received an additional year to phase in tariff elimination of sensitive products, while Paraguay was allowed to place 25 per cent more product categories on a temporary list of exceptions to the agreement's common external tariff (CET), with six additional years to incorporate them. Permanent derogations also exist — for example, Bolivia is outside the Andean CET — but they are not common.[21]
- Cascading. Discovery of new markets, good experiences and strategic considerations have led to cascading effects in which one agreement leads to another with upgrading of liberalisation beyond the old integration's traditional free trade in goods to include so-called new issues. One example is Chile. It began by integrating with Mexico in a simple FTA. After signing a number of similar agreements with other countries in the region, it attempted to enter the more comprehensive NAFTA. When this failed due to the refusal of the US Congress to authorise fast track authority, it signed a NAFTA-like agreement with Canada. Chile then upgraded its simple Mexican FTA to NAFTA-like standards and is currently in new discussions with the USA. It also is discussing full membership in MERCOSUR. Good experiences in the hemisphere also led to negotiations with South Korea and the EU.
- Scaled Down Architecture. The old integration tended to foster prematurely a complex and costly institutional structure. The new agreements tend to promote minimalist inter-governmental arrangements. Moreover, the more traditional agreements such as the Andean Community and the CACM have reformed the over-scaled institutional structures inherited from the past.
- More sustained. The resurgence of regional integration appears to be

---

[21] For a complete summary of special and differential treatment in the new regional accords, see OAS (1996). For the old accords, see Lizano (1982); and Devlin, Estevadeordal and Katona (2001).

more sustained than the early post-war experience. The commitments to liberalisation processes have, on the whole, been effectively implemented and have stayed on track with little back-pedalling, even during the difficult economic conjuncture of 1998–99. This is a major contrast with the old integration that was big on agreement but short on implementation.

Trade Indicators

There are some additional structural differences between the early and more recent integration initiatives that are revealed by looking at selected trade indicators. The measures presented below are, as usual, open to interpretation and can only offer some indication of possible trends, or underlying forces, behind the implicit dynamics of any trade agreement. It is also difficult to separate causality between periods, although in this case one can take advantage of the 1980s debt crisis, which served as a kind of 'laboratory trick', equivalent to a temporary shutdown of regionalism to be restarted again a few years later. Attention is focused on three areas. First, an examination is undertaken of which type of agreements made more sense from the point of view of their degree of 'compatibility' with trade structures at the time of the implementation of the agreement. Second, an evaluation is carried out of the existence of some *ex ante* 'anticipatory effects' on trade flows even before the agreement was implemented. Third, the two periods of regionalism are examined in terms of the 'intensity' of regional integration achieved over time.

Trade Compatibility

The degree of compatibility between the trade structures of potential partners entering into an agreement can be examined by using indices of compatibility that follow the work of Michaely (1996). The range of the index (Sx_jm_k)[22] is defined between zero and unity. It is zero when trade flows have no similarity whatsoever: there is no good imported at all, by one country, which is exported to any extent by the potential partner. On the other hand, the index reaches unity when the structures of the two trade flows are identical: one country exports proportionately precisely what the other imports. Some authors have used this index as an indication of potential trade diversion. In other words, if the export

---

[22] $Sx_jm_k = 1 - \sum_i [|x_{ij} - m_{ik}|] / 2$

where

Sx_jm_k = index of compatibility of exports of country j with imports of country k
x_{ij} = share of good i in exports of country j
m_{ik} = share of good i in imports of country k

structure of one country is very similar to the import structure of a potential partner, there exists the danger that the importing country will replace its third country imports with the potential partner's exports. Conversely, if the trade structures of two potential partner countries are vastly dissimilar, no trade diversion would be possible. However, it also must be noted that compatibility could indicate opportunities for intra-industry trade and enhanced specialisation and efficiency.

We calculated and compared compatibility indices using COMTRADE data at the three-digit product level for most of Latin America. The first year for which we have data (usually 1962)[23] corresponds to the old agreements, while 1990 is our benchmark year for the New Regionalism. Data are organised by exporting country. The results are fully reported in Devlin, Estevadeordal and Katona (2001). The plotted data show that in general the country indices with respect to other potential Latin American partners have risen over the stated time period for all countries. Mexico, Brazil and, to a lesser extent, Argentina, appear to be the partner countries in the region for which there has been a consistent increase in the index across our sample of Latin American exporters. As such, a preferential trade agreement with one or more of these three partner countries might prove most relevant to any other exporting country. It is interesting to note that Mexico has increasingly been a hub country in the formation of Latin American trade agreements and Brazil is a hub market in the Southern Cone.

Anticipatory Effects

This type of analysis compares the agreements in terms of the presence of the so-called anticipatory effects in the trade pattern. We follow Freund and McLaren (1999) in order to examine the existence of trade ratios with a 'S' shape pattern, indicating an accelerating and then decelerating growth of intra-regional trade around the formation of a trade agreement.[24] The evolution of the trade orientation of selected Latin American countries[25] is reported in Devlin, Estevadeordal and

---

[23] For most countries there are data beginning in 1962. The exceptions are the five Central American countries (beginning in 1963 or 1965) and Uruguay (beginning in 1970).

[24] The share of a country's total trade with the members of a given bloc is defined as follows:

$\text{tr}\,^t_{i,j} = \text{trade}\,^t_{i,j} / \text{trade}\,^t_{i,\text{world}}$

where

$\text{tr}\,^t_{i,j}$ = share of country i's trade with block j at time t

$\text{trade}\,^t_{i,j}$ = i's imports from j plus i's exports to j at time t

$\text{trade}\,^t_{i,\text{world}}$ = i's imports from the world plus i's exports to the world at time t

The indices are computed as the difference between actual shares at time t with respect to the share at the time when the agreement is implemented using aggregate trade data from the IMF's Direction of Trade Statistics (DOTS) database.

[25] Argentina, Brazil, Colombia, Venezuela, Mexico and the CACM and NAFTA (averages).

Katona (2001). The orientation focuses on trade with respect to a particular regional bloc(s) with which the country has been (early post-war agreements), or is currently, a member (1990s agreements). The work also examined the average relation for the CACM and NAFTA over the same time period.

Figure 1.4: Old and New Regionalism: Anticipatory Effects
Trade shares normalised with respect to the year of implementation.

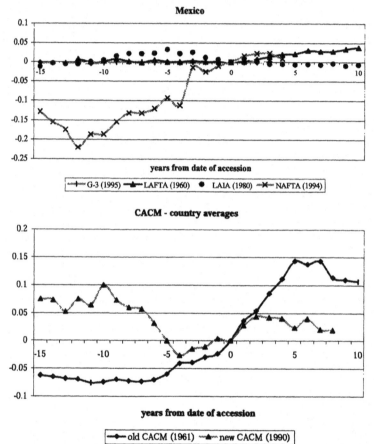

Source: Division of Integration, Trade and Hemispheric Issues, Integration and Regional Programs Department, IDB.

Freund and McLaren found an 'S'-shaped curve for some agreements (EU, European Free Trade Area (EFTA), MERCOSUR and NAFTA). The interpretation is that, when the initiative is credible, as the date of accession looms near, a country will accelerate trade with its future partner countries, and after accession, trade with the said members should flatten out. Recent theoretical work on the existence of sunk investments made in anticipation of accessions supports this view. Given the different scope, modalities and credibility of the older versus the new agreements, those effects may be of different magnitude, much stronger in the case of the new agreements, partly because of the greater credibility and domestic receptiveness to the openness of the New Regionalism.

For the purpose of this chapter, it is interesting to note that in general countries entering 'old' agreements exhibited the 'S' behaviour to a lesser degree than when the same countries entered into 'new' agreements.[26] Mexico is a striking example of this (Figure 1.4). This may reflect the fact that the 'old' regionalism was used as a means of extending the domestic import substitution industrialisation (ISI) model to the regional level rather than enhancing trade among partners as such. The exception is the CACM (Figure 1.4), perhaps because some of the features of its 1960 intra-regional liberalisation scheme approximated the commitment structure of the New Regionalism. In any event, significant anticipatory effects can be observed in most cases of New Regionalism, indicating that the current regional liberalisation processes are perhaps more credible: they are integrated into the three-tier liberalisation process described earlier and form an integral part of commitments to structural reform.

Trade Intensity

To measure the degree of regional integration over time one can deploy two regional intensity ratios, one based on exports and another based on imports. The regional intensity indexes that we have used were developed by Anderson and Norheim (1993) and are defined as the share of country i's exports (imports) to (from) region j relative to the share of region j's imports (exports) in world imports (exports), net of country i's imports/exports.[27]

Trade intensity indices are a better measure of reorientation than trade shares because they control for the overall growth in members' trade relative to world trade as well as for the number of members in the accord by controlling for the size of the bloc. The index describes how much a country trades with other members of the agreement relative to

---

[26] Devlin, Estevadeordal and Katona (2001).

[27] The import (IM) and export (IX) intensity indexes, respectively, are as follows:

$IM_{ij} = x_{ij}/m_j$

where

x_{ij} = the share of country i's exports to the region j

m_j = the share of region j in world imports (net of country i's imports)

$IX_{ij} = m_{ij}/x_j$

where

m_{ij} = the share of country i's imports from the region j

x_j = the share of region j in world exports (net of country i's exports).

how much it trades with the rest of the world. A trade intensity index of unity implies that country i's share of trade with the other members of the agreement is identical to the partner's share of trade with the rest of the world. When the index takes on values above (below) unity the countries have greater (less) bilateral trade than would be expected based on the partner's share in world trade.

Figure 1.5: Old and New Regionalism: Regional Intensity Indices (R11), 1960–98

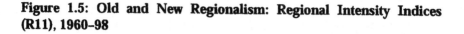

MERCOSUR Countries

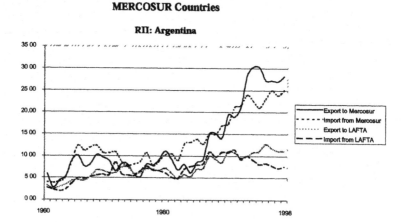

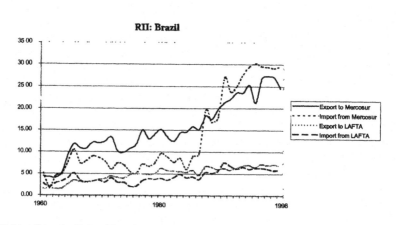

Source: Division of Integration, Trade and Hemispheric Issues, IDB.

Devlin, Estevadeordal and Katona (2001) report the intensity indices for all countries in Latin America during 1960–98, with respect to their immediate subregional agreements as well as LAFTA/ALADI (except for

Central American countries). In order to illustrate the potential effect of regional trade agreements, the analysis depicted the development of the index for each country for all years, even though not all of them participated in the specific agreement during the whole period (i.e., Chile in the Andean Group and MERCOSUR).

The index is very useful in order to analyse the long run dynamics of intra-bloc trade, since implicitly one is controlling for factors such as relative income growth, distance, language and other factors, which would be typically included in a gravity model.[28] Then, examination of trade intensity indices over time accomplishes the same purpose as estimating a gravity equation in a more parsimonious way.[29]

For some countries the effect of the new regional initiatives seems to have been very important; particularly noteworthy are the cases of the major trading partners in the South American agreements, i.e., Argentina and Brazil in the case of MERCOSUR (illustrated in Figure 1.5) and Colombia and Venezuela in the case of the Andean Community. Moreover, the fact that there is a co-movement of the import and export series indicates that there is not a systematic bias between the two, and therefore there is less risk of potential systematic trade diversion effects. Other studies also have suggested that the New Regionalism in Latin America and elsewhere has, in general, not been trade diverting.[30]

Some 'Old' Dimensions of the New Regionalism

Notwithstanding the advances of the New Regionalism, it still exhibits some lingering 'old' characteristics which could be undermining the full potential dynamic and non-traditional effects of the new approach to regional integration.

Latin America still often makes excessive use of 'irregular' unilateral measures to deal with disruptive trade imbalances in their regional agreements. This is sometimes due to the fact that the agreements have made no provision for safeguard clauses even during periods of tariff

---

[28] Assuming that the elasticity of trade with respect to income and distance are constant over time, the gravity equation defines the movements in excess trade over time as those movements that cannot be explained by income growth since distance does not change. There are of course other factors that can explain those movements, among others, the real exchange rates. However, we take the view that some of those price effects will be more important in the short to medium run. In other words, we interpret the long run trends in the indices as due more to structural factors in the way different economies are linked through formal trading arrangements, while short-to-medium run fluctuations can be attributed to variables such as exchange rate movements.

[29] See Freund and McLaren (1999) for an analytical derivation of trade intensity indices using a gravity equation.

[30] Soloaga and Winters (1999); Robinson and Thierfelder (1999); Nagarajan (1998); and Devlin, Estevadeordal and Katona (2001).

phase-out (Table 1.3). Although there have been some signs of improvement,[31] there has been insufficient attention to the use of formal dispute settlement. Past practice in Latin America was to settle disputes in back rooms through diplomatic channels. The diplomatic route is still heavily used today. This approach perhaps made sense when the state was the primary economic actor in the region. However, today integration is market driven; growth of private sector investment in the regional markets would be enhanced by more modern and transparent rules-based systems.

Table 1.3: Available Unilateral Trade Measures Applicable to Intra-Agreement Trade

MEASURE	LAIA	ANDEAN PACT	CACM	CARICOM	GROUP OF THREE	NAFTA	MERCOSUR	MERCOSUR Bilaterals BOLIVIA	CHILE
Increase in tariffs[1]		No[2]	No[3]	No[5]	No	No	No	No	No
Import Surcharges	No	No	No[4]	No	No	No	No	No	No
Minimum import prices	WTO rules	WTO rules	No		No	No	WTO rules	WTO rules	WTO rules
Anti-dumping tariffs	Yes	Yes	Yes	Yes	Yes	Yes	Yes	Yes	Yes
Countervailing duties	Yes	Yes	Yes	Yes	Yes	Yes	Yes	Yes	Yes
Safeguards									
General rules	Yes	Yes	No	Yes	Yes	Yes	No	Yes	No
Sector-specific rules	No	No	No	No	No	Yes[6]	No	No	No[7]
Safeguards or other measures triggered by balance-of-payments problems	Yes	Yes	No	Yes	No	No	No	No	

[1] Other than under a safeguard clause.
[2] Exceptions for Bolivia and Ecuador.
[3] However, products can be removed from the free-trade list. In that case the MFN tariff is applied.
[4] Nicaragua applied a temporary protection tariff (ATP) to intra-regional trade that was eliminated in 1999, except for some products for reasons of fiscal revenue in 2001.
[5] Can be raised to MFN level with consensus of all CARICOM states.
[6] Textiles and apparel goods.
[7] Under negotiation.
Source: OAS (1996), IDB (1999a).

The old regionalism was characterised by significant selectivity in its tariff liberalisation process. While the New Regionalism is more universal and automatic in this regard, there is considerable sectoral

---

[31] For example, the AG Tribunal was created in 1984, but went unutilised until 1996. Starting in this latter year activity has increased significantly, with some 30 cases of non-compliance being sent to the Tribunal (authors' communication with the Andean Community Secretariat, 1999).

selectivity in some product specific tariff phase-outs and preferences across different partners. Another source of selectivity is the increasing use of product-specific rules of origin. Moreover, rules of origin lack the transparency of a tariff. All the above — but especially rules of origin — are contributing to a 'spaghetti' bowl of agreements that raises transaction costs and reduces transparency. There is a clear need to evaluate empirically the effects of rules of origin. The WTO could help by putting rules of origin under the umbrella of Article 24 and expanding its development of a system of non-preferential rules of origin to include the preferential type.[32] Meanwhile, creation of an FTAA in 2005 would help to clean out and harmonise many of the more shallow FTAs in the hemisphere.

One solution to the ROO problem is the formation and consolidation of a customs union. The old regionalism encountered tremendous difficulties in establishing and maintaining a CET. It has proved difficult in the New Regionalism too. The CET in all subregions were 'imperfect' when established in the early 1990s and some have suffered serious perforations since then. In Central America the CET established in the 1990s began at 95 per cent of the tariff universe, but now involves only 50 per cent, or 70 per cent if Nicaragua is excluded.[33] MERCOSUR started out with a CET on 88 per cent of the tariff universe; the current situation is very fluid and difficult to assess, but a significant number of perforations have occurred in recent years.[34] In the Andean Community about 85 percent of the tariff lines were incorporated in the CET; exceptions were to be eliminated in 1999, but this was postponed. Meanwhile, aside from a significant number of items outside the CET, rules of origin are also necessary because no subregion has a common system for collection of tariff revenue.

Conclusions

The New Regionalism contrasts fundamentally with the old. Its instrumental role is geared to supporting structural reforms to make economies more open, market-based, competitive and democratic. Given that regional liberalisation has worked in tandem with unilateral and multilateral trade opening and a liberalised economic environment for the private sector, the new trade agreements enjoy a credibility that the old did not due to their preference for protection and state intervention. The scope of liberalising disciplines in the New Regionalism tends to be comprehensive and more rapid, universal and sustained in terms of effective application. The New Regionalism is meant to attract foreign

[32] Serra et al. (1996).
[33] Granados (1999).
[34] INTAL (1996).

investment, not restrict or control it. The New Regionalism also has more functional and cost-effective institutional arrangements. Finally, the new initiatives also better support important non-economic objectives such as peace, democracy and effective participation in international forums.

Regional integration, like any major structural transformation, has costs that must be assumed and should be minimised to the extent possible. However, with the new setting for, and role of, regional integration in LAC countries the matrix of objectives and expected benefits have changed dramatically. In this sense Ethier (1998) is correct to argue that the simple Vinerian approach to the evaluation of regional schemes is overly narrow and development of a broader conceptual framework is needed. What else is needed is an increased analytical capacity to evaluate effectively events in this broader framework. This will require, among other things, much better empirical observation and analysis than we have today of what is actually happening on the ground.

CHAPTER 2

Regional Integration and the Investment Effect

Sheila Page

Even without special arrangements for capital, the formation of a region will affect investment within the region and outside it. Foreign investment can be to serve a local market: this replaces exports to that market; or to exploit a resource that is more abundant in the host than the home country, whether a natural resource or an economic one like different types of labour: this increases exports from the host.

- Investment to supply a market is a substitute for trade; if lowering trade barriers within the region makes it more efficient to supply markets through exports, this type of investment will *fall within the region.*
- Investment may increase and perhaps relocate within the region, to exploit opportunities for trade creation or any increased income. If there is trade diversion, investment to exploit this may be diverted from non-member countries. Outside investment will respond in the same ways as regional investment to trade creation or diversion opportunities; in addition, increased growth (relative to the rest of the world) could make the region more likely to attract investment. This could suggest an *increased share for the region in total world investment,* which might include an increased share within the region by regional investors if they have advantages of proximity and familiarity, or if there is institutional preference for regional investors.
- Particularly for relatively small or poor countries forming a region, the increase in total income or the potential for more rapidly increasing income in the future may give the necessary minimum size for an *investment in production* capacity or for investment to have cost advantages over exports to supply the market, and cause more than marginal increases in investment. Increases in the integration of the market, including reductions in non-tariff barriers, but also increased similarities, will reinforce this effect.
- The relative fall in growth outside the region could affect regional investors more strongly, *lowering their share in external* investment.
- Any general reduction in barriers to foreign investment could *increase* both regional and non-regional *investment.*
- Investment to exploit a natural resource *may increase within a*

region. If the resource extends across more than one member, increasing returns to scale mean that there is a potential for increased efficiency in its use.
- Because lowering internal barriers effectively raises the relative protection against the rest of the world, investment to get behind tariff barriers, the direct *substitution of investment for exports,* may also rise within a region.

Other types of integration within regions can also have effects on investment through their trade or growth effects. These include regional preferences for services trade, special rules on government procurement, common standards or regulations for products (or for companies), deeper macroeconomic integration, or the establishment of common legal approaches. Investment is also probably even more sensitive than trade to the 'new partner' or awareness effect. The increased information and discussion of the fellow members of a region may give a stimulus to look for investment opportunities there, rather than in already well-known or still unfamiliar areas. This may be encouraged by closer contacts between business groups.

An analysis of intra-regional and inter-regional investment in the years up to 1990, before the period examined here, found a tendency by most major investors to become less regionally orientated.[1] For the USA, Western Europe became a more important destination, replacing Canada and Latin America, while Japanese investment shifted from Asia to North America and Europe. This is attributed partly to the fact that 'companies competing in global markets were increasingly likely to establish a local presence in the three main markets' (p. 108), with the exception that there was no growth in investment in Japan. If new multinational companies in Latin America and the Caribbean (LAC) countries follow a similar pattern of investing first in their own region before diversifying, we could observe an apparent increase in regional investment, but this could indicate only a step in the first stages of expansion.

We expect, therefore, to observe increased investment, within countries, intra-regional and from outside, but there are some forces which could reduce intra-regional investment. The expected direction of effects is therefore more ambiguous than for trade, and it is more difficult to find a simple measure of integration.

Traditional theory on customs unions and FTAs does not deal with the consequences of freer movement of capital flows among members of a regional group. In the pre-Viner regions, capital movements were either completely free, within and outside the group, or controlled within each country.

---

[1] Wyatt-Walter (1995), pp. 106–9.

1. Investment Policy

Policy towards capital flows may reinforce these effects of regions on investment. Many of the Latin American and Caribbean regions have had an objective of freer, and eventually free, capital movement within the region, and some now have special arrangements for investment, giving discrimination between the region and the rest of the world for investment as well as trade.

However, other influences act against an increased effect of regions on investment flows. As well as the market and resource use motives for foreign investment, investors may be seeking access to local information, not only about markets, but about technology. This may be a particularly important motive for developing country exporters.[2] They may benefit from both direct access and the availability of labour with experience in new technologies. They may therefore have a preference for investment in a more developed country. If markets improve and company sizes increase sufficiently to make foreign investment a possible strategy, there may be a conflict between the conventional assumption that firms choose more familiar (by assumption, nearer) destinations first and their desire for access to technology. There is some evidence, however, that developing country investment in developed regions has been more conventionally motivated, seeking access to protected markets.[3]

In parallel with trade liberalisation, countries have tended to reduce their barriers to both inward and outward investment in the last 50 years. Since the 1950s, both on their own initiative and under pressure from major investors, countries have also signed bilateral agreements to restrict their ability to control foreign investment, requiring either minimum standards of liberalisation or full national treatment (these were first encouraged by the European countries; the USA only began to sign them from 1982). Both general liberalisation and bilateral treaties cut across regions and therefore reduce their relative liberalisation as trade liberalisation reduces their effective degree of preference. The growth of the bilateral treaties, like that of bilateral most favoured nations (MFN) trading agreements in the late nineteenth century, is starting to give a *de facto* common minimum standard for investment regulation at international level and by including access to international dispute procedures, they provide some enforceability. Both the regional agreements and the proposals for multilateral agreements build on this.

At the time the GATT was established, most countries had tight controls on capital flows, and there was no attempt to include either liberalisation or regulation of the controls in the GATT. There was therefore no equivalent of MFN rules for regulation of investment,

---

[2] Adams (1998).
[3] Page (1998).

leaving countries free to give special access or apply special controls to all investment, or on a discriminatory basis, whether by bilateral agreements or regional arrangements. There were provisions attempting to regulate the use of trade-related restrictions on investment, in particular the imposition of minimum export or local content rules, because these could be held to interfere with commitments on non-discriminatory treatment of trade and national treatment of traded goods, but these were not enforced. In the Uruguay Round, Trade-Related Investment Measures (TRIMS) were one of the major issues in the opening stages, but the final agreement did little more than restate the GATT provisions.

The increasing awareness of the roles of international investment and of large multinational companies has led to attempts to regulate both their activities and the potentially conflicting attempts by national governments to control the companies. The move to include services within the WTO was used to bring in increased regulation of investment in service industries. It was argued that 'establishment', a commercial presence in the importing country, was likely to be an essential part of trade in services, and therefore that the General Agreement on Services (GATS) should include commitments to permit investment for this purpose. The importance of the agreement to investment was, first, that it made the regulation of at least some types of investment clearly part of the multilateral regime and, second, that it required countries to specify in advance, when they adopted the GATS, any partner countries to which they wished to give special, non-MFN, treatment. In order to give special treatment to fellow members of a region, therefore, the group must either conform to the full integration requirements of including most services or have recorded the exceptions by 1995.

The World Bank has sponsored a series of agreements on different aspects of foreign investment. There are procedures for settlement of disputes (the Convention on the Settlement of Investment Disputes between States and Nationals of Other States), and for providing insurance against political risks (the Multilateral Investment Guarantee Agency, MIGA), but effectively these apply only when countries agree that they should, or apply for coverage. There are also extensive guidelines on aspects of treatment of foreign investment by host states, but these are advisory. Under the UN system, there are guidelines on the regulation of foreign investment and on the activities of multinational firms, but again these are voluntary. There are also agreements among the OECD countries on particular aspects of the treatment of investment, with proposals for a new agreement on investment, which could be expanded to other countries.

All these multilateral agreements indicate the growing consensus that the regulation and legal treatment of investment, as for trade, are no longer exclusively matters for national governments and that there are limits to countries' discretion in discriminating among investors, by company or by country of origin. The agreements limit the scope and the potential effect of regional initiatives, but also help to legitimise them. Regions can still differ in whether they liberalise more to the region.

2. Investment Flows

The factors outlined above suggest that the effects of a region could appear as an increase in non-regional foreign investment and perhaps in intra-regional investment within the region. The strongest evidence of diversion would be a decrease in regional investment outside the region. The general reduction in barriers to inward and outward investment, as well as other economic changes (including, in the 1990s, the formation of other regions), could mask any of these effects.

Even in countries which are not members of regions, there have been important increases in foreign investment in recent years. The total more than tripled between 1990 and 1998 (Table 2.1). The share of developing countries in receipts, which had fallen sharply in the 1980s, recovered, reaching a peak of 38 per cent in 1996–97, although it fell to 28 per cent in the Asian crisis of 1998. The share of LAC countries, which had received about half the total to developing countries in 1970, fluctuated by less and has now returned to over 40 per cent. For the world as a whole, foreign investment now accounts for 6–7 per cent of total investment (compared to 2–3 per cent in the 1970s and 1980s) and two per cent of GDP. Latin America, however, in contrast to developing countries as a group, has not had a rising share of investment in output so that on the simplest measure of a response to the formation of regions, that it should lead to improved growth and therefore investment, there is no evidence of an effect.

Latin American countries' outward investment has also risen in the 1990s, but by less than inflows (Table 2.2). It doubled between 1995 and 1998. It is still only 30 per cent of the total for developing countries, although this has risen from the 1995 figure of 14 per cent (the most recent figures for its distribution by destination are from 1992, UNCTAD 1999, p. 24, when half was in Latin America and half in developed countries).

The increasing number of large firms, in developing countries as well as traditional foreign investors among the developed countries, means a growing number of potential investors with a global view, and therefore demand for production facilities that encourage foreign investment. Increased liberalisation gives more scope for the growth of these firms.

Table 2.1: Foreign Direct Investment (US$ million) and Percentage of Gross Domestic Investment (GDI)

	Value				Percentages of GDI			
	1970	1980	1990	1998	1970	1980	1990	1998
Argentina	11	678	1,836	6,150	0	3	9	10
Aruba	—	—	131	81	—	—	—	—
Barbados	9	3	11	15	18	1	3	4
Belize	0	0	17	20	—	0	15	12
Bolivia	-76	47	27	872	-26	10	4	51
Brazil	421	1,911	989	31,913	5	3	1	19
Chile	-79	213	590	4,638	-5	4	8	22
Colombia	43	157	500	3,038	2	2	5	15
Costa Rica	26	53	163	559	13	4	10	19
Dominica	—	—	13	21	—	—	19	33
Dominican Republic	72	93	133	691	25	6	7	17
Ecuador	89	70	126	831	29	2	7	17
El Salvador	4	6	2	12	2	1	0	1
Grenada	0	0	13	21	—	0	15	15
Guatemala	29	111	48	673	12	9	5	22
Guyana	9	1	0	95	15	0	0	46
Haiti	3	13	8	11	6	5	2	3
Honduras	8	6	44	84	6	1	6	5
Jamaica	162	28	138	369	35	7	12	18
Mexico	323	2,156	2,634	10,238	4	4	4	11
Nicaragua	15	0	0	184	10	0	0	27
Panama	33	-47	132	1,206		-4	15	40
Paraguay	4	32	76	256	4	2	7	14
Peru	-70	27	41	1,930	-6	0	1	13
St Kitts and Nevis	—	—	49	24	—	—	56	18
St Lucia	—	—	45	46	—	—	44	39
St Vincent and the Grenadines	0	1	8	40	—	5	14	40
Trinidad & Tobago	83	185	109	730	39	10	17	52
Uruguay	0	290	0	164	0	16	0	5
Venezuela	-23	55	451	4,435	-1	0	9	24
Latin America & Caribbean	1,091	6,148	8,188	69,323	3	3	4	16
Developing	2,207	4,400	24,130	170,942	2	2	2	12
World	9,206	50,684	193,382	619,258	2	3	4	n/a
Developing as % of world	24	9	12	28				
Latin America as % of developing	49	140	34	41				

No data available for Antigua and Barbuda, Cayman Islands, Cuba.
Source: World Bank (2000).

Strategic alliances between firms are in fashion. These trends mean that increased investment, even at a very high rate, cannot be assumed to derive from reasons peculiar to a region.

The investment observed in LAC regions will also be affected by changes in the investment strategies of the major investing countries. The trade liberalisation by Latin American countries has permitted a change in focus of US investment in the region, from investing in order to have access to protected markets to greater emphasis on investing to find competitive advantages.[4] This may obscure any influence from better access because of regional markets. Japanese investment, however, still seems to be principally directed at the local and regional markets, although this may be beginning to change, and French investors have moved away from natural resource investment to market-seeking.[5]

Table 2.2: Outflows of Latin American Investment: Selected Countries (US$m)

	1994	1995	1996	1997	1998	1999
Argentina	1013	1497	1600	3656	2166	1195
Brazil	618	1163	520	1660	2609	1401
Uruguay	0	-26	11	13	5	10
Bolivia	2	2	2	2	3	3
Chile	911	752	1188	1866	2797	4855
Mexico	1058	-263	38	1108	1363	800
South America	3139	3773	4140	8642	8428	8329
Developing Countries	42124	50259	57763	64335	33045	65638
Total	282902	357537	390776	471906	687111	799928
Share in total outflows (%)						
Developing Countries	14.9	14.1	14.8	13.6	4.8	8.2
S. America & Mexico	1.48	0.98	1.07	2.07	1.42	1.14
S. America & Mexico / Developing	9.96	6.98	7.23	15.15	29.63	13.91

Source: UNCTAD, 1999.

The large-scale sales of public sector industries to the private sector in Latin America, especially in Argentina and Brazil, have provided a new opportunity for investment by foreign service providers. Investment to

---

[4] IDB/IRELA (1998).
[5] *Ibid.*

take advantage of this will explain part of any foreign investment in MERCOSUR countries. A high share of this has been by Spanish investors, whose investment in Latin America grew strongly in the 1990s.[6]

There are two difficulties for analysing investment in a way similar to that for trade. The first is the extreme concentration of all direct investment. This makes the use of any measure of intensity difficult.[7] There are likely to be very uneven flows by and to countries, so that we would not expect to find similar ratios among members of a region, or to find that comparisons among regions can be made directly. The USA accounts for a quarter of foreign investment, the UK for 15 per cent; if Germany, France, Japan and Hong Kong are added, these six countries make up 70 per cent of the total. This is very different from the pattern of trade. Among recipients, the USA is again a quarter of the total, with the other important recipients being the UK, France and China. Among developing countries, ten countries, six in Latin America and four in Asia, account for three-quarters of receipts. If a region contains one of these major investors or recipients, as NAFTA and MERCOSUR do, the numbers will be distorted.

The second obstacle is the poor quality of the data. There is no equivalent to 'seeing' trade at the border. Many countries rely on samples or surveys. Many countries lack data by source and destination. Data on investment flows on a comparable basis by direction and source are only available in one Latin American series, with detailed figures only to 1990,[8] supplemented by an UNCTAD Directory (1994). These can be supplemented by more recent data from ECLAC and individual countries, but these rarely permit the detailed analysis by sector which can be done for trade data, and tax havens and investment through subsidiaries or in joint ventures make geographical identification difficult. There are no regions for which there are sufficient comparable data to make intensity calculations. The data are becoming less reliable because of the liberalisation of capital flows, which means there is often no compulsory notification.[9] This report will therefore examine the available data, without a formal measure of integration.[10]

---

[6] Toral (2001).

[7] For trade, it is customary to measure a region's integration by comparing the share of intra-regional trade to the region's trade with the world. See Bulmer-Thomas and Page (1999).

[8] CEPAL (1993).

[9] 'Al no registrar más la entrada de inversiones extranjeras, se pierde casi toda posibilidad de analizar éstas en cuanto a su lugar de procedencia y a su destino sectorial. Cada vez son más los países que tienen tan sólo una noción global de los montos de recursos financieros que acuden desde afuera, a partir de los cálculos que efectúen para elaborar sus balances de pagos'. CEPAL (1997), p. 16.

[10] Using correlation among interest rates as a proxy would be an alternative way of measuring the integration of capital markets, but there are now few regions where capital

3. MERCOSUR

MERCOSUR requires national treatment of almost all intra-regional investments, following the Colonia Protocol of 1994.[11] This includes equal treatment of the transfer of profits and repatriation. Although this may add little to the requirements for all foreign investors, the sectoral promotion provisions, especially the special rules for the car sector, effectively encourage investment in the region, although the car sector is the only sector in which performance requirements are still permitted on intra-MERCOSUR investment.[12] The final goal of MERCOSUR is a single economic market, including full liberalisation of capital (and labour) movements. One of the MERCOSUR working groups is elaborating harmonising policies in banking and stock markets.[13]

There are still restrictions on foreign investment in both Argentina and Brazil which apply to the MERCOSUR countries as well as to non-members. Argentina restricts investment near the frontier, in naval construction, nuclear energy and uranium, and also in insurance and finance. Brazil restricts it in mining, hydroelectricity, health services, radio and telecommunications, banking and insurance, construction and shipping and its restrictive provisions on government procurement further limit opportunities for all foreign investment.[14] In MERCOSUR, however, as elsewhere in the LAC region, there has been a major shift from a regime of controlling foreign investment to trying to promote it. This is true also of the associate members, Chile and Bolivia.

The member states had already moved to fewer restrictions on national treatment before the establishment of MERCOSUR, and all the countries (including Chile and Bolivia) have recently signed a large number of bilateral agreements. Most give what is effectively national treatment and have few controls on profit remittances and disinvestment. They also recognise the World Bank dispute settlement procedures; these can still be used for intra-MERCOSUR disputes, as well as for disputes with third countries. Argentina has joined the World Bank MIGA scheme. Brazil still requires authorisation for investment, although Argentina has dropped this.[15] Their GATS services offers were also restricted to only five to seven sectors so these have not encouraged

---

flows have been more liberated within the region than with the rest of the world, and in these internal controls suggest that interest rates are unlikely to move freely. There would also be the usual difficulties of finding comparable rates and ensuring that they were not correlated because of other influences, perhaps from outside the region.

[11] Blomström and Kokko (1997), p. 32; UNCTAD (1997).

[12] There are also legislative provisions for a common company regime, dating from the Argentine-Brazilian agreement of 1985 (Lucángeli, 1996, p. 92). These have full national treatment, but the provisions have not been much used: there are 12 in Brazil.

[13] Organisation of American States (OAS) (1996a).

[14] Lipsey and Meller (1996), p. 110.

[15] Bouzas in de la Balze (1995), p. 320.

investment.

MERCOSUR has the intention of setting up a common competition policy (it is in the 1991 Asunción Treaty). In 1996, a framework was established.[16] It provides for controlling anti-competitive practices which affect competition at the MERCOSUR level, by harmonising domestic legislation, but the division of responsibilities between national and regional agencies has not yet been determined and Paraguay and Uruguay do not have internal competition laws, so this is not an important contribution to integration.

In MERCOSUR, therefore, there is some discrimination in favour of members, but the major changes in recent years have probably been its general liberalisation. This explains some increase in foreign investment, both intra-regional and from other countries; this has been reinforced by substantial inflows in both Argentina and Brazil because of their privatisation programmes. Only a marginal advantage for intra-regional investment would be expected from the limited bias of regulation in favour of regional investment. The rise in intra-regional trade, however, could suggest an increase in trade-induced investment.

There has been a sharp increase in investment in the MERCOSUR countries, especially Brazil, followed by Argentina; outflows have risen slightly, but the net inflow is significant (Table 1.1). These are two of the six major Latin American recipients of foreign investment, with Chile a third.

For Argentina, the rise occurred in the 1980s, even before MERCOSUR was formed. Paraguay has seen a rise, but Uruguay has not. Only for Brazil is there a strong surge in the 1990s, and especially after 1995, but here privatisation has been an important influence. UNCTAD (1997, p. 73) estimates that a quarter of investment inflows to Latin America were accounted for by privatisation in the first half of the 1990s, but the shares for Brazil and Argentina are estimated to be much higher, perhaps as much as a half. It accounted for about 25 per cent of inflows to Brazil in 1998,[17] and 17 per cent for Argentina.[18] The Chilean purchases of electricity companies indicate that regional investors are also participating in the privatisation process, but this is more likely to reflect common interests and experience than regional preference. Only Brazil has a strikingly above average share of foreign investment in total investment (Table 1.1).

Some foreign investors that entered for a single country market in the 1980s, however, expanded because of MERCOSUR.[19] Formally, this has been marked by the establishment of separate Latin American

---

[16] Tavares and Tineo (1997), pp. 9–13.
[17] UNCTAD (1999).
[18] Giordano and Santiso (1999).
[19] *Ibid.*

divisions. The availability of a regional market was particularly important for the car industry, giving international producers a much stronger base to use as part of a global strategy of production. In contrast to the pre-1990s situation, the country markets have been consolidated and new models have been introduced. That these investments are primarily for the regional market is supported by the evidence that their share in domestic sales is higher than their share in exports, although individual firms have a high propensity to export.

Data on intra-regional investment are only available in non-comparable forms, and for selected years. For Argentina, investment by other members accounted for one per cent of foreign investment in the 1980s and only 1.3 per cent in 1990, but it was 5.7 per cent of the capital stock by 1992, when investment was starting to rise. By then investment inflows from Chile had risen to six per cent of the total.[20] Measured by stocks, Brazil was an important investor in Argentina before 1992. Using data on individual projects, Chudnovsky found that Brazilian investors accounted for about five per cent of foreign investment in 1990–94, and Chile for 14 per cent.[21] These figures support the aggregate data. A survey by an Argentine investment institute[22] of investments planned in 1994–95, found only two per cent (by value) from Brazil, mainly in breweries, and six per cent from Chile. There was one investment, worth 0.2 per cent, from Uruguay, but the major investor was the USA, accounting for 40 per cent of the total. A third of the Chilean investment was the purchase of a privatised electricity plant, with other investments in improving other electricity plants.

Argentine surveys of investors show increasing interest in MERCOSUR, rising from five per cent in 1991 to 45 per cent by 1995.[23] The increase in Argentine outflows coincided with the formalisation of MERCOSUR in 1994, but also with the domestic liberalisation which was putting pressure on firms to find new markets.[24] Chile, not at this time even an associate of MERCOSUR, had seen a similar increase in the early 1990s, while Brazil's rise was much later (Table 2.2). Some of the Argentine investment, however, was more clearly targeted at the MERCOSUR market, in particular the oil investment by the privatised national oil company, YPF.

In contrast to the Argentine inflows, there was no comparable rise in the early 1990s in MERCOSUR investment in Brazil. In 1991, under one per cent of investment in Brazil came from the other MERCOSUR countries or went to them. A Brazilian survey suggested that only 70

[20] IDB (1996); and IRELA (1996).
[21] Chudnovsky, López, Porta, in Chudnovsky (1996), pp. 124–5.
[22] Fundación Invertir Argentina (1996).
[23] Lucángeli (1996), p. 93.
[24] UNCTAD (1999), pp. 66–7.

companies from the other three countries had invested in Brazil.[25] There had been some investment by Argentina in Brazil in the 1980s,[26] but this ended by 1990, with the recession in Brazil and expansion in Argentina. Most Brazilian investment is in developed countries, especially the USA, although it has been argued that MERCOSUR is an 'incubator for Brazilian emerging multinational companies. Depending on the source, one-third to one-half of all Brazilian emerging multinational companies started their overseas operations in the MERCOSUR region.'[27] This suggests that some of the investment is not because of MERCOSUR as an institution, but merely as a step to world investment, the 'infant multinational' model.

Most foreign investment by Brazil is in services (about 60 per cent) with manufacturing accounting for about 30 per cent,[28] but in Argentina Brazil invests mainly in manufacturing.[29] 139 Brazilian companies are operating there, principally in transport equipment, financial services, and metal products. The importance of transport is consistent with the importance of this sector in trade. Financial services have been liberalised in Argentina, making this a logical direction for investment, especially as the large Brazilian banks are among the largest in Latin America, and are taking advantage of a more advanced use of automation. It is, however, still impossible for Argentine banking and insurance companies to operate in Brazil on the same basis as Brazilian firms in Argentina. The investment in breweries, visible in both Argentine and Brazilian data, is because the Brazilian firm already held almost half the Brazilian market, and was looking for expansion.[30] In Paraguay, almost all Brazilian investment is in services. In Uruguay, two-thirds is in services, but there is also investment in chemicals, wood, and textiles,[31] similar (except for the absence of transport equipment) to the investment in Argentina.

The greater investment by Brazil in Argentina than by Argentina in Brazil is partly because of lack of liberalisation in Brazilian services, but it may also indicate the advantage, at least initially, of a country with larger companies, already accustomed to operating on a wide geographical scale. Surveys of Brazilian industry in 1994 and 1995[32] suggested that, while almost all sectors saw MERCOSUR having an important effect on

---

[25] Neto and Bannister (1997), p. 13.

[26] Lucángeli (1995), p. 89.

[27] Neto and Bannister (1997), pp. 7–8.

[28] *Ibid.*, p. 6.

[29] Brazilian data for investment in Argentina are lower than Argentine data for investment from Brazil; this is attributed by Brazilian authors to lack of controls and poor data (Neto and Bannister (1997), p. 6).

[30] Neto and Bannister (1997), p. 11.

[31] IDB (1996), p. 16.

[32] Confederação Nacional da Indústria (1994), (1995).

exports (the only exceptions were mining, leather, food and drink), those expecting to invest abroad as a response were mainly in transport followed by other manufactures, with less consistency between the two years, except in chemicals, perfumes and drink.

The MERCOSUR countries are important investors for Paraguay. In 1992, about a third of inward investment there came from Brazil, and Chile had been important in 1991. However, both these observations date from before regional integration. MERCOSUR countries account for seven per cent of investment in Bolivia.

MERCOSUR investors already accounted for 3.7 per cent of flows and two per cent of the stock in Chile in 1992. Chile's important role is as an investor, particularly in Argentina. There have been parallel investments by two Chilean power companies, perhaps — like the Brazilian breweries — finding the Chilean market too small for expansion. For Chile, in contrast to Brazil, Argentina represents a much larger market than the domestic one. Chile, however, has also been investing in other Latin American countries. A total of 78 per cent of Chilean investment went to Latin American countries in 1990–96. While Argentina received most of this, other important recipients were Brazil, Peru, Bolivia, Colombia, Mexico and Panama,[33] so again the explanation for investing in Argentina may not be the regional access. The investments recorded here preceded Chile's associate membership, and most preceded even the beginning of negotiations. For Argentina, Brazil and Chile account for almost all its receipts of investment from Latin America; Brazil and Chile have more sources (and destinations). On investment, therefore, Argentina seems more 'regional' than the others.

4. CARICOM, Andean Group and CACM

The only Caribbean regional liberalisation of investment applies to banking, although there are provisions in the agreement for a regional regime for investment and for looking at the possibility of national treatment.[34] The CARICOM countries also have joint agreements on the regulation of third-country investment. They issued joint Guidelines on Foreign Investment in 1982, and have specified performance criteria (including employment, local content and external financing) and the conditions for expropriation, etc.[35] The Caribbean countries have signed very few bilateral agreements (even the major recipients of investment, Jamaica and Barbados, have fewer than any of the MERCOSUR countries). Jamaica liberalised only seven services in the GATS.

---

[33] IDB (1997), p. 6.
[34] OAS (1996a).
[35] *Ibid.*

The CARICOM regime is still restrictive, for both intra-regional and external foreign investment. With no reduction in restrictions on regional or other investment, recent changes in trade do not provide a strong reason for new investment. Trinidad and Jamaica have seen significant increases in investment in the 1990s (Table 2.1), and the increase in the foreign share is particularly important for Trinidad. But it seems unlikely that this is associated with intra-Caribbean trade. There are no data on intra-regional investment for CARICOM, and the data on investment in the region are too distorted by the presence of financial centres to be useful. There has been some increase in investment in the region, but it is unlikely that this is associated with regional incentives.

The Andean Pact in its original 1970s form had extensive joint regulation (Decision 24 of the Pact) of foreign investment, including its direction and requirements on performance and remittance of profits. The region was seen as the appropriate target for development strategy, which necessarily included the regulation of investment and of the balance of payments. This lapsed, and was formally changed in the revisions of the 1980s. The current rules date from Decision 291 of 1991. This represents a complete reversal of the previous regime, with an emphasis on liberalisation and minimal controls, and, although a joint Andean initiative, it gives equal treatment to third-country investors. The purpose was to encourage foreign investment, including offering the advantages of a regional market and common rules, rather than to regulate it. Like the MERCOSUR countries, most of the Andean countries have signed a large number of bilateral investment treaties. However, also like the MERCOSUR, their services regimes, within the Andean region and under the GATS, remain restricted. Andean countries give investors national treatment, permit profit remittances and do not allow performance requirements. There are still a few reserved sectors, which apply to Andean and other investors. Decision 291 revived the old concept of the Andean company, a multinational operating in the region, which was given some preferences.[36]

Andean liberalisation is now explicitly directed at attracting investment from outside, not at promoting intra-regional investment. The level and the increase of intra-regional trade, however, could have encouraged regional investment. Total investment in the region has increased spectacularly since the second half of the 1980s (Table 2.1). Investment flows, however, have fallen back since 1996. Except for Venezuela (oil), the share of foreign investment in total investment is not much above the developing country average.

The most recent intra-regional investment data date from 1992. Only about one per cent of investment in Colombia and Ecuador came from

---

[36] *Ibid.*

the region, but there was significant investment by Venezuela in Peru. The pattern had not changed greatly from 1990. The high percentages for Peruvian investment in Bolivia and Colombian investment in Venezuela show mainly how little these countries invest outside, but do suggest a strong preference for regional investment by small investors. Other Latin American countries, already important in 1990, notably Chile, are important, and are more important in the Andean countries than in the larger countries, MERCOSUR or Mexico (Table 2.3). The figures for stocks support the view that some of the increase was coming from other Latin American countries, and show clearly that investment by Colombia is largely confined to Latin America.

The Central American countries do not have a common investment regime, either within the region or with respect to the rest of the world. They have tended to sign fewer bilateral agreements than the MERCOSUR or Andean countries, although more than the Caribbean. Investment does not seem to be an important part of the regime, and there has been little opening on services.

Table 2.3: Latin America: Origin of Capital Stocks, 1995 (%)

	USA	LAC	Europe	SE Asia	Other
Bolivia	59.5	22.1	9.0	0.4	5.0
Brazil	36.7	6.2	44.0	7.7	5.4
Chile	40.0	7.4	24.7	3.9	24.1
Colombia	55.7	21.7	18.4	1.9	2.3
Ecuador	66.9	9.2	21.6	0.3	2.0
Mexico	59.5	0.0	23.4	5.1	12.0
Paraguay[a]	9.8	46.3	38.9	0.9	4.1
Peru	14.5	11.2	69.0	0.7	4.6
Venezuela[b]	53.2	10.3	29.1	3.8	3.6
Costa Rica[c]	75.1	11.8	9.3	3.6	0.2
El Salvador	36.0	19.8	24.6	1.9	18.3
Guatemala[d]	55.2	8.8	5.8	5.2	25.1
Panama[e]	74.5	6.0	3.5	3.8	12.2[f]
Dominican Republic	29.2	3.2	10.0	0.3	57.3

Notes: (a) 1992–94; (b) 1993; (c) 1990–94; (d) 1990–94; 'Other' includes some European countries; (e) 1994; (f) Canada.
Source: CEPAL, 1993.

Investment in this region will not have been stimulated by the regulatory regime, but the high and increasing level of intra-regional trade could encourage regional investment. There are no data on this. Costa Rica and Guatemala have seen large increases in inflows in this period, and Honduras and Nicaragua have had some rise (Table 2.1). Except for Honduras, all now have above average shares of foreign investment in the total.

Table 2.4: Foreign Direct Investment (FDI) in and by the USA (%)

	Inflows from the Rest of the World				Outflows to the Rest of the Word			
	1990	1994	1995	1996	1990	1994	1995	1996
NAFTA	4.22	13.21	9.52	6.63	18.81	15.28	13.38	11.25
Canada	3.76	10.55	10.20	7.19	12.59	9.90	9.91	8.04
Mexico	0.46	2.66	-0.68	-0.57	6.22	5.38	3.47	3.21
MERCOSUR (4)	0.01	0.05	0.30	-0.13	4.03	6.57	8.51	4.07
Argentina	0.10	0.08	0.19	0.00	1.22	1.36	2.69	0.49
Brazil	-0.09	-0.02	0.14	-0.13	2.83	5.15	5.76	3.58
Paraguay	—	0.00	0.00	0.00	0.01	0.00	0.00	0.00
Uruguay	0.00	-0.01	-0.03	0.00	-0.03	0.05	0.05	0.00
Chile	-0.07	-0.02	-0.03	0.00	1.68	2.28	1.65	1.16
Bolivia	0.00	0.00	0.00	0.00	0.06	0.11	0.14	0.00
MERCOSUR (6)	-0.07	0.03	0.28	-0.13	5.76	8.95	10.30	5.23
ANDEAN	-0.15	0.25	-0.01	0.29	0.51	2.20	1.55	2.58
Bolivia	0.00	0.00	0.00	0.00	0.06	0.11	0.14	0.00
Colombia	—	-0.03	-0.03	0.00	0.25	0.54	0.23	1.16
Ecuador	0.00	-0.01	—	0.00	-0.10	0.27	0.16	0.03
Peru	—	—	0.01	0.00	-0.27	0.34	0.37	0.94
Venezuela	-0.15	0.29	0.00	0.29	0.57	0.94	0.65	0.46
CACM	0.00	-0.05	-0.02	0.00	0.27	0.52	0.32	0.44
Costa Rica	-0.01	-0.03	0.01	0.00	0.14	0.39	0.31	0.39
El Salvador	—	-0.01	0.00	0.00	0.07	0.05	-0.03	0.00
Guatemala	0.01	-0.01	-0.02	0.00	0.03	0.03	0.03	0.08
Honduras	0.00	-0.01	—	0.00	0.01	0.06	0.02	-0.04
Nicaragua	—	—	—	0.00	0.03	—	—	0.00
CARICOM	3.46	-0.73	-4.51	0.04	1.16	0.74	0.07	-0.04
Bahamas	3.25	-0.17	-4.33	0.04	-0.10	0.17	-0.53	-0.37
Barbados	0.21	-0.57	-0.18	0.00	0.36	0.10	0.29	0.14
Guyana	—	0.00	0.00	0.00	0.02	—	—	0.00
Jamaica	—	—	—	0.00	0.91	0.37	0.17	0.00
Trinidad and Tobago	0.00	0.01	—	0.00	-0.03	0.10	0.14	0.18
All countries	100.00	100.00	100.00	100.00	100.00	100.00	100.00	100.00

Countries with 0 omitted.

Source: USA, Department of Commerce *Survey of Current Business* (various years).

5. NAFTA

Mexico traditionally exercised extensive regulation on foreign investment, with major sectoral exclusions, but the NAFTA agreement required it to remove most restrictions. The NAFTA agreement goes much further than the average bilateral treaty; it requires national and MFN treatment, and removes pre-investment authorisation and other obstacles. It covers the normal subjects — remittances and expropriation. It also forbids performance requirements, both in general and as a condition for special privileges.[37] Given the nature of previous Mexican regulation, among the most important elements is the removal of sectoral restrictions on financial services and mining.

Following the negotiations, and before NAFTA was implemented, Mexico liberalised its general investment regime to almost the same extent. Previously, it had signed very few bilateral treaties. The USA and Canada already had few restrictions on investment flows, except in specified sectors. Mexico included nine of the 11 services sectors in its offer under the GATS (more than Canada, at seven, but fewer than the USA at 11) and more than the other Latin American countries.

Therefore, at the outset of NAFTA there was a general liberalisation of investment by Mexico, not restricted to the other NAFTA members. The special advantage of NAFTA was that it introduced dispute procedures for investors at the national level, as well as the facility to use the international mechanisms.

Mexico liberalised its investment regulation at the time of the establishment of NAFTA, but to the rest of the world as well as to NAFTA. This could give an increase in total investment in Mexico. The increase in trade, particularly the evidence of diversion and increased integration of sectors like cars and clothing, could be expected to lead to an increase in intra-regional investment. In recent years, Mexico has returned to its position as one of the major recipients of foreign investment among developing countries (Table 2.1). Foreign investment remains, however, a relatively low share of total investment in Mexico. The share of NAFTA in US foreign investment was high in 1990, but then declined (Table 2.4). The flows were largely to Canada, but Mexico has shared first place among Latin American recipients with Brazil. The US share to Mexico relative to the rest of Latin America in the first half of the 1990s was not very different from that of Japan.[38]

The rise in the rate of total foreign investment in Mexico (Table 2.1) was largely complete by 1995. US investment in Mexico has risen, but the rise began in 1988, earlier than even the announcement of a possible

---

[37] Parra (1993); and OAS (n.d.).
[38] 30 per cent for both, IDB/IRELA (1998).

NAFTA.[39] If there was a policy explanation, it was probably a combination of the trade liberalisation of the 1980s and expectations of a change in Mexican investment law (the actual change came after the increase in investment).[40] Since 1994, which marked not only the beginning of NAFTA but at the end of the year a strong devaluation of the Mexican currency, US investors in Mexico have increased their sales to third countries, more than to either Mexico or the USA, suggesting that investment is of the cost-reducing, rather than market-seeking type.[41] The rise in sales to the USA could be attributed partially to NAFTA, although most of the planned liberalisation of trade is still to come.

In investment in the USA, the NAFTA share also rose in 1994, and fell back in 1995 and 1996; this was because of increases in Canadian investment in the USA, not Mexican, and probably not for regional reasons: the Canadian-US FTA had been in force for several years. Mexican investment in the USA remains low. Not only do these small and fluctuating changes not suggest a strong regional effect, but the small overall share of NAFTA in US inward and outward investment is strikingly lower than its share in trade. The share of MERCOSUR in US outflows also rose in the early 1990s, although with a decline in 1996; the only other developing region with a significant share is ASEAN. Both of these are much closer in share to NAFTA on investment than they are in trade. There are, however, no other developing countries with as high a share in inward investment in the USA as Mexico.

Table 2.5: Investment in Mexico (%)

	US	Canada	Japan	EU total	UK	Germany	Netherlands
Stocks							
1994	61	2	5	—	7	5	—
Investment							
1993	72	2	2	—	4	2	—
1994	50	2	9	18	6	3	7
1994–99	—	—	3	21	5	4	7

Source: Mercado de Valores, April 1994; April 1995; May 1996; September 1996; July 2000.

In 1994 and 1995, most US investment in Mexico was in manufacturing equipment, and within that in transport. In 1996, however, there was a

---

[39] Graham and Wada (2000), p. 781.
[40] *Ibid.*, p. 784.
[41] *Ibid.*, p. 789.

sharp fall in the latter, while investment in food products became much more important. Mexican investment in the USA has also been mainly in manufacturing. US investment in Canada has also been largely in manufacturing, with a high share of transportation equipment, and showed the same fall in 1996. Canadian investment in the USA has been more varied, with a high share in services.

The USA is the principal foreign investor in Mexico, with 61 per cent of past investment by 1992, and a share of about 60 per cent in most years (Table 2.5). Canada, however, has been only a minor investor. Post-NAFTA figures for 1994 show a decline for the USA and a rise in the share for non-NAFTA countries. Three EU countries are major investors: Netherlands, UK and Germany. Data by investor country and type of investment are not available, but for all foreign investment, manufacturing accounts for a third to a half of the total in the 1990s, suggesting that the US share in manufacturing may be relatively high.

Conclusions

For MERCOSUR, the Andean Group and NAFTA regional liberalisation has accompanied or been closely followed by full liberalisation. There are some regional advantages in simplicity, common company rules, and sometimes in disputes procedures, but these are much less important than the general reductions. For CACM, in contrast, neither the regional nor the multilateral regime has been liberalised. The only region where there is significant discrimination in favour of members is CARICOM (Table 2.6).

Table 2.6: Changes in Regional Investment, Summary

	MERCOSUR	CARICOM	Andean	CACM	NAFTA
Investment high?	Yes	No	Yes	No	YES
Regional effect:					
on outward	Yes	No	Yes	No	Yes
on inward	Possibly	No	No	No	Yes
Rules on integration?	Some	Limited	Yes	No	Yes
Different from the rest of the world?	Little	Little	No	No	Limited

The lowering of trade barriers, within and to outside the regions, has not increased total investment in the regions. Total foreign investment has increased in most of the regions, in absolute terms and relative to the rest of the world and to developing countries in particular, but in many cases other influences have also stimulated this, for example privatisation. There are some increases in intra-regional investment, and this is particularly important for some smaller countries. There is no evidence of increased investment flows to outside the region. Some new or revived industries (notably cars in both MERCOSUR and NAFTA) have seen important regional restructuring.

The other changes in the countries and in investor preferences which would also be expected to increase investment seem to have been more important: lower restrictions on all foreign investment, privatisation, the growing integration of world production and the emergence of world companies.

In MERCOSUR and NAFTA there is some evidence, from both intra-regional flows and inflows and outflows for other countries, of a regional effect on investment but this explains only part of the increase in inflows to those countries. In the Andean countries, there is what seems to be more a neighbouring country effect: newly investing countries have gone first to nearby countries, but this is not associated with formal regional pacts, and other investors are more important. In CARICOM there has been little regional or general liberalisation and little change in investment.

Investment effects are sometimes given great importance in support for regional initiatives. These dynamic effects are expected to emerge both from the growth stimulated by the region and from new opportunities. Both the theoretical arguments and the data, however, suggest that these may be less significant than other changes in policy or in the climate for investment.

CHAPTER 3

Regional Integration and
Intra-Industry Trade

Victor Bulmer-Thomas

The stylised facts for intra-industry trade (IIT) are now well known. Since the creation of GATT in 1948 and the subsequent rapid growth of world trade in goods, the proportion classified as manufactured has risen steadily with developed countries (DCs) accounting for nearly 80 per cent of the total. With regard to the trade in manufactured goods between developed countries, the proportion classified as intra-industry rose steadily until the mid-1980s, since when it has either stayed the same or fallen slightly. Nevertheless, on the standard Grubel-Lloyd (GL) indices,[1] IIT still accounts for almost two-thirds of DC trade in manufactures with each other.

Trade in primary products between all pairs of countries is subject to much lower GL indices, which is usually explained by reference to comparative advantage based on natural resources. Nevertheless, the GL indices for primary products are not zero. This is often explained in terms of seasonal factors, e.g. trade in fruits and vegetables between southern and northern hemisphere countries. However, it is also a reflection of trade distortions as a result of export subsidies (e.g. the European Union's Common Agricultural Policy) or border trade.

International trade in services is a growing proportion of world trade and now accounts for some 20 per cent of the total. I have not seen any calculations of GL indices for trade in services. As with manufactured goods, however, it is highly probable that trade between DCs in services is increasingly intra-industry or more accurately intra-activity. Most DCs now both export and import financial services, insurance, transport and telecommunications to and from each other. And tourism is subject to a high level of intra-activity trade between DCs.

Since DCs are supposed to have similar factor endowments, it is also widely accepted that IIT in manufactured goods between DCs cannot be explained in terms of the Hecksher-Ohlin (HO) theorem. Instead, it is explained by a combination of product differentiation, economies of scale and imperfect competition. However, these arguments could be applied just as readily to intra-activity trade in services between DCs

---

[1] The GL index has now become established as the 'industry standard' despite its well-known deficiencies and numerous attempts to improve it. On the problems of measuring IIT, see Greenaway and Milner (1983).

where factor endowments are assumed to be similar while product differentiation, economies of scale and imperfect competition are all important.

Since product differentiation is greater the higher the level of income of the consuming country and since IIT presupposes similar consumption patterns, it is expected that the GL index will be higher (lower) for pairs of countries with (dis)similar income levels and that it will rise with the average income of the two countries. However, one should not accept this stylised fact too quickly. The GL indices for DCs have not been rising since the mid-1980s despite the rise in income per head and only a small proportion of trade is in final goods. As we shall see below in the case of NAFTA, this stylised fact may be incorrect.

The assumptions of economies of scale and imperfect competition are much easier to accept. At least in DCs, the production of manufactured goods is almost always subject to economies of scale and firms are almost invariably price-makers. Under these circumstances, firms have an incentive to concentrate on some production lines at the expense of others and have the ability to price differently in home and foreign markets. Both these conditions make IIT among DCs very plausible.

These widely accepted explanations of IIT in manufactured goods (and services?) between DCs lead to a major policy implication: intra-activity trade imposes lower adjustment costs than inter-activity trade since it is easier for firms to shift resources towards the production of different goods in the same activity than to shift resources towards new activities. As an analytical point, this is surely correct — it must be easier to shift from ladies' high fashion shoes to children's shoes than to textiles. Nevertheless, at the level of aggregation at which GL indices are usually calculated (3-digit SITC), this assumption should also not be accepted too quickly. As we shall see below, the 3-digit categories are quite broad and can include goods that are by no means close substitutes.

There are many fewer stylised facts about IIT for less developed countries (LDCs). Most of their trade is with DCs rather than other LDCs. There is still an important school of opinion which argues that trade between DCs and LDCs can be explained by differences in factor endowments along HO lines. This is obviously true of the exchange of primary products for manufactures, but could also be true of trade in manufactured goods between DCs and LDCs. Trade between LDCs (South-South trade) is less easy to explain in terms of HO theory, but it must always be remembered that LDCs are much more heterogeneous than DCs so that factor endowment differences can still be important.

GL indices for LDCs are in general much lower than for DCs, but they are rising — they have not peaked — and they are often not negligible. High GL indices are sometimes dismissed as categorical aggregation error and therefore not necessarily a reflection of 'true' IIT (Haiti's trade in manufactured goods with the United States is a good illustration; the high GL index arises because of assembly operations that reflect different factor endowments and different factor prices).

Whether IIT in LDCs has the same benign policy implications as in DCs depends on its nature. The adjustment problem is less severe when IIT takes a horizontal form, i.e. the products exchanged are close to each other in quality as measured by price. Where the price (or unit value in trade statistics) is very different, IIT is of the vertical — not horizontal — form. Vertical IIT can be high or low; the former occurs when the unit value of the exported product is significantly higher than the unit value of the imported good, while the opposite occurs with low vertical IIT.

Vertical IIT is less benign because it is consistent with international trade flows determined by differences in factor endowments. It is not a simple matter, for example, for Caribbean countries to switch from sewing blue jeans — a labour-intensive operation — to exporting the fabric from which blue jeans are made — a capital-intensive operation. Thus, the presence of high levels of IIT should not necessarily be a cause of rejoicing unless it is unequivocally of the horizontal kind.

The phenomenon of IIT — at least between DCs — has been linked to new research in industrial organisation and the microeconomics of competition. However, it has not been closely linked to another well-known phenomenon: the growing dominance of multinational corporations (MNCs) in international trade and the rise of intra-firm trade (IFT). MNCs now account for over 40 per cent of world trade in goods and 25 per cent of world trade in goods is intra-firm. It would be surprising, therefore, if there is not a link between IIT and IFT and we return to this point below.

The other phenomenon in world trade with which IIT has not been closely linked is regional integration. This is partly because, in the case of the European Union (EU), it seemed to add little to the explanation of IIT since other DCs outside appeared to have similar trends in GL indices. However, the spread of regionalism to other parts of the world makes it appropriate to explore the relationship between integration and IIT. This is done in the next section.

1. Intra-Industry Trade and Regional Integration

Most of the arguments used to explain IIT are more likely to be relevant in the presence of regional integration. There is one important counter-argument, however, as we shall see below, so that the impact of regional integration on IIT cannot be known *ex ante*.

IIT is much more likely when countries trade manufactured goods with each other rather than primary products. Regional integration schemes tend to promote trade in manufactured goods since it is much easier to lower or eliminate tariff barriers on secondary than primary products. LDCs in particular have a long history of giving preference to trade liberalisation in manufactured goods. Indeed, some regional schemes in LDCs have specifically excluded agricultural products. Thus, the fact that regionalism tends to promote trade in manufactured goods should *ceteris paribus* lead to higher levels of IIT.

Consider now the issue of factor endowments. Regional integration schemes usually, but not always, involve countries with similar factor endowments. Examples are the European Union (EU), the Caribbean Community (CARICOM) and the Central American Common Market (CACM). Intra-regional trade among the members of these schemes cannot be easily explained by differences in factor endowments and must therefore have other explanations. The alternative explanations need not necessarily lead to IIT, but they may do so.

This argument is particularly powerful when a large proportion of trade is intra-regional. This is clearly the case with members of the EU. No integration scheme in the Americas can match the EU in terms of the share of intra-regional trade in total trade, but the importance of intra-regional trade for some countries (e.g. Uruguay, Paraguay, El Salvador and Mexico) comes close to the mean for EU states (60 per cent). Paraguay, however, has very low GL indices with its MERCOSUR partners (see below), so IIT is not an inevitable consequence of high ratios of intra-regional trade.

Regional integration schemes usually, but not always, embrace countries with similar levels of income per head. Where there is a divergence, the scheme may provide for mechanisms to narrow the differentials. The EU is the best known example, but revenue-sharing from tariffs in the Southern African Customs Union (SACU) is another example.[2] Similar income levels are a necessary, but not sufficient, condition for IIT based on product differentiation. They are not sufficient, because two very poor countries could have unsophisticated demand patterns that would not justify high levels of product differentiation (Haiti and Guyana, for example, are both members of CARICOM with similar — very low — levels of income per head). However, provided that average incomes are rising, similar standards of living in partner countries should promote IIT.

Product differentiation itself may also be promoted by regional integration independently of the level of income per head. Since partners in schemes are usually close geographical neighbours, often sharing a common language, producers can be expected to know the markets in much more detail than would be the case for more distant

---

[2] See Page (2000).

countries. This means that differences in tastes — an important basis for product differentiation — can be catered to more easily in regional integration schemes than outside them.

This argument should not be exaggerated; Taiwanese and South Korean manufacturers have learnt how to react swiftly to changes in taste in the crucial US market without being linked to the United States in an integration scheme and the subsidiaries of MNCs should be able to adjust production lines swiftly throughout the world as consumption patterns change. Nevertheless, the argument does carry some weight. Uruguayan producers of consumer goods, for example, have far greater knowledge about the Argentine and Brazilian markets than about the US or EU markets.

The counterpart to product differentiation as an explanation of IIT is economies of scale. Membership of regional integration schemes is clearly irrelevant in this context. Production of a certain good is either subject to increasing returns or it is not. However, the ability to exploit economies of scale may depend on transport costs. If the fall in unit costs from larger production runs is small, but transport costs are high, then it may not be in the interests of profit-maximising entrepreneurs to specialise. The lower the costs of transporting goods to foreign markets, the greater the opportunity to reap economies of scale.

Transport costs are usually a function of distance, so that they are lower between neighbours than between distant trade partners. Since geographical proximity is often a feature of integration schemes, it follows that regionalism should facilitate the exploitation of economies of scale. Coupled with product differentiation, this is a powerful reason for arguing that regional integration will promote IIT.

There is one possible qualification to this argument. If economies of scale are less important in LDCs than in DCs, then we would not expect regional integration *ceteris paribus* to lead to IIT. This is an empirical question, but a recent survey article by James Tybout has questioned the degree of increasing returns in LDCs in contrast to DCs.[3] This is an important qualification that may help to explain the low levels of IIT in manufactured goods among members of some integration schemes.

What is less in doubt is the extent of imperfect competition in LDCs. Subject to high degrees of concentration, firms in the manufacturing sectors of LDCs are almost invariably price-makers. This is particularly so when the leading firm (firms) is (are) linked to MNCs. The need for oligopolies to be represented in all the main markets of a regional integration scheme is very strong; this creates opportunities to promote brands, build product awareness and purchase consumer loyalty. The supra-normal profits that accompany imperfect competition provide an

---

[3] See Tybout (2000).

opportunity for price discrimination in different markets. Even in the presence of constant returns, it may still be in the interests of an oligopolist to discriminate on price, offering lower prices in neighbouring countries in order to build a presence.

All of this assumes that trade between partners in integration schemes takes place in manufactured consumer goods. Product differentiation and price discrimination are much less important in the case of intermediate and capital goods. Between DCs, with or without the presence of a regional integration scheme, the share of manufactured trade that is classified as capital or intermediate goods is high and rising (this may help to explain why IIT peaked in the mid-1980s for such countries). Among LDCs, however, the share of consumer goods in manufactured trade is much higher and is particularly high in the case of partners in regional integration schemes. The reason for this is simple. Tariffs on consumer goods are invariably higher than on capital and intermediate goods. The shift to zero tariffs for intra-regional trade, therefore, has more of an impact on consumer goods than on other kinds of products.

If the small country assumption holds, local producers set prices equal to the cif import price plus the external tariff and only lower prices after all imports from third countries have been eliminated. This — the elimination of imports of consumer goods from third countries — is certainly a possibility. However, the small country assumption is not particularly appropriate in the presence of imperfect competition and product differentiation, so that in practice firms respond to zero tariffs on intra-regional trade by lowering prices. This stimulates trade in all manufactured goods, but particularly trade in manufactured consumer goods because the scope for price reductions is that much greater.

Nothing has been said so far about MNCs and intra-firm trade. However, it has long ago been accepted that the formation of an integration scheme will stimulate investment by MNCs in order to circumvent the tariff wall. Tariff-hopping by MNCs has been proven for the European Economic Community as early as the 1950s, the CACM in the 1960s and CARICOM in the 1970s. It was clearly important in NAFTA in the 1990s and is undoubtedly relevant in several sectors in MERCOSUR today. Where MNCs are represented by more than one subsidiary, there will be scope for IFT and very probably IIT. In the 1970s, for example, the Latin American Free Trade Association (LAFTA) abandoned multilateral tariff cuts in favour of complementarity agreements that provided opportunities for subsidiaries of MNCs to engage in free trade at the regional level. Since this IFT was typically in a specific sector, it is very likely to have led to IIT.

So far all the arguments have pointed to a positive impact of regional integration — particularly among LDCs — on IIT. However, as mentioned above, there is one counter-argument. Regional integration schemes are associated with a move towards both trade creation (the replacement of expensive domestic production by cheaper imports from a partner) and trade diversion (the replacement of cheaper imports from the rest of the world by more expensive imports from a partner). In their original Vinerian formulation, neither trade creation (TC) nor trade diversion (TD) leads to IIT. However, TC **could** be associated with IIT if the domestic firm shifts to a different product in the same Standard Industrial Trade Classification (SITC) category.

The problem is therefore TD. The product is now no longer imported from a third country, so that IIT will only occur if two countries in the regional integration scheme produce it simultaneously. This is improbable unless the product is subject to managed trade. The latter can be very important (consider, for example, the automotive regime in MERCOSUR which provides for both Argentina and Brazil to replace cheap imported cars from the rest of the world with more expensive imports from each other). Thus, in the absence of managed trade, a trade-diverting integration scheme will not promote IIT and may even reduce it. This will happen if the previous division of labour involved assembly operations that led to two-way trade without a change of SITC category. This type of IIT, often known as vertical IIT, is very important in Latin America (see below).

To the extent that regional integration schemes are net trade creating rather than trade diverting, they can be expected to lead to higher degrees of IIT. The risk of trade diversion rises in proportion to the height of the external tariff. When such tariffs have been high, as in Latin America in the 1960s and 1970s, net trade diversion was important and this will have reduced the scope for IIT. In the 1990s, however, regionalism has been accompanied by trade liberalisation towards the rest of the world leading to modest tariff rates on all but a handful of products. New regionalism is therefore less likely to be associated with TD and therefore more likely to be associated with IIT.

2. Intra-Industry Trade and Latin America

There have been a number of studies on IIT in Latin America.[4] Many of these, however, are for a single year or a single country and are not necessarily comparable with each other. Even when different studies use the GL index, the results are not necessarily comparable because of different levels of aggregation or different data sets used for international trade. In this section I use the results presented in Rodas (1996). These cover a 15 year period using the same index (GL), the same level of aggregation and the same trade classification (SITC).

---

[4] See, for example, Behar (1991); Baumann (1992); and Inter-American Development Bank (1992).

Table 3.1: Grubel-Lloyd Indices for 3-digit SITC Activities (All Sectors): 1978–93

	1978	1981	1984	1987	1990	1993
Argentina	23	19	18	25	26	29
Brazil	22	26	21	30	35	41
Chile	11	11	10	11	13	18
Colombia	15	13	15	15	18	24
Mexico	24	16	32	37	44	63
Peru	10	11	10	12	15	16
Uruguay	14	15	17	23	20	17
Venezuela	02	04	05	09	13	15

Source: Rodas (1996).

The results for the eight main Latin American countries are given in Table 3.1. The data refer to all SITC categories including primary products. In the first year (1978) the pattern is very clear: low levels of IIT for all countries with a level close to zero in Venezuela. The latter is explained by Venezuela's dependence on oil exports unmatched by imports of oil. The implication of the data for 1978 is that trade at that time was inter- rather than intra-activity and almost certainly consistent with Hecksher-Ohlin factor endowment theories.

Since 1978 the GL index has risen in all countries (see Table 3.1). In the case of Mexico, the increase has been spectacular and by 1993 had reached a level normally found only in DCs. Elsewhere, however, despite the increase from 1978 levels, the GL index was still very low. This suggests that — outside of Mexico — international trade in Latin America is still largely inter-activity and not inconsistent with the Hecksher-Ohlin theory.

The rising trend in Table 3.1 has two possible explanations. The first is that Latin American countries are now importing more of the same primary products as they are exporting. The second is that the share of total exports accounted for by primary products is falling. There is some truth in the first explanation; trade liberalisation has made border trade in bulky agricultural products more profitable and the relaxation of foreign investment rules has made cross-border trade in energy products more important. Nevertheless, the second explanation is almost certainly more relevant. The share of manufactured goods in total Latin American exports has been steadily rising and manufactured goods are assumed to have higher GL indices than primary products.

The data in Table 3.1 are based on all SITC categories. Table 3.2

limits the analysis to SITC 5–8, i.e. manufactures including agro-industrial products, and the analysis is again carried out at the 3-digit level. The assumption that manufactured trade is subject to higher levels of IIT than primary trade gains some support.[5] In 1978 most trade in manufactured goods was **not** intra-industry and in many cases (e.g. Chile, Peru and Venezuela) was extremely low. This is almost certainly because SITC 5–8 includes processed primary products that accounted for the bulk of exports in many countries. The GL indices do show the same trends as in Table 3.1 with Brazil as well as Mexico now having an index over 50 by 1993. Elsewhere, however, even in the 1990s, the importance of IIT in trade in manufactured goods has been modest.[6]

Table 3.2: Grubel-Lloyd Indices for 3-digit SITC Activities (Manufacturing Sectors Only): 1978–93

	1978	1981	1984	1987	1990	1993
Argentina	42	26	36	36	53	33
Brazil	38	51	44	45	49	54
Chile	10	09	10	13	14	19
Colombia	20	19	16	21	19	29
Mexico	32	17	60	55	56	71
Peru	10	11	10	08	09	12
Uruguay	22	22	27	34	33	38
Venezuela	03	09	14	17	34	27

Source: Rodas (1996).

The long-run trend and pattern of trade revealed by Tables 3.1 and 3.2 is clear. There has been an increase in intra-industry trade in all countries that is explained by the growing importance of IIT in trade in manufactures, by the declining importance of exports of primary products and by increasing intra-activity trade in primary products. This increase has made a **qualitative** difference only in Brazil and Mexico, where exports are now dominated by manufactured goods subject to a high degree of IIT. Elsewhere, the pattern of trade is still consistent with differences in factor endowments (including natural resources). The clearest example is Peru, but Chile, Colombia, Uruguay and Venezuela are similar cases.

---

[5] This is because the entries for manufactured trade in Table 3.2 are almost invariably greater than the equivalent entries in Table 3.1 for all trade.

[6] Rodas (1996) also contains data on the GL index at 5-digits for SITC 5–8 for six countries (Argentina, Brazil, Chile, Colombia, Mexico and Peru). The absolute levels are lower, but the trends and the ranking are the same. In the case of Mexico, for example, the index is 51 in 1993. This does not suggest a serious problem of categorical aggregation.

The long-run trend may be clear, but the GL indices are not monotonically increasing. There are short-run reversals that hint at measurement problems. The most obvious examples are provided by Argentina, where the GL index in Table 3.1 falls sharply between 1978 and 1981. This also happens in Table 3.2, where the index declines not only between 1978 and 1981, but also between 1990 and 1993. These cases illustrate the difficulty the GL index faces when overall trade becomes unbalanced.[7] In both periods, Argentina experienced a sharp increase in the trade deficit as a result of an overvalued real effective exchange rate (REER). This led *ceteris paribus* to a fall in the GL index as a result of the increase in imports of manufactured goods unmatched by an increase in exports of the same goods. The same measurement problem occurred in Mexico between 1984 and 1987 (see Table 3.2). This time, however, the problem was the increase in the trade **surplus** as a result of the undervalued REER.

Table 3.3: Number of Manufacturing Sectors (Maximum 107) with High GL Indices (a): 1978–93

	1978	1981	1984	1987	1990	1993
Argentina	29	23	23	25	42	26
Brazil	29	37	39	36	42	47
Chile	9	5	5	13	16	17
Colombia	17	19	12	18	26	32
Mexico	27	27	45	49	48	61
Peru	6	13	6	6	9	17
Uruguay	5	15	8	13	18	20
Venezuela	0	3	10	14	32	21

(a) High GL index defined as >50 and > US$1 million.
Source: derived from Rodas (1996).

SITC 5–8 includes 107 sectors at the three-digit level. It is of some interest to know to what extent high levels of IIT are spread across the different sectors and to what extent the phenomenon is concentrated in a handful of activities. This is done in Table 3.3, which lists the number of sectors where the GL index exceeded 50 and the value of trade was more than US$1 million. In 1978 not a single country had more than 30 sectors that met these — relatively undemanding — targets. By 1993 all countries except Argentina had increased the range of sectors, although

---

[7] When trade is unbalanced, there is a downward bias in the GL index since it is mathematically impossible for the aggregate GL index to reach 100. It is this bias that accounts for the (largely unsuccessful) attempts to improve on the GL index.

only in Mexico did it account for more than 50 per cent of all activities. In Argentina, by contrast, the number of sectors actually declined, although the fall is concentrated in the period after 1990 when manufactured exports suffered from the overvaluation of the REER.

The sectoral distribution of IIT is pushed further in Table 3.4. This shows the distribution of the 107 manufacturing sectors in each time period according to the number of countries in which a high GL index was recorded. The maximum score is therefore eight and the minimum is zero. Looking first at the trend over time, there has clearly been a deepening of IIT in Latin America. While 47 sectors (44 per cent) had a zero score in 1978, i.e. no country recorded a high GL index, this had fallen to 16 sectors (15 per cent) by 1993. Furthermore, the decline is monotonic after 1984, suggesting a causal link between export promotion under the New Economic Model and IIT.

No sector recorded a high GL index in all countries, but one (SITC 651 — textile yarns) was present in seven countries by 1993 (see Table 3.4). Several sectors were present in six countries: four in 1987, seven in 1990 and three in 1993. Nearly all of these sectors were from SITC 6 with two from SITC 5 (513 and 554), one from SITC 7 (723) and one from SITC 8 (893). A similar pattern was found for those sectors present in five countries; this reached a peak of ten sectors in 1993, mainly from SITC 6.

Table 3.4: Country Distribution of Manufacturing Sectors with High GL Indices

No. of Countries (a)	1978	1981	1984	1987	1990	1993
0	47	32	35	32	20	16
1	24	39	27	24	19	22
2	24	17	21	23	26	21
3	6	8	16	16	24	28
4	2	9	7	8	7	10
5	3	2	1	0	4	6
6	1	0	0	4	7	3
7	0	0	0	0	0	1
8	0	0	0	0	0	0

(a) For list of countries, see Table 3.1.
Note: The total for each column is 107 (the number of 3-digit manufacturing sectors).
Source: derived from Rodas (1996).

We have seen from Tables 3.1 to 3.4 some evidence of increasing levels of IIT in Latin America. However, doubts remain. First, IIT appears to be vulnerable to trade imbalances; secondly the dominance of SITC 6 in the sectoral pattern raises awkward questions about the possibility that IIT in Latin America may still be consistent with traditional theories of comparative advantage, since these are the sectors that process natural resources. Both of these questions will be addressed here.

The problem of unbalanced trade can be tackled by measuring the change in imports and exports for each sector between two years. This is known as marginal IIT (MIIT) and can be calculated according to a formula developed by Shelburn and Brulhart (SB). The SB (A) index where X_t in exports at time 't', M_t is imports at time t and 'n' is the number of years over which comparison is made is written as:

$$ A = \frac{\left|(X_t - X_{t-n}) - (M_t - M_{t-n})\right|}{\left|X_t - X_{t-n}\right| + \left|M_t - M_{t-n}\right|}, $$

The SB index has a minimum value of zero and a maximum of unity. The closer to zero, the lower the importance of IIT in the change in trade flows; thus, where a country continues to export the same value of a product in two years, while imports have risen, MIIT would be zero. It is therefore well-suited to exploring the issue of changes in IIT as a result of trade imbalances. This index can be aggregated across sectors, as in the case of the GL index, using as weights the increase in each sector's trade (exports plus imports) as a proportion of the total increase in trade.

The values of the SB index are given in Table 3.5 for the same eight countries over five time-periods for the manufacturing sector. It shows that MIIT has been very modest in five countries (Argentina, Chile, Peru, Uruguay and Venezuela). By contrast, Table 3.5 reinforces the impression that Mexico has become the key country in Latin America in terms of intra-industry trade with a SB index of nearly 70 per cent in the period from 1990 to 1993. When compared with Table 3.2, the results in Table 3.5 reinforce the notion of a robust trend towards IIT in Mexico, and to a lesser extent in Brazil and Colombia, coupled with a much more fragile increase — or even decrease (e.g. Peru) — in IIT elsewhere.

The second doubt raised above concerned the nature of IIT in Latin America and the possibility that it is not inconsistent with trade specialisation according to differences in factor endowments. This problem is usually tackled by calculating unit values of exports and imports for a range of products in sectors where IIT has been recorded on the GL index. Where unit values differ by less than 15 per cent, IIT is said to be horizontal since the products are assumed to be similar in quality. In this case, IIT is assumed to be inconsistent with trade specialisation based on differences in factor endowments. Where the unit value of exports is more than 15 per cent below (above) the unit value of imports, IIT is said to be low (high) vertical. In this case, the products are assumed to be dissimilar and IIT may not be inconsistent with the Hecksher-Ohlin theorem.

Table 3.5: Shelburn and Brulhart Indices for 3-digit Manufacturing Sectors: 1978–93

	1978–81	1981–84	1984–87	1987–90	1990–93
Argentina	11	14	25	5	15
Brazil	11	17	22	25	37
Chile	4	6	8	10	19
Colombia	12	21	13	10	31
Mexico	5	11	45	35	68
Peru	7	7	7	2	5
Uruguay	13	18	32	24	24
Venezuela	5	4	10	7	16

Source: Rodas (1996).

The results of these calculations are given for the five main Latin American countries in Table 3.6.[8] The unimportance of horizontal IIT is immediately apparent. Even for Mexico, the Latin American country where IIT appears to be most established, there is no evidence of horizontal IIT. Low vertical IIT has been dominant in Brazil and Chile, while Argentina, Colombia and Mexico switched from low vertical to high vertical after 1990.

Table 3.6: Horizontal and Vertical Intra-Industry Trade (%): 1987, 1990 and 1993

	Horizontal			Low Vertical			High Vertical		
	1987	1990	1993	1987	1990	1993	1987	1990	1993
Argentina	4	5	5	72	67	44	24	28	51
Brazil	2	3	2	78	78	78	20	19	20
Chile	2	5	5	58	56	52	40	39	43
Colombia	5	4	5	56	61	44	39	35	51
Mexico	3	5	4	77	60	46	20	35	50

Note: The sum of the row entries for each separate year is 100.
Source: Rodas (1996).

---

[8] Figures are not given in Rodas (1996) for Peru, Uruguay and Venezuela.

Both low and high vertical IIT imply an international division of labour in which trade specialisation may well be explained by differences in factor endowments. High vertical, however, suggests that the exporting country is specialising in high value added activities closer to the point of consumption. This is clearly encouraging for Mexico, where IIT is established as an important component of trade, and some consolation for Argentina and Colombia where IIT is much less important. Low vertical means that the exporting country is specialised in the first links of the commodity chain. This is a matter of concern for Brazil and Chile, although it is much less important for Chile where IIT is not particularly important in overall trade.

3. CACM, CARICOM and the Andean Community

The analysis so far has focused on IIT in Latin America at the multilateral level, i.e. without distinguishing between trade partners. In what follows, the analysis will focus on IIT at the bilateral level in order to explore the impact of regional integration on the pattern of trade. This section will look at the Central American Common Market (CACM), the Caribbean Community (CARICOM) and the Andean Community (AC).[9]

The CACM was created in 1960 at a time when there was virtually no intra-regional trade among the Central American countries (Costa Rica, El Salvador, Guatemala, Honduras and Nicaragua). The CACM was designed to stimulate industrialisation and tariff liberalisation was limited to manufactured products. It is not surprising, therefore, that intra-regional trade consisted almost entirely of industrial goods until the relaunch of the CACM in the 1990s created a modest space for trade liberalisation in agricultural products.

The first decade of the CACM was very successful and intra-regional trade jumped to one-quarter of total trade by 1970. This, it should be remembered, was achieved despite a brief war between El Salvador and Honduras in 1969 that paralysed trade between both countries for many years. Since intra-regional trade at that time consisted almost entirely of manufactured goods and since most manufactured exports were sold inside the region, the multilateral GL indices provide a first proxy for the evolution of IIT in the CACM. The results are shown in Table 3.7 at the usual 3-digit level.

It can be seen from Table 3.7 that by 1970 there already existed a clear difference between Honduras and the other four members of CACM. The GL index was extremely low in Honduras and this reflected the failure of Honduras to develop a modern industrial base at a time

---

[9] The data for the Andean countries given correspond to those years when they were known as the Andean Group.

when it was starting to import industrial products from its neighbours. Honduras therefore suffered from trade diversion and a growing trade imbalance with its partners to whom it was unable to sell primary products because of trade restrictions on agricultural goods. It is hardly surprising, under these circumstances, that Honduras withdrew from CACM at the start of the 1970s.

The period from 1970 to 1980 was marked by the growth of absolute trade in the CACM and a small decline in its relative importance (expressed as a share of total trade). The value of the GL index rose sharply in Costa Rica, approximating the value of the index in El Salvador and Guatemala, but fell in Nicaragua. This was due to the reconstruction of the Nicaraguan economy in 1980 after the collapse of the Somoza regime, with imports from partner countries unmatched by exports. IIT in Honduras remained insignificant.

Table 3.7: GL Indices for 3-digit Manufacturing Sectors in the CACM: 1970, 1980 and 1990

	1970	1980	1990
Costa Rica	29	40	28
El Salvador	40	43	27
Guatemala	41	39	31
Honduras	14	17	12
Nicaragua	29	19	6

Note: entries have been rounded to nearest whole number.
Source: IDB (1992).

In the first half of the 1980s intra-regional trade in the CACM collapsed because of the debt crisis and the regional conflicts. Trade began to recover after 1985, but the rate of recovery was very modest and did not recover its previous (1980) peak until 1994.[10] By the end of the 1980s the GL indices had fallen in every country (see Table 3.7), by which time IIT in manufactured goods was negligible in Honduras and Nicaragua.

The CACM was relaunched in 1990 and this is the first year for which we have bilateral GL indices without the need for proxies.[11] These are shown in Table 3.8 together with the bilateral indices for trade with Mexico and the developed countries. The pattern is very clear. IIT is much more important in trade with CACM members than in trade with other trade partners. This is partly because most (nearly 70 per cent in 1990) of manufactured exports go to the CACM and partly because of a

---

[10] Bulmer-Thomas (1998).
[11] A multilateral GL index measures IIT with all partners; a bilateral GL index measures it with a particular country or region.

'pure' regional integration effect. Thus, the dummy on CACM in all regression analysis of bilateral IIT is always highly significant and has an effect independent of the share of manufactured exports in total exports.[12]

Table 3.8: Bilateral GL Indices for 3-digit Manufacturing Sectors in the CACM: 1990

	CACM	Mexico	North America	Japan	Western Europe	DCs
Costa Rica	51	4	14	0	4	10
El Salvador	53	1	7	0	2	5
Guatemala	59	4	7	0	1	4
Honduras	22	13	7	0	9	6
Nicaragua	15	0	0	1	0	0

Note: entries rounded to nearest whole number.
Source: IDB (1992).

The GL indices in Table 3.8 refer to both vertical and horizontal IIT. In the case of CACM, however, it seems that horizontal IIT (unit values of exports and imports no more than 15 per cent apart) has been important — at least for Costa Rica, El Salvador and Guatemala. This is shown in Table 3.9 together with the range of GL indices for each country. Most products traded have GL indices below 25, but over 20 per cent of all products traded in El Salvador and Guatemala have horizontal GL indices in excess of 50.

Table 3.9: Bilateral Horizontal GL Indices for the CACM: 1994

Country	GL Index	Distribution of Traded Products by Size of GL Index (%)			
		0–25	25–50	50–75	75–100
Costa Rica	36	71.3	12.4	6.9	9.4
El Salvador	42	65.5	11.6	11.9	11.0
Guatemala	42	64.9	11.4	13.0	10.7
Honduras	20	85.4	3.8	5.2	5.6
Nicaragua	13	82.8	6.8	4.3	6.0

Source: Rodas (1998).

---

[12] See Inter-American Development Bank (1992), Table 9, p. 212; see also Havrylyshyn and Civan (1983), Table 2, pp. 124–5.

The Andean Community (AC) was created in 1969 (as the Andean Group) in frustration at the slow progress in trade liberalisation within LAFTA. The AC, as it has been called since 1995, was influenced by the ideology of industrial planning and emphasis was placed on the spatial distribution of industrial activities. It might seem, therefore, that the AC would enjoy high levels of IIT in intra-regional trade. This, however, has not been the case. Table 3.10 shows the GL index for manufactured trade between 1970 and 1990. There is the same pattern as for CACM of a rise in the 1970s followed by a fall in the 1980s, but throughout the period the levels are extremely low (except for Venezuela in 1990 — a figure that is almost certainly too high).[13]

Table 3.10: GL Indices for 3-digit Manufacturing Sectors in the Andean Pact: 1970, 1980 and 1990

	1970	1980	1990
Bolivia	10	21	6
Colombia	8	20	19
Ecuador	5	5	7
Peru	5	17	11
Venezuela (a)	4	7	(b)

(a)   Venezuela did not join until 1973.
(b)   The figure in the source is 38, but this must be an error as it is higher than the value of all bilateral indices in Table 3.11.
Source: IDB (1992).

The share of manufactured exports sold to other AC countries is not as high as in CACM, so the GL indices in Table 3.10 are not necessarily good proxies for the bilateral trade indices. However, when the GL index is calculated only for trade in manufactured goods with other AC countries (see Table 3.11), the levels are still modest. The only consolation is that the GL index with other AC members is nearly always much higher than with other trade partners (see Table 3.11). Indeed, with the partial exception of Venezuela, manufactured trade with all DC groups — North America, Japan, the European Union — is clearly inter- not intra-industrial.

Regression analysis suggests that the dummy for membership of the Andean Pact is positive and significant in explaining the level of bilateral IIT.[14] This does not mean that bilateral IIT is of much importance, but it does support the argument in the previous paragraph that IIT in

---

[13] See note (b) to Table 3.10.
[14] See Inter-American Development Bank (1992), Table 9, p. 212.

manufactured goods is more important with AC members than with other countries. Indeed, there are no sectors in which trade in manufactured products with DCs reached a GL index greater than 50 by the end of the 1980s.

Table 3.11: GL Bilateral Indices for the 3-digit Manufacturing Sector in the Andean Pact (AP): 1990

	AP	Brazil	North America	Japan	Western Europe	DCs
Bolivia	14	2	7	1	5	5
Colombia	37	7	12	0	4	7
Ecuador	25	2	4	0	1	2
Peru	30	3	9	1	4	6
Venezuela	31	18	30	5	17	24

Source: IDB (1992).

It might seem puzzling that IIT is so unimportant in the AC. The average income per head is higher than in the CACM and industrial diversification much greater. However, intra-regional trade is a very small part of total trade and the cost of transport between the major points of consumption is very high. Both these considerations work **against** high levels of IIT so that intra- and extra-regional trade are more easily explained in terms of inter-industry specialisation.

The Caribbean Community (CARICOM) was launched in 1968 as the Caribbean Free Trade Area (CARIFTA). It has expanded to 14 members, the most recent being Haiti, but its core remains former British colonies. These states inherited a trade pattern that reflected the imperial division of labour — exports of primary products and imports of manufactured goods — and CARICOM has been designed to help them diversify.

The bilateral GL indices for 1990 are given in Table 3.12 for four countries (Bahamas, Barbados, Jamaica and Trinidad & Tobago) and the indices for trade in manufactured products with CARICOM members are compared with the indices for trade with developed countries. As in the case of CACM and the AC, the index is higher for intra- than extra-regional trade. Surprisingly, however, the dummy for CARICOM in regression analysis of bilateral trade indices is not significant, although it is positive.[15]

CARICOM countries are increasingly caught up in the global

---

[15] *Ibid.*

commodity chain with production in export processing zones feeding into the trade flows between subsidiaries of multinational enterprises. Although the overall level of IIT with DCs may be low (see Table 3.12), there are several sectors where it is high. These include not just labour-intensive activities such as leather goods, clothing and footwear, but also chemicals and electrical machinery. It is safe to assume that this is vertical IIT rather than horizontal and does not undermine the view that trade in CARICOM is still largely based on differences in factor proportions.[16]

Table 3.12: GL Indices for 3-digit Manufacturing Sectors in CARICOM: 1990

	CARICOM	North America	Japan	Western Europe	DCs
Bahamas	0	6	0	9	6
Barbados	24	19	0	10	14
Jamaica	38	28	0	2	19
Trinidad & Tobago	46	7	0	7	7

Source: IDB (1992).

These three integration schemes — CACM, AC and CARICOM — have demonstrated that IIT is more important in trade in manufactured goods with regional partners than with other countries. However, in the case of AC and CARICOM intra-industry trade has been of limited importance even in intra-regional trade with the GL index always below 50 and almost always below 40. Only in CACM has the index been greater than 50 and even in CACM this is only true of Costa Rica, El Salvador and Guatemala. Since intra-regional trade is not of much importance for Costa Rica, it is fair to conclude that IIT in these three schemes is only of major importance in the case of El Salvador and Guatemala, where geographical proximity and similar income levels provide ideal conditions for horizontal intra-activity trade.

4. Mexico and MERCOSUR

In this section, the two most important Latin American experiments in regional integration are explored from the perspective of intra-industry

---

[16] Helen McBain (author of Chapter 12) has provided me with unpublished data on GL indices for Jamaica's trade with Trinidad in the 1990s. The data suggests a decline in IIT in many sectors over the course of the decade.

trade. The first case involves Mexico, whose integration experience is often assumed erroneously to be limited to NAFTA. While its free trade agreement with the European Union may be recent (1 July 2000), Mexico has in fact signed an impressive array of free trade agreements with other Latin American countries in the last ten years that also constitute a form of regional integration. The second case is MERCOSUR, which was transformed in the 1990s from a minor market for its members' exports to a major strategic trade issue. MERCOSUR passed through a period of intense stress after the Russian default in August 1998 and more particularly the Brazilian devaluation in 1999, but it is clearly here to stay and has irreversibly changed trade patterns in the southern half of South America.

Mexico's transformation from a semi-closed oil-dependent economy at the start of the 1980s to a global trader specialising in manufactured exports has been remarkable. Less than ten years separate the decision to join GATT and entry into force of NAFTA on 1 January 1994. Since the opposition to NAFTA in the United States was based on the assumption that bilateral trade would be dominated by Mexican labour-intensive exports based on cheap unskilled labour — a scarce factor in the United States — it was widely predicted that trade would be inter-industry based on differences in factor proportions.

Nothing could be further from the case. Mexico's trade with the United States records the highest levels of IIT found anywhere in Latin America. Indeed, the levels are comparable to those found in the European Union. However, this was true even before the formation of NAFTA, as Table 3.13 shows. Whether the analysis is based on all sectors or only manufactured products, there was a sharp increase in the value of the GL indices after 1981 and a further discrete jump after 1990.

The change in the trade pattern with the United States appears to have been unique. Trade with other Latin American countries has continued to exhibit low values for the GL indices. This is true, as Table 3.13 shows, both for those countries with which Mexico has signed free trade agreements (Chile, Colombia) and those with which it has not (Argentina, Brazil). Thus, trade with the United States, which accounts for 70 to 80 per cent of Mexico's total trade, is clearly subject to special considerations.

Those considerations include the presence of *maquiladora* plants that import semi-finished goods and re-export them as finished products. We have already seen in Table 3.6 that at the multilateral level high vertical IIT is very important in Mexico and horizontal IIT negligible. Since most of this trade is with the United States, it is safe to assume that the same applies to bilateral trade with Mexico's northern neighbour. However, even when GL indices are calculated at the four-digit level the pattern of high IIT with the United States and low everywhere else does not disappear.[17] This suggests that bilateral trade with the United States is based on an extremely complex international division of labour in which the degree of product transformation is often so small that commodities remain classified in the same product group. This division of labour reflects the needs of international capital — mainly US multinationals — and has brought Mexico closer and closer into the US production networks and commodity chains.

Table 3.13: Bilateral GL Indices (3-digit SITC level) for Mexico: 1978–93
(a) All Sectors

Partner	1978	1981	1984	1987	1990	1993
USA	18	16	35	33	44	63
Argentina	22	13	07	09	13	22
Brazil	36	15	13	33	22	20
Chile	4	5	2	3	5	10
Colombia	14	18	3	6	20	20

(c) Manufacturing Sectors

Partner	1978	1981	1984	1987	1990	1993
USA	29	16	61	46	57	71
Argentina	44	32	20	11	31	32
Brazil	38	25	52	44	26	20
Chile	12	6	3	3	7	12
Colombia	15	21	5	10	23	22

Source: Rodas (1996).

That process can only be reinforced by NAFTA. Indeed, NAFTA has had a small, but appreciable effect on the GL indices. It may also be significant that the GL index with Canada doubled with the launch of NAFTA — albeit from a low base. Mexico and the United States now have very similar patterns of bilateral exports. Eight of the top 11 Mexican imports from the United States now feature in the top 11 Mexican exports to the United States.[18] The GL index remains very high and this is true despite the unbalanced nature (in Mexico's favour) of the bilateral trade.[19] As trade becomes more balanced (the Mexican real

---

[17] See Buitelaar and Padilla (1996).
[18] The other three sectors are plastics, paper and paperboard and organic chemicals; these appear in the top 11 US exports, but not in the top 11 Mexican exports.
[19] Using the 1998 2-digit data, the GL index is 61; unpublished information from Ann Bartholomew (author of Chapter 10).

effective exchange rate has been appreciating since 1996 and the US economy will have to slow down), the GL index may increase even further.

Bilateral trade between the United States and Mexico, therefore, exhibits very high indices of IIT, but we should guard against misleading interpretations. First, this trade is not like bilateral IIT trade in the European Union where factor proportion and cost differences are of minor importance in explaining trade flows. The difference in hourly wage rates expressed in dollars between the USA and Mexico is still huge as is the difference in the real rate of interest on domestically-borrowed capital. It is therefore highly improbable that bilateral IIT contradicts Hecksher-Ohlin type explanations of trade specialisation and the low degree of horizontal IIT appears to confirm this.

Secondly, the high GL index for trade in manufactured products between Mexico and the United States clearly predates the launch of NAFTA. While the rise in the index after 1990 — when negotiations began — could perhaps be attributed to NAFTA, it is much harder to explain the rise after 1981 in terms of regional integration. It is much more likely that it is due to globalisation and the outsourcing by US capital of many of the activities that are no longer profitable in the United States. This globalisation effect has been reinforced by NAFTA, but it precedes it and would no doubt have continued even in the absence of NAFTA.

MERCOSUR was formally launched in 1991 by Argentina, Brazil, Paraguay and Uruguay. Thus, any observed MERCOSUR effect on bilateral GL indices for each country should be apparent in the 1990s. However, as with NAFTA, there was a period of preparation before the formal launch of the integration scheme; in addition, Argentina and Brazil signed a series of trade protocols from 1985 onwards so that there is a quasi-MERCOSUR effect to be taken into consideration in the second half of the 1980s. Finally, the expansion of MERCOSUR to include two associate members — Bolivia and Chile — after 1996 means that there is a greater MERCOSUR effect to be taken into consideration in the second half of the 1990s as well.

The bilateral GL indices for Argentina and Brazil are given in Table 3.14 for 1978 to 1993. For both countries there is a clear quasi-MERCOSUR effect with the signing of the bilateral trade protocols. Indeed, the index doubles for both countries between 1984 and 1987. However, this only brings the value of the index back to the level in 1978. Thus, the evolution of the index is as much a story about the disruption to bilateral trade caused by the debt crisis in the first half of the 1980s as it is about the quasi-MERCOSUR effect induced by the bilateral protocols.

Table 3.14: Bilateral GL Indices for 3-digit Manufacturing Sectors in Argentina and Brazil: 1987–93

(a) Argentina

	1978	1981	1984	1987	1990	1993
Brazil	49	36	21	41	50	45
Chile	12	19	18	16	21	28
Colombia	4	24	19	27	29	28
Mexico	50	24	23	12	29	32
USA	16	18	24	21	29	16

(b) Brazil

	1978	1981	1984	1987	1990	1993
Argentina	47	35	20	40	61	50
Chile	3	7	8	5	13	7
Colombia	6	4	2	8	10	16
Mexico	43	16	44	50	35	19
USA	30	35	34	31	44	46

Source: Rodas (1996).

From 1987 onwards, there is a perceptible increase in the value of the GL index for bilateral trade between Argentina and Brazil. The results in Table 3.14 must be interpreted carefully because the indices are not the same for both countries;[20] the upward trend appears to be stronger in Brazil than in Argentina, but in both cases the index is close to 50 by 1993. Since trade was unbalanced (in Brazil's favour) at that time, the index may underestimate the degree of bilateral IIT. Outside of MERCOSUR, Table 3.14 also shows a strong upward trend in the GL index for Argentina with Chile and Colombia, but not with Mexico and the United States. For Brazil, there is a clear upward trend with the United States and a sharp fall with Mexico.

Bilateral IIT for Brazil alone has been analysed in an important study by Baumann (1998), building on his earlier study of Latin American IIT. The indices have been prepared on the basis of all SITC categories, not just the manufacturing sectors. There is clear evidence of a MERCOSUL (as it is known in Brazil) and greater MERCOSUL effect at both the 3 and 5-digit level (see Table 3.15). This time, however, the effect is

---

[20] This always happens in studies of bilateral trade. It can arise for many reasons including differences in valuation and differences in timing.

concentrated after 1990; indeed, the quasi-MERCOSUL effect appears to be negative with a **decline** in the GL index between 1985 and 1990.[21] The study also records the sectors in which IIT with MERCOSUL and greater MERCOSUL were particularly important in 1996. Out of 50 sectors, 13 (26 per cent) are in chemicals, 12 (24 per cent) are in transport and 11 (22 per cent) in miscellaneous manufactured products.

Table 3.15: Brazil's Bilateral GL Indices (all sectors): 1985-96

(a) 3-digit

	1980	1985	1990	1991	1992	1993	1994	1995	1996
(1)	38	62	58	42	36	47	56	53	56
(2)	27	42	37	37	34	38	43	46	50
(3)	25	43	35	33	30	34	37	44	46

(b) 5-digit

	1980	1985	1990	1991	1992	1993	1994	1995	1996
(1)		48	41			41	48	43	45
(2)		34	27			30	35	38	40
(3)		36	25			28	31	36	38

(1)=Argentina; (2)=MERCOSUL (3)=MERCOSUL + Bolivia + Chile
Source: Baumann (1998).

The most recent study on bilateral IIT for MERCOSUR is by Bartholomew (2000). Based on SITC 3 (fuels) as well as SITC 5–8, this confirms the quasi-MERCOSUR effect in the second half of the 1980s for Argentine–Brazilian bilateral trade (see Table 3.16). However, there then appears to be no increase in the 1990s for IIT between Argentina and Brazil. Instead, both countries record a significant increase in the value of the GL index for bilateral trade with Uruguay (IIT with Paraguay remains negligible despite an increase in the index).

It is at first puzzling that the GL index for Argentine–Brazilian trade did not increase in the 1990s. This may be due to trade imbalances since real exchange rate movements produced a large surplus in Brazil's favour in the first half of the 1990s and a surplus in Argentina's favour thereafter. However, a more probable explanation, as proposed by

---

[21] This surprising result — repeated in the case of Brazil's trade with Argentina (see Table 3.15) — appears to contradict the evidence in Table 3.14, which suggests a sharp rise in the GL index between 1984 and 1990. However, Baumann's study considers only 145 products in 1985 compared with 480 in 1990. One suspects that this may explain the difference.

Bartholomew (2000), is that it is due to managed trade. Bartholomew calculates the GL index at the one-digit SITC level for both Argentina and Brazil. The only manufacturing sector in which there has been a significant increase is miscellaneous manufactured products. In the other sectors, the level of IIT has either fallen or remained the same — albeit at a high level. These are the sectors that include products covered by the bilateral protocols signed in the second half of the 1980s, where trade was both managed and balanced. Thus, IIT was already high before the launch of MERCOSUR in 1991 and in the 1990s bilateral trade in areas covered by the protocols has either been liberalised, raising the probability of unbalanced trade, or continues to be managed (e.g. automobiles) without much possibility of increasing IIT.

Table 3.16: Bilateral GL Indices for SITC 3 and 5–8 in MERCOSUR: 1987–98

(a) Argentina

	1987	1988	1989	1990	1992	1993	1994	1995	1998
Brazil	35	31	52	57	33	49	48	61	48
Paraguay	0	2	1	1	8	8	8	7	13
Uruguay	39	33	38	26	37	36	41	52	45
RoW	29	34	36	32	27	24	22	28	36
Total	34	41	44	41	29	33	33	45	46

(b) Brazil

	1987	1988	1989	1990	1992	1993	1994	1995	1998
Argentina	30	25	54	56	39	44	49	55	54
Paraguay	0	0	4	8	5	3	4	7	9
Uruguay	21	20	22	26	26	23	31	40	39
RoW	34	30	30	34	43	44	27	50	46
Total	36	33	34	38	43	49	34	45	39

Source: Bartholomew (2000).

If the GL index is high in MERCOSUR in part because of managed trade, this is not inconsistent with a positive effect of regional integration on IIT. The automobile regime, for example, is very much part of the MERCOSUR story irrespective of its impact on welfare. Furthermore, trade between Argentina, Brazil and Uruguay clearly has some features of horizontal IIT since factor proportions are similar between the three countries (particularly if we focus on the south of Brazil where most trade with MERCOSUL is located). Thus, MERCOSUR does seem to present the case of an integration scheme that has had a perceptible impact on IIT among its members.

Conclusions

This chapter has explored the phenomenon of IIT in Latin America and the Caribbean (LAC) and its relation to regional integration. Intra-industry trade in the LAC region has increased in the last two decades and there is no evidence that the GL indices have peaked — unlike the case of DCs. This is not surprising given the low level of IIT 20 years ago on the one hand and the impact of trade liberalisation on the other.

The second section of this chapter outlined a number of hypotheses with regard to the possible impact of regional integration on IIT. The evidence shows clearly that levels of IIT are much higher with partners in integration schemes than with third countries. There also seems little doubt that membership has had a positive effect on the trend in IIT despite the risk of lower IIT as a result of trade diversion.

Where IIT is high and/or rising, this does not necessarily contradict theories of international trade specialisation based on differences in factor proportions and factor prices. Most IIT in Latin America is vertical — not horizontal — and is not inconsistent with the Hecksher-Ohlin theorem. The adjustment costs of vertical IIT are not as easy to predict as in the case of horizontal IIT. Nevertheless, the costs should still be less than in the case of inter-industry specialisation.

Horizontal IIT appears to be of no importance in trade with DCs and only arises in trade with regional partners. It is only of proven importance in the case of Costa Rica, El Salvador and Guatemala; even in this case, it is much more important for El Salvador and Guatemala than Costa Rica, as the latter depends much less on intra-regional trade. It is probably gaining in importance in trade between Argentina, Brazil and Uruguay and is clearly of major significance in the automobile trade between Argentina and Brazil.

IIT in MERCOSUR appears to owe a great deal to the legacy of managed trade under the bilateral trade protocols implemented between Argentina and Brazil in the second half of the 1980s. The great leap in measured IIT occurred during those years, whereas there has been little or no increase in the 1990s. Trade between Uruguay and its MERCOSUR partners, however, has become increasingly intra-industry. This could become in the next decade one of the most interesting cases of IIT in Latin America, since factor proportions in the three countries are very similar and income levels are quite high.

Mexico's trade with the United States is for the present the most outstanding case of IIT in the LAC region. It is overwhelmingly vertical rather than horizontal, but has reached levels normally found only in trade between DCs. It is probably close to its peak, but it is unlikely to decline. Mexico has now been fully integrated into the US commodity chains and North America is becoming a single economic space. However, this process of integration began at least ten years before NAFTA. Thus, the impact of NAFTA on Mexico's IIT appears to have been quite small, since the big increase in IIT had already taken place. This increase, in turn, owed much to the intra-firm trade among subsidiaries of MNC.

It would be a mistake to exaggerate the importance of IIT for the LAC countries. In the new international division of labour brought about by globalisation and trade liberalisation, some LAC countries (e.g. Mexico) will have very high levels of IIT while others (e.g. Chile) will have very low levels. For all countries there are costs and benefits associated with this process of integration into the world and regional economies. However, the net benefits are only loosely associated with the degree of IIT. It may well be the case that Mexico's integration with the US economy is less costly as a result of (vertical) IIT rather than a division of labour based on inter-industry trade, but this does not mean that those countries exploiting a comparative advantage based on natural resources will necessarily suffer greater costs.

At the regional level, the future of IIT depends on the whether the next stage of integration involves deepening or widening. If the emphasis is on widening without deepening, there are no strong reasons to expect an increase in bilateral IIT; the new members are unlikely to have the same factor proportions as existing members and will almost certainly have different natural resource endowments. If the emphasis is on deepening — through adoption of regional currencies, elimination of non-tariff barriers and the embrace of trade in services — there may well be an increase in bilateral IIT. At present, the prospects for deepening are poor and therefore one should not expect much change in bilateral levels of IIT in the next few years.

PART 2:
INSTITUTIONS

CHAPTER 4

Institutions and Regional Integration:
The Case of MERCOSUR

Roberto Bouzas and Hernán Soltz

The Common Market of the South (MERCOSUR) was created by a brief framework treaty signed in March 1991 that fits in 25 pages (the Treaty of Asunción, ToA). In just two dozen articles it stated objectives, principles and instruments; created governing organs; established the duration of the pact and defined adhesion and repudiation procedures. The treaty had five annexes establishing: a) an automatic and across-the-board trade liberalisation programme; b) a general regime of rules of origin; c) procedures for intra-regional safeguards; d) a target date to enforce a dispute settlement mechanism; and e) ten working groups to advance the co-ordination of macroeconomic and sectoral policies. The matters ruled by these annexes would be in force during a 'transition period' scheduled to conclude on 31 December 1994. Before the end of the 'transition period' member states were expected to agree on a permanent institutional structure, decision-making procedures and specific responsibilities for each organ.

On 17 December 1994, member countries signed the Additional Protocol on the Institutional Structure of MERCOSUR (the so-called Ouro Preto Protocol (OPP). The OPP, also a short document including 53 articles and one annex, introduced modest organisational innovations: it created new organs and allocated more detailed responsibilities, gave MERCOSUR international legal personality and set up a mechanism to take decisions and implement agreements. The OPP also spelled out the legal sources of MERCOSUR, refined the dispute settlement mechanism (DSM) and postponed the adoption of a definitive DSM until full convergence towards the common external tariff takes place in 2006.

In contrast to the detailed, rules-based approach of the North American Free Trade Agreement (that includes a total of 245 articles crammed in over 1,200 pages), the ToA and the OPP laid out a broad and flexible framework to foster regional integration. They also differ from the Treaty of Rome in the detail of the commitments undertaken by the signatories, the nature of governing organs, the role given to an 'autonomous' legal order and the procedures adopted for decision-making.

This chapter examines the institutional record of MERCOSUR. The first section sums up its major institutional features, analysing the structure and role of organs, rules and the DSM. The second section assesses the performance of MERCOSUR institutions, identifying both strengths and weaknesses. The third section provides an eclectic view of the factors that have shaped MERCOSUR's institutional approach. A final section is devoted to the conclusions.

1. An Overview of MERCOSUR Institutions

The ToA created two collegiate and inter-governmental organs scheduled to operate on a periodic basis: the Common Market Council (CMC) and the Common Market Group (CMG). These organs were empowered to further develop rules and make room for institutional innovation and enhancement during the so-called 'transition period'. By 31 December 1994, member countries were expected to have agreed on a definitive institutional structure, including a definition of organs, responsibilities and decision-making procedures.

The Common Market Council, the top political and decision-making authority responsible for moving towards the common market, would bring together the ministers of the economy and foreign relations. The CMC was given power to create, modify or eliminate organs and further develop rules and institutions. The CMC would meet periodically and it would be co-ordinated by a semi-annual rotating chair. The heads of state would take part in the meetings at least once a year. The explicit and active involvement of the economy ministers aimed to make sure that the process would go beyond a diplomatic exercise and to ensure the implementation of decisions, the bulk of which would fall under the competence of economic agencies.

The Common Market Group was comprised of four officials (and four deputies) from each country's Ministry of Foreign Relations, Ministry of the Economy and Central Bank. The CMG was a sort of executive in charge of enforcing CMC 'decisions', undertaking and overseeing technical work required to further economic integration (including the co-ordination of macroeconomic and sector policies), issuing 'resolutions' in its areas of competence and making recommendations to the CMC. To develop the required technical work the ToA established ten working groups (*Subgrupos de Trabajo*) under the orbit of the CMG.

In 1994 the OPP created a Trade Commission (MTC), a Joint Parliamentary Commission and an Economic and Social Consultative Forum. The OPP also expanded the responsibilities of the Administrative Secretary and defined more precisely the role and duties of each organ. Like the CMC and the CMG, the new organs (except the Administrative Secretary, that was given a small staff and budget) were collegiate and would meet periodically. The only new decision-making organ (the Trade Commission) was also inter-governmental.

Apart from its previous duties the CMG was given responsibility to carry forward international negotiations under the guidelines set by the CMC and to participate in the operation of the DSM and the claims procedures (see below). Following approval of the OPP, the CMG restructured its operations into 11 working groups, specialised meetings and ad hoc Groups.[1] The new CMG guidelines required SGTs, specialised meetings and ad hoc Groups to submit negotiating proposals for the CMG to decide over priorities and a follow-up schedule.

Figure 4.1: MERCOSUR Decision-Making Organs

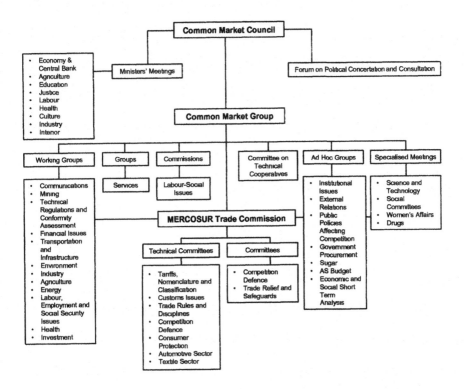

---

[1] The working groups (SGTs) created in 1995 were: SGT 1: Communications; SGT 2: Mining; SGT 3: Technical Regulations and Assessment of Conformity; SGT 4: Financial Issues; SGT 5: Transport and Infrastructure; SGT 6: Environment; SGT 7: Industry; SGT 8: Agriculture; SGT 9: Energy; SGT 10: Labour, Employment and Social Security Issues. In 1996 an eleventh SGT on Health issues was created. Specialised meetings include those on Science and Technology, Social Communication, Women's Affairs and Drugs. Ad hoc groups were created on Institutional Issues, External Relations, Public Policies Affecting Competition, Government Procurement, Sugar and Services. Since the CMG can create, change or eliminate organs, structure has changed over time (for an updated list see Figure 4.1). Trade-related issues were transferred to the Trade Commission and its Technical Committees.

Of the new organs, only the Trade Commission was given decision-making powers (called 'directives'). It consisted of eight officials from each member state (four permanent and four deputies). Its role would be to enforce common trade policies, administer intra-regional trade-related issues and run the new process of consultations. It was also given a role at the initial stages of the DSM. Ten Technical Committees operating under its orbit would be responsible for the technical negotiations required to design and enforce common trade policy instruments and to administer intra-regional trade affairs.[2]

The Joint Parliamentary Commission and the Economic and Social Consultative Forum were exclusively counselling and advisory organs. The former consisted of eight congressmen from each member state, chosen following the procedures set by each national legislature. Its duties would be to consider issues at the request of the CMC, make recommendations to the CMG and the CMC, oversee and request reports to other MERCOSUR organs and facilitate congressional procedures needed to enforce decisions.

The Economic and Social Consultative Forum would represent non-governmental actors. Its maximum authority would be a plenary bringing together delegates from the four 'national sections'. The plenary would meet at least twice a year to elaborate and put forward recommendations to decision-making organs (mainly the CMG). Each 'national section' would consist of representatives from business, labour and other sectors of civil society. It would be represented by nine delegates, with an equal number drawn from business and labour.

And last, the OPP extended the role of the Administrative Secretary (AS) as compared to that defined by the ToA. The AS would provide operational support to all MERCOSUR organs (and not exclusively to the CMG as established in Article 15 of the ToA), and help with the logistics of the meetings of all MERCOSUR organs. Apart from that, the AS would continue to be a depository of documentation, also in charge of publishing and disseminating regulations. The AS was the only organ to have a small budget (made up of member states' contributions) and a full-time staff.

The ToA established the principle of consensus as the sole decision-making procedure. The treaty also included provisions over the duration of the agreement and the mechanism to join and repudiate the pact.[3] The OPP made modest progress towards the definition of rules,

---

[2] The ten Technical Committees were: 1: Tariffs, Nomenclature and Goods Classification; 2: Customs Issues; 3: Trade Rules and Disciplines; 4: Competition Distorting Public Policies; 5: Competition Defence; 6: Safeguards and Unfair Trade Practices; 7: Consumer Protection; 8: Non-Tariff Restrictions; 9: Automotive Sector and 10: Textile Sector.

[3] Two annexes to the ToA established a safeguards and a rules of origin regime to be in force during the 'transition period'.

particularly regarding the implementation of decisions, resolutions and directives. The OPP also defined the legal sources of MERCOSUR.

Regarding implementation, Articles 38 and 42 of the OPP committed member states to 'adopt all measures necessary to ensure' the domestic enforcement of decisions, resolutions and directives (including 'internalisation' when required). The OPP also defined these acts as 'mandatory'. Article 40 established a procedure to ensure simultaneous implementation of norms in all member states through a notification mechanism run by the Administrative Secretary. Finally, Article 41 stipulated the legal sources of MERCOSUR, namely: a) the ToA, its protocols and related instruments; b) the agreements reached in the context of the ToA and other related instruments; and c) the decisions, resolutions and directives issued by MERCOSUR competent organs.

Less than a year after the ToA member states signed the Brasilia Protocol for Dispute Settlement (BPDS). The BPDS was regarded as a transitory arrangement to be used during the 'transition period', at the end of which definitive institutions and dispute settlement procedures should be in place. However, the OPP just extended the procedures of the BPDS and postponed the implementation of a permanent mechanism until full convergence towards the common external tariff in 2006. The OPP also defined the procedures to raise claims before the Trade Commission.

Dispute settlement in MERCOSUR includes three alternative procedures ranging from 'self-help' (consultations and claims) to non-binding third-party adjudication (the BPDS). Consultations offer a mechanism to solve disputes through direct negotiations subject to pre-determined procedures and terms. The mechanism enables member states to exchange information through the request of explanations and clarifications, and to manage trade frictions that do not warrant launching a claim or 'judiciary' procedures. Consultations can be initiated by member states on behalf of central and local administrations or the private sector.

Claims are a sort of pre-judiciary mechanism to settle trade disputes. Its procedures were defined in an annex to the OPP. Claims on behalf of member states, legal or physical persons must be initiated by a 'national section' and they must refer to trade-related matters falling under the authority of the Trade Commission (Figure 4.2). If a claim is not settled in the Trade Commission, it must be referred to a technical committee that has to reach a conclusion in 30 days. The report of the committee is not binding and it may include more than one recommendation. If the Trade Commission fails to reach consensus the claim can be taken to the

CMG, that has 30 additional days to settle the dispute.[4] If the claim fails to be settled the complaining member state can directly activate the arbitral procedure of the BPDS.

Figure 4.2: Sequence of a Claim before the Trade Commission

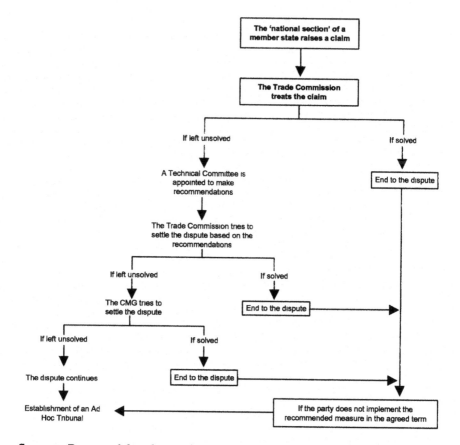

Source: Prepared by the authors on the basis of the OPP's annex on General Procedures to Make Claims Before the MTC (1994).

Finally, the Brasilia Protocol established a sequential DSM with separate procedures to treat controversies among member states and between a member state and a private party. Member states can open a dispute over matters of interpretation, implementation or violation of rules established by the ToA and any other legal instrument (such as

---

[4] If either the MTC or the CMG decide by consensus that the claim is appropriate, the 'accused' member state must adopt the measures recommended in a specified period of time. If it fails to, the member that raised the claim may directly invoke the judicial procedure of the BPDS.

protocols, agreements, decisions, resolutions and directives). Formal procedures contemplate three stages: direct negotiations, intervention by the CMG and a judicial mechanism, each subject to (relatively flexible) time limits. All disputes need to go through the first two stages (direct negotiations and intervention by the CMG) before the judicial mechanism can be triggered (except when the issue is already subject to a claim). The judicial procedure is undertaken by an 'ad hoc tribunal' of three members that makes 'mandatory and definitive' determinations (Figure 4.3).[5]

Figure 4.3: Sequence of a Dispute between Member States according to the BPDS

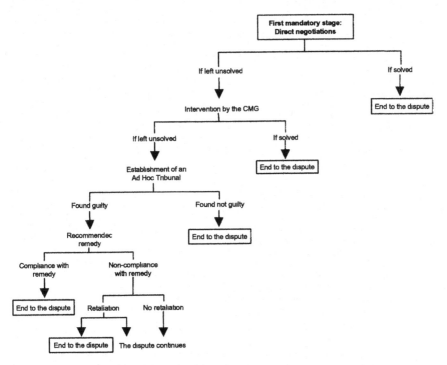

Source: Prepared by the authors on the basis of the BPDS (1991).

The private sector cannot directly trigger the DSM (Figure 4.4). All complaints must be first submitted to the 'national section' of the CMG, which may then take it before the CMG plenary. If the CMG does not

---

[5] Each side in the dispute will appoint one member of the Ad Hoc Tribunal. The third member cannot be a national of any of the parties involved. Each tribunal will define its own procedures. Decisions must be taken by a majority vote. Apart from the legal procedures of MERCOSUR, if the parties agree a tribunal may resolve a dispute on an *ex aequo et bono* basis, thus opening an additional door to inter-state negotiations.

reject the complaint (it must do so by consensus), it convenes a three-member committee of experts to decide on the next step. The committee (selected from previously agreed national lists) must reach its conclusion by unanimity and in a fixed term. If the complaint is found to be without foundation or the committee fails to reach an unanimous agreement, the complaining state may trigger the mechanisms set in the BPDS. If the complaint is found to be valid and the 'accused' party does not implement appropriate measures, the complaining member state can directly activate the legal procedures of the DSM between member states.

Figure 4.4: Sequence of a Dispute Initiated by the Private Sector according to the BPDS

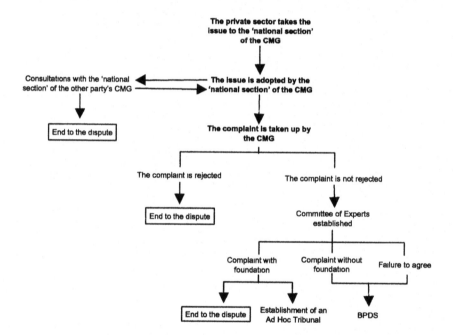

Source: Prepared by the authors on the basis of the BPDS (1991) and its *Reglamento* (1998).

The DSM adopted by MERCOSUR relies on third-party adjudication and a recommended remedy, with retaliation left as the only response for non-compliance.[6] This mechanism provides flexibility to the parties

---

[6] Yarbrough and Yarbrough (1997) classify DSM in four stylised categories, namely: a) DSM-I (a third party provides information on violations and disseminates that information, with retaliation as the only punishment); b) DSM-II (a third-party provides non-binding adjudication with retaliation as the only punishment); c) DSM-III (binding third-party

and stimulates compliance on the basis of the perceived benefits of an ongoing relationship. However, its major shortcoming is a limited ability to end disputes and a relatively high number of ongoing disputes.

2. The Institutional Performance of MERCOSUR

The discussion of Section 1 highlighted three major institutional traits of MERCOSUR, namely: a) its strong inter-governmental bias; b) the 'incomplete' character of its organs' legal acts; and c) the absence of an independent judicial body. This design gave governments a high degree of control over the process, ensuring graduality and flexibility.[7] This 'institutional model' was very effective at the initial stages, when interdependence was low and commitment at a peak, and it proved quite resilient for nearly a decade. However, clear signs of diminishing returns are evident. This section briefly reviews the performance of MERCOSUR institutions since the ToA. In the next section we attempt an explanation of their sources and evolution.

MERCOSUR organs were created as strictly inter-governmental. All decision-making authority rests in the hands of government officials. Except for a small Administrative Secretary with very limited logistic, depository and information gathering/disseminating responsibilities, there is no bureaucracy 'autonomous' from national administrations. The creation of strictly inter-governmental organs was aimed to prevent isolation of decision-making layers from the national agencies responsible for enforcement. The objective was to engage the national agencies and bureaucracies (particularly the ministries of the economy) in decision-making responsible for implementation. This approach built upon the poor results of previous experiences in Latin America, where 'integration bureaucracies' disconnected from the rest of the national public sector or diplomats with limited ability to push decisions forward within their own administrations usually undertook commitments with few chances of being implemented.

The semi-annual meetings of the CMC (regularly followed by presidential summits) were to be important 'signalling' and decision-making events. Since the members of the CMC are the ministers, usually working under very tight time-constraints, the effectiveness of each meeting has varied according to the quality and extension of the preparatory work. The latter, in turn, was influenced by the changing priority attributed by national administrations to the establishment of a

---

adjudication and an appeal process); and d) DSM-IV (third-party enforcement of the type common in domestic legal systems, with the right to retaliate abolished). According to this taxonomy the DSM of MERCOSUR resembles DSM-II. WTO's DSM and the European Court of Justice are, respectively, 'weak' and 'strong' versions of DSM-III. Figures 4.2, 4.3 and 4.4 were also inspired by Yarbrough and Yarbrough (1997).

[7] Boldorini and Zalduendo (1995).

regional regime, the initiative and resources of the member state in charge of the *pro-tempore* presidency and, more importantly, the nature of the issues involved.

Since 1991 the CMC issued an average of 19 decisions per year, with above average figures in 1994 (the last year of the 'transition period', when many decisions related to the implementation of the customs union were taken) and the 1997–99 period (Table 4.1). Two major conclusions emerge after examining the record of the CMC. First, while in the initial years of MERCOSUR trade and institutional issues accounted for most of the decisions, in the late 1990s a high and rising share was related to justice, culture, education and security. Second, while in the initial years of MERCOSUR the CMC produced detailed working mandates and set precise deadlines to guide the activities of lower-level organs (such as the 'Las Leñas Schedule' in 1992 and the 'Year 2000 Action Program' in December 1995), since the mid-1990s no new detailed route map with targets and deadlines for lower-level bureaucratic layers was agreed.

Table 4.1: Common Market Council: Summary of Decisions taken between 1991 and 1999

	1991	1992	1993	1994	1995	1996	1997	1998	1999	Total
NUMBER OF DECISIONS	16	11	13	29	9	18	26	23	27	172
OF WHICH, IN PERCENTAGE:										
Trade policy	18.8	18.8	30.8	62.1	0.0	27.8	30.8	13.0	3.7	25.6
Culture, Justice, Education & Security	0.0	27.3	2.0	10.3	22.2	38.9	23.1	43.5	37.0	23.8
Institutional Affairs	81.3	27.3	30.8	6.9	33.3	16.7	3.9	26.1	11.1	22.1
Other Issues	0.0	9.1	23.1	20.7	0.0	0.0	15.4	4.4	14.8	11.0
External Negotiations	0.0	9.1	0.0	0.0	11.1	11.1	23.1	0.0	25.9	9.9
'Deepening'	0.0	0.0	0.0	0.0	33.3	0.0	3.9	8.7	3.7	4.1
Technical Standards	0.0	9.1	15.4	0.0	0.0	5.6	0.0	4.4	3.7	3.5
TOTAL	100.0	100.0	100.0	100.0	100.0	100.0	100.0	100.0	100.0	100.0

Source: Authors' calculations based on CMC Decisions.

Over time, the credibility and effectiveness of CMC meetings diminished. The growing difficulty to iron out differences in lower decision-making layers led to issue-congestion and an over-burdened agenda at the top. The credibility of presidential summits, which started

as important 'signalling' events, also suffered as failures to implement
and agree on pending issues has mushroomed since the mid-1990s. The
regular intervention of the heads of state in trade and policy disputes
(labelled 'presidential diplomacy') served at critical times to unlock
blocked negotiations or de-escalate conflict. However, as implementation
and follow-up were usually poor, this method over-exposed top political
leaders and ultimately damaged credibility.

The effectiveness of the CMG to undertake technical negotiations, lay
the groundwork for substantive CMC meetings and enforce CMC
decisions also varied over time. The *Subgrupos de Trabajo* (SGTs) were
originally conceived as organs responsible for undertaking the daily
collaborative work necessary to meet the targets and deadlines set by
upper-level organs.[8] The SGTs were also regarded as the institutional
vehicles to engage national bureaucracies in the process, rooting
negotiations and technical work as firmly as possible in national
competent agencies. Since MERCOSUR lacks a mechanism to
automatically enforce legal acts, the active involvement of public sector
officials with the capacity to implement and push the agenda forward
within their own administrations was a prerequisite to effectiveness.
SGTs were also given responsibility for undertaking preparatory work,
thus performing a mixed role as technical and negotiating fora.[9]

Initially the activities of the CMG and the SGTs fostered mutual
knowledge between national officials and contributed to develop a
highly motivated team spirit, stimulating commitment and helping to
root negotiations as firmly as possible in competent national agencies.[10]
After the mid-1990s, however, the effectiveness of the CMG suffered due
to the large number of issues left unsolved at the top and the technical
layers' lack of authority to search for common ground in contentious
areas. When there was disagreement at the decision-making level as
regards the precise content of targets, technical layers replicated the
dissent and there was a failure to make progress. As a result, the morale
of those involved and the credibility of the process suffered. These
problems were made worse by the fact that national officials were
frequently over-burdened, as they added to their ordinary tasks new

---

[8] The Las Leñas Schedule set a detailed action plan for each SGT, including a sequence of
activities and deadlines to be completed by December 1994. However, in spite of the
precise targets set by the Las Leñas Schedule, SGTs performed heterogeneously.
[9] In theory, the role of the CMG and the SGTs can be compared to that of the Committee
of Permanent Representatives (COREPER) in the Council of the European Union.
However, COREPER is a more systematic and structured forum. According to Wallace
(2000), COREPER 'meets at least weekly to agree items on the Council agenda, and to
identify those that need to be discussed (and not merely endorsed) by ministers'.
[10] Active inter-governmental negotiations also provided the opportunity to train human
resources in activities complementary to their routine tasks (such as international
bargaining; development of interpersonal skills; drafting, understanding and
communication abilities).

international negotiating responsibilities. The effectiveness of the SGTs also suffered because each technical negotiating forum was disconnected from the rest, even when issues at stake were closely intertwined.

Failure of the CMG to reach consensus at the decision-making level and to set precise guidelines and targets to guide the work of technical fora was a major factor behind decreasing effectiveness. The informal exchanges that during the initial years of the process laid the ground for substantive CMG meetings were gradually replaced by formal plenary sessions (particularly in the critical 1998–99 period) that simply reproduced disagreement over time.[11] In this latter period the co-ordinators of the 'national sections' of the CMG even failed to meet regularly, as was previously the rule (usually once a month).

As explained in Section 1, the need to administer trade-related issues on a daily basis and to implement and follow-up common trade policies led to the establishment of a Trade Commission (MTC) in 1995. The MTC was created as the institutional locus where trade officials would meet and interact on a regular basis. However, the MTC (and the Technical Committees under its orbit) suffered many of the same problems faced by the CMG and the SGTs. In particular, although technical committees combined the task of carrying forward technical negotiations and administering trade disputes, the latter in practice distracted energies from the former.[12] Although the MTC was instrumental in channelling trade disputes through the consultations mechanism, their number fell markedly precisely at the most critical period (1998–99) (Table 4.2).

Table 4.2: MERCOSUR Trade Commission: Summary of Consultations, 1995–99

	1995	1996	1997	1998	1999	Total
Total number of consultations	134	85	65	32	39	355
Pending consultations*	0	7	16	15	8	46
Pending consultations as a share of total consultations (percentage)	0	8.2	24.6	46.9	20.5	13.0

* October 1999.

Source: Authors' calculations based on data from the MTC.

---

[11] Peña (1999).

[12] Except for TC 5 (that drafted and administers the Protocol on Competition Defence) and TC 6 (that drafted the common anti-dumping regime), the activity of TCs suffered from the same bias as the Trade Commission: their members got involved in dealing with market access problems rather than with the enforcement of common trade policies. Therefore, controversies over non-tariff barriers, common external tariff perforations, sector issues (like the special regime for motor vehicles) and rules of origin became the cornerstone of the TCs' negotiations and energies.

The inter-governmental structure of MERCOSUR made the process flexible and cost-effective at the initial stages. However, it also stimulated governmental (and executive) 'encapsulation', limiting the permeability of the decision-making process to non-governmental actors. The establishment of a consultative regional organ (ESCF) in 1995 failed to fill the gap, as private actors correctly perceived that their ability to influence outcomes could be maximised if exercised at the national rather than the regional level. The fact that the ESCF had no budget to finance its operations also conspired against representation. In effect, only those organisations able to support and finance a continuous involvement were in a position to be active participants.

The record of the legislative consultative organ (the JPC) has been equally modest, failing to play either a proactive or an advisory role to technical negotiation layers as well as to decision-making organs. Moreover, the JPC was unable to block (or even react to) measures unilaterally taken by national legislatures, such as Argentine legislation excluding sugar from free-trade commitments.[13] The activities of the Administrative Secretary were also kept to a minimum.

Although all 'acts' undertaken by MERCOSUR decision-making organs are mandatory, they are neither 'immediately applicable' nor have 'direct effect'.[14] In practice, this means that member states undertake the commitment to 'internalise', but not necessarily to enforce, these acts. They can be conceived, therefore, as 'incomplete' legal acts, equivalent to signed but not yet ratified international agreements.

In MERCOSUR all norms need to be transposed ('internalised') through domestic legislative or administrative acts in accordance with the mechanism and procedures established by domestic legislation.[15] Since there are neither mandatory time limits to 'internalise' nor effective procedures to ensure it, the process has been slow, uneven and highly vulnerable to the goodwill and the effective (legal, administrative

---

[13] In 1997 the Argentine legislature passed legislation excluding sugar from free trade commitments until Brazil phases out the subsidies granted to the sugar and alcohol industries.

[14] The principles of 'immediate applicability' and 'direct effect' are easier to refer to than to define. As a matter of fact, the European Court of Justice often uses both terms interchangeably. The principle of 'immediate applicability' is more 'formal' and means that norms produced at the international level do not need to be 'transposed' into domestic legislation in order to 'apply fully' to (or develop all their effects upon) individuals. The effect of norms immediately applicable can vary according to their nature and content. The principle of 'direct effect' is more 'material'. It gives individuals the right to invoke before domestic (or community) jurisdictions norms produced at the international level even if these norms need to be transposed *fully* to develop *all* their effects. With the usual caveats we are indebted to Professor Ramón Torrent for his useful clarifications.

[15] Strictly speaking, not all norms need to be 'internalised'. That would be the case, for example, of a technical standard identical to the one domestically enforced.

or political) obstacles faced by each government.

Frequently, delays in 'internalisation' were aggravated by the fact that MERCOSUR decision-making organs did not take into account the administrative, legal or constitutional obstacles faced by each national government to enforce a decision, resolution or directive. Therefore, decision-making organs could easily turn out norms with few chances of being rapidly enforced. Moreover, since to become fully operative a decision, resolution or directive would need to be 'internalised' by all member states, the uneven pace of 'internalisation' led to significant delays in enforcement. Implementation was also postponed due to failure to report progress to the Administrative Secretary and to the 'internalisation' of modified versions of the original norm.[16]

After the loose mechanisms established by the OPP failed to improve performance, member states took steps to speed up and facilitate 'internalisation', but mostly through exhortation. In July 1998 the CMG agreed to 'undertake the maximum possible efforts' to 'internalise' rules requiring only administrative decisions and asked the JPC to facilitate congressional treatment of decisions requiring legislative changes.[17] The CMC, in turn, asked the JPC to speed up legislative procedures in those cases where 'internationalisation' required the participation of Congress.[18] Technical negotiating groups (SGTs and TCs) were also asked to inform 'national sections' of any decision, resolution or directive under consideration to facilitate the identification of potential legal or administrative obstacles to 'internalisation'. It was also established that all norms requiring only national administrative acts to be 'internalised' should include an explicit term to complete the process and, whenever possible, an identification of agencies involved and steps required.[19]

Since these initiatives were basically exhortative and established only indicative terms, they had very limited impact upon performance. In order to have a mechanism to follow-up the process of 'internalisation', in 1998 the Administrative Secretary was requested to prepare regular reports identifying the current status of each norm passed. However, since these reports were confidential they made no contribution to increased transparency.

Member states made intensive use of consultations as a first step before triggering the claims procedure or the judicial dispute settlement mechanism of the Brasilia Protocol, which have been used more sparsely. Many disputes were also managed through straight 'self-help' mechanisms, such as diplomatic bargaining and direct involvement of high-level political authorities ('presidential diplomacy').

---

[16] Jardel (1998).
[17] Resolution 22/98.
[18] Decision 3/99.
[19] Resolution 23/98.

The option to hold consultations in the Trade Commission was established in 1995 and the procedures to initiate, follow-up and terminate them were established one year later.[20] In an attempt to prevent lengthy consultations, at the end of 1999 a directive established new procedures to speed up the process.[21] Consultations were actively used as a mechanism to exchange information and promote adjustment, generally in non-fundamental trade-related matters. During the initial years the mechanism was used actively, but the number of consultations fell markedly after 1998 (Table 4.2).

By October 1999 only 13 per cent of total consultations were pending resolution, nearly half of which had been initiated during 1998. The relatively low level of unfinished consultations has been taken as an indicator of effectiveness. However, the termination of a consultation is not the same as the effective settlement of the underlying dispute.[22]

The OPP also established a general procedure to make claims before the Trade Commission aimed to speed up trade-related complaints raised either by member states or by the private sector. Between 1995 and 1999 the mechanism was used 11 times, most frequently by Argentina (nine times as against two by Brazil).[23] Of the 11 claims raised six were settled within the mechanism, while by October 2000 three were still pending. The remaining two were taken to the dispute settlement procedures established by the Brasilia Protocol. For the claims mechanism to lead to the settlement of a dispute the parties need to reach consensus either at the MTC or the CMG. The 'self-help' nature of the procedure is reinforced by the fact that technical committees do not play the role of a third-party, as they are composed of national officials. The claims procedure has been slower than expected.[24]

In December 1998, after two years of negotiation, member states finally agreed on a code to regulate the implementation of the Brasilia Protocol. The code defined key terms, notification and confidentiality procedures, qualifications for both judges and experts and conditions to

---

[20] Directive 6/96.

[21] Directive 17/99. However, the two parties can decide not to conclude the consultation by consensus.

[22] A consultation may end satisfactorily although the underlying problem has not been solved (e.g.: a request for information about a member state's restrictive measure may be answered satisfactorily, even though the underlying measure is not removed). Most disputes treated through the claims mechanism or through judicial procedures started as consultations.

[23] Argentina raised five claims against Uruguay and four against Brazil, on issues such as internal taxation, sanitary restrictions, failure to 'internalise' regulations, import licenses and production and export subsidies. The two claims raised by Brazil were against Argentina and referred to the imposition of anti-dumping duties on aluminium wire imports and treatment of the sugar sector.

[24] The Ad Hoc Group on Institutional Affairs is working on a code to increase its effectiveness.

be fulfilled in order for the private sector to make presentations. Member states started to use the DSM shortly after the code was promulgated: in less than two years the DSM dealt with three cases, two raised by Argentina and one by Brazil.[25]

The operation of the BPDS has faced numerous problems. One has been the possibility of delayed negotiations: if member states agree, they can extend the mandatory fifteen-day term to undertake bilateral negotiations in the CMG almost indefinitely. In practice, this means that the triggering of a third-party adjudication procedure can be delayed and replaced by political and diplomatic bargaining. Although it is quite desirable that a DSM provides ample room for direct negotiations, the possibility of long delays before a third-party adjudication mechanism is activated may create uncertainty on the part of the private sector.[26]

A second problem has been that the ad hoc character of the tribunals conspires against the development of a 'body of common interpretation'. Although there is nothing like case law in the legal arsenal of MERCOSUR, permanent tribunals (as opposed to ad hoc ones) are more likely to take decisions consistent with their previous commitments.[27]

Finally, there is the critical issue of enforcement. Although the verdict of the ad hoc tribunals are formally final (they are not subject to an appeals procedure) and binding, the practical meaning of 'binding' in each member state differs according to the domestic constitutional background. Since these verdicts do not have equivalent 'supremacy' over domestic legislation in all member states, enforceability is subject to different practical (legal) requirements.[28] The limit case is Argentina,

---

[25] The issues raised by Argentina (import licenses and subsidies to the production and export of pork) had been previously subject to claims procedures. In contrast, the case raised by Brazil (over Argentine safeguards on textiles) did not go first through the claims process. In what can be taken as a confirmation that the MERCOSUR DSM is regarded as a 'weak' one (certainly weaker than WTO's), Brazil also took the case before the WTO. INTAL (2000).

[26] The private sector cannot directly trigger the dispute settlement mechanism. If there is a private sector complaint, it has to be first taken up by a member state. However, as has been noted, the latter can in practice postpone third-party adjudication, extending negotiations indefinitely. In the BPDS the private sector cannot invoke a derived rule as contrary to the Treaty of Asunción or any other agreements. All private parties can do is to challenge measures adopted by member states in violation of the Treaty of Asunción.

[27] The verdicts of the tribunals are not considered to be part of the legal sources of MERCOSUR.

[28] It is said that the conflict stems from the opposition of 'monist' legal systems, where obligations acquired under international law automatically become part of domestic legislation (such as in Argentina and Paraguay), and 'dualist' ones, where international law obligations have no domestic force until they are 'internalised' through domestic implementing legislation (such as in Brazil). While some jurists maintain that enforcement does not require a domestic act in the case of Brazil, others disagree (González, 1999). However, it is interesting to point out that the European Union has put in place common procedures even though some members are 'monists' and others 'dualists' (such as the UK). This suggests that the issue is political rather than procedural.

where international agreements have supremacy over national law and can be directly enforced by private parties before the local courts.

3. Accounting for Institutional Design in MERCOSUR: an Eclectic View

Except for institutionally-based accounts (such as property rights theory, economic history and new institutional economics), economists have not devoted much time or energy to account for variation in regional institutions. In effect, most of the contributions have come from the camp of international relations theory and/or political science. In these disciplines the major divide has been between functionalist/neo-functionalist theories vis-à-vis realists and neo-realists. According to the former the incentive to co-operate, further liberalise, lower transaction costs and develop common regulatory regimes is related to the intensity of economic interdependence. Realists and neo-realists, in turn, underline concepts such as hegemony, leadership and relative gains to help understand the strengths and weaknesses of regional institutions.

However, available empirical evidence does not seem to support fully any of the contending explanations. Grieco (1997) argues that in contrast to the functionalist story, the evolution of interdependence does not appear to be a reliable predictor of the existence and success of regional institutions. While in some regions interdependence has risen without a parallel increase in institutionalisation (such as in APEC), in others there has been modest regional institutionalisation even in the absence of a marked increase in interdependence (such as in ASEAN). Alternatively, the existence of an hegemonic leader does not seem to have been either a necessary or a sufficient condition for regional institutions. In the European Union, a paradigm for 'dense' regional institutions, the largest economy (Germany) accounts for only a quarter of regional GDP and provides a market for less than a fifth of total regional exports. In contrast, in the Pacific Basin (where we see modest institutionalisation in the case of APEC) the USA accounts for over half of regional output and is the market for more than a third of total regional exports.

Mattli (1999) tried to integrate these contending approaches into an eclectic framework that takes into account the role of both 'supply' and 'demand' factors in shaping regional institutions. According to this author, functionalist, neo-functionalist and institutional theories provide useful insights about the factors that create a 'demand' for regional institutions. But for regional institutionalisation to proceed, political leaders have to be willing and able to accommodate and respond to existing pressures towards integration. Thus realist and neo-realist explanations help to understand the strengths and weaknesses of 'supply-side' conditions in the establishment and success of regional institutions.

A complete account of the incentives and dynamics of regional integration requires not only an adequate understanding of the internal logic of discrimination, but also of its reactive components. In effect, regional arrangements can also be fostered by 'defensive' motivations and 'domino' effects.[29] Since discrimination is the essence of preferential trade arrangements, outsiders may feel enticed to react to the formation of regional agreements in one of two forms: they can either try to join the agreement or to create their own regional group.[30] In the first case the outcome will depend on whether the original partners are prepared to share the benefits of the arrangement and on the size of the 'entry fee'. In the second case success will be closely related to the degree to which 'internal supply and demand conditions' are satisfied. Mattli maintains that the fact that 'internal demand and supply conditions' are generally weak can help to account for the modest progress usually recorded by 'defensive' regional integration arrangements.

To understand properly the establishment and development of regional institutions in MERCOSUR, two key factors need to be taken into account. One is the relatively low starting level of interdependence between member states. The second is the weight of 'defensive' considerations behind economic integration: although the formation and development of MERCOSUR cannot be fully accounted for by external events, these played a key role in shaping the evolution of regional co-operation. In effect, the launching of NAFTA negotiations in 1990 set the background to the signature of the Acta de Buenos Aires (1990) between Argentina and Brazil and, shortly after, to the formation of MERCOSUR. In 1994 the preparation of an hemispheric presidential summit and the launching of negotiations towards a Free Trade Area of the Americas (FTAA) stimulated adoption of a common external tariff at the end of the 'transition period', when many doubted that MERCOSUR would effectively adopt the structure of a customs union.

The shape of regional institutions in MERCOSUR can be partly explained by the lack of strong functional demand pressures to reduce market fragmentation and stimulate policy harmonisation. In effect, economic intercourse in the region has been traditionally low measured either by conventional 'trade encapsulation' indexes or by other indicators of macroeconomic interdependence. Although for the smaller economies (Paraguay and Uruguay) Argentina and Brazil have been relevant trade partners for decades, this was not the case either for Argentina or Brazil. Therefore, in a context of relatively low interdependence the primary purpose of MERCOSUR was to raise

---

[29] Bouzas and Ros (1994); and Baldwin (1993).
[30] Mattli (1999) labelled the two options the 'first' and 'second integrative response', respectively.

economic intercourse rather than to administer its effects.

Despite the fact that 'demand pressures' were not significant, structural reform in the late eighties raised the potential to benefit from increased economic exchange. In effect, market-oriented policies opened new opportunities for intra-regional specialisation and widened the potential to benefit from scale economies. The nearly two-fold increase in the aggregate 'trade encapsulation' index during the 1990s confirms the significant potential for larger trade flows (Table 4.3). Interdependence also increased through monetary and financial channels, as 'demonstration' and 'contagion' effects spread throughout the region.[31]

Table 4.3: MERCOSUR: Indicators of Interdependence, 1991–99

	1991	1992	1993	1994	1995	1996	1997	1998	1999
Trade 'Encapsulation Index' (exports to MERCOSUR as a share of total exports, %):									
Argentina	16.5	19.0	28.1	30.3	32.3	33.3	36.2	35.6	30.2
Brazil	7.3	11.4	14.0	13.6	13.2	15.3	17.1	17.4	16.4
Paraguay	35.1	37.5	39.6	52.1	57.1	63.2	60.9	61.2	41.6
Uruguay	35.5	33.6	43.5	47.0	47.1	48.1	49.7	55.4	45.1
MERCOSUR	11.1	14.3	18.6	19.4	20.5	22.7	24.8	25.8	20.4
Exports to MERCOSUR to GDP Ratio (%):									
Argentina	1.04	1.02	1.56	1.87	2.62	2.91	3.26	3.16	2.49
Brazil	0.57	1.05	1.22	1.08	0.87	0.94	1.12	1.14	0.89
Paraguay	4.14	3.82	4.17	5.43	5.85	6.86	8.49	7.89	3.64
Uruguay	5.56	4.59	5.06	5.53	5.50	6.03	6.86	7.59	5.03
MERCOSUR	0.83	1.13	1.44	1.46	1.46	1.58	1.84	1.86	1.41

Source: Authors' calculations on the basis of national official figures.

The rapid rise in trade interdependence was made possible by the broader policy environment (i.e.: the overwhelming priority of unilateral trade liberalisation during the early 1990s) and the mechanism adopted to implement preferential trade liberalisation during the 'transition period' (the so-called Trade Liberalisation Programme, TLP). The TLP was ground-breaking compared to other precedents in the region because of its calendar of automatic, across-the-board and linear tariff cuts, scheduled to grant a 100 per cent preference over most favoured nations tariff rates by the end of 1994. In effect, once the treaty was

---

[31] For an analysis of macroeconomic interdependence, see Heymann (1999).

ratified by each national Congress, tariff-cutting commitments became binding domestic legal obligations. In practice, the TLP did not mean that national governments lost all flexibility to deal with special circumstances, as suggested by episodic ad hoc interventions in 1992–93 and by the implementation of the '*régimen de adecuación*' as of 1995.[32] However, the traditional logic of preferential trade liberalisation in Latin America was turned upside-down through the adoption of a 'negative' instead of a 'positive' list approach.[33]

In contrast to tariffs, commitments in the area of non-tariff barriers (NTBs) were looser: member countries agreed to eliminate all NTBs by the end of the 'transition period', but left the critical issues of definition and identification to technical negotiations to be undertaken by national bureaucracies. The ToA also committed member countries to negotiate and adopt a common external tariff (CET) by December 1994 and to co-ordinate macroeconomic and sector policies. However, the ToA made no provision about specific targets or procedures. While some objectives were met (e.g., negotiation of a CET by December 1994), others were missed (e.g., sector and macroeconomic co-ordination).

As unilateral and preferential trade liberalisation raised inter-dependence, the demand for more formal, substantive and centralised institutions began to mount, particularly on the part of smaller countries, ambiguous and unilaterally changeable rules (particularly in the realm of market access) produced uncertainty and limited the benefits of the larger market. By the same token, the disagreement over what constituted a 'level playing field' produced conflicts over investment location (such as in the motor vehicles industry). The slow pace of 'internalisation' and a weak DSM aggravated these grievances. The critical year of 1999 demonstrated the limited institutional resources (rules) to deal with a shock (the sizeable devaluation of the Brazilian currency). Unilateral initiatives and 'presidential diplomacy' were the preferred modes of response, constrained only by reputational considerations and domestic legal obligations. As the credibility of MERCOSUR organs and procedures suffered, the asymmetry of the constraints posed by domestic legal arrangements was made more evident.[34]

---

[32] The '*régimen de adecuación*' established a new automatic schedule to liberalise trade in a small group of sensitive products from 1995 to 1999.

[33] Bouzas (1998). The TLP illustrates how 'loose' institutional arrangements can provide a framework to take 'hard' policy decisions.

[34] The (relative) restraint to implement trade restrictive measures on the part of Argentina after the devaluation of the *real* in January 1999 is accounted for by the limits posed by the domestic legal system rather than by any rule or MERCOSUR organ. Since the violation of any 'legal norm' derived from the ToA or its associated instruments would be easily challenged in domestic courts, the Argentine government had few options but to show restraint.

In sum, weak 'demand pressures' for regional institutions at the start of MERCOSUR helps to account for the 'lean' institutional design originally adopted. But this did not prevent member states from taking 'hard' decisions and successfully implementing them. The ensuing rapid rise in interdependence was not strong enough to alter one basic feature of MERCOSUR, namely structurally asymmetric interdependence produced by large differences in size. Although Brazil was the member that experienced the largest relative increase in 'trade encapsulation', its absolute level remained too low to shift the balance from the preference for flexibility to more formal and procedural institutions (Table 4.3).[35] This structural feature, combined with a leadership gap on the 'supply side', helps to account for the current impasse in MERCOSUR institutional development.

'Supply' factors (the conditions under which political leaders are willing and able to accommodate demands for functional integration or respond to external events) provide the other side of the coin to account for the type and pace of institutionalisation that has taken place in MERCOSUR. Again following Mattli (1999), 'willingness' depends greatly on the expected payoff of economic integration to political leaders. This, in turn, tends to be positively correlated with the prevalence of economic difficulties as a background condition.

This explanation is consistent with the record of MERCOSUR during the first half of the 1990s, when the ToA was signed and the bulk of the trade liberalisation programme implemented. On the one hand, the opposition to preferential liberalisation from adversely affected domestic interests (one of the 'political costs' of economic integration) was lowered in the context of a broader trade policy environment that emphasised unilateral trade liberalisation and structural reform.[36] On the other, the expected 'benefits' rose stimulated by 'defensive' considerations and the perception of an economic performance that lagged behind that of other regions in the world.

But 'willingness' is not enough. Politicians and member state governments also need to be able to overcome collective action problems typical of economic integration.[37] Repeated interactions, issue-linkage and reputation can help to overcome collective action problems typical of trade relations. However, in a world of uncertainty and incomplete information these mechanisms are unlikely to provide enough guarantee against violation of agreements. This makes 'commitment institutions'

---

[35] However, aggregate 'trade encapsulation' indices do not tell the full story. In effect, a more detailed analysis shows that MERCOSUR has turned into a key outlet for Brazilian manufacturing exports. See da Motta Veiga (1999).

[36] After 1995 unilateral trade liberalisation (that had contributed to dissolving opposition to preferential trade liberalisation) ceased to be an over-riding policy priority in all member states, and particularly in Brazil. See da Motta Veiga (1999).

[37] See Snidal (1985).

(such as a DSM) necessary to improve the chances of compliance. Commitment institutions can monitor or help enforcement of rules among a group of countries seeking regional integration, enhancing the chances of successful co-operation by limiting the range of possible choices in cases when self-restraint is insufficient to ensure compliance. In more demanding 'co-ordination games', the ('supply') condition for success is even stronger: a focal point is needed to co-ordinate rules, regulations and policies and to ease distributive tensions. The role of the focal point and facilitator is normally performed by an undisputed regional leader, who is able to provide 'collective goods' and perform other tasks on behalf of the group of countries seeking closer ties.

Analysed from this standpoint 'supply conditions' in MERCOSUR have been very weak. During its first decade of existence repeated cajoling, arm-twisting and brinkmanship have been the most widely used vehicles to stimulate co-operation and constrain defection, possibly aided by the conviction that size asymmetries would create strong centrifugal forces towards the alignment of other member states behind Brazilian preferences. However, opacity and 'self-help' mechanisms have remained dominant as member states (and particularly Brazil) have been reluctant to move towards more transparent and formalised regimes that would have raised the cost of non-compliance.[38] Weak 'supply' conditions help to account for lean 'commitment' institutions and the practical absence of enforceable co-ordination initiatives at the regional level. In particular, they help to explain the fragility of centralised monitoring and third-party enforcement procedures in the DSM, a feature that has failed to provide certainty to private sector agents.

The fulfilment of the more demanding conditions typical of co-ordination games has been even rarer. Except for isolated episodes of ad hoc trade policy in the early 1990s,[39] distributive issues have been mostly managed on a national basis with little consideration given to 'collective' needs. The meagre progress recorded in policy co-ordination and/or harmonisation on issues such as effective implementation of a CET, common customs procedures, production and investment subsidies, macroeconomic and exchange rate policy and trade negotiations with third parties suggests that member states have been inclined to maintain autonomy and flexibility. In particular, the incentives for the larger member state to provide the leadership required (and pay the costs for it) have been very weak.[40]

---

[38] One outstanding example is the confidential character of the Administrative Secretary reports on the progress of 'internalisation'.

[39] These episodes (for example, accepting Argentina's increase of its statistical import surcharge in 1993) can be interpreted as an acceptance of derogations in exchange for the right to benefit from derogations at some time in the future.

[40] The firm opposition of the Brazilian government to the inclusion of an 'escape' clause or a safeguard mechanism after the end of the transition period illustrates more than the

The existing gap in the provision of leadership can be thus explained by the modest payoff perceived by the Brazilian government (the most obvious candidate to exert such a role) as obtainable from doing so. More formal, centralised and substantive institutions in MERCOSUR would have constrained flexibility and discretion, in a context of limited interdependence, a volatile economic environment and not fully convergent national preferences.[41]

4. Conclusions

The main institutional traits of MERCOSUR are the strong inter-governmental bias of its organs, the key role of consensus in decision-making and the non-existence of an 'autonomous' legal order (including a jurisdictional body to settle disputes). These features have been consistent with an institutional model that emphasises continuous bargaining, flexibility and adaptability. This institutional approach was very effective in increasing interdependence in a context where functional demands for integration were weak. As Khaler (1995) argues, 'state-like' institutions (emphasising the role of explicit rules and injunctions) may not be the most efficient institutional form in all environments. Decentralised and informal institutions can be more effective when scarce and expensive information requires substantial information gathering before additional institution-building can occur or, alternatively, when plentiful and cheap information about the preferences and reputation of partners make reputation-based systems sufficient to ensure compliance.

In the initial years of MERCOSUR institutions with the ability to adapt rapidly and easily to changes in the environment proved to be both effective and durable, helping to increase interdependence and develop a 'learning process' that may eventually lead to more formal, centralised and substantive institutional forms as demand and supply conditions develop. Moreover, this institutional design did not prevent taking 'hard' policy decisions, such as the TLP.

From the standpoint of furthering economic integration in the region the institutional design of MERCOSUR seems to have reached a point of diminishing returns. Since the mid-1990s a growing wedge between commitments and implementation has developed *pari passu* with a growing credibility gap. The sharp increase in interdependence has created new functional demands for institutionalisation, most evident in the case of the smaller partners. This has made more obvious the

---

formal argument that such mechanisms are alien to a customs union. The defence of such a rigid stance — even after the sizeable devaluation of the *real* in 1999 — is hard to reconcile with the exercise of constructive, benevolent leadership in the region.

[41] For a discussion of the factors (including changing national 'preferences') explaining the contrasting record of MERCOSUR in the 1990s, see Bouzas (1999).

shortcomings that dominate the 'supply' side, still constrained by low and asymmetric levels of interdependence, macroeconomic fragility, vulnerability to external shocks and divergent national preferences. This has given a premium to the maintenance of flexibility, particularly on the part of Brazil. In the future these structural factors will continue to shape the context in which MERCOSUR institutions will evolve. Progress towards more 'dense' institutional forms will therefore at best be gradual and slow.

CHAPTER 5

The Winner's Curse: Premature Monetary Integration in the NAFTA

Valpy FitzGerald

The progress of the North American Free Trade Agreement (NAFTA) since its inception in 1994 has considerable implications for Latin American economic integration as a whole.[1] Mexico now accounts for over half of the trade between the USA and Latin America. Mexico is the destination for most US investment in the region, and the origin of the bulk of immigration — both legal and illegal. NAFTA also represents a new standard for integration initiatives, particularly for those between developed and developing countries and has had a profound effect on the design of multilateral trade and investment treaties. The three NAFTA countries — Canada, Mexico and the USA — now account for nearly a quarter of world trade; while trade between its members represents 40 per cent of their total trade.

The NAFTA also represents a major departure in the economic and institutional relationship between the United States and the other nations of the Americas. On the one hand, it involves an explicit commitment to market integration — not only in goods but also in services and capital markets — with significant additional agreements in employment and environmental standards. On the other hand, NAFTA appears to involve an implicit step back from the traditional US commitment to multilateral agreements on free trade and open capital markets on a global scale — and possibly even a retreat into a regional trade and currency zone.

The first seven years of NAFTA have seen not only a rapid trade expansion between the partners, but also a major financial crisis in Mexico. While the US administration has been willing to support the Mexican economy in crisis, very little institutional change has taken place in order to reflect the real degree of economic integration between the two countries. This policy of 'benign neglect' seems to have been justified in the case of commodity trade: the NAFTA passed a major 'stress test' in the form of a major peso devaluation in 1994–95 and a

[1] The support of the MacArthur Foundation for the research programme at Oxford University, from which this chapter is derived, is gratefully acknowledged. I would also like to thank my student Anne Vandenbeele for stimulating ideas arising from her own research on this topic and participants at the 50th Congress of Americanists, Warsaw, July 2000, for their comments on an earlier draft.

subsequent import surge into the USA, without serious protective reaction. Although trade remains seriously unbalanced and the export of services such as road transport is still constrained by state-level restrictions, the periodic inter-governmental meetings seem capable of handling differences in an effective manner and furthering the integration process.

The same cannot be said of financial policy, where both the scale and direction of flows and the institutional arrangements are highly problematic, in view of the potential for macroeconomic disruption caused by periodic monetary crises. The increasing dollarisation of the Mexican economy and the exogenous nature of capital flows have severely reduced the capacity of domestic authorities to stabilise the economy. The need for greater understanding of the implications of the use of the dollar for the Mexican economy is evident. However, this is not just a matter of monetary cost-benefit in terms of seignorage loss and lower interest rates; or even only an issue of increased credibility and loss of adjustment capacity. The central issue is in fact the nature of the institutional arrangements that underpin any currency system — particularly the provision of liquidity and the regulation of capital markets.

This chapter sets out to address this issue by examining a range of historical models for the use of an 'external currency' and then applying their implications for monetary relations between Mexico and the USA in the NAFTA context. Section 1 defines the nature of currency substitution, looks at some evidence on the use of the dollar and the peso, and sketches the main elements of the current debate on dollarisation in the region. The lessons of the gold standard and more recent currency board ('dollar standard') systems of apparently 'unmanaged' use of external money are drawn in Section 2. These suggest that last resort lending and supervisory co-ordination are still required except in special cases such as Panama. In Section 3 the post-WWII sterling area and the Franc Zone on the one hand, and the European Monetary Union on the other, are examined as examples of 'managed' external currency systems with varying degrees of participation by the member countries. Despite the provision of liquidity, the need for common fiscal rules and the problem of asymmetric response to exogenous shocks are evident.

In Section 4 of this chapter these two strands are brought together to provide an assessment of the monetary options available to Mexico, suggesting that membership of an extended Federal Reserve system would be both feasible and preferable in economic terms. However, the political economy considerations mentioned in the conclusions seem to imply that the institutional implications of further monetary co-operation may be unacceptable. This is the 'winner's curse': the success of North American market integration is itself leading to a degree of institutional co-operation and implicit fiscal support that US legislators desired to avoid when establishing NAFTA.

1. Financial Integration and Currency Substitution between Mexico and the USA

Market integration lies at the heart of the explanation for the growth in both Mexican exports and imports. This might seem surprising under the conditions of currency volatility, which is why the increasing dollarisation of the private sector may be related to trade expansion. The dollarisation of the Mexican economy is evident, but difficult to measure, for two reasons. The first, and most obvious, is that the use of the dollar as currency in circulation within Mexico is not registered by either monetary authority and Mexican assets in Mexico tend to be under-reported for fiscal reasons. The second, and possibly more important reason, is because money does not just act as a means of exchange and store of value, but also as a unit of account. In other words, most large contracts and transactions in Mexico are now carried out implicitly in dollars, and peso prices will be varied automatically with the exchange rate — except of course wages.

The literature makes an important distinction between: (a) 'normal' currency substitution based on the services supplied by both currencies and the risks of parity shift (including risk aversion), in other words a risk/return motive for holding assets and transactions motives; and (b) 'pathological' currency substitution based on uncertainty and a change in expectations thereof.[2] Normal substitution can take place due to changes in return or risk, and also if markets are completed so that new assets are available.[3]

This leaves 'pathological' substitution essentially undefined. In the case of Mexico, at least, a more convincing explanation might be that dollarisation is the path-dependent consequence of four factors:

(a) cumulative macroeconomic shocks leading to asset composition changes as wealth-holders (firms, banks and rich households) hedge their positions;

(b) reduced costs of dealing in foreign assets and liabilities, due to technological change, capital account liberalisation and the experience of doing so;

---

[2] See Calvo and Vegh (1992); Giovannini and Tutelboom (1994); Guidotti and Rodriguez (1992); McKinnon (1982); Ortíz (1983); Ramírez (1985); and Tavlas (1997). Finally, IMF (2000) even has a 'box' on dollarisation, but appears to confuse it with a fixed exchange rate regime, which misses the central point.

[3] Thomas (1985) suggests that this normal/pathological distinction can be defined in quantitative terms as the point where the elasticity of substitution in response to exchange rate change is greater than unity.

(c)   fear of continued macro-shocks of the 'new' type;
(d)   the transnationalisation of households themselves, in the form of migration (and remittances) for the poor, and reliance on education, health and consumer goods from the US (requiring large balances there) in the case of richer households.

The official estimate of the extent of dollarisation (see Table 5.1 below) in Mexico is that no more than seven per cent of total money supply was in dollar form in 1999, with a peak at 27 per cent in 1994.[4] However, if to this 'dollar-M4' we add the US bank deposits and securities holdings by Mexican residents recorded by the US Treasury (see Table 5.2) then the figure is closer to 20 per cent in 1999 with a peak of 44 per cent in 1994. Vanderbeele (2000) carries out tests for the degree of dollarisation in Mexico since 1980 under this wider definition. Structural factors such as trade integration and regulatory changes explain the dollarisation trend over the long term, while 'pathological' factors such as exchange rate expectations and hysteresis are also present, especially during crisis periods. Nonetheless, structural factors determine changes in the parameters of the money services function and have altered the substitutability of both currencies and thus the elasticity of currency substitution.

Table 5.1: Aggregate Money Supply in Mexico

	1993	1994	1995	1996	1997	1998	1999
M4 (bn pesos)	580.4	724.2	869.3	1116.2	1405.4	1769.0	2115.6
National Currency	527.2	530.3	754.7	985.6	1283.5	1627.0	1971.5
Foreign Currency	53.1	193.9	114.6	130.6	121.9	142.0	144.0
Deposit Rate	15.1	13.3	38.1	24.7	14.7	13.8	9.6
Inflation Rate	—	—	—	—	—	—	—
Depreciation rate	—	—	—	—	—	—	—
GDP	1256.2	1420.2	1837.0	2503.8	3179.0	3791.2	4622.8
Foreign/total M4	9%	27%	13%	12%	9%	8%	7%
M4/GDP	46%	51%	47%	45%	44%	47%	46%
Real interest rate: peso prices							
Real interest rate: dollar prices							

Source: Banco de México.

---

[4] This also the definition used by the World Bank in its webpage on dollarisation (http://www.worldbank.org/dollarization).

Table 5.2: Reported Monetary Assets of Mexican Residents

US $ billions	1993	1997	1999
M4: Domestic Currency	169.6	158.8	207.2
Foreign Currency	17.1	15.1	15.1
Total	186.7	173.9	222.4
Liquid Claims on US	20.7	36.0	36.0
Banks	20.0	35.3	35.1
Non-banks	0.7	0.7	0.9
Total Monetary Assets			
Pesos	169.6	158.8	207.2
Dollars	37.8	51.1	51.1
Total	209.4	209.9	258.3
Dollars/Total	**18%**	**24%**	**20%**

Sources: Banco de México and US Treasury.

However, there is good reason to believe that dollarisation is much more extensive in Mexico than these figures indicate. The recorded holdings of US securities seem much too low in view of at least two decades of capital flight, while there is no estimate of dollars in the hands of the Mexican public. The implicit portfolio balance between US bank deposits and securities seems implausible. If we allow for some US$10bn in securities (rather than the US$1bn recorded) plus a further US$5bn for circulating currency (the reserve money in pesos is equivalent to US$20bn), then the true 'dollar money supply' available to Mexican residents would be of the order of one-third of the dollar equivalent of the domestic money supply.

The main concern in the early literature in the 'monetary approach to the balance of payments' tradition was the effect of currency substitution in reducing the effectiveness of monetary policy. This argument was then developed in order to explain the lack of effect of monetary expansion on the exchange rate: increased money supply was held to lead to increased currency substitution. Mundell (1961) also stresses the importance of factor mobility (both labour and capital) as a shock absorber within a currency even if production structures are not symmetrical; this mobility can compensate for the loss of the exchange rate instrument. Mexico would clearly qualify here. Wage flexibility will also be important insofar as labour cannot move freely. During the crisis after 1994, real wages fell by some 30 per cent, similar to the real exchange rate adjustment. Openness of the economy is also held to be important and would clearly be a positive factor for Mexico.[5]

---

[5] McKinnon (1963).

However, the experience of European Monetary Union (EMU) has raised a number of other factors, particularly the credibility of exchange rate arrangements and time-inconsistency in governments' fiscal and monetary policy. Countries with similar economic structures are held to respond similarly to shocks (whether trade or financial); in this case symmetrical (i.e. common) responses will be appropriate. If structures are different, then disturbances will be asymmetrical and the policy response should be asymmetric too. Further, with a dominant economy (e.g. US) in the currency area, shocks will be transmitted to the other members (e.g. Mexico) rather than the other way around.

In contrast, the need for similar inflation rates (e.g. EMU convergence criteria) is clearly not met at present; although it should be noted that high-inflation countries can converge very rapidly under a *credible* currency conversion — as the Argentine experience indicates. Finally, fiscal integration is held to be important (e.g. replacing devaluation by transfers for adjustment and tax harmonisation), but there is little or no prospect of this. In consequence, currency union would force adjustment back on real wages, unemployment and public expenditure. This may seem regressive, but of course in a semi-dollarised economy devaluation has an asymmetric effect in any case — benefiting those with dollar assets and prejudicing those paid in pesos.

The function and power of the central bank are clearly undermined by dollarisation. As the central bank cannot issue the external currency, the domestic money supply is no longer a policy instrument and the economy may be forced to operate without a 'lender of last resort (LLR)'.[6] Banks lose asset value during crises, but retain their liabilities; so LLR is brought in to transfer wealth to depositors/creditors. Some access to assets, tax receipts, credit lines or the issue of currency/reserves must be available to the LLR in order to buy assets at prices which the market considers unrealistic at the time. As these crises usually involve a shortage of liquidity and the central bank creates this, the LLR function is typically assigned to the central bank.

This function can be carried out by other actors with access to external funds who can make corresponding asset purchases: the government (the treasury or even an agency such as the state pension fund); another central bank; or even the private sector — typically the head offices of banks with branches or subsidiaries in the host country. Dollarisation of the private sector would eliminate exchange rate risk, and thus one of the major causes of liquidity crises (from attacks on the exchange rate affecting institutions with unhedged balance sheets) and bank runs. It does not, however, eradicate credit risk or the effect of exogenous interest rate (or price) shocks.

---

[6] Caprio et al. (1996).

However, as Calvo and Vegh (1992) point out, continued fiscal imbalances may force the private banks to lend to the government and to those previously relying on liquidity provision, which increases their bad loan book and then causes bank runs. A high interest-rate T-Bill market as an alternative 'solution' to the fiscal problem leads to longer-term solvency problems and causes the banks to disintermediate.[7]

2. Using an 'External Money': the Gold Standard and Currency Boards

The 'classical' gold standard system that operated between 1870 and 1914 was, for the participating countries, an apparent equivalent to moving to a 'dollar standard' today. Participating countries declared parities against gold, with implicit cross-rates to be enforced by arbitrage in bullion. Capital controls were largely absent, and although governments did try to influence international lending levels, they had little information on their balance of payments position and thus could not target the current account. In fact, capital flows were very large relative to the size of national economies and their mutual trade during this period. There was also a remarkable co-movement of domestic prices between the leading economies during this period, including long episodes of deflation, due mainly to the flexibility of nominal wages and a large pool of reserve labour. Long-term interest rates were remarkably stable and converged gradually to the three–four per cent range, due not only to the gold and capital arbitrage but also to increasing confidence that the system would be maintained.[8]

During the Great War the system broke down, and although it returned in the mid-1920s it proved unsustainable as persistent payments imbalances threatened to exhaust the reserves of deficit countries and deflationary pressures worsened unemployment and augmented the burden of mortgage debts.[9] In this inter-war period it was the 'periphery' — that is, Latin America and the Dominions — that was most seriously affected. Argentina and Uruguay suspended payments in 1929, while Canada introduced monetary restrictions equivalent to devaluation. Brazil, Chile, Paraguay, Peru, Venezuela, Australia and New Zealand all suspended gold convertibility, and their currencies immediately fell below par.

Thus, although the gold standard system did stabilise exchange rates and had a dramatic effect on balance of payments deficits, it did not

---

[7] This was the result of the currency board system in Argentina during the 1990s, where the government was forced to abroad not only to cover its own fiscal deficits but also in order to provide liquidity to the banks, leading eventually to debt insolvency and an IMF bailout in 2000.

[8] Eichengreen (1994).

[9] Eichengreen (1992).

engender much stability in domestic variables such as money supply or growth or employment. In consequence, it failed to stabilise price levels and real interest rates — in other words, output and employment were unnecessarily sacrificed to external equilibrium.[10] It is also evident that the gold specie flows, through which adjustment was to take place in principle, were quite low compared to the balance of payments adjustments that took place. In practice, the adjustment mechanisms were a combination of Keynesian output shifts and trade multipliers on the one hand, and large capital flows between banking centres and participating countries on the other.

The gold standard system was of considerable advantage to the 'core countries' (UK and France) which managed the system, as the world's capital markets were thus in London and Paris, with depth on which their governments could borrow cheaply and massively.[11] They could also use this dominance in order to influence the policies of smaller European and other peripheral countries. The two central banks intervened heavily in the market to stop volatility; they issued government bonds to bolster their reserves, which were always low, and co-operated closely — both before 1914 and more intensely after 1919.[12] However, the system relied extensively on *private* banks such as Rothschilds using their gold balances as the two central banks never had sufficient gold and in particular they were needed to support the Bank of England and the Bank of France in the 1907 crisis.[13] The point here is that private capital flows were not entirely guided by immediate arbitrage gains, but by the longer-term advantages to large banks of supporting international monetary stability.

The adoption of the gold standard by the industrialised countries meant that Latin America did not have to balance bilateral trade: exports to the USA which were used to pay for imports from Europe until the breakdown of the gold standard in 1914 led to severe disruption.[14] On independence Latin America had inherited a motley circulation of silver and gold coin; and the decline of silver prices after 1870 left those countries that were not on the gold standard on a de facto silver

---

[10] See Hallwood and MacDonald (1994), Chapter 13.

[11] Note that the main source of fiscal deficits then was military, not social expenditure.

[12] 'The biggest difference between the pre-1914 gold standard and the old exchange system of the 1920s was that two of the most important players — the United States and France — bent the rules by sterilising additions to their reserves in order to avoid domestic inflation. Without central bank co-operation, the system could not survive.' (Ferguson (1998), II, p. 462).

[13] Indeed as early as 1825 the Bank of England itself was bailed out by Rothschilds (Ferguson (1998), I, p. 136). Rothschilds became involved in forcing stabilisation policies on Brazil throughout the nineteenth century, including large coffee purchases (Ferguson II, pp. 346–7); gold mining for supply in South Africa and gold price 'fixing' (Ferguson II, pp. 352–3).

[14] See Bulmer-Thomas (1994).

standard. As this latter became indefensible so they retreated onto paper money. However, subsequent inflation led to most countries attempting to get onto the gold standard by the end of the century, even though many did not have sufficient gold reserves. Argentina, Brazil and Chile solved this problem by collecting taxes in gold and entered early. Others — Costa Rica, Ecuador and Peru — had hardly joined by 1914, while Caribbean countries adopted the dollar instead. However, rising commodity prices during the pre-war decades meant that lack of export competitiveness was not a general problem. Where domestic inflation in non-traded sectors affected costs, tariffs were often used to achieve effective devaluation.

The Great War meant the end of the gold standard system and the movement of capital, leading to suspension of convertibility and wholesale debt default. However, even in the classical period, the way in which the gold standard (supposedly) operated between industrialised economies was not really relevant to Latin America. Balance of payments difficulties arose from terms of trade shocks rather than fiscal imbalance and could not be corrected by relative price shifts domestically in order to promote exports. Any inflow of gold after export price rises led inevitably to unsustainable import levels. Thus even in the classical gold standard period, Latin America tended to suspend convertibility in periods of gold outflow.

During the 1920s, some countries adopted the gold standard for the first time (e.g. Bolivia) and others returned (including Argentina, Brazil and Mexico) precisely because of the automatic stabiliser it provided.[15] However the decline in exports was so severe after 1929 that gold reserves evaporated and three countries (Argentina, Mexico and Uruguay) suspended the gold standard before the British decision to stop selling gold and foreign exchange on demand in 1931. Most countries introduced exchange controls and rationed imports until forced off the standard by US suspension in 1933. The result was relatively positive because declining fiscal receipts from trade duties led to expansionary monetary stances, which stimulated domestic demand and promoted a rapid recovery from the Great Depression despite the massive trade shock.[16]

In contrast, Australia and Canada stayed on the gold standard without excessive strain between 1890 and 1914. Unlike Latin America, Australia and Canada had no independent monetary authorities and thus could neither play by 'the rules of the game' or break them. As neither Dominion could sterilise capital flows, it was the international mobility of capital rather than adherence to gold standard rules as such

---

[15] Díaz-Fuentes (1999).
[16] See Thorp (1984).

which made the system work smoothly.[17] This may suggest that Argentina being driven off the gold standard in the 1890s while Australia was not, despite its depression in that same period for much the same reason, was due to sustained capital market access. This access in turn can be seen as a reputational benefit of credible membership of the sterling-gold zone derived from Dominion status, which made exit more difficult and ensured support from London.

Currency boards may appear to provide a modern parallel to the gold standard system based on the dollar or a basket of international currencies. Although the domestic money supply is no longer a policy instrument in the sense of being linked to the external reserve position, there is no open access to foreign money. There is no *official* lender of last resort (LLR) in the form of a central bank under a currency board system.[18] However, in practice other actors with access to external funds can make the corresponding asset purchases: the government (the treasury or an agency such as the state pension fund); another central bank; or even the private sector (head offices of banks with branches or subsidiaries in the host country). This tends to cause further instability because continued fiscal imbalances[19] may force the private banks to lend to the government and to those previously relying on liquidity provision, which increases their bad loan book and then causes bank runs. A high interest-rate treasury bill as an alternative 'solution' to the fiscal problem leads to longer-term solvency problems and causes the banks to disintermediate.[20]

For instance, Berg and Borensztein (2000) examine the costs and benefits of full dollarisation as compared to a currency board, taking Argentina as the test case. The benefits include lower international borrowing costs, which they quantify by looking at the effect of currency risk on the default risk component of international (i.e. dollar) borrowing costs. The quantified costs are the loss of seignorage (much less than the interest rate gain) but the effect of having no easy exit option and the absence of a lender of last resort are only discussed

---

[17] Dick, Floyd and Pope (1996) use a portfolio model of balance of payments adjustment that treats asset markets in a world-wide general equilibrium framework with imperfect capital mobility, which gives a better understanding of the way in which the gold standard really worked than the price-specie-flow mechanism of adjustment espoused by Taussig and Viner.

[18] Banks lose asset value during crises, but retain their liabilities; so a lender of last resort (LLR) is brought in to transfer wealth to depositors/creditors. Access to assets, tax receipts, credit lines or the issue of currency/reserves must be available to the LLR in order to buy assets at prices which the market considers unrealistic at the time. As these crises usually involve a shortage of liquidity and the central bank creates this, the LLR function is typically assigned to the central bank.

[19] Which themselves may result from the need to bail out fragile banks by taking over their bad loan books.

[20] As Calvo and Veigh (1992) point out.

qualitatively.[21] They also argue that optimal currency area criteria such as convergence with the US economy are not relevant to this case. For instance from 1996 the monetary authorities in Hong Kong assumed explicit responsibility for the provision of LLR facilities to banks experiencing day-to-day liquidity shortages. In 1998 banks were given unrestricted access to liquidity through repurchase agreements using the Exchange Fund (which holds the Hong Kong foreign exchange reserves).[22] However, it should be noted that 90 per cent of deposits are concentrated in one bank and its subsidiaries; and as this bank was well diversified internationally, systemic risk was reduced and the LLR function was implicitly provided 'internally'. Again, with Argentina in the early 1990s strict application of the currency board system shifted LLR responsibilities to the private sector (as had been the case of Canada before 1935, or indeed Scotland under the free banking system during the eighteenth and nineteenth centuries). This was made viable by the fact that all but one of the domestic banks were foreign-owned, and could thus rely on their head office (or in the last resort, the home country central bank) as LLR.

Finally, there is the case of Panama. Under treaty arrangements established on independence, dollars serve as legal tender and are the only (paper) fiat money.[23] There is no central bank, money creation or exchange rate, or interest rate policy as such — the minimal differential reflects the (low) default risk. The treaty arrangements ensure the supply by the US Treasury of fiat money to meet banks' requirements to replace old notes or for cash against deposits in US banks. There is no provision for LLR as such, although most banks are foreign affiliates and thus can rely on home country facilities. Moreover, in Panama the money supply (deposit money in this case) is comparatively small and the banking system has a very strong reserve position, as the large dollar inflows were mostly converted into external assets. Above all, Panama represents no systemic risk to the US economy. The implications are two: on the one hand this model requires the core country to assume explicit responsibility for fiat money supply; and it is also only viable in small economies where the banking system is not heavily committed to the domestic economy — that is, in offshore financial centres.

One should also note that in Panama, the money supply (deposit money in this case) is comparatively small: in 1999 'deposit money' (the only type recorded) was US\$1bn as opposed to US\$42bn in Mexico and

---

[21] In fact, as mentioned above, Argentina has two lenders of last resort: the Argentine treasury borrowing on New York and London, and the foreign banks located in Buenos Aires borrowing from their head offices.

[22] The HK authorities also bought up (with the public sector pension fund) a third of the stock market index to provide non-bank liquidity and confidence.

[23] The only other such treaty is with Liberia.

US$1462bn in the USA. However, the banking system has a very strong reserve position (by definition), to match the very low official foreign exchange reserves of less than US$1bn (Mexico is US$32bn) in 1999. Panamanian interest rates are only 1–2 per cent above those of the USA. Above all, Panama represents no systemic risk to the US economy.

3. Constructing a Currency Zone: the Sterling Area, the Franc Zone and the EMU

The heyday of this dollar standard was the 1950s and 1960s, and as the dollar was the only reserve currency, it was the rest of the world (RoW) which intervened in foreign exchange markets in order to stabilise parities. The RoW held their reserves in US Treasury securities rather than Federal Reserve liabilities, which implied a passive sterilisation of US payments imbalances, while the RoW was unable to sterilise the effects of capital flows on their own money base. In consequence, currency substitution out of (into) the dollar raised (lowered) the world's money base as a whole.[24] Significantly, the Bretton Woods system broke down because of the costs to the core member (the USA) of maintaining the stability of the core currency (the dollar) in the face of fiscal deficits.[25]

An alternative approach to the use of an external currency in the post-WWII period was the arrangement in place between the UK and the Sterling Area participants during the 1950s.[26] Post-war arrangements with the aftermath of empire were dominated by the desire to retain trading arrangements and the role of sterling as an international reserve currency in the face of the 'dollar shortage'. The UK maintained capital controls for all payments outside the Sterling Area, whose members kept their reserves in London (in sterling) and enforced common currency controls with the UK. The sterling balances were liabilities for the UK, of course, and exceeded UK foreign exchange reserves (i.e. dollar balances) by four or five times; although they were to some extent matched by UK direct investment (i.e. fixed assets) in member countries. The currency zone was thus underpinned not only by trade flows, but also by capital movements. The system was finally undermined by the desire of members to switch to a stronger reserve currency (the dollar) and to lift capital controls on the one hand. The relative economic weakness of the

---

[24] McKinnon (1982) supposes that world money demand is a stable function of income but that substitution into and out of the dollar is unstable and depends on exchange rate expectations. Under these circumstances (an extreme case of the so-called 'N + 1 Problem') only the US money base is directly controlled; so that of the rest of the world depends on the domestic assets of the Federal Reserve.

[25] The parallel with the US current account deficit 30 years later is cause for concern — dollarised economies can only hope for a 'soft landing'.

[26] See Schenk (1994) for a complete account. The members included the Commonwealth (except Canada) and related countries in the Middle and Far East.

'central banker' for the zone (the UK) relative to both members and to the rest of the world was also a key causal factor.

The other post-colonial model, which has survived rather better, is the CFA franc/euro arrangement in West and Central Africa.[27] The members benefit from a fixed exchange rate against the French franc (now the euro) which is adjustable in consultation with the French authorities. Full convertibility is guaranteed by the French Treasury for those currencies emitted by the Bank of Central African States and the Bank of West African States, respectively. In turn, these two central banks deposit at least 65 per cent of their foreign exchange reserves with the French Treasury, at market-related yields. As these balances can be both positive (from accumulated external earnings and aid transfers) and negative, an automatic 'overdraft' facility is available; but member countries enter into formal commitments to limit fiscal deficits. The key consequence is the unlimited convertibility of the CFA franc into euros, which is complemented by full cross-convertibility of currencies within the zone and free capital movements.

Although the CFA system came under strain with the devaluation of 1994 (after various commodity price shocks), leaving a legacy of debt, it has performed well as a whole. One of its shortcomings is that the countries inside the zone do not form an optimal currency area between themselves. The strength of the system is its market credibility, which is provided not so much by the backing of the French Treasury (which in practice manages the system so that member balances remain positive) as the economic and political cost of withdrawal. Although the euro does not appear to circulate as such, it certainly 'backs' domestic money in a more effective way than a currency board (with no external discipline of LLR) would do — while allowing for devaluation in response to a persistent misalignment. The equivalent setup in the case of Mexico would involve the central bank holding its reserves with the Federal Reserve against an overdraft facility and some sort of stability pact as 'operating rules' as in the CFA. Full convertibility at a fixed (but not irrevocable) rate would be ensured in this way.

Early debates on the European Monetary System and Monetary Union were not dissimilar to current discussions of dollarisation in the Western Hemisphere. Initial expectations were that member countries would not meet the fiscal targets necessary nor legislate for the required labour market flexibility. [28] These were felt to be necessary because price stability in the region as a whole would require a strict limit on aggregate money supply, and that individual members should not be allowed to

---

[27] Created in 1939 as the Franc des Colonies Françaises d'Afrique, it is now called Franc de la Communautée Financière d'Afrique. It covers 14 African countries. See Hadjimichael and Galy (1997).

[28] Hallwood and MacDonald (1994), Chapter 14.

borrow directly from the central monetary authority in order to prevent moral hazard. In consequence, with unified interest rates the only adjustment mechanism available to asymmetric shocks would be labour costs. Given the level of social entitlements built into the 'European Project', the only option was employment flexibility.

The benefits of monetary unification were held to include: (i) increased allocative efficiency due to reduction of exchange rate risk, although shocks might be transmitted to the bond market; (ii) risk adjusted interest rates would fall, leading to increased investment and growth; (iii) avoidance of overshooting, misalignment of exchange rates and currency speculation; (iv) payments can be made in own currency rather than in dollars requiring trade surpluses with the USA; (v) savings in transactions costs estimated at half of one per cent of European output; (vi) gains in monetary credibility for high inflation countries, above all in Southern Europe; (vi) trade promotion effects due to reduced price uncertainty.

The costs of monetary unification were considered to include: (i) the loss of adjustment capacity, which depends upon how well demand and supply shocks are correlated — it was felt that these were better correlated in the USA than in the EU;[29] (ii) built-in fiscal and wage inflation pressure would force excessive deflation for long time after unification; (iii) low wage member countries would attract 'broadening' investment while high income ones attract 'deepening' (high wage and value added) investment so that structural subsidies would be necessary to ensure productivity convergence; (iv) a single monetary policy would not suit all members due to very different financial structures;[30] (v) the strong constraints on fiscal policy would be politically unsustainable.

The central point in the traditional analysis was that factor mobility is crucial in order to keep the real exchange rate steady as well as the nominal parity.[31] The example given (of course) is labour mobility, and without wage flexibility, unemployment can result. However, the experience of EMU has raised a number of other factors, particularly the credibility of exchange rate arrangements and time-inconsistency in governments' fiscal and monetary policy. If countries with similar economic structures are held to respond similarly to shocks (whether trade or financial), then symmetrical (i.e. common) responses will be appropriate. If structures are different, then disturbances will be asymmetrical and the policy response should be asymmetric too. Further, with a dominant economy (e.g. Germany, or in our case the USA) in the currency area, shocks will be transmitted to the other members (e.g. to Spain or Mexico) rather than the other way around.

---

[29] This was also felt to be due to the faster adjustment of *non-traded* prices in the USA.
[30] Which disrupted the EMS in 1992.
[31] E.g. Mundell (1961).

Subsequent theoretical advances in the analysis of market expectations on the one hand and the experience of fiscal adjustment (the Maastricht Treaty) and the relatively smooth introduction of the euro, have led to a considerable shift in opinion as to the relevant criteria.[32] It is clear that members must agree on the monetary policy rules, but a problem of credibility remains if the new monetary institutions (i.e. the European Central Bank (ECB)) have no reputation in capital markets.[33] Moreover, if one member is economically dominant, the transmission of the business cycle to the periphery will be exacerbated — particularly if the latter is subject to asymmetric terms of trade shocks.[34] However expectations are central to success: the credibility of low inflation cause lower interest rates and thus outweigh the increased adjustment costs. The gains to the core economy (or economies) are not quite so clear; indeed its own credibility will be diminished by its LLR role — or at least the pressure to adapt interest rate policy to the broader needs of the zone.

The size of the euro capital market now approximates that of the USA.[35] In fact, European monetary unification is about capital market integration as much as fixed exchange rates as such: it is profoundly changing the financial structure of Europe.[36] In consequence, the direct effects, such as the elimination of currency risk foreseen in the Ceccini Report,[37] are now considered to be less important than the indirect effects such as larger bond and equity markets, mergers of banks and stock markets. These in turn lead to greater pressure to introduce further reforms in order to reduce the cost of intra-EU transactions and to increase the depth and liquidity of European financial markets. Finally, appropriate regulatory structures are gradually emerging in response to these changes, despite the fact that the powers of the European Central Bank were originally confined to money supply in the pursuit of price stability.

---

[32] See de Grauwe (1992); Danthine, Giavezzi and von Thadden (2000); and Detken and Hartmann (2000).

[33] If the Federal Reserve exercised these functions for a dollar zone, this would not be such a problem.

[34] Which in the case of dollarisation would include relative price shifts *within* the US economy.

[35] Danthine, Giavezzi and von Thadden (2000).

[36] Detken and Hartmann (2000) find that for most market segments, the euro immediately became in 1999 the second most widely used currency for international financing and investment. International bond and note issuance overtook the dollar in the second half of the year. The investment role of the euro is not so dynamic, as most of the early external asset supply of the euro was actually absorbed by euro-area residents.

[37] EC (1990).

4. Assessing the Mexican Options for Monetary Integration

Although the Mexican economy is increasingly integrated to the US economy, their business cycles are not highly correlated because of the vulnerability of Mexico to repeated financial crises. These in turn are followed by large demand adjustments (as in 1983 and 1995) and although trade recovers quickly, investor confidence tends to recover much more slowly.

The benefits to Mexico would thus be the reduction of the risk premium, possibly towards Canadian levels. This would reduce foreign and domestic borrowing costs considerably (Table 5.3). As Table 5.3 and Figure 5.1 suggest, the gains would be very large — affecting both fiscal resources and domestic investment levels very positively. On government debt alone, a 100 basis point reduction in the dollar yield spread costs would be equivalent to a saving of US$1 billion a year. Probably as important would be the reduction in variability of interest rates and thus in business uncertainty, leading to a stimulus to fixed investment and thus competitiveness.

Table 5.3: Spreads on 'Americas' Bonds in New York

	Jan 2000	Jan 2001
US Treasury 10 years	6.75	5.14
Spreads (basis points):		
Canada (2010)	+28	-19
Mexico (global 2010)	+327	+356
Brazil (global)	+655	+701
Argentina (global)	+542	+737

Source: IMF, International Financial Statistics.

A major concern in European (and other) discussions of currency unification has been the seignorage loss, and specifically the cost of replacing the money supply. The net cost depends on how money supply is interpreted, because reserves are no longer necessary. At the simplest level, reserve money in Mexico is equivalent to US$20bn, and is backed by US$32bn of official reserves (see Table 5.4). However, if wider money supply M4 in national currency is *all* a potential liability against the Banco de México (Banxico), then this has a value of some US$200bn — five times reserves. It should also be noted that the large net exposure position of the banks is only just balanced by the Banxico reserves. Further, there is a short-term government debt rollover of at least US$100bn a year (which triggered the 1994–95 crisis). In other words, the reserves are collateral for a number of different things at the same time.

Figure 5.1: Mexico Bond Spread 1997–2000

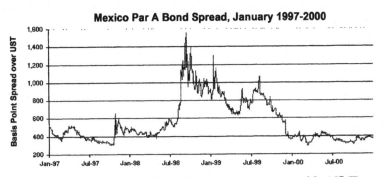

Note: Sovereign benchmark (Par A) spread to comparable US Treasury.
Source: Bloomberg.

Unlike in the EMU — and possibly Canadian — cases, seignorage is not really an issue here. US$30 billion in reserve money implies US$1 billion a year in increased money supply in real terms for three per cent GDP growth. This is about 0.2 per cent of GDP, and one per cent of fiscal income. However, in terms of the risk premium on foreign borrowing, with external government debt at US$100 billion, then a reduction of 100 basis points in the spread would exceed this cost — while the present spread is in the order of 400 basis points. In other words, the likely reduction in the risk premium would far outweigh the seignorage loss.

Further, as Table 5.5 indicates, overall Mexican debt has stayed remarkably stable in dollar terms at around US$100 billions: the main change is the shift from domestic to foreign holdings up to 1995; and then the switch back afterwards, so 1999 looks very much like 1993. However two thirds of this is held by residents abroad.[38]

The 1994–95 peso crisis clearly indicates the importance of the LLR function in Mexico. The Mexican banking system was extremely vulnerable, and *dollar* as well as peso liquidity had to be supplied by the national authorities; the latter was not too problematic (although pressure for restrictive monetary and fiscal policy difficult) and ultimately took the form of the government taking on banks' bad loan books. Dollar liquidity was provided in the event by the US authorities, although without sufficient speed (or advance warning) to support the peso and prevent the collapse of the banking system.[39]

---

[38] Note that in the case of Spain (1998) 25 per cent of debt is held by non-residents.

[39] The degree of Federal Reserve concern and involvement is evidenced in the minutes of Federal Reserve meetings at the time. See www.bog.frb.fed.us/fomc/Transcripts/1994/940324ConfCall.pdf [24 March conference call on Mexico]; /941220Meeting.pdf [20 December meeting]; /941230ConfCall.pdf [post-crisis emergency conference call on 30 December1994].

Table 5.4: Monetary Survey

	1993	1995	1997	1999
MEXICO				
International Liquidity				
(US$bn)				
Official Reserves	25.1	16.9	28.8	31.8
Bank Assets	2.4	3.3	2.9	2.8
Bank Liabilities	36.6	44.4	35.2	31.2
Net Balance	(9.1)	(24.3)	(3.5)	3.4
Monetary Survey				
(US$bn equivalent)				
Reserve Money	15.2	8.7	13.5	19.8
Money Supply	46.3	19.7	33.0	41.6
Domestic Credit	94.9	67.6	112.7	106.9
Exchange Rate (per US$)	3.106	7.643	8.083	9.514
CANADA				
International Liquidity				
(US$bn)				
Official Reserves	12.5	15.0	17.8	28.1
Bank Assets	41.1	64.1	84.4	79.2
Bank Liabilities	67.2	77.1	109.0	95.6
Net Balance	13.6	2.0	(6.8)	11.7
Monetary Survey				
(US$bn equivalent)				
Reserve Money	23.3	23.5	24.2	31.7
Money Supply	88.8	101.2	119.0	138.6
Domestic Credit	383.5	423.7	488.3	485.1
Exchange Rate (per US$)	1.324	1.365	1.429	1.443
USA				
International Liquidity				
(US$ bn)				
Official Reserves	62.3	74.8	58.9	60.5
Bank Assets	552.3	606.5	791.3	808.8
Bank Liabilities	828.2	1011.9	1208.1	1264.3
Net Balance	(213.9)	(330.8)	(357.9)	(395.0)
Monetary Survey				
(US$bn equivalent)				
Reserve Money	400.2	453.8	513.2	652.4
Money Supply	1231.0	1220.7	1280.2	1462.1
Domestic Credit	5026.0	5674.8	6493.7	7693.4
Exchange Rate (per US$)	1.000	1.000	1.000	1.000

Source: IMF, International Financial Statistics.

In view of the size of the Mexican economy and financial system, the simple 'panamanian' solution of a currency treaty to allow Mexico to use dollar bills is hardly a feasible solution. On the one hand, the Mexican financial system would require an enormous capital expenditure (in the order of US$200 billion) to convert peso into dollar assets; Panama built these up over nearly a century and was in receipt of large dollar inflows which were converted into external assets. This contrasts with membership of a federal reserve system (when the US authorities would simply exchange peso notes for dollar notes at nominal printing cost) or CFA-type system where only the external reserves are handed over (with monetary rules) in exchange for parity underwriting. In short, it would require a tripling of Mexican external debt. On the other hand, the US authorities would — by allowing use of the dollar — be committed not only to supply of currency but also to an implicit support for the economy (which could no longer adjust thorough devaluation); and this could not be conceded without some control over monetary policy.

Table 5.5: Mexico: Government Debt by Residence of Holder

	1993	1995	1997	1999
Total Govt Debt (bn pesos)	318.0	751.6	821.8	1126.2
Domestic	134.8	155.4	273.7	466.1
Foreign	183.2	596.2	548.1	660.1
(Foreign Share)	58%	79%	67%	59%
Exchange Rate	3.106	7.643	8.083	9.514
Total Debt (bn US $)	102.4	98.3	101.7	118.4

Source: Banco de México.

This argument, in combination with the high degree of trade and investment integration between the USA and Mexico, would seem to imply that a dollar equivalent to the euro/CFA area is the logical solution. Moreover, the reserve currency in question (the dollar) is fully convertible and the US economy is much stronger in relation to Mexico. It is true that the present overvaluation of the dollar and the chronic US current account deficit (as well as the recovery prospects of the euro and the yen) imply a considerable potential for dollar devaluation. However, this would not have the same effect on Mexico (or Canada) as it did on Sterling Area members because the former are far more integrated with the US economy than the latter were with the UK. As in the case of the CFA, the key steps would be three: first, the transfer of Mexican reserves to the Federal Reserve or the US Treasury in some agreed proportion of the peso money supply; second, the fixing of an exchange rate which can be credibly maintained; and third, a commitment by the US authorities to maintain the agreed exchange rate. This in turn would require agreement on the operating rules for fiscal and monetary policy in Mexico.

Whatever the principles of optimal currency areas might indicate, in view of the degree of dollarisation in practice in Mexico, and the extent of US intervention during the 1994–95 crisis, a logical step worth examining is that of the Banco de México (Banxico) being called upon to assume the functions of the '13th US Federal Reserve Bank'. Membership of the Federal Reserve System includes depository, supervisory and government serve functions as well as the contributions to monetary policy (and the right to call on other members for liquidity). Examining these functions is important because it indicates not only the scope of Fed membership, but also implies that if (as is very probable) this does not occur, then the functions will have to be taken on by another institution.

The depository function of the member banks include the replacement and circulation of fiat money and the management of the reserves required of depository institutions. Reserve banks also handle receipts of Treasury funds (e.g. income tax payments), and issue and redeem public debt in various forms. These are functions that Banxico carries out at the national level 'in pesos'; and these could also be carried out for the Mexican authorities under an integrated monetary system; indeed it could carry out similar functions for other US federal agencies.

The supervisory and regulatory functions of reserve banks include the monitoring of domestic and foreign banks and bank holding companies in their territory. Banxico does not do this, but the Superintendencia de Bancos does, and the function could be transferred. The Superintendencia also regulates securities markets, which would require a link with the US Securities Exchange Commission (SEC). Indeed, this latter step is probably inevitable anyway as most stocks are traded on US markets. Nonetheless, participation in the federal supervisory system (involving information exchange and taking part in the drafting of financial regulations) does pose constitutional problems for both countries in principle — although in practice the political problem would be greater north of the border.

The crucial issue is thus the ability of a federal bank to set and influence monetary policy. There are two quite different features of this relationship. On the one hand, Banxico would lose its own reserves and the ability to set interest rates through open market operations, and would be thus be unable to help domestic banks in difficulty unless the governors of the Federal Reserve approved of such an action — committing the overall 'pool' to such support. This would, of course, have far more market credibility than at present. On the other hand, the president of Banxico would presumably serve, in rotation, on the Federal Open Market Committee, which makes monetary policy for the US economy as a whole — which would raise important constitutional issues (taken up below) but not economic ones. As we have seen the former loss would not be significant, the problem being the latter gain.

Finally, the relative size of the two economies means that the implicit expansion of the dollar money supply would not be sufficient to mean that any future Mexican difficulties would affect the value of the dollar as such, which would continue to be underpinned by the strength of the US economy. The Mexican money supply is only equivalent to 3 per cent of that of the US; the reserve money ratio is similar.

Of course similar considerations apply to Canada. Buiter (1999) considers a North American Monetary Union (NAMU) from the point of view of Canada, which currently has a flexible exchange rate and looks at (a) the adoption of the US dollar, and (b) full monetary union. Transactions costs savings arise with either, but the seignorage loss in (a) is more than (b). Macroeconomic stabilisation aspects of a *permanent* fixed exchange rate are key to optimal currency area arguments;[40] these effects are equal in (a) and (b). The loss of a lender of last resort is the main cost of unilateral dollarisation, which makes (b) better than (a). Integration of the capital markets, moreover, eliminates the extraneous instability and excess volatility inherent in the market-determined exchange rate. Buiter argues that 'on balance the economic argument favours a full, formally symmetric monetary union, but not the unilateral adoption of the US dollar'. However, 'because of the absence of any democratic political institutions spanning both Canada and the USA, the political arguments against any form of monetary union are overwhelming'.

Conclusions

NAFTA trade expansion has been much faster than that originally contemplated (or estimated in simulation models), and it cannot be explained by price effects — that is the 1995 devaluation. Market integration appears to be proceeding in a more 'direct' fashion associated with cross-border investment and the process of de facto currency substitution. This 'winner's curse' was not contemplated by the architects of NAFTA.

The process of currency substitution ('dollarisation') is difficult to measure, but clearly marked; it affects not just asset holdings but also the basis for financial transactions and price calculations. This currency substitution is part of a secular trend reflecting trade integration and capital account liberalisation. It is driven by the private sector, and accelerated by exchange rate uncertainty. However, Mexico and the USA clearly do not meet the usual criteria for a currency area — unlike Canada and the USA.

The ideal solution might be for the Banxico to become the thirteenth member of the Federal Reserve, i.e. for the US authorities to underwrite the monetary stability of the Mexican economy. This would be difficult to achieve, because of the need for the US government to act as both lender of last resort and financial supervisor. There are, however, a number of intermediate solutions — equivalent perhaps to the Franc Zone or the Sterling Area — that could perform the necessary functions without implying Mexican participation in US monetary policy decisions.

---

[40] Mundell (1961); and McKinnon (1963).

The problem appears to lie in the District of Columbia (DC) rather than in the Distrito Federal (DF) in Mexico. The de facto dollarisation of the Mexican economy and the widespread desire for monetary stability mean that there almost certainly exists sufficient political support for the ceding of legal sovereignty. US public opinion is probably not ready for such an option, because of the implications of constructing new cross-border institutions — which in this context would be regarded as a constitutional issue — although there are signs of change.[41]

Trade and financial rules and regulatory agencies would have to take into account the legitimacy of their Canadian and Mexican counterparts (in essence the European 'passport' system), which would require legislation that would be regarded by opponents as having profound constitutional implications. NAFTA harmonisation of trade and financial services regulations will eventually require major changes at the level of individual US states, if only to prevent regulatory arbitrage and regulatory capture: this might be even more politically difficult than changes in federal legislation. In a sense, the USA is coming to terms with having neighbours for the first time. This does not just require alterations in external economic relations ('border controls') but also to internal economic organisation — the fabric of civil society itself.[42]

In sum, there seems to be an inescapable tension between de facto dollarisation in Mexico — and by extension in the Americas — pushed by private sector portfolio composition decisions, on the one hand, and the evident drawbacks to de jure dollarisation as a government policy on the other. This tension does not just arise from the need to retain exchange rate flexibility in order to adsorb external trade shocks and respond to shifts in the parities of the main reserve currencies (dollar, ecso and yen). Dollarisation will not stabilise domestic output or bring the Mexican (or Latin American) business cycle into line with the USA, if historical experience is any guide. An active fiscal policy will be necessary to maintain growth and employment, which will in turn require a shift away from the current orthodoxy on budgetary balance and flexible access to capital markets unencumbered by debt.

Finally, the current debate underestimates the institutional problems of liquidity management in response to changes in private sector asset demand. This requires central banking commitments by the USA which it is currently unwilling to assume, even though it does appear to be prepared to permit the dollarisation of small economies such as Ecuador and El Salvador. This commitment is more likely to arise from repeated and cumulative response to emergencies rather than from a considered strategy of monetary integration, which is unfortunate.

---

[41] Both the Federal Reserve Bank of Dallas and Senator Mack (Florida) now support the extension of a 'dollar area' southwards.

[42] See FitzGerald (1999) for further discussion.

Chapter 6

Open Regionalism and Institutional Developments among the Smaller Integration Schemes of CARICOM, the Andean Community and the Central America Common Market

Shelton Nicholls, Garnett Samuel, Philip Colthrust and Earl Boodoo[1]

The process of globalisation is having a profound impact on regionalism and has contributed to some reform in thinking in Latin America and the wider Caribbean about the role that institutions should play in the process of regionalism. The orthodox notion[2] of regional integration as developed in Vinerian thought has been especially silent on the role that institutions play in the process of regional integration.[3] Indeed, modern thinking on regional integration is placing much greater emphasis on the functional role that institutions should play in determining the likelihood for success of regional integration efforts. Several critical questions arise about the role, functions and performance of the institutions of integration. First, are these institutions failing because the norms and preferences to which they subscribe make little sense in the emerging global village? Second, are they failing because valid alternatives have emerged elsewhere in the regions or the wider world which have made them redundant?; or third, are they failing because they have demonstrated a lack of capacity to perform and implement their responsibilities satisfactorily? This chapter compares the institutional changes that have taken place in the smaller integration schemes during the period of closed and open regionalism. The objective of the comparison is to discern whether major institutional changes have been made in the smaller integration schemes of the Caribbean Community (CARICOM), the Andean Group and the Central

[1] The authors wish to thank Victor Bulmer-Thomas, Sheila Page, Penelope Forde, Chris Milner, Bob Hine, Compton Bourne and participants at the Workshop on Regional Integration in Latin America and the Caribbean (Institute of Latin American Studies, School of Advanced Studies, University of London) and those at the Symposium on Regional integration, 50th Congress of Americanists, University of Warsaw, Poland for helpful comments and criticisms. We are also grateful for the financial and research support provided by the University of the West Indies, St Augustine Campus and the Institute of Latin American Studies, University of London.
[2] The Vinerian notion of integration has been at the centre of thinking about the static welfare effects of trade integration using the concepts of trade creation and trade diversion.
[3] Viner (1950).

American Common Market (CACM) to support the goals of open regionalism.

The chapter contains five sections. Section 1 provides a discussion of the concept of open regionalism and broadly assesses the impact that globalisation is having on regionalism, while Section 2 presents some pertinent notions of the theory of institutional design paying specific attention to the desirable properties of good institutions that have been advanced in the work of Goodin (1997) and North (1990, 1994). Section 3 discusses the institutional developments during the closed period of regionalism, highlighting the shortcomings that these developments have had on the progress of economic integration. Section 4 examines the new institutional developments that have occurred in the decade of the 1990s and discusses the relevance of these developments for the process of globalisation. Section 5 highlights some critical areas that need to be addressed if the institutional infrastructure is to support the process of open regionalism. The chapter then ends with the conclusions.

1. Open Regionalism in the New Global Order

The decade of the 1990s has witnessed significant reorganisation of the world economy following the disintegration of the Soviet Union and the gradual easing of 'east–west' or 'capitalist–communist' tensions. The hegemonic domination of the United States has also been on the wane as the European Union and China have sought to increase their participation in political, economic and military affairs at the global level. The new and emerging global order is characterised by some fundamental restructuring of production, finance, communication, politics, identity and culture. This restructuring is being accomplished through the rapid elimination of barriers to trade in goods, labour and capital as well as significant commercialisation of the innovations in information technology and telecommunications. Ohmae (1995), for instance, refers to the emergence of the borderless world in which the sovereignty of nation states is being gradually effaced by transnational capitalists who are systematically reorganising the distribution and management of natural, human and financial resources. These new developments are placing greater emphasis on open markets that are characterised, in the main, by increased trade and financial liberalisation, privatisation of state enterprises, deregulation of public control over the economy as well as the reform of *law, culture, ideology and institutions* to support greater global interdependence.[4]

These configurations in the global balance of power have spurred

---

[4] Marchand and Boas (1999) discussed the expansion in cross-border alliances and strategic management arrangements that have resulted in the increased interconnectedness of the global economy.

development of regional trading blocs as countries jockey for economic, military and political supremacy. According to Roy (1999), these global changes have produced three major politico-economic blocs: (i) a *European Bloc* with the unified Germany as the hub; (ii) a *Western Hemispheric Bloc* with the United States of America as the hub; and (iii) a *Pacific Rim Bloc* with China and/or Japan as the hub. These major trading blocs have encouraged renewed growth in regionalism especially among the smaller countries of the globe. There is considerable disagreement over the definitions of the terms 'regionalism', 'old regionalism' and 'new regionalism' (see Chapter 1). Mansfield and Milner (1997), for instance, define regionalism as '*the disproportionate concentration of economic flows or the co-ordination of foreign economic policies among a group of countries [that are] in close geographic proximity*'.

There is, however, a substantial difference between the meaning of the terms '*old regionalism*' and '*new regionalism*'. Old regionalism (that is 'inward-looking' or closed regionalism) involves substantial discrimination by member countries of an integration scheme against trade with non-member territories. This type of regionalism tends to be biased towards countries in close geographical proximity with similar levels of development. New regionalism, or what is often termed 'open regionalism', seeks, according to Bergsten (1997), **to discriminate against non-member countries while accommodating multilateralism and the process of globalism.**[5] Open regionalism therefore attempts to liberalise intra-regional trade in goods and services and intra-regional movements in labour, capital, information and knowledge in congruence with multilateralism and the process of globalism. It is this concept of open regionalism which has served as a catalyst for the simultaneous deepening and widening of several of the small integration efforts in the Western Hemisphere. The question of the compatibility between regionalism and the forces of multilateralism/globalism has led to the eruption of an interesting debate between those that support multi-lateralism like Jagdish Bhagwati, Anne Krueger and T.N. Srinivasan and those that support regionalism.[6]

Bhagwati (1991) has proffered the view that the compatibility between the processes of regionalism and multilateralism can be characterised in two important ways.[7] If, on the one hand, the preferential trading areas contribute to the multilateral freeing of trade by the

---

[5] In short, the new regionalism tries to serve 'two masters' — protectionism and free trade. The incompatibilities which arise are directly related to the dual nature of this service. The old biblical adage that one cannot serve two masters has for a long time recognised this incompatibility.

[6] See arguments presented by Summers (1991); and Krugman (1990), (1993).

[7] This is really the dynamic time-path issue.

progressive addition of members or through the promotion of accelerated multilateral trade negotiations, then they represent a building block towards multilateral free trade. If, on the other hand, the establishment of tariffs and non-tariff barriers increases the level of discrimination against non-members, then preferential trading arrangements can be a stumbling block to multilateral free trade.[8]

Following the conclusion of the Uruguay round in 1994, substantial changes have been introduced into the conduct of multilateral trade affairs. Indeed, a number of new trade issues now fall under the purview of the World Trade Organisation (WTO). This new trade arrangement has introduced new disciplines for trade in services (including maritime, financial and telecommunications services); new rules for competition policy and for the protection of intellectual property, as well as a supposedly stable rule-making structure for dispute resolution. If open regionalism is to be compatible with multilateralism as advocated by the WTO, then new organisational and institutional structures attuned to the requirements of the new regionalism should be erected within the existing regional integration schemes.

2. Institutional Design and Regional Integration

The literature on economic integration has ignored the critical role that institutions play in the process of integration although this role has been implicitly recognised in the non-mainstream economic literature for quite a number of years. The 'Balassian' taxonomy,[9] which has provided the framework for the development of European integration, implicitly accepts the notion that institutions are important in the achievement of the final stage of integration — the attainment of complete political and economic unification. In this stage, the principle of supranationality has emerged as a critical ingredient for the successful achievement of European integration. The process of European integration has had its influence on the institutional architecture of integration that has emerged in the Caribbean and Latin America since the 1960s. One of the real differences, however, between the institutional design among

---

[8] Bhagwati has been especially dismissive of what he describes as the 'gung-ho' approach to regionalism that has surfaced in Dornbusch's article published by Eastman Kodak (see Dornbusch (1989)). In a recent paper, Srinivasan and Bhagwati (1999) have continued to extol the virtues of an outward-oriented trade regime (export promotion strategy) and have emphasised the importance of trade openness for accelerating development and growth. The contrasting view advocated by Rodríguez and Rodrik (1999) has been much more cautious about the positive relationship between openness in trade and economic growth. The free trade philosophy recommended by Bhagwati is only commendable, however, if all participants on the world stage adhere to its tenets and commit themselves to playing fairly by the rules. It remains an utopian ideal in the existing imperfect world. Regionalism is therefore a natural second best response to the current imperfections in the global trade market.

[9] See Balassa (1961).

the smaller states of Latin America and the Caribbean and those of Europe relates to the supranational nature of the structures for regional governance. It is therefore important at this stage to develop conceptually our relevant definitions of institutions and organisations and to describe the process of implementation and decision-making that is required for successful goal attainment.

North (1990) in his influential book considers institutions to be the formal or informal rules and their enforcement mechanisms that shape the behaviour of individuals and organisations in society.[10] Formal rules relate to explicit codes such as constitutions, laws, regulations and contracts while informal rules consist largely of implicit codes of conduct that encompass religious precepts, norms, ethics, trust and the like. Institutions thus play a major role in our society in the sense that they reduce uncertainty through the establishment of a stable structure to human interaction. Organisations, on the other hand, are composed of persons who act collectively in the pursuit of shared objectives. These organisations therefore take advantage of the opportunities that are created by institutions. One of the fundamental questions that must be dealt with in the context of the new regionalism relates to the institutional design that is necessary to support the process of open regionalism. In this process, the concept of the society extends beyond the immediate national and regional borders and encompasses other global actors. Goodin's (1997) 'desiderata' suggest that the principles which should guide institutional design should relate not merely to the functional 'goodness of fit' of the various institutions but as well to the manner in which these institutions incorporate, by consensus, the norms and moral beliefs of the society. The core principles of a good institution are therefore:

(i) **Revisability**: Institutions should be structured in such a manner that they adapt to errors and learn by doing. Given the inherent fallibility of humans in the process of decision-making, potential errors that are attributable to human frailties should never be set in stone. Institutions should learn from these errors.

(ii) **Robustness**: Institutions should be capable of adapting to new and unknown situations. They should not be easily demolished when presented with new and unknown challenges. At the same time, this requires that if society changes in fundamental ways then institutions should adapt their formal and informal rules to reflect these changes.

(iii) **Sensitivity to Motivational Complexity**: Institutions should respect the plethora of motives that influence the decisions of persons in the society and should expect that principled and even altruistic motives will co-exist with egoistic motives.

---

[10] See also Pierson (2000); and Reich (2000) for useful discussions on institutionalism.

(iv) **Publicity**: Institutions should always be ready and prepared to defend their decisions publicly by appealing to reason.

(v) **Variability**: Institutions should embrace the desire for variability as a central principle of design. Experimentation, within reason, with different institutional structures should be encouraged and supported.

Institutions adjudged to have functioned well in society are those that have been able to accomplish their objectives and tasks successfully without requiring social actors to undertake unnecessary, burdensome and strategic actions to achieve those objectives. Indeed, according to North (1990), institutions should not burden 'other social actors with the need for purposive and strategic actions'. As such, the emergence of such actions often signals that the institution cannot be trusted to yield beneficial or at least tolerable outcomes. In the final analysis, 'good institutions are expected to provide rules that are clear, widely known, coherent, applicable to all, predictable, credible and properly and evenly enforced'.[11]

Although one can glean relatively useful characteristics of what constitutes a good institution from the foregoing philosophical definitions, establishing relevant criteria for adjudging good institutions at the policy level is often not so straightforward a task. At the policy level, some of the more important ingredients for 'good' institutions of integration should include (i) the system of governance (supranational or national); (ii) the form of decision-making (centralised or de-centralised); (iii) record of implementation (number of decisions successfully executed); (iv) financial viability and performance; and (v) flexibility.

3. Institutional Developments under Closed Regionalism: The Experience of the Andean Group, the Central American Common Market and CARICOM

To have a proper appreciation of the major institutional arrangements that have occurred under open regionalism, it is necessary to examine, first of all, the institutional structures which existed under closed regionalism as well as to describe the functions and performance of the integration arrangement under the specific institutional structure. In this section, an attempt is made to describe the institutional architecture that was created to support the process of closed regionalism in the various schemes. This period of closed regionalism was dominated by the functionalist and neo-functionalist ideas which were influenced in large measure by the process of European integration. Indeed, the institutional design of the European integration process provided a blueprint for the regional integration schemes in Latin America and the

---

[11] Burki and Perry (1998).

Caribbean. Also, the Economic Commission for Latin America, under the influence of Raúl Prebisch, was particularly influential in promoting an agenda for regionalism behind temporary protectionist barriers as a mechanism to support the structuralist development strategy of import-substitution industrialisation. All of the integration efforts in these three small integration schemes incorporated in significant ways this development strategy.

(a) The Andean Community

The Andean Group was created by the Cartagena Agreement which was signed in 1969 between Bolivia, Chile, Ecuador and Colombia. Venezuela joined the Group in 1973, while Chile withdrew in 1975. The Cartagena agreement sought to promote economic development through sectoral planning, regional trade liberalisation and multilateral control of foreign investment.[12] The Agreement created two main institutions — the Andean Commission and the Junta — at the political level for the promotion and development of regional integration. The Andean Development Corporation (Corporación Andina de Fomento) was also established in 1970 to provide technical assistance as well as financial assistance for pre-feasibility studies and investment projects. At the time of its creation, the Andean Commission consisted of one plenipotentiary representative. Although the agreement did not create a special institution comprising the heads of government, the presidents of the member states collectively provided overall direction on an ad hoc basis.

The Commission was supported both administratively and technically by the Junta, which was responsible for implementing the agreement, executing the decisions of the Commission as well as conducting studies and developing proposals for the advancement of the Andean Community. To execute its function, the Junta drew on various advisory councils in the areas of planning, money, finance, trade and fiscal policy. The decisions that were undertaken by the Commission were adopted automatically and did not require congressional ratification nor approval. Although there was much dynamism in intra-regional trade in the decade of the 1970s, the institutional apparatus was only partially functional with respect to the objectives of the agreement. Ocampo et al., (1994) argued, for instance, that the common external tariff was never approved, that liberalisation of competitive goods was systematically postponed and that the sectoral programmes proved to be rather cumbersome from an operational standpoint. By the mid-1970s, therefore, it was clear that a new organisational structure was required to refocus the process of Andean integration.

---

[12] Hufbauer, Schott and Clark (1994).

In 1979, three important institutions were created in the Andean Group — the Andean Parliament, the Council of Foreign Ministers and the Andean Court of Justice.

Andean Parliament: This Parliament consists of five representatives each of whom is elected from the respective national congress of the Andean member country. The Parliament promotes the harmonisation of legislation of the various member countries and the growth of co-operative and co-ordinated relations with the Parliaments of the Andean countries.

Council of Foreign Ministers: This council is largely charged with the responsibility of formulating joint approaches to foreign policy as well as co-ordinating actions of the Andean Group vis-à-vis third countries, groups of countries and international organisations.

Andean Court of Justice: This judicial body is comprised of five judges each representing one of the member countries of the group. The court's main responsibility lies in overseeing the application of the laws in the settlement of disputes among member states and in ensuring that laws of the group are applied uniformly in the various member territories.

Table 6.1: Institutional Structure of Smaller Integration Schemes: Andean Community

Type of Institution	Period of Closed Regionalism	Period of Open Regionalism
Political	• Andean Parliament (1979) • Andean Council of Foreign Ministers (1979)	• Andean Presidential Council (1996) • Andean Council of Foreign Ministers (1996) • Commission of the Andean Community (1996) • Andean Parliament (1996)
Legal	• Andean Court of Justice of the Cartagena Agreement (1979)	• Court of Justice of the Andean Community (1996)
Administrative	• Andean Commission (1969) • Andean Junta (1969)	• General Secretariat of the Andean Community (1996)
Social Education Health	• Universidad Andina Simón Bolívar • Hipólito Unanue Agreement	• Universidad Andina Simón Bolívar • Hipólito Unanue Agreement
Economic Monetary / Finance Business Labour	• Andean Development Corporation (ADC) • Andean Reserve Fund (1976) • Andean Business Advisory Council • Andean Labour Advisory Council • Simón Rodríguez Agreement	• Andean Development Corporation (ADC) • Latin America Reserve Fund • Andean Business Advisory Council • Andean Labour Advisory Council • Simón Rodríguez Agreement

The 1970s also witnessed the creation of two important development finance institutions — the Andean Development Corporation and the Andean Reserve Fund. The member countries of the Andean Group recognised quite early that the successful implementation of the integration programme required a substantial infusion of financial resources. The Andean Development Bank was created to provide development finance, while the Andean Reserve Fund was established to provide financial support to group members that were experiencing structural balance of payments deficits.

Of the smaller integration schemes, the Andean Group gave considerable attention to the co-ordination of social activities among member countries of the group and four important social agreements were signed during the 1970s and the first half of the 1980s. The Andrés Bello agreement of 1970 provided for joint co-operation in the areas of science, technology, culture and education, while the Hipólito Unanue Agreement of 1971 developed a series of programmes to manage health and sanitation problems. Issues relating to the improvement of social and labour conditions in the various countries were addressed by the Simón Rodríguez Agreement of 1976, which developed a number of proposals and programmes for improving labour conditions in the member states, while food security, agriculture and the environment were important features of the José Celetino Mutis Agreement of 1983 (see Table 6.1).

(b) Central American Common Market

After various efforts at functional co-operation between 1950 and 1960, the four Central American countries of Guatemala, Honduras, El Salvador and Nicaragua signed the General Treaty of Central American Integration in 1960, and along with Costa Rica completed the ratification process by 1963. The Treaty provided a framework for fostering the development of the region through the establishment of a free trade area, customs union and common market. In order to co-ordinate the integration of economic activity and policies within the region, a Central American Economic Council was created comprising the ministers of economy of the contracting parties. This Council represented the highest political authority of the system. An Executive Council, comprising vice-ministers of economy, was also created with specific responsibility for the implementation of the commitments made under the agreement. The Executive Council along with other advisory councils dealt with sectoral issues affecting agriculture, transport, finance and science and technology.

At the administrative level, the Treaty established the Permanent Secretariat of the System of Central American Economic Integration (SIECA) to serve as administrative secretariat and to provide technical support to the principal organs. SIECA also had the task of ensuring the correct application of the treaty at the regional level and of undertaking studies on behalf of the Executive and the Economic Councils. Besides the political and administrative organisations, the integration system also included a number of autonomous regional bodies which functioned in a wide variety of areas. To facilitate the promotion and financing of integrated economic growth, the Central American Bank of Economic Integration (BCIE) was founded, while the Central American Monetary Council (CMCA) was created to provide advice on monetary policy and to attempt to harmonise monetary policy through a process of regional consultations. Regimes were also established for settling payment imbalances (Central American Clearing House) and for financing member territories that experienced persistent balance of payments deficits (Central American Monetary and Stabilisation Fund).

After 1963, a plethora of institutions was added to the basic structure of the General Treaty to deepen the process of integration through functional co-operation. These institutions covered the areas of education, scientific and technical development, telecommunications and air and sea transport, among others. In the field of education, the Central American Council for Higher Education (CSUCA) and the Central American Industrial Technology and Research Institute (ICAITI) co-ordinated research in technology as well as tertiary education in the region. Several infrastructural development organisations were also established to improve intra-regional transportation and communications and include the Central American Commission for Maritime Transportation, the Central American Corporation for Air Navigation Services, the Central American Railways Commission and the Central American Technical Commission for Telecommunications. A significant proportion of the funding of these institutions came from the United States Agency for International Development (USAID) and its Regional Office for Central America and Panama (ROCAP). Unlike the Andean Group, there was no significant emphasis on the development of institutions to support social development and environmental management (see Table 6.2).

In 1987, in an attempt to return lasting peace to the region which was embroiled in civil conflicts, three important political fora emerged that later became fundamental pillars of Central American integration. These were the Meeting of Central American Presidents, the Meeting of Central American Vice-Presidents and the Central American Parliament.

Since 1991, the role of SIECA has been expanded with its incorporation within the System for Integration in Central America (SICA). The SIECA not only provides administrative and technical support to the SICA, but is the institution that oversees all economic aspects of Central American integration. The membership of SIECA is

Table 6.2: Institutional Structure of Smaller Integration Schemes: Central American Common Market

Type of Institution		Period of Closed Regionalism	Period of Open Regionalism
POLITICAL		• Central American Economic Council (CEC) (1960) • Executive Council	• Meeting of Presidents • Council of Ministers • Meeting of Vice-Presidents • Central American Parliament (PARLACEN) (1993)
LEGAL		None	• Central American Court of Justice (CCJ) (1992)
ADMINISTRATIVE		• Permanent Secretariat of the System of Central American Economic Integration (SIECA) (1960)	• Secretary General of the Central American Integration System (SG–SICA)
SOCIAL Education		• Central American Institute of Public Administration (ICAP) (1954) • Central American Institute of Research and Industrial Technology (ICAITI) (1955) • Central American Secretariat of Educational and Cultural Coordination (SG–CECC) (1975) • Commission for the Scientific and Technological Development of Central America and Panama (CTCAP) (1976) • Central American Council for Higher Education (CSUCA) (1963)	• Central American Institute of Public Administration (ICAP) (1954) • Central American Institute of Research and Industrial Technology (ICAITI) (1955) • Central American Secretariat of Educational and Cultural Coordination (SG–CECC) (1975) • Commission for the Scientific and Technological Development of Central America and Panama (CTCAP) (1976) • Central American Council for Higher Education (CSUCA) (1963)
Health and Sanitation		• Central American and Panamanian Institute of Nutrition (INCAP) (1949)	• Central American and Panamanian Institute of Nutrition (INCAP) (1949) • Regional Co-ordinating Committee of Potable Water and Sanitation of Central America, Panama and the Dominican Republic (CAPRE) (1991)
Social Security		None	• Central American Council of Social Security Institutions (COCISS) (1992)
Social Integration		None	• Central American Secretariat of Social Integration (SISCA) (1995)
Sports and Recreation		None	• Central American Council on Sports and Recreation (CODICADER) (1992)
Housing & Settlements		None	• Central American Council of Housing and Human Settlement (CCVAH) (1992)
ECONOMIC Agriculture		• Regional Council of Agricultural Cooperation of Central America, Panama and the Dominican Republic (COCATRAN) (1980)	• Regional Council of Agricultural Cooperation of Central America, Panama and the Dominican Republic (COCATRAN) (1980) • General Secretariat of the Council of Agriculture and Farming (SCA) (SG–CAC) (1991)
Banking / Finance		• Central American Bank of Economic Integration (BCIE)	• Secretariat of the Central American Monetary Council (SCMCA) (1993)
Energy		None	• Temporary Secretariat of the Committee of Energy Corporation of Central America (CCHAC) (1991)
Tourism		None	• Central American Secretariat for Tourism Integration (SITCA) (1965)
Transport		• Central American Commission of Maritime Transport (COCATRAN) (1980) • Central American Corporation for Air Navigation Services (COCESNA) (1960)	• Central American Commission of Maritime Transport (COCATRAN) (1980) • Central American Corporation for Air Navigation Services (COCESNA) (1960)
INFRA-STRUCTURE		• Regional Committee of Water Resources (CRRH) (1966) • Regional Technical Commission of Telecommunications (COMTELCA) (1966) • Executive Secretary of the Council of Electrification of Central America (SE-CEAC) (1979)	• Regional Committee of Water Resources (CRRH) (1966) • Regional Technical Commission of Telecommunications (COMTELCA) (1966) • Executive Secretary of the Council of Electrification of Central America (SE-CEAC) (1979)
ENVIRONMENT		• Executive Secretary of the Central American Commission of Environment and Development (SECCAD) (1989) • Co-ordinating Centre for the Prevention of Natural Disasters in Central America (CEPREDENAC) (1988)	• Executive Secretary of the Central American Commission of Environment and Development (SECCAD) (1989) • Co-ordinating Centre for the Prevention of Natural Disasters in Central America (CEPREDENAC) (1988)
NARCO-TRAFFICKING			Permanent Central American Commission against Drug Trafficking (CCP) (1996)

limited to the original five countries, but SICA also includes Panama and Belize joined in 2000.

(c) The Caribbean Community (CARICOM)

The road to economic integration in the Caribbean commenced in 1968 when the Caribbean Free Trade Agreement (CARIFTA) was signed by a number of Caribbean territories. The CARIFTA arrangement emphasised only trade liberalisation and it was felt that a deeper form of co-operation was needed among the English-speaking territories of the Caribbean Basin. The Caribbean Community (CARICOM), which was formed in 1973 with the signing of the Treaty of Chaguaramas, placed great emphasis not only on market integration but as well on the co-ordination of foreign policy, the provision of common services, co-ordinated or joint actions in production and special and differential treatment for the less developed countries of the community. The institutional arrangements established by this community were relatively complex.[13] The Conference of Heads of Government and the Common Market Council of Ministers were the principal organs of the community. The Conference of Heads of Government (CHG) is the supreme decision-making body of the community and is responsible for the formulation of policy for the community through a system of unanimous votes of heads of the various government delegations. It is also responsible for the conclusion of treaties on behalf of the community as well as conducting relations between the Community and international entities.

In addition, specific institutions of the community were responsible for various sectors of regional co-operation. These institutions comprised the Conference of Ministers responsible for health as well as Standing Committees of Ministers responsible for education, labour, finance, foreign affairs, agriculture, energy, mines and natural resources, industry, transportation, legal affairs, science and technology and tourism. These institutions were responsible for the identification and execution of programmes to be undertaken by the CARICOM Secretariat and the specific regional entities. Decisions on economic integration fell under the jurisdiction of the Common Market Council which was made up of ministers or alternates, one from each member country, who met at the Heads of Government Conference to discuss the operations of the Common Market.

The Council of Ministers also consulted with the Joint Consultative Group comprising the Caribbean Association of Industry and Commerce (CAIC), the Caribbean Congress of Labour (CCL) and the Caribbean Council of Consumers (CCC) on matters of significance to the region.

---

[13] See Mills et al. (1990) for a comprehensive review of institutions in CARICOM.

Table 6.3: Institutional Structure of Smaller Integration Schemes: Caribbean Community

Type of Institution	Period of Closed Regionalism	Period of Open Regionalism
POLITICAL	• Conference of Heads of Government • Common Market Council of Ministers	• Conference of Heads of Government • Community Council of Ministers • Association of Caribbean Community Parliamentarians (ACCP) • Caribbean Regional Negotiating Machinery (CRNM)
LEGAL	None	• Caribbean Court of Justice
ADMINISTRATIVE	• Caribbean Community Secretariat • Caribbean Centre for Developmental Administration (CARICAD)	• Caribbean Community Secretariat • Caribbean Centre for Developmental Administration (CARICAD)
SOCIAL **Education**	• Standing Committee of Ministers for Education • Caribbean Examinations Council (CXC) • Council of Legal Education (CLE) • University of the West Indies (UWI) • University of Guyana (UG) • Caribbean Law Institute (CLI)	• Council for Human and Social Development (COHSOD) • Caribbean Examinations Council (CXC) • Council of Legal Education (CLE) • University of the West Indies (UWI) • University of Guyana (UG) • Caribbean Law Institute (CLI)
Health	• Standing Committee of Ministers for Health • Caribbean Food and Nutrition Institute (CFNI)	• Council for Human and Social Development (COHSOD) • Caribbean Food and Nutrition Institute (CFNI) • Caribbean Environmental Health Institute • Caribbean Regional Centre for the Education and Training of Animal Health and Veterinary Public Health Assistants (REPAHA)
ECONOMIC **Agriculture**	• Caribbean Agricultural Research and Development Institute (CARDI) • Caribbean Food Corporation (CFC)	• Caribbean Agricultural Research and Development Institute (CARDI) • Caribbean Food Corporation (CFC)
Industry	• Standing Committee of Ministers of Industry	
Finance/Banking	• Standing Committee of Ministers of Finance • Caribbean Multilateral Clearing Facility (CMCF) • Caribbean Development Bank (CDB)	• Council for Finance and Planning (COFAP) • Caribbean Centre for Monetary Studies (CCMS) • Caribbean Development Bank (CDB)
Business/Private Sector	• Caribbean Export Development Program	• Caribbean Export Development (CEDP) • Caribbean Tourism Organisation (CTO)
TRANSPORTATION	• West Indian Shipping Company (WISCO)	
ENVIRONMENTAL	• Caribbean Meteorological Institute (CMI) • Caribbean Meteorological Organisation (CMO)	• Caribbean Meteorological Institute (CMI) • Caribbean Meteorological Organisation (CMO) • Caribbean Disaster Emergency Response Agency (CDERA)

The CARICOM Secretariat had the key responsibility of servicing the meetings of the various committees and conferences of CARICOM implementing decisions of the meetings, initiating and undertaking studies and executing any assignments mandated by the Heads of Government Conference. The treaty also provided for the establishment of a group of Associate Institutions of the Community. Those established under the treaty were: the Caribbean Development Bank (CDB); the Caribbean Investment Corporation; the West Indies Associated States Council of Ministers; the East Caribbean Common Market Council of Ministers; the Caribbean Examinations Council (CXC); the Council of Legal Education (CLE); the University of Guyana; the University of the West Indies; the Caribbean Meteorological Council and the Regional Shipping Council (see Table 6.3). In general, these associations formed the backbone of a relatively successful strategy of functional co-operation in the decade of the 1970s and 1980s.

4. Institutional Developments under Open Regionalism

The integration process in Latin America and the Caribbean experienced some form of revival in the 1990s. Following the dismal performance of integration schemes in the 1980s, the smaller integration schemes all embarked on a process of revitalisation of the integration arrangements. This revitalisation in the process of integration in Latin America and the Caribbean emphasised the liberalisation of goods and service markets as well as greater policy co-ordination. The core components of the new agenda entail:

• Free trade in goods and services
• Free movement of capital (elimination of barriers and restraints to investment)
• Free movement of labour services
• Co-ordination of monetary and financial policy
• Co-ordination of fiscal policy
• Co-ordination of foreign and external relations

A process of institutional reform was also initiated in several of the smaller schemes to support the new thrust towards open regionalism. It may therefore be useful at this juncture to discuss the integration reforms that occurred in each of the separate schemes and to assess the impact that these reforms had on the institutional arrangements within each of the selected regional schemes.

(a) Andean Community

The 1980s were particularly difficult years for the Andean Community. Intra-regional trade experienced a prolonged crisis during which time the Andean Community was in a state of near collapse.[14] The road to the revitalisation of the Andean scheme commenced in 1987 with the Quito Protocol. This introduced significant reforms to the Cartagena Agreement and attempted to provide a greater element of flexibility to investment procedures and industrial programming schemes, as well as to reform the safeguard measures that restricted intra-regional trade. Public investment programmes were to be replaced by programmes which encouraged greater private sector participation.

In 1989, a strategic plan for the re-organisation of the Andean Group was devised in a bid to consolidate the process of economic integration. The Galapagos Declaration emphasised co-operation on a range of non-economic matters which included joint negotiations at the international level, strengthening of the democratic process and reducing the threat of terrorism. It was also decided that the three largest economies, Venezuela, Colombia and Bolivia, would work towards the establishment of a customs union by 1995 while the remaining economies, Ecuador and Peru, were expected to do so later. At the La Paz meeting in November 1990, a decision was taken to accelerate the time frame for the formation of a customs union.

Since 1996, several significant institutional changes have been introduced. This followed the Act of Trujillo (1996) and the Modifying Protocol of the Andean Subregional Integration Agreement. At the political level, the Andean System of Integration now comprises the Andean Presidential Council, the Andean Council of External Ministers, the Commission of the Andean Community and the Andean Parliament. The Presidential Council is the highest level body of the integration system and comprises the various heads of states of the member countries of the group. The Presidential Council meets once a year to review the actions undertaken by the various bodies and institutions of the Andean Community. The Commission consists of a plenipotentiary representative from each of the member states[15] and an alternative member. This Commission is responsible for evaluating integration policy in the areas of trade and investment; for co-ordination of the joint position of the member countries in international fora; and for negotiations with international bodies. It is also responsible for evaluating the budgetary performance of the General Secretariat and the Court of Justice and for setting the contributions of the member territories.

At the administrative and executive level, the Junta has been converted to a General Secretariat which now gives technical support to the other bodies and institutions of the Andean Integration System. This secretariat is entrusted with the responsibility of undertaking technical

---

[14] Ocampo and Esguerra (1994).
[15] This representative has the full power to act independently.

studies as well as co-ordinating and managing the work programme of the integration movement in accordance with the mandates of the various political arms of the movement.

In a bid to broaden participation of civil society, the Andean Community has expanded the roles of the business and labour advisory councils. These councils, on their own initiative or on the request of the political organs of the community, bring the opinions of business and labour into the deliberations of the community. The Labour Advisory Council is actively participating in the updating of the documents and regulations on Social Security (Decision 113 and 144, respectively) as well as on Labour Migration (Decision 116). The Andean Community has placed a great deal of emphasis on social policies and has developed a broad range of policies covering employment generation, education, health and housing.

The Community has been moving much closer in recent years towards the status of a common market and the Guayaquil Act of 1998 has established general guidelines for deeper integration by the year 2005. Given the trend towards greater global liberalisation in trade and finance, the Community has liberalised capital flows (Decision 291) and has decided also to liberalise the telecommunications market by 2002. All in all, the institutional structure of the Andean community is relatively less complex when compared to CARICOM and the CACM.

(b)   Central American Common Market

For much of the period between the General Treaty and the 1990s, Central American integration performed below expectations. This is not to say that certain gains were not made. During the first decade of integration, the intra-regional exports of the Central American integration system had risen by nine times although some 30 per cent of the exchanges had been between Guatemala and El Salvador.[16] Economic difficulties played a significant part in the under-performance and helped to thwart the effectiveness and dynamism of the integration movement. Towards the end of the 1960s, global recession led to a fall in the demand for the products of the region and a weakening of product prices. Moreover, in the decade of the 1970s, the international oil crisis stimulated an increase in the costs of imported raw materials, negatively affecting internal economic activity. The economic recession that continued into the 1980s was accompanied by regional political instability.

In 1991, the revival of the CACM was initiated with the signing of the Treaty of Tegucigalpa which created the Central American Integration System (SICA). This Treaty provided the legal and institutional

---

[16] Bulmer-Thomas (1997), (1998), (1998a).

framework for the revamping of the Organisation of Central American States (ODECA) to facilitate its adaptation to the needs and realities of modern times. Certain economic and social goals were also reaffirmed as an expression of the recommitment of the contracting parties to the independence and integrated development of the region. Thus Article 3 highlighted the goal of the SICA of consolidating Central America as a region of peace, democracy and development. The Treaty of Tegucigalpa instituted as organs of the SICA, the following:

The Meeting of Presidents: This is the supreme organ of the SICA and is made up of the presidents of member states who ordinarily meet every six months or when it is deemed necessary. Decisions in this forum are by consensus. The role of this body is to establish and direct policies of integration and to harmonise the external relations of member states. Importantly, the presidents have been given the role of strengthening the Central American identity.

The Council of Ministers: This council is made up of the ministers of the various ministries and has responsibility for following up on and execution of the decisions taken in the Meetings of the Presidents. The ministers also prepare the subjects to be discussed by the presidents. The ministers of foreign relations have the task of co-ordinating the work of the various organs and the Meeting of the Presidents. The Council is also responsible for co-ordinating the processes of democratisation, peace and regional security. Within this council, important decisions are taken by consensus while for procedural matters majority voting is adopted.

The Executive Committee: The president of each member country appoints a member to this committee, which is charged with the efficient execution of the decisions of the Meetings of Presidents. This organ acts in close co-ordination with the ministers of foreign relations through whom they submit sectoral policies which they develop in response to the directives of the Meeting of Presidents. Other duties of the Committee include the preparation of the budget of SICA and making recommendations to the ministers of foreign relations on the formation of subsidiary organs.

The Secretariat: The secretary general, nominated by the Meeting of Presidents for a period of four years, heads the Secretariat. The Secretariat has a technical and administrative role and is the only organ with supranational status. It performs the function of secretary to the Meetings of Presidents and facilitates inter-institutional communication. The secretary general represents SICA in the international arena and executes the mandates of the Meetings of Presidents, the Council of Ministers and the Executive Committee.

The revisions under the Protocol of Tegucigalpa also contemplated the establishment of a **Central American Court of Justice** to guarantee the respect for the rule of law in the interpretation and execution of the Protocol. The statutes establishing the Court stipulate that judges must be sent from their respective national courts to assure their independence. The functions of the Court include decisions pertaining to disagreements among member states, complaints between juridical persons or against organs of SICA and judicial matters relating to integration. The **Consultative Committee** is the institution which tries to incorporate civil society in the process of integration. It includes sectors such as business, labour, academia and other representatives in the economic, social, and cultural realms. The **Central American Parliament** which was proposed as an organ of proposal, analysis and recommendation is a forum for the analysis of political, economic, social and cultural matters.

In the Protocol of Guatemala, signed in 1993, the Central American States effectively attempted to renew the General Treaty of Integration of 1960. The countries have committed to a gradual attainment of economic union through the co-ordination, harmonisation and convergence of economic policies, extra-regional trade negotiations, infrastructure and services. The Protocol created within the SICA a Central American Sub-system of Economic Integration. This sub-system comprises a number of technical-administrative organs and institutions. Among the most important is the **Secretariat of the Central American Integration System** (SIECA). SIECA is the technical-administrative organ of the process of Central American Integration and the Executive Committee of Economic Integration. This organ has responsibility for all the economic aspects of integration.

(c) Caribbean Community

Following the dismal performance of the Caribbean Community in the 1980s, a special meeting of the Heads of Government was convened in Grand Anse, Grenada, with the specific purpose of advancing the process of Caribbean integration. This meeting established the West Indian Commission, under the chairmanship of Sir Shridath Ramphal, which was given a mandate by the heads of government to develop a proposal to prepare the Caribbean society for the challenges of the twenty-first century. After a number of consultations throughout the Caribbean region, the committee prepared a comprehensive proposal for the deepening and widening of Caribbean integration. The deepening of integration was to be achieved by the formation of a single market and economy in CARICOM, while the widening of integration required the development of formal co-operative arrangements with other regional groupings, especially in Europe, North America, Central

and Latin America.[17] The achievement of this revised agenda for
Caribbean integration required some significant alterations in the
existing institutional architecture and the West Indian Commission
proposed seven key institutional 'Super-structures of Unity' for the new
thrust of Caribbean integration. The recommended superstructures
comprised:

- The Conference of Heads of Government
- The Council of Ministers
- The CARICOM Commission
- The CARICOM Assembly
- The CARICOM Charter of Civil Society
- The CARICOM Supreme Court
- The CARICOM Commission

Although the heads of governments of CARICOM recognised the
importance of this superstructure of unity, they rejected completely the
need for a CARICOM Commission but proceeded to implement other
pillars in the institutional infra-structure of CARICOM. The main
institutions that exist at the political level are the Conference of Heads of
Government, the Community Council of Ministers and the Association of
Caribbean Parliamentarians. The 'Conference' is the supreme organ of
the community and provides overall policy direction. It possesses the
final authority for concluding treaties on behalf of the community and
for entering into relationships with the international organisations. It is
also responsible for establishing the necessary financial arrangements to
meet the expenses of the community. The Community Council of
Ministers now replaces the Common Market Council of Ministers and is
responsible for the development of community strategic planning and
co-ordination in the areas of economic integration, functional co-
operation and external relations. Given the poor reporting by
governments to their national parliaments, the Association of Caribbean
Parliamentarians has been created to provide a mechanism by which
parliamentarians could update their respective national parliaments
about regional developments.

At the legal level, CARICOM has proposed a regional judicial
tribunal, the CARICOM Court of Justice, to serve as a replacement for
the Judicial Committee of the Privy Council. This Court is vested with
powers of original and appellate jurisdiction in respect of the
interpretation and application of the treaty establishing the Caribbean
Community. It is seen in many quarters as a major supporting pillar for
the successful implementation of the single market programme in the
Community.

---

[17] See Nicholls et al. (2000).

The revisions to the Treaty of Chaguaramas have also necessitated some fundamental restructuring in other organs. The plethora of standing committees which existed prior to the single market programme has been replaced by four new councils which are intended to streamline and improve the decision-making processes in the community. The Council for Finance and Planning is now charged with the responsibility of co-ordinating issues relating to financial intermediaries, the development of regional financial markets, regulatory issues of a prudential nature, monetary policy and investment initiatives and policy. The Council for Trade and Economic Development (COTED) is responsible for the promotion of trade and economic development in the region and co-ordinates policy relating to rules of origin, the common external tariff, trade disputes and trade in services. Relations with external states and international organisations are managed by the Council for Foreign and Community Relations (COFCOR). The Caribbean Regional Negotiating Machinery has been created as an advisory arm of this council with special responsibilities for developing a cohesive trade negotiating strategy for the region. The Council for Human and Social Development manages several areas that were formerly under the jurisdiction of various standing ministerial councils. Matters relating to health, education, culture, women and development, youth empowerment and sports now fall under the purview of this council.

All administrative matters relating to the single market programme and the widening of the Caribbean Community are handled by the Secretariat, whose work programme has been expanded to incorporate the new developments. The Caribbean Community also possesses a range of affiliate institutions, which are engaged in various aspects of functional co-operation in the region (see Table 6.3).

It is clear that all the smaller integration systems have attempted to restructure the nature of their institutions to cope with the new configurations of the global economic system. The Andean Community is furthest along the road to devising a supranational architecture and has been quite parsimonious in the design of its institutional architecture as compared to CARICOM and SICA. It has placed great emphasis on devising an elaborate institutional framework for social integration that encourages significant participation from civil society. By contrast, both CARICOM and SICA have placed greater emphasis on the restructuring of their political, legal and administrative institutions. The institutional structure of SICA is by far the most complex and unwieldy of the smaller schemes that has been discussed in this chapter.

5. Institutional Challenges in the Process of Open Regionalism

Despite the flurry of new institutional initiatives and reforms that have been taking place in the smaller integration schemes, the institutional architectures of integration are confronted by several important challenges.

(a) Financial Support for Institutional Development and Goal Attainment

One of the really difficult problems that is limiting the ability of the various institutions to execute their functions effectively relates to the inadequacy of financial support for the process of integration. In general, the programmes and activities of the various regional institutions are funded in three ways: (i) from contributions of the various member states; (ii) from extra-regional grants; and (iii) from donor contributions. In the case of CARICOM, a substantial proportion of the budget for financing the activities of the various regional institutions comes from donor finance. For instance in 1995, 49.1 per cent of the budget of the CARICOM Secretariat which is in charge of managing the various regional programmes and activities was obtained from donor finance, while 16.8 per cent and 17.4 per cent were obtained from contributions by member states and grants from external agencies, respectively.[18]

Although estimates are more difficult to obtain for the Andean Community and the Central American Common Market, the picture is not significantly different. As regards the Central American Common Market, the official subscription of each member government amounts to only US$200,000 making the official budget of the secretariat just US$1 million. Moreover, given weaknesses in their fiscal positions, several member states are unable to provide much by way of additional financial support to these institutions. Indeed, the financially weak institutions that constitute the regional institutional architecture are often unable to implement effectively the various tasks to which they have been assigned or may have to alter their priorities so radically that complementary aspects of their programmes vital for the attainment of goals have to be postponed. Institutions that are unable to implement their agendas quickly lose credibility and often find themselves in further financial difficulty.

An important danger that looms large in this process of integration is that the programmes and policies of the various regional institutions can be unduly influenced by external or donor agencies that have their own agendas. In addition, one of the glaring limitations that arises is the

---

[18] Information obtained from discussions with officials in CARICOM.

almost complete absence of public information on expenditures of the various programmes and activities of the regional institutions as well as on their budgetary processes. The very composition and efficiency of the expenditures by these institutions does affect, in the final analysis, the growth and development prospects of the various member states of the integration grouping. A critical question therefore arises as to how the various regional programmes should be funded. In the past, development banks have played a vital role in partially funding the programmes of these institutions at concessional rates. However, the development of regional capital and money markets could also provide avenues for financing of regional programmes.

(b) Democracy and the Participation of Civil Society in the Integration Process

The current process of integration remains highly centralised and organised around state-led and intergovernmental institutions. Indeed, the integration schemes are especially 'top-heavy' with respect to political, legal and administrative institutions. This highly centralised system has weakened the interface between the integration movement and various constituent elements of civil society, and there is now considerable asymmetry in the relations between these centralised institutions and the ordinary citizenry that they have been designed to serve. One striking example of this is the almost complete level of *unimportance* or sometimes *annoyance* that the ordinary citizens of these integration movements accord to the various presidential summits, meetings, communiqués and declarations organised by the regional secretariats. In the Caribbean, and to some extent in Central America and the Andean Community, the meetings of heads of government, though announced and advertised in the media, fail to attract the same level of interest or attention from constituent groups in civil society as do cricket, football or foreign political developments. The real problem here is that the 'common man' does not easily identify with the various aims of the integration movement and sees these as mere tasks or concerns for government bureaucrats. This raises an important concern as to the extent to which our formal institutions capture the concerns of the less fortunate in our society and allow them to participate meaningfully in the integration process. Although all of the smaller integration schemes have followed the lead of the European Union and have introduced various social charters modelled on the European example, the ordinary citizens have not voiced their support for these charters and are quite often ignorant of their content and intentions.

*(c)   Co-ordination of Work Programmes and Activities of the Various
        Institutions*

Another major difficulty which confronts the smaller integration
schemes is the lack of systematic co-ordination of the work programmes
and activities of the formal institutions of integration and those of the
affiliated bodies. This problem of co-ordination appears to be more
acute for the more complex institutional arrangements in CARICOM
and the Central American Integration System than for the Andean
Community. Indeed, as the institutional architecture becomes more
complex, it becomes more difficult for the associate institutions to
systematically ensure congruence between their individual work
programmes and the agenda that has been set by regional policy-
makers. Furthermore, the breadth of some of these programmes and
activities leads quite often to disagreements over areas of responsibility.

The new integration thrust also requires separate institutions to
address competition policy, intellectual property, information
technology, e-commerce and e-business, entertainment services,
genetically modified organisms, labour mobility, entertainment services,
trade in a host of other service categories, procurement practices and
dispute settlement. Given the range of issues that have been introduced
in the emerging global village, it is doubtful whether the existing
regional bureaucracies have the capacity to manage effectively the
complex range of deep reforms that have been envisaged. It is
imperative that a systematic evaluation of the regional institutions be
undertaken to ensure that their functions, programmes and activities
mirror these new developments.

(d)   Governance and Implementation

The question of accountability, responsibility and transparency are
important issues for the governance of the smaller integration schemes
as well as for the success of their member economies. In some instances,
ordinary citizens are unable to obtain important financial information
about expenditures on various regional programmes and activities as
well as on outcomes, whether these be good or bad. Moreover, the sheer
complexity in the structure and programmes of the various institutions
often has a negative effect on the process of decision-making as well as
on the pace of implementation.

Conclusions

The process of integration in the smaller integration schemes of
CARICOM, the Andean Community and the Central American
Common Market has undergone a radical metamorphosis from the
tenets of closed regionalism (with its emphasis on import substitution

and greater protectionism) to one of open regionalism that is supportive of export promotion and deeper integration within the existing global economy. This shift has necessitated some modification in the institutional architectures of the various schemes. Although some significant changes have been introduced into these schemes, they have occurred more at the political, legal, administrative and technical levels. There are still significant weaknesses in the capacities of the regional institutions and their affiliates to manage the new issues that confront the global economy. Furthermore, there has not been a significant birth of new organisations and institutions to handle new issues such as competition policy and intellectual property. These new issues are already making the existing modifications to the institutional architecture ineffective and redundant. Unless some careful attention is devoted to the redesign of the institutional architecture of integration to encourage more effective implementation, the new regional arrangements in the smaller integration schemes may never achieve their intended objectives.

PART 3:
POLITICS

Business Politics and Regional Integration: The Advantages of Organisation in NAFTA and MERCOSUR

Ben Ross Schneider[1]

Callers put on hold at SOFOFA,[2] Chile's industrial association, hear various recorded exhortations to join. Primary among the pitches is the invitation to let SOFOFA handle the caller's complex trade negotiations. This recording is but one indication of how fully SOFOFA had thrown itself into trade negotiations by the late 1990s. In 1995 SOFOFA hired an ex-government official with long experience in international trade who in turn transformed SOFOFA's international trade department from a skeleton crew of two people into SOFOFA's largest department with over a dozen professional staff. SOFOFA members and staff worked closely with government officials in all aspects of trade negotiations. Across the cordillera in Argentina, the Unión Industrial Argentina (UIA) had no recorded exhortations and only minimal staff. UIA's part-time co-ordinator for international trade and a clerical assistant hosted regular meetings with staff at various member associations, but UIA did not do much more than discuss trade issues. Some UIA members participated occasionally in negotiations, but others complained of neglect and exclusion.

With the end of many industrial policies and the dismantling of the developmental state, previous points of connection between business and government, or sources of potential collaboration, have disappeared. Trade negotiations are now one of the key points of contact, or potentially key, between business and government. However, the type and level of contact between government negotiators and business has varied widely across the major countries of Latin America. Among the four countries examined here, business associations in Mexico and Chile participated actively and consistently in regional trade negotiations in the 1990s, while their counterparts in Argentina and Brazil had at best uneven and sporadic input.

Why do association activities vary so much across Latin America and

[1] I am grateful to the Institute for Latin American Studies at the University of London and the Center for International and Comparative Studies at Northwestern University for research support, to the interviewees listed in the appendix for their time and insights, and to Roberto Bouzas and Victor Bulmer-Thomas for comments on previous drafts.
[2] See Appendix to this chapter for the full name of all abbreviations and acronyms.

why is business input so variable in trade negotiations? Generally business participation in trade negotiations varies primarily according to: 1) the receptiveness of government to business input; and 2) the overall strength of associations (or the intensity of collective action in them) and their capacity to represent business. Two more specific aspects of the strength of associations are important to trade negotiations: the institutional capacity of the association (mostly the number and quality of technical staff), and the ability of associations to co-ordinate intersectoral participation and reconcile intersectoral differences. These factors tend to vary together, but some of the case histories illustrate the problems for business participation if one or more of these elements is missing (see Table 7.1).[3]

Table 7.1: Factors Affecting Industry Participation in Trade Negotiations in the 1990s

	Mexico	Brazil	Argentina	Chile
Government receptiveness to business input	High	Low	Low	High
Capacity of associations to represent industry	High	Low	Medium	High
Number and quality of technical staff in associations	High	High	Low	High
Association ability to mediate intersectoral differences	High	Low	Low	Medium

Note: the bases for these rankings are discussed further in the country sections.

Government receptiveness to organised business participation was generally higher in Mexico and Chile than in Argentina and Brazil in the 1980s and 1990s. Particular governments sometimes deviated from these patterns; the Alfonsín government in Argentina (1983–89), and to a lesser extent the Sarney government in Brazil (1985–90) sought business input, while the Zedillo government in Mexico (1994–2000) was somewhat more aloof than its predecessors. In cases of higher

---

[3] The Chilean and Mexican economies already traded more before the initiation of regional agreements. Hathaway (1998) argues that trade liberalisation and increasing import competition make business less protectionist rather than more. The direct application of this argument to regional integration is problematic since regional agreements sometimes offer more protection than the pre-existing tariff structure.

receptiveness to business input, government officials admitted that they sought business input due in part to past conflicts which generated distrust on the part of business. In Mexico, for instance, the bank nationalisation of 1982 generated deep distrust. In Chile business worried about what a centre-left government would do after Pinochet left power. And, in Argentina, the Radical Party had a historically rocky relationship with business. However, as President Menem (1989–99) showed, inviting business associations to negotiate is not the only way to attempt to overcome business fears. Menem chose instead to appoint representatives of big business to run his government's economic policy. The government's receptiveness also depends in part on the preferences of top economic ministers. So, for example, Jaime Serra in Mexico and Alejandro Foxley in Chile favoured close contact with organised business, whereas Pedro Malan in Brazil and Domingo Cavallo in Argentina avoided it. Of course, government receptiveness to collaboration with business depends a lot on whether officials think associations are strong and capable.

On the private side, business seems to have been more favourably disposed to regional integration in the 1990s than it was in the previous attempts. This pro-integration preference partly reflects a rational preference for protection and favoured access to export markets. In the 1960s and 1970s when most producers enjoyed national protection, regional integration potentially opened them up to more competition. Regional agreements by the 1990s meant something different. Since most tariff and non-tariff barriers in Latin America had dropped dramatically in the 1980s and early 1990s, regional integration sometimes offered producers shelter from wide-open free trade. However, beyond general support, business participation depended much more on how well they were organised. For purposes of trade negotiations, associations needed to be able to say that they represented their members effectively (a claim that is surprisingly difficult for many associations to make). In addition they needed to demonstrate a capacity for data collection and analysis as well as internal conflict mediation and integration among their members.

By way of summary, encompassing associations in Chile and Mexico are very well organised; they are voluntary, enduring, well staffed and often able to mediate divergent preferences among their member associations. Chilean associations are strongest at the level of peak sectoral associations in industry, agriculture, mining and construction, and weaker at the economy-wide level (CPC).[4] In comparison, economy-

---

[4] I distinguish among three levels or types of associations: 1) *sectoral associations* that represent specialised producers, textiles or sugar, for example; 2) *peak sectoral associations* for the major sectors of the economy, such as industry, agriculture, finance, or commerce, whose members are usually narrower sectoral associations; and 3) *economy-wide peak*

wide, encompassing Mexican associations (CMHN and CCE) are very strong — the strongest of the large countries in Latin America — while most peak sectoral associations are comparatively weak, especially the corporatist industry associations CONCAMIN and CANACINTRA. In Brazil peak sectoral associations, especially CNI and FIESP, appear very strong at first glance and have large professional staffs, but they do not represent members well or resolve conflicts among them, largely because they are still regulated by corporatist legislation dating from the 1940s (which makes membership compulsory and over-represents marginal sectors). In Argentina peak sectoral associations like the UIA are weaker in terms of staff, and suffer from other problems in representation and conflict resolution. Neither Brazil nor Argentina has an economy-wide association that brings together the major sectors in the economy.

The next sections proceed in rough chronological order through four case studies of business participation in regional integration, beginning with Mexico and intense business participation in the NAFTA negotiations. The next sections examine Brazil and Argentina where business was sidelined during much of the negotiations over MERCOSUR save for some sporadic and piecemeal participation by sectoral associations or individual firms. The final case is that of close participation by business associations in negotiating Chile's associate membership of MERCOSUR in the late 1990s. The penultimate section addresses the consequences of variations in business participation and argues that collaboration was mutually beneficial for both business and government, and may accelerate regional integration. The conclusion takes a step back to consider why business in Mexico and Chile is so much more organised in the first place.

1. Mexico: COECE and the Room Next Door

Since the Mexican Revolution, business in Mexico has been comparatively well organised and the state has been the main force encouraging business to organise.[5] In the 1930s and 1940s state leaders organised business through compulsory sectoral associations that were in turn obliged to affiliate with the national confederations CONCANACO (commerce) and CONCAMIN (industry). Later, in the 1960s and 1970s threatening state actions had the unintended consequence of strengthening non-corporatist voluntary associations, especially the employers' association COPARMEX, the small elite club of the CMHN, and the economy-wide peak association, CCE. Born of conflict, these voluntary associations became, in the 1980s and 1990s, the privileged

---

associations whose members are usually six to eight peak sectoral associations. The focus in this chapter is primarily on the last two levels.
[5] See Schneider (2002).

interlocutors of negotiations over market-oriented reform.

The closest collaboration in the 1980s came in the stabilisation pacts.[6] In late 1987, as fiscal accounts and inflationary pressures worsened, government officials called on representatives of the peak associations of business and labour to negotiate prices and wages in an anti-inflationary pact. Despite heavy initial scepticism, especially by business, the pact yielded significant reductions in inflation over the course of 1988, an electoral year. Observers were nearly unanimous in crediting the agreement with rapid inflation reduction without a deep recession. Among other benefits, it co-ordinated private sector price increases, greatly enhanced the flow of information (and over time trust and credibility) between business and government and expanded political support for the government's stabilisation policies.[7] The success of the pact set a positive tone for subsequent collaboration on trade.

In Mexico consultations between business and government over trade policy began before 1988 and grew more intense as liberalisation proceeded and especially after the government entered into negotiations over NAFTA. In 1987 the government accelerated the tariff reductions unilaterally, but made trade liberalisation an integral part of the stabilisation programme and an item on the agenda for pact meetings. When the Mexican government announced plans in March 1990 to pursue NAFTA, the CCE (with government approval) quickly created COECE (Coordinadora Empresarial de Comercio Exterior). COECE and the government in turn created advisory committees comprised of five or so officials and eight–ten representatives from business to accompany negotiations in about 20 sectors. In the two years following the March 1990 announcement, various groups of representatives of business and government negotiators had 1,333 meetings or roughly a dozen a week.[8] Business representatives were not allowed at the bargaining table with the United States and Canada but were figuratively, and often literally, 'in the room next door'.[9]

Consensus-building through these multiple fora, especially through COECE and the NAFTA negotiations, contributed to consolidating trade reform by building support in the private sector, increasing the flow of information between business and government, and allowing business the opportunity to propose complementary and compensatory policies. The acquiescence of business to trade liberalisation was surprising, considering that business blocked Mexico's entrance into the GATT in

---

[6] See Kaufman et al. (1994); Zuckerman (1990); and Milor et al. (1999). This section on Mexico draws heavily on Schneider (1997).

[7] On the various benefits of co-ordination, monitoring, enforcement, credibility, flexibility, and trust, see especially Kaufman et al. (1994); and Lustig (1992).

[8] Puga (1994), p. 9.

[9] 'Cuarto de junta', interview with Raúl Ortega, COECE, 16 November 1993; Puga (1994); and Thacker (1999) and (2000).

1979.[10] Other factors contributed to muting opposition, but the fact that business felt consulted and included in negotiating the opening was also significant.[11] Government leaders felt such consensus building was important enough in the 1990s to invest a lot in campaigning in favour of liberalisation by sending officials out to talk with business groups.[12] Support by big business for NAFTA was nearly unanimous by 1993.

The process of dialogue increased the flow of information from business to government and vice versa. Generally, the advisory committees allowed for a lot of communication (everybody was linked up by e-mail) and mostly harmonious negotiation between business and government.[13] When NAFTA negotiations began, government negotiators knew less about North American business and trade than did Mexican exporters. Beyond this familiarity, the government needed more systematic data which COECE and member associations set about to collect. Initially, the government relied on the CCE's research unit to conduct a first national survey to find out what business wanted from a trade agreement.[14] Over time, sectoral associations began collecting more complete data on their respective sectors to use in the negotiations.[15] Through these negotiations, the state enhanced business capacity for interest intermediation. Within various advisory groups, representatives of upstream and downstream firms realised that they had to work out differences before taking joint proposals to government, otherwise business would lose influence.[16] From the business side, dialogue gave investors a better sense of where the government was headed and hence provided greater certainty for planning and investment.[17] COECE was due to close after the negotiations ended in 1993, but it survived in part to accompany negotiations over other possible trade agreements. Moreover, the model of consultation in COECE was so popular that government and business leaders favoured extending it to other areas.[18]

---

[10] Story (1982); and Kaufman et al. (1994).

[11] Interview, Fernando Canales Clariond, vice-president of IMSA, 19 November 1993. Other factors include the coercive powers of the state, the linkage of stabilisation and liberalisation, and the pre-existing support for trade liberalisation (see Kaufman et al., 1994).

[12] Interview with a trade negotiator, November 1993.

[13] For a favourable review of COECE and trade liberalisation from the business side, see COPARMEX's magazine *Entorno* (June 1991) p. 12, and the interviewees cited in Puga (1994), p. 10.

[14] Puga (1994), p. 7.

[15] *Ibid.*, p. 15.

[16] Interview with Raúl Ortega, COECE, November 1993. See Puga (1994) for further analysis of the impact of the NAFTA negotiations on Mexican business associations.

[17] Interview, Fernando Canales Clariond, vice-president of IMSA, 19 November 1993.

[18] Puga (1994), p. 16.

COECE was never intended to amplify the voices of smaller firms. The high costs in both time and money to participate in the regular meetings of COECE, separately and with government, priced many smaller firms out of the meetings.[19] State actors had some ideas about the sectors they expected to win and granted those sectors favoured access and benefits in negotiations. A study of business-government relations in six agroindustrial sectors during the NAFTA negotiations found that sectors like beer were well organised (not hard given the handful of firms), had good access to the negotiations, and gained longer adjustment periods than other sectors like canned foods and chocolate, where numerous producers were unable to organise, felt shut out of negotiations and were subjected to earlier import competition.[20]

While beyond the scope of this chapter, it is worth noting that business participation in NAFTA negotiations was the norm and intense on all three sides of the negotiating table. This common, 'North American' practice may have encouraged Mexican officials to include their business representatives to counter participation by firms in the United States and Canada. The organisers of COECE in fact directly copied the structure Canadian business had used in earlier negotiations with the United States. In the United States major firms and associations formed the USA–NAFTA Coalition to lobby in favour of the agreement. In addition, government negotiators set up a private sector advisory system (first mandated by Congress in the Trade Act of 1974). The top level, the Advisory Committee for Trade Policy Negotiations (ACTPN), consists of 44 members,

> mostly top business leaders, representing a cross-section of the United States' major economic sectors. The second level comprises seven committees charged with providing sector-specific advice, such as industry, agriculture, labor, and the like. The third level includes numerous technical and sectoral advisory committees that provide the detailed information needed to assess the likely impact on specific sectors of trade policy.[21]

James Robinson III, chair of ACTPN and head of American Express, said they met nearly 1,000 times with government officials and negotiators and he praised the Bush administration (1989–93) for working so closely with business.[22]

---

[19] Thacker (1999) and (2000); Shadlen (2000); and Martínez and Schneider (2000).

[20] Martínez and Schneider (2000).

[21] Avery and Friman (1999), pp. 93–94.

[22] *Ibid.*, p. 94.

In sum, Mexico set the standard for close collaboration between business and government in trade negotiations, a standard that would not be matched until Chile negotiated its affiliation with MERCOSUR. All the conditions in Mexico favoured close collaboration. The government was generally predisposed to incorporate business, and the minister responsible for NAFTA, Jaime Serra, was especially keen to involve business. On the private side, big business in Mexico had for decades been investing in strong voluntary associations, especially CMHN and CCE. These associations took the lead in structuring, staffing, and funding COECE. CMHN, CCE and COECE had sufficient staff resources to provide timely and high quality information. Moreover, they had the experience and fora necessary to talk through intersectoral differences and sometimes coerce consensus (big firms, for example, used their resources and leverage to marginalise smaller firms that had more reservations about NAFTA).

2. Brazil: State-led Integration

Business-government relations in Brazil have sometimes been close, but they have never been organised, consistent, or institutionalised. In some periods and sectors, business and government have collaborated intensely and sometimes productively (what Cardoso called 'aneis burocráticos') to fashion and implement industrial policies and projects.[23] With the advent of democracy after 1985 many business people became politically active, but business associations languished. Despite exceptions like the sectoral *cámaras* in the early 1990s, relations between business (especially business associations) and economic policy-makers has been distant, both generally and in trade policy in particular.[24]

Despite the appearance of strong industrial associations in organisations like FIESP and CNI, Brazilian business is probably less organised than anywhere else in Latin America.[25] FIESP, CNI, and other comp-ulsory corporatist associations have huge buildings, staffs, and budgets, but they do not represent their members well. Corporatist regulations governed by national legislation greatly over-represented small, agricultural regional associations in the CNI and marginal sectoral associations in state-level federations like FIESP. The distortions in representation are such that policy-makers often bypass them to consult

---

[23] See Schneider (1991); and Evans (1995).
[24] See Schneider (1997) and; Cason (2000). The câmara setorial was a tripartite negotiation with representatives from unions, government, and business associations convened sporadically in various sectors like toys or automobiles to negotiate wages, prices, and investments. See especially Arbix (1995).
[25] See Kingstone (1999); Weyland (1996); and Schneider (1997–98).

directly with businessmen, and association leaders rely on surveys of members rather than internal consultations to find out member preferences. In other instances, prominent business leaders in São Paulo have created rival associations like PNBE and IEDI in an attempt to compensate for the distortions in FIESP.[26]

Despite these organisational weaknesses, São Paulo business was indirectly 'represented' in the Sarney government through numerous top level appointees, including several cabinet members. These contacts gave São Paulo industrialists access to discussions about economic integration with Argentina. However, capitalists were generally more concerned about macro-stabilisation policies (short-lived, ineffective and numerous) and the drafting of the new constitution than in gradual integration with Argentina.[27] The disorganisation of business undermined its capacity to participate effectively in either stabilisation pacts, as in Mexico, or in influencing the constitution writing.[28]

In mid-1986 the Alfonsín and Sarney governments endorsed the Programa de Integración y Cooperación Económica (PICE). According to Cason, 'from the beginning the [PICE] initiative was clearly state led. The private sector was generally not involved in the early negotiations, and only when its economic sectors were put on the agenda by trade negotiators did the private sector become involved'.[29] This was a pattern that would be repeated in both Brazil and Argentina: presidents and their foreign ministers sign bold agreements on integration to which business later gains concessions and exemptions. The foreign ministries took the lead in implementing and administering PICE,[30] and historically Itamarati (the Brazilian foreign ministry) has been more distant and insulated from business than other ministries, in part because it recruits almost exclusively from within its own ranks. The initial PICE agreement did open the door for business to propose further integration. For example, in late 1987 associations representing the chemical industries in the two countries signed agreements designed to create common markets in three products.[31]

PICE began with great fanfare but further integration had largely stalled by 1988.[32] Argentine exports to MERCOSUR did grow rapidly, nearly tripling from US$668mn in 1985 to US$1.8bn in 1990. Brazilian exports to MERCOSUR also grew rapidly from US$990mn to US$1.6bn in 1988 before dropping to US$1.2bn in 1990 (just above the US$1.1bn

---

[26] See Kingstone (1998).

[27] See Gomes (1998).

[28] Weyland (1996) and (1998).

[29] Cason (2000), p. 207; Manzetti agrees (1990), p. 110.

[30] *Ibid.*, p. 115.

[31] *Ibid.*, p. 127.

[32] *Ibid.*, p. 120.

Brazil exported to Argentina in 1979.[33] By the late 1980s integration had stalled due largely to increasing macroeconomic stability in both countries and because PICE was 'not reinforced by supportive economic and social groups, which were not organised either spontaneously or by the government'.[34] This lack of support would re-emerge as a problem in the late 1990s when MERCOSUR ran into problems, a lack of support that contrasts sharply with the stronger positive consensuses in Chile and Mexico. Moreover, the piecemeal approach to integration 'was stymied by sectoral lobbies in both countries that made negotiations more difficult'.[35]

Fernando Collor came to the Brazilian presidency attacking many perceived abuses of power, including undue business influence in policy-making. Collor rejected a campaign endorsement from FIESP before his election and afterward called FIESP one of the most retrograde institutions in Brazil.[36] Much of Collor's economic team lacked the business networks of their predecessors in the Sarney government. Business felt excluded though they did not complain much initially (beyond the freezing of their accounts in 1990), because much of Collor's neoliberal agenda coincided with public business demands.[37] The Collor government, especially the foreign ministry, pushed forward a bolder plan for integration, without business input. This push culminated in the Treaty of Asunción in early 1991. Itamarati's traditional insulation from political pressures in its design of foreign economic policy combined with Collor's public exclusion of organised business meant MERCOSUR was designed without much consultation with business.[38]

Top economic policy-makers in the Cardoso government also kept their distance from organised business.[39] Some cabinet members (Luiz Carlos Bresser Pereira, Celso Lafer, Alcides Tapias and Andrea Calabi, for example) had close business connections, but the main economic ministers did not invite contact with associations. However, Brazilian business from the beginning was generally predisposed to integration with Argentina. A small survey in 1991 revealed that 82 per cent of Brazilian businesses expected to gain from MERCOSUR (versus only 45 per cent of Argentine business respondents).[40] Overall MERCOSUR was

---

[33] Cason (2000), pp. 206, 210.

[34] Manzetti (1990), p. 133.

[35] Jenkins (1999), p. 39.

[36] Kingstone (1994), p. 88.

[37] *Ibid.*, (1994), p. 104.

[38] Cason (2000), p. 215 and Pfeifer and Oliveira (2000).

[39] Dorothea Werneck, minister of industry was one of the few top policy-makers in the 1990s who sought to structure business-government dialogue through *câmaras setoriais* (the most famous in the auto sector). However, Werneck did not last long in government and her enthusiasm for negotiation was not shared by other economic ministers. By 1995 the *câmaras* had fallen into disuse (see Schneider, 1997).

[40] Coopers and Lybrand study cited by Jenkins (1999), p. 42.

less important to Brazilian business because of the smaller relative size of the economies of its trading partners. The other three countries considered here, Argentina, Mexico and Chile, were all seeking integration into larger economies.[41]

Brazilian business was later incorporated into several formal fora for subsequent rounds of MERCOSUR negotiations. In 1994 negotiators created the Foro Consultivo Econômico Social (FCES) to bring together representatives from peak sectoral associations, unions, and consumer groups. This Foro is large, cumbersome and meets only rarely to accompany big MERCOSUR meetings. Interviewees from Chile and Argentina claimed it was a forum more for general speeches rather than effective negotiation. MERCOSUR negotiators also encouraged the formation of the Consejo Industrial MERCOSUR (CIM) comprised of the peak industry associations in the four countries. Interviewees had similar disdain for CIM, claiming it met infrequently, discussed broad issues, and was not an effective conduit for channelling private sector representation.

Overall, Brazil's participation in MERCOSUR was 'state-led' with business playing a minor role.[42] Alfonsín and Sarney started the process for their own political and state reasons. Menem and Collor (1990–93) added in ideology, geopolitics, and competing regionalisms (i.e., exclusion from NAFTA and the European Union). However, once states had started negotiations rolling, businesses, especially narrow sectoral associations, geared up to push states to protect hard hit sectors, slow integration, and/or compensate losers. Politically, the government's strategy seems to have been less one of building a strong pro-MERCOSUR coalition (comparable to the pro-NAFTA coalition in Mexico) and more one of undercutting the formation of an anti-MERCOSUR coalition by granting exceptions and concessions.[43] This model of state initiation followed by business parti-cipation also characterised the Argentine process, though perhaps with fewer concessions to business.

3. Argentina: More State-led Integration

As in Brazil, decision-making in Argentina on regional integration through PICE and MERCOSUR was largely 'top-down', state-led and dependent on presidential initiatives.[44] Business participation in

---

[41] One indication of the relative lack of importance of MERCOSUR was the fact that CNI's annual surveys of business preferences did not always cover MERCOSUR issues in the early 1990s but focused instead on other government policies.

[42] Cason (2000) and (2000a); Burrell and Cason (2000); and Manzetti (1994).

[43] See Jenkins (1999).

[44] Manzetti (1994), p. 117.

negotiations over integration was uneven, both over time and across sectors, but in contrast to Mexico and Chile business participation was not mediated by strong encompassing associations. When business did participate it was usually through narrow sectoral associations or as individual firms or capitalists.

Argentine business associations are comparatively weak, like those in Brazil, but in different ways and for different reasons. Neither country has an economy-wide peak association, though sectoral associations in Argentina periodically meet to try to co-ordinate joint actions. Argentine associations, especially voluntary ones like SRA (Sociedad Rural Argentina) and UIA do not suffer the corporatist distortions in internal representation of Brazilian associations. However, Argentine associations have been highly politicised and subject to chronic internal conflicts and, occasionally, splits. Argentine associations are often characterised more as movements than organisations, which reflects the fact that they have, in some periods, enormous influence and ability to mobilise coalitions, but they lack institutional capacity and staff. Both problems — internal divisions and institutional incapacity — limited the effective participation of business associations in trade negotiations.[45]

Industrialists appear to have a strong, voluntary association to represent them. The UIA has a long history dating well back into the nineteenth century.[46] By 2000 it had several hundred member associations representing nearly all major sectors and regions of industry. UIA had prominent downtown offices, a budget of around US$2 million and a staff of around 30.[47] However, UIA's past is also laced with political conflicts, both external with various (Peronist) governments and rival associations, and internally between smaller, more protectionist industries and larger, more liberal members. UIA's partisan conflicts resulted in several 'interventions' when Peronist governments in the 1950s and 1970s, and even the military government in the 1970s, closed UIA or appointed its leaders. Even when it was not closed, UIA was suspect because of its partisan ties, and some

---

[45] The CEA, like the CMHN in Mexico, is a very elite club of owners and chief executives of top corporations from all major sectors of the Argentine economy. Like the CMHN, the CEA's primary activities are dining with government officials and funding studies. However, unlike the CMHN, the CEA is not active in co-ordinating other business associations. Moreover, CEA was generally not vocal on MERCOSUR issues. According to ex-president and long-time member Alfredo Martínez de Hoz, CEA was not interested in MERCOSUR because it is less free market than unilateral openness (interview 5 May 2000). Felix Peña, a key government negotiator in the early 1990s and again in the late 1990s, had regular contact with CEA but confirmed their general disinterest in regional integration (interview 5 May 2000).

[46] See Schwarzer (1991); and Birle (1997).

[47] Interviews with Jorge Blanco Villegas, Eduardo Casullo, and Dario Pons. The SRA has more staff and resources, and provides more direct services to members. SRA's budget is US$12 million, nearly six times that of UIA (SRA, 1999: 274).

industrialists, especially the largest firms, bypassed UIA in contacting the government. After 1980 UIA attempted to broaden its membership base to bring in both large and small, central and provincial industries and designed a cumbersome internal structure that split representation between sectoral and regional associations. Moreover, UIA developed two internal factions, MIA and MIN, representing respectively liberal and protectionist factions.[48] On the one hand, UIA seems to have a great capacity to manage internal divisions; on the other, it seems to have little capacity to do much else. And, as discussed later, UIA often cannot come to an agreement among its members, thus immobilising UIA in policy debates.

Beyond the organisational weaknesses of UIA, the overall political and economic context also mattered, though in different ways in the 1980s and 1990s. In the Alfonsín government, policy-makers were open to business participation, but macroeconomic and political instability shifted attention to immediate survival issues, especially by the late 1980s when regional integration was an issue. Alfonsín and his top economic policy-makers made many efforts to consult with organised business on the full range of policy initiatives. The Alfonsín government was open in part because of a tradition of distance and mutual mistrust between business and the Radical Party.[49] Consultations with business proceeded on multiple levels and in multiple fora. Foreign minister Dante Caputo called together a small, informal group of the largest firms, later called the 'captains of industry'.[50] The Ministry of Economics also convened several social pacts in attempts to stem inflation, but none lasted. Moreover, the immediate and recurrent crises of hyperinflation made efforts to establish longer-term collaboration uncertain.

However, it was in the context of the short stability of the Austral plan in mid-1986 that Alfonsín launched the idea of integration with Brazil. Business was not involved in the initial decision nor in the overall framework for the PICE, but later had input into implementation. Government officials decided which sectors to include in the PICE and then told business associations in these sectors to work out agreements with their counterparts in Brazil. This sector by sector integration moved slowly in the mid-1980s, but stalled by the end of the decade as the Alfonsín government unravelled, precisely because PICE was so dependent on presidential initiatives.[51] By 1988 a protectionist lobby was arguing that Brazil was gaining unfair advantage.[52] Thereafter, business participation in negotiations over integration were uneven; access varied

---

[48] See Calvo (2000); and Schvarzer (1991).
[49] Interview with a top official in the Alfonsín government.
[50] See Ostiguy (1990).
[51] Manzetti (1990).
[52] *Ibid.*, p. 120.

over time and was generally better for top capitalists and particular sectoral associations than for encompassing associations like the UIA. For example, the head of the Centro de la Industria Lechera as well as Jorge Blanco Villegas, then president of UIA, complained of inadequate consultation between business and government, and the head of a smaller dairy association claimed there was no channel for consultation between business and government.[53] In contrast Santiago Soldattí, head of one of Argentina's largest conglomerates, contrasted the failure of previous attempts at regional integration (due in part according to Soldattí to the lack of co-operation between business and government) to the success of MERCOSUR 'where business and the state participated very closely'.[54]

Like Alfonsín, Menem started his government with overtures to business in order to establish some confidence and overcome capitalists' historic fears of Peronism. However, Menem's style was quite different. Rather than consult with organised business, Menem appointed executives from the Argentine firm Bunge y Born to run economic policy in the first years of his government. When Menem announced MERCOSUR and a rapid acceleration in the timetable for integration (tariff reductions in five years instead of ten, as last agreed by Sarney and Alfonsín), he did not consult with business. According to a government negotiator, Félix Peña, organised business had a lot of input negotiating exceptions in 1989, but no input in the lead up to the Treaty of Asunción in 1991,[55] in part because business did not think that the Asunción meeting would be anything more than a lot of fanfare to sign onto an agreement with no real teeth.

By the end of Menem's term business was more involved in (re)negotiating MERCOSUR, especially in the wake of Brazil's devaluation in January 1999. By the end of the decade business lobbying had become much more sophisticated: some businesses, for example, would build coalitions of provincial governors, labour leaders and representatives in Congress that they would mobilise to lobby MERCOSUR negotiators.[56] However, at the same time UIA became increasingly marginalised and lacked regular institutionalised channels to consult with government negotiators.[57] Félix Peña described two episodes that reveal the lack of capacity in UIA, both technical and in terms of reconciling conflicting interests. In the first instance, Peña convened a meeting of 32 representatives from business associations to

---

[53] Luján (2000), p. 5, and personal interview with Blanco Villegas.
[54] *Ibid.*, (2000), pp. 4–5.
[55] Interview 5 May 2000.
[56] Interview with Félix Peña.
[57] Various formal bodies like CACE, and later FCES and CIM, did not meet often and were not viewed as crucial forums for negotiations between government and business.

discuss co-ordinating macroeconomic policies with Brazil. He requested written papers before the meeting, but not one of the associations submitted anything. In a second case, he asked UIA to give him an opinion on a temporary change in MERCOSUR regulations. UIA wrote him back a week or so later saying that UIA had no opinion because affected members could not come to agreement. Félix Peña, after long experience as a government negotiator, concluded that business interlocutors were most effective in helping government negotiators when the business association: 1) was well organised nationally; 2) had a good 'technocracy', i.e., qualified staff; 3) was con-centrated and had few member firms; and 4) had high levels of 'bilateral intimacy' (close contacts with counterpart associations in Brazil).

Overall, business in Argentina has been less enthusiastic about regional integration than business in Brazil, Mexico and Chile. From the beginning only 45 per cent in one survey of business expected to gain from MERCOSUR.[58] Thereafter the Menem government largely denied business associations access to ongoing negotiations. Worse, by 1999 Argentine business was under pressure from Brazil's devalued exports, and business was so divided over MERCOSUR that even the 'winners' would not come to an open defence of MERCOSUR in 1999 when the clamour of criticism was growing.[59]

4. Chile: Business Mobilisation for MERCOSUR

Chile is a case of especially close collaboration between business and government in trade negotiations, as in other major economic and social issues of the 1980s and 1990s. Overall collaboration is primarily a function of two factors: 1) the political desire by governments (both military after 1984 and civilian after 1990) to seek business support and negotiate compromises on contentious policies; and 2) the high level of organisation achieved by Chilean business, especially industry, prior to the 1990s.[60]

Chilean capitalists invest far more in their associations than their counterparts in most countries of Latin America. And their past investments accumulated by the 1990s into substantial endowments (both institutional and financial). The organisation of the economy-wide CPC is surprisingly straightforward, by Latin American standards, comprising the six associations for all the major sectors of the economy: industry (SOFOFA), commerce, finance, mining (SONAMI), agriculture

---

[58] Jenkins (1999), p. 42.

[59] Interview with Félix Peña.

[60] See Silva (1995) and (1996); and Rehren (1995) for overviews. P. Silva writes that business was 'fully integrated into negotiations' for trade agreements with Colombia, Venezuela and Mexico (1995), p. 22.

(SNA), and construction.[61] The strength and activism of the CPC has varied with the overall political context.[62] CPC's visibility and activism waxed in moments of political conflict in the 1930s and late 1960s and early 1970s, as well as during periods of political transition where governments sought business collaboration, especially from the mid-1980s through the early 1990s. By the late 1990s sectoral associations, especially SOFOFA, had gained strength relative to the CPC, especially in issues of trade negotiations and regional integration.

The decade from the outbreak of mass protests against Pinochet in 1983 through the first years of the democratic Concertación government (1990–94) put the CPC at the centre of business-government relations. After 1984 the military government's new economic ministers, especially Hernán Büchi, actively sought consultation and collaboration with business associations, in particular the CPC.[63] Then the CPC became a privileged location for deliberating a common position of the private sector for the plebiscite and presidential elections, as well as for negotiating major changes in tax and labour laws in the early 1990s.[64] Manuel Feliu, president of the CPC in the late 1980s, called this the 'golden age' of the CPC (interview, 10 May 2000). Of course the issues in this period were big and encompassing: political transition, new forms of political representation, new institutions for economic policy-making (e.g., central bank autonomy), taxes and labour law. Most of these issues affected most or all of the private sector, which made reaching a consensus in the CPC more valuable. However, trade issues had more uneven sectoral impacts and ultimately exceeded CPC's capacity for reconciling intersectoral differences and building consensus. The shift in policy issues over the course of the 1990s from broad, economy-wide policies to narrower sectoral issues, shifted power away from the CPC.[65]

Regional integration became a major policy concern by the mid-1990s. The military government had opted for unilateral trade opening in the 1970s and 1980s. By the 1990s policy-makers became concerned about the trend towards regionalism and the possible exclusion of Chile

---

[61] Cámara Chilena de la Construcción, Cámara Nacional de Comercio, Servicios y Turismo de Chile, and Asociación de Bancos e Instituciones Financieras de Chile. The peak sectoral associations like SOFOFA are voluntary and mostly represent larger subsectoral associations and large individual firms. Other associations have emerged to represent smaller firms, but they are not affiliated with CPC. Conupia organises some 35,000 small manufacturing firms (Rehren (1995), p. 16). Asexma is a recently formed association dedicated to helping small manufacturing firms export.

[62] See Cusack (1972); and Silva (1996).

[63] See Silva (1996).

[64] See Rehren (1995).

[65] The biannual reports of the CPC (1992, 1998) show a drop in activities related to international trade. In the 1992 report several commissions and the president reported studies, activities, meetings, and position papers. In 1998 the Commission on Agreements and International Economic Relations had very little to report.

from emerging trading blocs. The initial inclination of the Aylwin government (1990–94) was toward NAFTA. However, by 1995 the Frei government had shifted attention to MERCOSUR. Several factors contributed to this shift. Within the Aylwin government there were advocates for both regional agreements; those favouring NAFTA were strong in the Ministry of the Economy, while many in the Ministry of Foreign Relations favoured MERCOSUR. And, over the 1990s the private sector became increasingly vocal and active in pressing for MERCOSUR in part because export opportunities, especially for industry, were expanding rapidly.[66] In 1990 trade with MERCOSUR countries accounted for eight per cent of Chilean exports and 16 per cent of imports. By 1994 the value of exports had doubled and MERCOSUR accounted for 12 per cent of total exports and 18 per cent of imports.[67] MERCOSUR was perceived as a major source of growth for Chilean trade. Moreover, Chilean industries perceived greater opportunities for export growth. Manufactured exports like stoves and refrigerators could compete in Argentina and Brazil, but not in Mexico and the United States.[68]

From 1994 through 1996 associations like CPC, SOFOFA and ASEXMA (exporters) mounted a multipronged campaign to press the government to negotiate Chile's entry into MERCOSUR.[69] Leaders from these and other associations wrote letters, called meetings, and made public declarations in favour of MERCOSUR over NAFTA. Moreover, business leaders said they wanted to be included from the start; Víctor Manuel Jarpa, president of the construction association, said 'we are not going to limit ourselves to revising agreements made by the government, as we did in the past. This time, we will participate in the whole meal, including the entrée, instead of just the dessert'.[70] Business associations then began making specific recommendations on tariff schedules, timetables and exceptions that they pressed the government to push in negotiations. When it became clear in late 1995 that the US Congress was not going to authorise fast track negotiations, the pro-NAFTA coalition in Chile faded and business succeeded in pushing the government to pursue MERCOSUR more aggressively. By mid-1996 negotiators had worked out an agreement for Chile's entry into MERCOSUR that extended protection for Chilean agriculture while reducing the initial obstacles proposed to slow manufactured exports from Chile.

---

[66] See Burrell and Cason (2000), for a full account.
[67] Meller and Donoso (1998) p. 25; see also Duran (1996), p. 193.
[68] Interview with Hugo Baierlein, 9 May 2000. The biggest gains after 1996 in fact went to sectors like electric goods, textiles, plastics, and equipment. See Mellor and Donoso (1998), p. 2.
[69] Burrell and Cason (2000).
[70] *Ibid.*, (2000), p. 20.

The consultations on NAFTA, the association of Chile to MERCOSUR and other ongoing trade negotiations induced major changes in the internal organisation of Chilean business. Overall, trade negotiations shifted investment in associations to sectoral chambers, opened rifts between sectors and weakened the economy-wide CPC. While some Chilean manufactures might be able to compete in MERCOSUR, agricultural producers in Chile — it was argued — could not compete with the extremely competitive agricultural sectors in Argentina and Brazil. Divisions between SNA (agriculture) and SOFOFA (industry) exceeded the consensus-building capacity of the CPC, which abandoned discussions with the government on trade. SOFOFA and SNA agreed to disagree and pursue their separate lobbying efforts with government negotiators. SOFOFA staffers felt this breakdown of consensus-building hurt industry because agriculture was able secure a gradual opening to free trade over decades. In return, MERCOSUR industries sought and received compensatory protection from Chilean manufacturers in exchange for the concessions on agriculture (interview with Hugo Baierlein, 9 May 2000).[71]

At the same time, participation in trade negotiations strengthened sectoral associations. As noted at the outset, SOFOFA recast itself as the negotiating representative for its members and also increased staff in the international trade department from two in 1995 to 15 in 2000. Moreover, by entering into various trade agreements, Chilean negotiators committed exporters to abide by the rules of origin stipulated in these various agreements. Certifying manufacturing exports then became a major administrative task that the government decided to delegate to SOFOFA. The association charges for this service, open to all manufacturers whether or not affiliated with SOFOFA, and these charges not only cover costs but contribute another ten per cent to SOFOFA's overall operating budget.[72]

The regional and formal consultative fora for business–government discussion of MERCOSUR such as CIM and CES are not highlighted by business interviewees. The most important connections to government come at the negotiating table. Here business was always very close to government negotiators throughout the 1990s; just how close depended

---

[71] Although not directly related to divergent positions on trade, differences between SOFOFA and CPC widened over the 1990s. In the mid-1990s Walter Riesco (ex-president of SONAMI, with support from SNA) defeated Pedro Lizana (ex-president of SOFOFA) in the first contested elections for the presidency of CPC. By late 1998 relations had deteriorated to the point where SOFOFA president Lamarca stopped attending CPC meetings. Then after a year of abstention, SOFOFA withdrew its economic contribution in early 2000. The crisis was apparently resolved in May 2000 through some tinkering with the CPC statutes (mostly designed to exclude past presidents) and streamline decision-making within the CPC (see *El Diario*, 10 May 2000, p. 27).

[72] Interview with Pedro Lizana, 10 May 2000.

on the official protocols for negotiations. In some cases, business was not allowed at the table, but was in the room next door (with cellular phones to call back to the office to check on SOFOFA positions). In other cases business was at the table next to government negotiators. In the most extreme case, the government deputised SOFOFA staffer Hugo Baierlein to negotiate an agreement with Bolivia, gave him a diplomatic passport, sent him to La Paz and rubber stamped the agreement he negotiated. This kind of access gives associations very strong incentives to invest in institutional capacity, as SOFOFA has done through expanding the staff of its international trade department.

In sum, general receptivity by government to the idea of consultation with organised business combined with strong pre-existing business associations yielded close collaboration over MERCOSUR and other trade agreements. Over the course of the 1990s a virtuous, or at least self-reinforcing, cycle developed: the government granted business associations a place in the negotiations, which encouraged associations to invest in institutional capacity for negotiating, which made associations even more valuable interlocutors for government officials. That is, associations by virtue of their participation became more specialised in trade. This specialisation of course prompted changes in internal organisation and in external relations with other associations and with member firms. The strains within CPC are at least partly a reflection of the divergence of opinion and activity with respect to trade. Put differently, CPC is dispensable when it comes to trade, and to the extent that trade tops the list of member's concerns, CPC loses relevance. At the same time SOFOFA is disagreeing with SNA and CPC, it is also attracting non-industrial members, and, again, to the extent SOFOFA becomes encompassing it has even less need for interest aggregation in CPC.

5. Some Consequences of Intense Business Participation

Overall, closer collaboration between business and government in negotiating NAFTA and MERCOSUR yielded benefits for both sides.[73] Government officials received better information on sectoral capabilities, intersectoral problems and preferences, and probable economic outcomes. They also enlisted stronger political allies in their conflicts with other opposed political and social groups. Business sometimes obtained more protection (usually in the form of temporary concessions or exemptions) to ease adjustment and promote expansion. Importantly, though, this protection was not necessarily extended to the least

---

[73] These benefits were mentioned by many of the interviewees listed in the appendix. See Schneider and Maxfield (1997) for a general discussion of the positive and negative economic effects of close collaboration between business and government.

competitive and most vocal sectors.[74] Moreover, business had a better sense of where the government was headed and a stronger expectation that government officials would take their interests into account in future trade negotiations.

Government negotiators in Chile and Mexico relied more on information from business associations than could officials in Brazil and Argentina. Many government negotiators on the Mexican side of NAFTA were young economists without any training or experience in managing trade agreements, and in interviews some negotiators acknowledged the quality and timeliness of the information they received from business, both formally in documents and informally in frequent meetings and contacts. After President Salinas (1988–94) announced his intention to pursue a free trade agreement with the United States, officials in the trade ministry (SECOFI) immediately asked COECE and member associations to prepare extensive background reports on their sectors, markets and preferences. SECOFI also asked the CCE's research department to conduct a survey of business to gauge initial preferences on NAFTA. How much this information really affected the outcomes of negotiation is hard to measure, but the fact that government officials continually requested it in Mexico and Chile suggests that they found it helpful (and judged the associations capable of delivering the kind of information they needed).

Regional integration has complex effects across related sectors, a complexity that is difficult for negotiators to foresee. This generates both informational and political problems that powerful associations can help resolve. Associations in Chile and Mexico were strong enough technically (i.e., had staff and resources to collect and analyse the data) and in terms of internal representation (they could broker compromises among sectors) that then helped negotiators. If insulated from business input, negotiators may in principle reduce protection more than if business is involved, but insulated officials may also just open themselves up subsequently to more intense lobbying if they misjudge the effects of the agreements they sign.

The political benefits for the government seem clearest: business associations were publicly more supportive of regional integration in Chile and Mexico, while their counterparts in Brazil and Argentina have been equivocal, lukewarm or downright critical.[75] Chilean business in fact led the charge for MERCOSUR and pulled the government along with it. In contrast, as one Argentine official lamented, when the going

---

[74] As noted above, our study of six agro-industrial sectors found that the more competitive sectors (beer and sugar) got longer protection in NAFTA than less competitive sectors like chocolate and canned foods (Martínez and Schneider, 2000).

[75] For in-depth analysis of coalition building and political support, see Thacker (2000); Pastor and Wise (1994); Kingstone (1999); and Calvo (2000).

got tough in MERCOSUR after the Brazilian devaluation of early 1999, even the major beneficiaries of MERCOSUR in Argentina did not come out to defend it against the rising chorus of critics. In Brazil and even more so Argentina, visible political support for MERCOSUR is hard to drum up. Had political leaders like Alfonsín, Menem and Collor not been willing to pay the political price, MERCOSUR would probably not have gone far on its own. Moreover, the lack of broad political support for integration in Brazil and Argentina made negotiators more vulnerable to pressures from hostile business, labour or other social groups in favour of exceptions. In explaining the failure of integration between Argentina and Brazil to progress in the late 1980s, Luigi Manzetti wrote that 'governments should actively encourage the creation of a pro-integration lobby that can serve to counterbalance protectionist and isolationist groups... To this end, governments should broaden the base of support for integration by promoting greater involvement of economic interests in shaping the negotiation process...'.[76] Manzetti's recommendations sound very much like what officials were setting up at that very moment in Mexico.

For business the benefits of collaboration were largely more information, and hence greater predictability, on government preferences and plans. In general economists find a strong, positive correlation between investment and policy credibility (or overall political stability).[77] Presumably regional integration is more credible and predictable to business when business has been closely involved in the negotiations, and business should therefore invest more in anticipation of the integration, but isolating the impact of this credibility on investment is very difficult empirically. Some scattered interview evidence suggests that credibility did help business plan investments. Over time, if business feels that government negotiators are sympathetic to business concerns, they may develop a broader trust that economists again think facilitates higher investment. The high rates of investment in Chile in the 1990s, in a period of rapid policy change (though always negotiated) and regional integration, provides some macro evidence for such a correlation.

Carol Wise (1999) argues that post-liberalisation economic performance has varied in the major countries of Latin America according to whether or not governments adopted a pro-active, pro-export, competitive strategy versus a laissez-faire, passive strategy. Chile is the best example of the competitive strategy. The government used tax policy, exchange rates, training, and close business–government relations to increase investment, productivity, and exports. Argentina, in contrast is the most 'passive' case; the government has not used policy

---

[76] Manzetti (1990), p. 136.
[77] See for example Borner et al. (1995); and World Bank (1997).

and close business–government relations to expand exports and raise productivity. Brazil and Mexico are intermediate cases, Brazil because the government pursues multiple strategies and Mexico because policies were laissez-faire but shifted after 1996 to a more competitive strategy. Overall, the competitive strategy for Wise requires close business–government relations — something governments constructed in Chile and Mexico much more than in Brazil and Argentina.

Conclusions

Encompassing business associations in Chile and Mexico had access to government trade negotiators and participated actively in shaping the terms of regional integration into MERCOSUR and NAFTA, respectively. In contrast, peak industry associations in Brazil and Argentina rarely enjoyed easy access and had little influence, especially in the early 1990s when much of MERCOSUR was negotiated. These variations in business–government collaboration over regional integration depend first on government openness to, and sometimes promotion of, collaboration. Beyond idiosyncratic issues of style and personality, government openness to business participation depended on an anomalous mix of strength and weakness. On the weakness side, officials in Mexico and Chile felt they needed the trust and support of business, though for different reasons. In Mexico, technocrats in the de la Madrid (1982–88) and Salinas (1988–94) governments were still trying to overcome deep business suspicions of government that came from the acrimonious 1970s and culminated in the bank nationalisations of 1982. In Chile, Concertación governments (1990–) suffered a historic deficit of trust or confidence and consulted with business nearly every step of the way.

However, this overall vulnerability (as perceived by political leaders) was coupled with the expectation of state (or bureaucratic) strength to withstand particularistic pressures. That is, government officials had both strong political backing to stand up to lobbying and they were also dealing with strong encompassing associations that had incentives to discourage particularistic pressures by member firms and associations. In contrast, presidents (save Alfonsín) in Brazil and Argentina felt less need to assuage business preoccupations, or did so by appointing business executives to the cabinet rather than opening up negotiations to business associations. And, despite moments of overall political strength (Menem especially), leaders in Brazil and Argentina knew that their executive bureaucracies were weaker and more porous. They also recognised that business was more fragmented and hence more likely to infuse negotiations with intersectoral infighting.

The second main variable, therefore, in explaining contrasting patterns of business–government collaboration is prior patterns of business organisation, especially the extent of investment in encompassing associations, both for industry and for the economy as a whole. Why are associations like CMHN and CCE in Mexico and CPC and SOFOFA in Chile so much stronger than the UIA and CNI in Argentina and Brazil, countries which also have no economy-wide encompassing associations? The full answer requires historical institutional analysis on the evolution of encompassing voluntary associations over the course of the past 50 years.[78] The short answer is that SOFOFA, CPC, CCE and CMHN were strengthened by alternating periods of conflict and close collaboration with their respective governments. By the 1980s the collaboration increasingly took institutionalised forms for regular access and input in economic policy-making. This access in turn provided powerful centripetal incentives for business to invest in institutional capacity for their associations. This capacity was very strong by the 1990s in terms of interest aggregation (intersectoral negotiation) and technical staff. Both of these strengths were instrumental in business participation in regional integration.

Looking ahead, there are some grounds to expect business associations to take a more pro-active role in pushing further regional integration. To the extent that firms become more internationalised (on multiple dimensions of trade, ownership and financing), they may start to put new items on the negotiating agenda. Regional integration in the 1980s and 1990s almost always started with some state initiative, not only in the cases of Mexico, Brazil and Argentina considered here, but also Colombia and Venezuela.[79] Subsequent business participation in negotiations, public debates and political support varied, but business rarely took the lead in pushing governments into trade agreements.

The significant exception was Chilean industry, which was more aggressive in seeking new integration opportunities, and business pushed government away from NAFTA to MERCOSUR. Chilean industry had functioned in an open economy for longer than business in the rest of Latin America, and may be a harbinger of more pro-integration orientations and activities by business in other countries. Another indication of increasing business pressure for further integration was the surprise proposal by top Mexican capitalists for dollarising the Mexican economy. In the spring of 1999 members of the elite CMHN met at the presidential residence for their annual announcement of projected investment.[80] However, the president of the CMHN took advantage of the press attention to call for dollarisation. Officials in the Zedillo government quickly dismissed the idea as

---

[78] See Schneider (2000) and (2002).
[79] Giacalone (1999).
[80] *Reforma*, 12 March 1999, p. 1.

impractical. A common currency in any regional bloc is not likely in the near future, but given the damaging consequences of currency fluctuations, the idea is not likely to disappear.[81]

---

[81] Discussions of common currencies have not gone far in MERCOSUR. In late 1987 Sarney and Alfonsín announced the creation of a trading currency, the *gaucho*, that did not prosper (Manzetti, 1990: 119). At the end of his term President Menem also proposed dollarisation for Argentina, though without generating much enthusiasm in the business community.

ABBREVIATIONS AND ACRONYMS

ACTPN	Advisory Committee for Trade Policy Negotiations (United States)
ASEXMA	Asociación de Exportadores de Manufacturas y Servicios (Chile)
CACE	Consejo Asesor de Comercio Exterior (Argentina)
CANACINTRA	Cámara Nacional de la Industria de Transformación (Mexico)
CEA	Consejo Empresarial Argentino
CCE	Consejo Coordinador Empresarial (Mexico)
CEES	Centro de Estudios Económicos del Sector Privado (Mexico)
CGE	Confederación General Económica (Argentina, proscribed 1955–58, 1976–84)
CIM	Consejo Industrial del MERCOSUR
CMHN	Consejo Mexicano de Hombres de Negocios
CNI	Confederação Nacional da Industria (Brazil)
COECE	Coordinadora de Organismos Empresariales de Comercio Exterior (Mexico)
CONCAMIN	Confederación de Cámaras Industriales (Mexico)
CONCANACO	Confederación de Cámaras Nacionales de Comercio (Mexico)
CONUPIA	Confederación Nacional de la Pequeña y Mediana Industria y Artesanado (Chile)
COPARMEX	Confederación Patronal de la República Mexicana
CPC	Confederación de la Producción y del Comercio (Chile)
FCES	Foro Consultivo Económico Social (MERCOSUR)
FIESP	Federação da Indústria do Estado de São Paulo (Brazil)
IEDI	Instituto de Estudos para o Desenvolvimento Industrial (Brazil)

MERCOSUR   Mercado Común del Sur, (March 1991–)

MIA   Movimiento de la Industria Argentina

MIN   Movimiento de la Industria Nacional (Argentina)

NAFTA   North American Free Trade Agreement (1994–)

PICE   Programa de Integración y Cooperación Económica.
                 Also known as ABEIP—Argentine Brazilian
                 Economic Integration Program (1986–91)

PNBE   Pensamento Nacional das Bases Empresariais
                 (Brazil)

SECOFI   Secretaría de Comercio y Fomento Industrial
                 (Mexico)

SNA   Sociedad Nacional de Agricultura (Chile)

SOFOFA   Sociedad de Fomento Fabril (Chile)

SONAMI   Sociedad Nacional de Minería (Chile)

SRA   Sociedad Rural Argentina

UIA   Unión Industrial Argentina

LIST OF INTERVIEWS

Argentina

Blanco Villegas, Jorge. President of UIA. 3 May 2000.

Casullo, Eduardo. Executive Director of UIA. 4 May 2000.

Eurnekian, Murat. UIA. 4 May 2000.

Martínez de Hoz, José Alfredo. Long-standing member (1972–) and
    several times President of the Consejo Empresarial Argentino; Ex-
    Minister of Economics (1976–80). 5 May 2000.

Peña, Félix. Government negotiator (1990–92, 1998–2000). 5 May 2000.

Pons, Dario. Head of MERCOSUR, UIA (1999–). 3 May 2000.

Sourrouille, Juan. Minister of Economy (1985–89). 5 May 2000.

Chile

Baierlein, Hugo. Head of International Trade Department at SOFOFA
    (1995–). 9 May 2000.

Feliu, Manuel. President of CPC (1986–90). 10 May 2000.

Guzmán, José Antonio. President of Cámara Chilena de Construcción (late 1980s); President of CPC (1990–). 9 May 2000.

Lizana Greve, Pedro. President of SOFOFA (1993–97). 10 May 2000.

Marfan, Manuel. former Finance Minister, 8 May 2000.

Mexico

Francisco Calderón, Executive Director of CCE (1976–97). 12 June 1996; 19 May 1998.

Fernando Canales Clariond. Executive Vice-President, IMSA. 19 November 1993.

Aslan Cohen, SECOFI; CFC. 7 June 1996.

Guillermo Güemez. Banamex (1974–92); Director of COECE (1990–95); Director of Banco de Mexico (1995–). 7–8 June 1996.

Santiago Macias, Director General, SECOFI, November 1993.

Roberto Sánchez de la Vara, President of Canacintra (1990–92). 8 June 1996.

Raúl Ortega. Director, COECE. 16 November 1993.

Jaime Serra. SECOFI (1988–94); Minister of Finance (1994). 15 July 1996; 16 July 1998.

Fernando Villareal Palomo. General Director, CAINTRA, Nuevo León. 18 November 1993.

CHAPTER 8

The Politics of Regional Integration in MERCOSUR

Andrew Hurrell

When regional economic arrangements prosper, politics recedes into the background. Through the mid-1990s MERCOSUR saw a sustained growth of regional trade, the expansion of cross-border investment and important changes in the regional strategies of firms. There were certainly voices pointing to divergences in the strategic outlooks or foreign policy 'visions' of Brazil and Argentina and to the lack of institutional solidity. But economic success seemed to be carrying the project forward, establishing MERCOSUR's place as a natural and increasingly important part of the regional political landscape. However, when regional economic arrangements hit troubled waters, as MERCOSUR has done since 1999, politics returns with a vengeance. It is through political mechanisms that economic difficulties become destabilising problems and through politics too that those difficulties may, or may not be, contained, managed or resolved. Definitions of politics are, of course, contested. But whereas economic or economistic accounts lay primary emphasis on interests (of states, of private actors, of bureaucracies), political accounts are concerned with the relationship between three dimensions: power, interest and values.

This chapter seeks to draw together the most important political forces at work within MERCOSUR; to explore how they play into the tensions and frictions that have been such a salient feature of the period since early 1999; but to suggest too the important ways in which they point to the durability of continued regional co-operation. To do this the chapter lays out four stylised, analytical stories of what drives integration and of how one might have expected MERCOSUR to develop through the 1990s. Each one stresses a different dimension of politics — interest groups, institutions, identity, and power and state interest. The idea is not to test these contending theoretical approaches in any detailed way against the MERCOSUR case. It is rather to help identify the ways in which politics might matter and the balance between supportive and disruptive political forces and pressures.

1. Interest Groups and Integration

It is entirely plausible to suppose that interest group activity might be a potentially important factor in regional integration schemes. There is, of course, a large and flourishing literature dealing with interest groups within the European Union (EU). On this account it is only by looking at lobbies and interest groups and at the networks in which they are active that we can understand the development of EU rules and policies into policy domains and into structures of governance that member states acting simply in inter-governmental mode would not have negotiated.[1] In terms of the comparative study of regionalism, Mansfield and Milner highlight preferences among interest groups as one of the factors that explain institutional variation across regional integration schemes.[2] More ambitiously, Solingen has proposed a coalitional model to explain the emergence of regional orders. Her account stresses two broad kinds of coalitions:

> Internationalist coalitions favour economic liberalisation and, where they are strong at home and in their region, they often create co-operative regional orders. Statist-nationalist and confessional coalitions often oppose economic liberalisation and are prone to create and reproduce zones of war and militarised disputes, particularly where they prevail throughout a region.[3]

Coalitional accounts suffer from a number of well-known problems. First, they are often weakest at explaining how regional schemes begin: what causes new coalitions to form and how do they come to coalesce around new regional strategies? Second, even if the analyst can identify liberalising coalitions *post hoc*, how do we know that they were instrumental in actually pressing policy in a particular direction? Third, and most important, coalitional accounts underplay the power and autonomy of the state and the capacity of the state and of state elites to develop and implement their own perspectives and policies towards regional integration. This is likely to be a particular difficulty in the case of MERCOSUR. Brazil's foreign and foreign economic policy had long been associated with a strong and relatively autonomous state and with rather weak input from political parties, business or other societal groups. And in both Brazil and Argentina the development of MERCOSUR coincides with the predominance of presidentialist politics (including presidentialist diplomacy in managing problems within the grouping).

Some accounts, especially of Brazil, give very little space for interest groups. Thus Jeffrey Casson argues: 'But trade policy... has not been changed much by the participation of actors in civil society. These actors might be heard but, with regard to foreign trade policy, they are heard

---

[1] See, for example, Sandholtz and Stone Sweet (1998).

[2] Mansfield and Milner (1999), pp. 602–8.

[3] Solingen (1998), pp. 119–64.

largely to further the goals of policymakers.'[4] Such a claim is a little too hasty, in part because of the general need to guard against an image of the state that is too disconnected from society; but in part because we have, as a matter of fact, seen a good deal of interest group activity around MERCOSUR, especially during the strains of 1994–95 and the far more serious crisis of 1999 and 2000. So we need to isolate the factors that explain when and how interest-group pressures might come to matter.

One factor concerns the availability of different **locations** for influence and the possible role of regional institutions as sites of influence. Does critical interest-group pressure take place at the level of the state or at the level of regional institutions? Once established, regional institutions become significant arenas or venues for public policy-making, for lobbying and for interest-group activity.[5] Interest-groups lobby at the regional level because this is where important public-policy decisions are made. Regional bureaucracies need to develop relations with interest groups in order to establish a stable policy environment, to reduce the risks of opposition and to secure effective compliance. In the case of MERCOSUR, this possibility can be disposed of quite quickly. It is true that MERCOSUR institutions have included provision for broader social involvement (for example the Economic and Social Consultative Forum). Nevertheless, at the level of regional institutions, this has not had any significant impact on important decisions. So if interest groups matter, it is within the national political systems.

A second factor concerns **timing**. Is interest-group pressure important at all stages of regional integration or does it grow over time? Here there is a clear consensus. In the phase of initiation and early development the project was statist in both conception and implementation; government and government agencies (above all the respective ministries of foreign affairs and economy) dominated the process of policy-formation and implementation; and in both Brazil and Argentina, political (rather than economic or commercial) motivations were central to the way in which integration policy was understood. As Vigevani puts it:

> The Treaty (of Asunción) created a structure of decision-making power concentrated in the ministries of foreign relations and economy…whilst other organs and social sectors only participated in the period [from 1991–1995] when summoned to do so and exercising the role of those consulted with the right, in some cases, to make recommendations.[6]

---

[4] Cason (2000), p. 205.
[5] See, for example, Mazey and Richardson (1996).
[6] Vigevani (1998), p. 34; see also p. 52 and 73.

If this is the case, then the question becomes: how far has interest-group politics developed as a response to successful integration? As economic integration develops, so two things happen: first, winners and losers emerge and seek to voice their support or opposition; and second, regional integration increasingly becomes an organising basis for domestic political mobilisation, cleavages and coalitions. Regional developments and regional politics come to shape and define the domestic political landscape.[7] Almost all versions of integration theory argue that high and rising levels of regional exchange will involve shifts in patterns of political mobilisation, both within and (especially in neo-functionalist variants) across states.

This picture clearly picks up important aspects of the MERCOSUR story. There is little doubt about the absence of participation of business in the early phases of the integration process: this is true both of the 1986 bilateral programme between Argentina and Brazil as well as the process of negotiation leading to the Buenos Aires Act of June 1990 and the Treaty of Asunción of March 1991. Equally, as mentioned above, direct input into decision-making remains limited in the first half of the 1990s. Yet, as trade expands, so industrial support grows. Thus, for example, the growth of Brazilian exports in automobiles, chemicals and textiles to Argentina represented an important compensation for the loss of domestic markets as a result of trade liberalisation. Other supportive sectors included soya, cellulose and paper, orange juice, and iron and aluminium producers. In addition, there is a widening of the public debate within Brazil that involves a broader range of actors, including, for example, the trade union movement.[8]

In the case of Argentina, economic reform under President Menem (1989–99) was heavily centralised in and around the executive and with the president playing a particularly central role in the overall direction of foreign policy. Nevertheless, as integration proceeded business voices become more audible. In 1991 to 1994, for example, as the trade balance favoured Brazil, so complaints from Argentine industry grew, reinforcing the arguments of those pressing for a strategy of joining NAFTA. In this period opposition was managed partly by protectionist measures (for example the statistical tax — see Chapter 4) and partly by political bargains whereby Brazil would purchase wheat and petroleum from Argentina. More importantly, the political construction of the exceptions and of the adjustment periods to the common external tariff in the process leading up to the 1994 Ouro Preto Agreement (see Chapter 4) reflected what the administration saw to be politically viable, not least in the light of the positions taken by the Argentine Industrial Union.

---

[7] See Hix (1999); and Hurrell and Menon (1996).

[8] Vigevani (1998), pp. 77–82.

It is clear, however, that there is no automatic rise in interest group influence as integration proceeds. Clearly as governments came to negotiate detailed schemes of co-operation there was a need for consultation with industry on technical and specific issues.[9] Equally, there was a growth of political participation in and across the frontier provinces. However, higher-level influence depended on a further range of factors.

One further factor concerns the stability and **solidity of the regime**. For example, following the 1999 elections in Argentina, the formation of the de la Rúa government, the political difficulties of the new administration, and the protracted economic crisis — all this led (as one might expect) to a weakened government being forced to adapt more directly and more immediately to the demands of those industries and sectors damaged by changing patterns of trade that followed the Brazilian devaluation. A second factor concerns **access to the state**. States are rarely monolithic and the success of interest groups depends heavily on the existence of important figures or groups who share perspectives and have an interest in cultivating ties.

A very good example concerns Brazilian policy in 1994–95 in relation to the automobile regime. After the launch of the Real Plan in mid-1994, the minister of economy (Ciro Gomes) distanced himself from São Paulo industrialists; there was a clear predominance of liberalisers within the government's economic team; and the car industry felt that its interests had been ignored in the negotiation of the Ouro Preto agreements of December 1994. In early 1995, however, the government increased tariffs and imposed a temporary quota on car imports, a decision that owed much to the balance of power within the government and the support of key political figures such as Serra and Werneck who adopted a more traditionalist developmentalist approach and a harder-line towards MERCOSUR.

This leads to the final factor, namely the degree to which influence depends on the broader overlap between the goals of interest groups and the goals of state elites. Throughout the 1990s the Brazilian government saw integration in strategic terms: as a means of taking forward a national industrial project under new global conditions; of increasing international bargaining power; and of attracting foreign capital and direct foreign investment. It consistently refused to allow regional economic integration to threaten established industrial sectors. This picture strengthened with the significant hardening of Brazilian policy after 1994: partly following the reintroduction of a clearer industrial policy; and partly as a result of increased external vulnerability. Thus, in relation to this period, Motta Veiga talks of 'the

---

[9] See Costa Vaz (1999), pp. 69–94.

hegemony of a strategic vision of foreign policy, that is expressed in notions such as 'building a regional power' and in concepts such as 'autonomy of development', to the detriment of considerations informed by a geoeconomic and commercial perspective.[10]

If this is how the state elites view integration, there is a natural coincidence between the interests of powerful business sectors such as automobiles, auto-parts, capital goods, computers or telecommunications and the vision of integration pursued by the executive (and by particular ministers within government). We do not need interest groups to explain Brazilian policy moving in this direction, although they may have played a supporting and reinforcing role. So the hardening of Brazilian policy is not the result of the growing influence of import-competing sectors, pushing policy in a more mercantilist direction. It is rather that foreign economic policy was based throughout the 1990s on an awareness of the need for economic reform and liberalisation but combined with powerful elements of the older developmentalist-nationalist project.

Equally, in the case of Argentina in 1999 and 2000, almost any government would have been concerned with the negative impact of the Brazilian devaluation and would have moved towards administrative controls and counter-measures against the rapid increase in Brazilian imports across a range of sectors from shoes to iron, textiles and paper. Lobbying and interest groups may explain why particular frictions emerge at particular times. But, again, we do not need interest group analysis to understand the overall picture.

It is important to distinguish between weaker and stronger versions of interest-group thesis. In a weaker version the executive maintains overall control of integration, but has increasingly to compromise with important societal interests in order to secure support or acquiescence. This has certainly been an important part of the picture, especially in Argentina and, at times, in Brazil. In the case of Brazil, however, the state has consistently maintained its agenda power and its leading role in terms of policy towards MERCOSUR. In November 2000, for example, the agreement on the dispute within the automotive regime over local content rules that fixed the percentage at 48 per cent was concluded without direct consultation with the most important firms. In a stronger version, interest-group pressure grows sufficiently strong so as to shift executive policies away from their pre-existing goals and preferences. In neither Brazil nor Argentina is there any clear and consistent evidence for this stronger image of interest group success.

---

[10] Da Motta Veiga (1999).

2. Institutionalism

Varieties of rationalist institutionalism dominate mainstream political science theory on international co-operations and regimes and have played a particularly important role in shaping understanding of European integration.[11] Institutionalists base their analysis on a number of core arguments. In the first place, increasing levels of interdependence generate increased 'demand' for international co-operation. Institutions are viewed as purposively generated solutions to different kinds of collective action problems. As Robert Keohane puts it:

> Institutionalists do not elevate international regimes to mythical positions of authority over states: on the contrary, such regimes are established by states to achieve their purposes. Facing dilemmas of co-ordination and collaboration under conditions of interdependence, governments demand international institutions to enable them to achieve their interests through limited collective action.[12]

Norms, rules and institutions are generated because they help states deal with common problems and because they enhance welfare. Second, neo-liberal institutionalism is heavily statist, concerned with ways in which states conceived of as rational egoists can be led to co-operate.[13] In contrast to the pluralist networks stressed by the neo-functionalist, the state is viewed as the effective gatekeeper between the domestic and international. Indeed this approach emphasises how the successful collaborative management of common problems strengthens the role of the state. Thus the dominant strand of rationalist institutionalism has sought to retain neo-realist assumptions, but to argue that they do not preclude co-operation. The aim is to analyse and isolate the particular constellations of power, interests and preferences likely to explain the sources and constraints of co-operative behaviour.

There are various problems that emerge when we try and apply this kind of thinking to the origins and formation of MERCOSUR. In the first place, institutionalists are concerned with understanding co-operation after the parties have come to perceive the possibilities of joint gains. Yet this misses out what is often most puzzling: how historic enemies and rivals come to view each other as legitimate players in a potentially co-operative enterprise or game? Before we get to active co-

---

[11] See Keohane and Hoffmann (1990). See also the most important recent theoretical study of the EU, Moravcsik (1998).

[12] Keohane (1993), p. 274.

[13] Because it takes states as central this is often seen as a realist theory. Unlike realism, however, institutionalism accords a major role to institutions and accepts that sustained co-operation is possible.

operation we have to explain the joint acceptance of co-existence and the willingness of the parties to live together within a framework of agreed legal and political rules. In the case of Brazil and Argentina reaching a situation where institutionalist logics might 'kick in' was not obvious and poses significant theoretical challenges.

Second, institutionalists stress the extent to which co-operation is viewed as a functional and self-interested response by states to the problems created by regional interdependence and they are keen to stress the extent to which increasing interdependence creates the 'demand' for regimes. This idea remains extremely powerful both within institutionalism and in modified versions of neo-functionalism.[14] Yet in this case *rapprochement* developed against a background of, and as a response to, declining regional interdependence. This was true of the first phase of economic agreements in 1986 and also of the moves towards the Treaty of Asunción, which also took place against the background of that first phase having stalled. Regionalism was a political instrument to promote economic exchange, not a response to the problems that it created.[15]

We might acknowledge these limits, but still expect that institutionalist logics would become more salient after MERCOSUR was created in 1991, as economic interdependence grew through the 1990s, and as the scope and intensity of co-operation deepened. International institutions are made up of two elements. In the first place, they are made up of clusters of connected norms, principles and rules (constitutive, transactional and societal). These rules can be analysed and compared across various dimensions.[16] In terms of scope, the MERCOSUR agreements are far-reaching and, as is often noted, go well beyond economic liberalisation to include physical integration, macro-economic co-ordination and shared political values. The 1990s saw substantial progress in expanding the scope of rules, for example the 1997 decision to begin negotiations on freeing trade in services. In terms of clarity and precision, the MERCOSUR treaties are less detailed and precise than, for example, NAFTA. But, while they do contain generalised exhortations to deepening co-operation and deliberately ambiguous formulations, they contain many obligations that have a high degree of clarity and precision. In terms of obligation and authority, the rules are intended to be formally binding and are hence expressed in hard law (although traditional international law rather than any variety of community law). Finally, in terms of the degree to which they formally delegate authority to implement and interpret rules or to make further rules, there is clearly much less delegation than in the EU but arguably

---

[14] Sandholtz and Stone Sweet (1998).
[15] See Hurrell (1995), pp. 258–9.
[16] Stone Sweet (1994), pp. 441–74; and see K.W. Abbott et al. (2000), pp. 401–19.

more than in the case of NAFTA. Partly this follows from the creation of the dispute resolution mechanism (see Chapter 4); and partly from the expectation that, even if strictly inter-governmental, MERCOSUR was always intended not as a static, one-off bargain but as an on-going process of regional co-operation.

Second, rules are organised within stable and on-going social practices. Those practices may have no organisational structure or may be built up into formal inter-state or supranational bodies. In many ways institutionalisation within MERCOSUR is remarkably dense — certainly relative to other forms of international institutions — with a complex network of formal institutions and less formal negotiating and consultation procedures. These involve regular presidential summits; regular ministerial meetings of the Common Market Group; the growth of institutionalised interaction among bureaucratic actors within the Common Market Group and the related networks of working groups; the creation after 1994 of the MERCOSUR Trade Commission and the Administrative Secretariat (see Chapter 4).

On an institutionalist account, rules and institutions such as MERCOSUR make a difference because they alter incentives and affect calculations of interest; provide a way of linking issues; act as focal points for co-ordinating behaviour; reduce transaction costs; and provide information to counter defection and free-riding. They 'matter', then, because they perform valuable functions for states (and private actors). On such an account, for example, the clarity, precision and obligation of the rules governing economic liberalisation are important in promoting transparency, in restraining strategic behaviour and in sending credible signals of a stable co-operative environment, especially to private economic actors.[17] Preferences over outcomes remain stable, but preferences over options and policies can be influenced by the existence and nature of norms and institutions.

It is certainly true that, in some cases, there is a powerful utilitarian logic within MERCOSUR and a link between the problems of increasing interdependence and the necessity of co-operation (dealing with the cross-border spread of cattle diseases in the frontier zones would be a classic recent example). It is also the case that there has been progress on developing and tightening juridical means of dispute settlement. (Again, note that, in comparative institutional terms, the Dispute Settlement Procedure (DSP) established under the Brasilia Protocol is a relatively strong mechanism. Its main weakness is that it does not provide a stable or direct system of redress for private actors.)[18] Thus, although the

---

[17] For an application of this logic to NAFTA see F.M. Abbott (2000), pp. 519–47.
[18] On the DSP in MERCOSUR and beyond see Cameron and Campbell (1998), especially Chapter 13, Marta Haines Ferrari, 'MERCOSUR: Individual Access and the Dispute Settlement Mechanism'.

structure is clearly inter-governmental, there is nothing in principle that would prevent this kind of institution from 'mattering' in the way in which institutionalists expect. Indeed there are elements of the kind of story that can be told in precisely this way.

But, and this is the crucial but, as MERCOSUR has developed, its institutional structures have not functioned as institutionalist theory would expect. Its institutions have not done very much to alter the patterns of power and interest of the member states. Indeed what is striking is the gap between the rather far-reaching commitments of the treaties and the inability of MERCOSUR to discipline the policies of its members, especially of its largest member, Brazil. Moreover, if anything, the institutions have declined in dynamism and become more formally politicised as the 1990s progressed, reflecting both the emergence of specific tensions but also the absence of any overall integrationist logic to replace the great success of automatic tariff reductions in the 1991–94 phase.

Thus, trade and economic interdependence certainly developed very substantially between 1996 and 1999. But so did awareness (especially in Argentina) of a significant failure to consolidate institutions, to ensure rule-compliance, to place limits on state discretion and to narrow the gap between the formal commitments in the black-letter texts of the treaties and their actual delivery.[19] On almost any institutionalist account, one would expect the economic dynamism of MERCOSUR in the 1990s, and the consequent complex spill-over and spill-around problems to which that dynamism gave rise, to have had political effects on the character of MERCOSUR and its institutions. And yet this has not happened, at least not to the extent predicted by the theory.

Does this rather bald and negative summary capture the whole picture? Not quite. For all of the conflicts and frictions, Brazil and Argentina find themselves embedded in a well-structured process of on-going negotiation. Institutions are not strong, but there is a still-expanding process of interaction in which an increasing range of topics have to be negotiated and in which the framework of MERCOSUR is seen as the (at least up to now) unquestioned option. Thus the period since January 2000 has seen many agreements to disagree. Both sides have agreed on the tactic of pushing difficulties into the future and of repackaging problems in order to avoid direct and immediate clashes (as with chickens, sugar and cars). No doubt much of this has to do with the broader structure of power and interests. But institutionalised embeddedness has played a role: dense and regular meetings at many levels; a strong expectation that problems should be resolved within the framework of MERCOSUR; the extent to which the members are able to

---

[19] See de la Balze (2000), pp. 18–24.

pick up on earlier proclaimed objectives (as in the case of macro-economic co-ordination). Institutions, then, may not constrain. They may not even alter incentives. But they do provide a useful menu of alternatives (including formal DSP when it is politically convenient to use, as in the case of chickens in 2000); and a platform for negotiation. Institutions, in other words, provide established and helpful opportunities for purposive action.

But if interest-groups and institutions can only take us so far, then we are pushed back to institutionally-unmediated constellations of state power and state interest (both political and economic). Here it is useful to pick up the two perennial criticisms of rationalist institutionalism: first, a constructivist one that stresses the variability of state preferences and the links between interests and identity; and second, a realist one which stresses the neglect or downplaying of power and of power-political interests.

3. Constructivism

Instead of focusing solely on power and material incentives, constructivists emphasise the importance of shared knowledge, learning, ideational forces, and normative and institutional structures. Understanding inter-subjective structures allows us to trace the ways in which interests and identities change over time and new forms of co-operation and community can emerge. As Wendt puts it: 'Constructivists are interested in the construction of identities and interests, and, as such, take a more sociological than economic approach to systemic theory. On this basis, they have argued that states are not structurally or exogenously given but constructed by historically contingent interactions.'[20] So looking at a specific case such as MERCOSUR, a constructivist account would suggest the need to look much harder at the sources of state interest, at the critical junctures and break points when actors come to redefine and reinterpret the nature of their relations, and at the role of interaction and institutions in reinforcing these redefinitions.

I have argued elsewhere that constructivism does provide very important analytical resources for making sense of the tremendous changes that took place in the international political landscape in the Southern Cone through the 1980s.[21] We cannot tell a convincing story of the Brazil–Argentine *rapprochement* and of the road to MERCOSUR without examining the redefinition of state interests and state preferences as a result of both democratisation and changed understandings of economic and development policy. Moreover

---

[20] Wendt (1992) and (1999).
[21] Hurrell (1998).

interaction and institutions within the political and security field are associated with quite a radical shift in how the two countries view each other and the move from historic rivalry to co-operation. Even if each stage was driven by instrumental calculations, the overall change in the character of relations is larger than the sum of its parts. This is particularly important in explaining Argentine willingness to embark on both increased security co-operation and deep economic integration with the erstwhile threatening hegemon.

And yet in the case of MERCOSUR in the 1990s the picture is rather different. Although not as theoretically precise as institutionalism, constructivism does lead to certain sorts of expectations of how integration processes might develop. Thus we would expect to see deeper economic interaction leading to the construction of stronger institutions, to broader societal integration and to a continuing shift in attitudes and sense of regional community.[22] In contrast to the rationalist stress on integration as a series of discrete bargains among states, constructivism stresses process. Ongoing processes of integration change the context within which interests are understood. Actors are not able to predict exactly where they will end up and the full consequences of their choices. This account focuses on the on-going process of legal and institutional enmeshment and impact of integration on actor properties. Theoretically, the focus is on notions of socialisation and internalisation rather than optimisation. Empirically, we look to see how institutions provide channels for the operation of policy or legal networks through which norms are diffused and internalised (bureaucratically, legally, psychologically). The most convincing accounts of this kind have taken this rather general picture and shown how, for example, dispute settlement processes may be initially based on rational self-interest, but may expand over time into more complex governance systems.[23]

In overall terms, it is difficult to make this sort of picture work within MERCOSUR during the 1990s (in contrast to Europe and to at least elements of NAFTA). And yet it would be wrong to throw out all elements of constructivism. Whether or not we need to use the phrase, it matters how actors interpret the world and how their understandings of 'where they belong' are formed. We do need to be alert to the ways in which both interests and identities are shaped by particular histories and cultures, by domestic factors and by on-going processes of interaction with other states.

In the 1990s, the integration process continued to be shaped by broader sets of foreign policy interests, values, and ideologies in both

---

[22] In contrast to NAFTA and elements of Europe it is very hard to place any weight on transnational social networks and the kind of social transactions that played such an important role in the original Deutschian versions of functionalism.

[23] Stone Sweet (1999); and Sugden (1989).

Brazil and Argentina. The strategic visions of the two countries towards the region diverged sharply. After 1991 the degree of divergence varied in importance and in intensity but never disappeared: in the case of Argentina its heavily ideological stance as a member of the 'western strategic relationship', its very clear pro-US alignment, and its strong commitment to market-liberalism; the view that co-operation with Brazil was important but that 'integration is not identification'; in the case of Brazil, its more ambivalent and ambiguous position especially in terms of relations with the USA. Of course there have been major shifts in the foreign and foreign economic policies of Brazil since the late 1980s. Economically, the rhetoric has been of using MERCOSUR as a 'platform' for modernisation and competitive insertion in the world economy and as a way of bringing together the internal and external agendas of economic liberalisation. But, despite the rhetoric, Brazil remained far more interested in closed regionalism and in adapting older autonomy and power goals to a different environment. And in terms of foreign policy, the elements of continuity are just as striking as the changes, not least in relation to the United States and to its role within South America.

What of the more recent period? Here the optimist would point to the change in foreign policy brought about by the election of de la Rúa in December 1999: the toning down of the stridency of the previous emphasis on close relations with the USA and the proclaimed desire to relaunch MERCOSUR and to give a higher priority to regional relations than was the case under Menem and his foreign minister Guido Di Tella. This would seem to bring the strategic visions and foreign policy values of the two countries more firmly into line with each other. There are, however, some grounds for doubt. The recent period has also seen a greater self-confidence in Brazilian foreign policy and a greater willingness to play an activist, managerial role in the international relations of the region. This has been most visible in the process leading to the presidential summit in Brazil in late August 2000 and in the accompanying rhetoric: more open talk about its leadership role (although disclaiming all hegemonic pretensions); the development of a specifically 'South American' perspective on international matters; and a greater willingness to challenge US policy more openly. This rhetoric found a notable resonance within press and political commentary in Brazil.

Now on a strict interest account one might argue that this is a good thing for Argentina: larger regional agreements, in this case covering more of South America, contain more potential partners and provide the means for diluting the country's direct dependence on Brazil. But, on an identity-calculus, the picture looks rather different: Brazilian self-assertion, in the context of on-going economic frictions, runs the risk of reawakening older suspicions of Brazilian regional ambition; and, even if not intended, an expanded MERCOSUR involves a dilution of Argentina's role at the heart of the regional integration process. How much weight should we attach to these admittedly very 'soft' factors to do with image and identity? They do not in themselves determine outcomes; but they do provide the prism through which questions of power and interest are understood and can have a powerful domestic political resonance; and, as we have clearly seen in Argentina through 1999 and 2000, they work to complicate the domestic politics of managing tensions within MERCOSUR.

4. Power-Political Interests and Hegemony

Although a vast amount of effort has been expended in analysing the general relationship between hegemony and co-operation, links between hegemony and regionalism remain under-theorised. Clearly the existence of a powerful hegemon within a region may undermine efforts to construct inclusive regional arrangements involving all or most of the states within a region. India's position in the sub-continent and the chequered history of Southern African regional integration provide a powerful illustration. But the picture is far more interesting and complex than this. There are at least four ways in which hegemony may act as a powerful stimulus to regionalism and to the creation of regionalist institutions.

First, subregional groupings often develop as a response to the existence of an actual or potential hegemonic power. Thus, in many parts of the world there is a tendency for subregional groupings to form as a means of improving the balance of power vis-à-vis a locally dominant or threatening state. Although varied in scope and character, examples of this include ASEAN (against Vietnam, and more recently China), the Gulf Co-operation Council (against Iran), SADCC (against South Africa). This has historically been the most powerful factor behind political and economic regionalism in South America. Second, regionalism can emerge as an attempt to restrict the free exercise of hegemonic power through the creation of regional institutions. Many would see the position of Germany within the European Community (EC) as the classic illustration of this 'regionalist entrapment', designed to mitigate and manage the unavoidable impact of German preponderance. If European integration was pressed from outside by the threat of the Soviet Union on the one side and by the hegemonic leadership of the USA on the other, it was also explicitly promoted as a means of managing German power. Although the division of Germany mitigated the fears of other Europeans, it certainly did not remove them. Europe needed German economic power to fuel post-war recovery and German military power to counter the Soviet threat. Indeed the specific project of regional integration arose precisely as the preferred means of dealing with this problem: permitting rearmament and economic rehabilitation by tying a semi-sovereign Germany into an integrated network of institutions in both the economic field (EC) and the military (e.g. NATO).

This kind of behaviour is often closely linked to a third possibility, namely the tendency of weaker states to seek regional accommodation with the local hegemon in the hope of receiving special rewards ('bandwagoning' in the realist jargon). Neo-realist theory predicts that this kind of behaviour is most likely when power differentials are very great, when there are few external alternatives to accommodation with the hegemon, and when the small state finds itself in close geographic proximity. Although prompted by actual or potential vulnerability, such a strategy offers the smaller state the possibility of material benefits. Clearly the greater the degree to which the dominant power is prepared to accept a rule-constrained hegemonic order, the more likely is a strategy of bandwagoning for the weak states.[24]

Fourth, the hegemon itself may seek to become involved actively in the construction of regional institutions. On several accounts hegemonic leadership is a necessary condition for successful regional integration. This builds on the various strands of writing on hegemonic leadership and regionalism. Although plausible, cases of this kind often have to be stretched to make the thesis fit (e.g. Mattli's overemphasis on the idea of German leadership in Europe; and the MERCOSUR case where Argentina has consistently been more pro-active than Brazil).[25] And we need to press a good deal further to find out how this kind of link between hegemony and regionalism actually works.

More importantly, large states may well press towards the creation of common regional institutions with smaller neighbours in order to share burdens, to solve common problems, and to generate international support and legitimacy for their policies. To a much greater extent than crude versions of realism acknowledge, states need international institutions both to share the material and political costs of protecting their interests and to gain the authority and legitimacy that the possession of crude power can never on its own secure. And yet powerful states also have more options (choice of different regional forums, of global forums, of bilateralism or unilateralism). Hence, even

---

[24] On traditional realist accounts in which states will always be fearful of unequal power, bandwagoning will be an exception. However, if, as Stephen Walt argues, states seek to balance **threats** rather than simply power and if factors such as ideological commonality and institutionalisation play a role, then accommodation with the hegemon becomes a less anomalous policy. For Walt's modification of the traditional balance of power logic, see Walt (1987) especially Chapter 1. For a restatement of the view that states will always balance unequal power, see Waltz (1993).

[25] Mattli (1999).

when there are potential gains, there is very little incentive to agree to the creation of strong regional institutions that will constrain their autonomy or formal legal sovereignty. Both regionally and globally, the trade-off for powerful states in multilateralism is to invest institutions with sufficient autonomy to be both effective and legitimate on the one hand, while also seeking to maintain as high a degree of control and insulation as possible on the other

Power-political interests have been, and remain, of central importance in understanding the dynamics of MERCOSUR and the relationship between Brazil and Argentina. But regional and global power considerations point in somewhat different directions. Within the region, inequality of power explains a good deal of the character and limits of institutionalisation: first, Argentina's desire for stronger dispute settlement (an active user of dispute procedures before the Brasilia Protocol and active pusher of moves to tighten the DSP system), and a more rule-governed process; and, second, Brazil's reluctance to restrict its own freedom of action and unilateralist tendencies. Thus, as the crisis of 1999 developed, Brazil's dominant response was to offer negotiations and potential compensation on a case-by-case, sector-by-sector basis, rather than a more formal compensatory mechanism or any attempt at structural renovation.

But broader power considerations and the structural political and economic vulnerabilities of both Brazil and Argentina work to reinforce the political logic of MERCOSUR. For Argentina at the end of a period in which it has become clear that the much vaunted 'special' or 'strategic relationship' with Washington is neither very special nor very strategic, and in an economic context of high vulnerability, there are no obvious alternatives. When we add political factors to the country's economic stake in MERCOSUR, there is indeed structural dependency.

Brazilian policy towards MERCOSUR has two faces. On the one hand, it is the largest player and the asymmetry of power gives it the means to press its own interests and to play 'economic hardball'. Thus it has consistently refused to allow regional economic integration to threaten established industrial sectors, and certainly not to constrain national economic policy autonomy. Pressed by domestic industrial lobbies, by the external vulnerability that followed the Asian and Russian crises, but also by the continued existence of a developmentalist project, Brazil has been willing to adopt unilateral protectionist measures, including against Argentina. As with other large states, it has also been resistant to the creation of regional institutions that would constrain its freedom of action. It has shown a penchant for unilateralism, believing that Argentina is economically vulnerable and has few alternative foreign or foreign economic policy options. This tendency to play economic hardball has been consistently visible in the disputes of 1999 and has continued even as the overall mood moved towards damage limitation and the containment of disputes, as in the case of negotiations over the automotive regime.

But, on the other hand, MERCOSUR is extremely important to Brazil's overall economic and foreign policy goals and this provides a major incentive to solve problems, often by means of intense, high-level presidential diplomacy. First, the direct costs of any reversion to rivalry with Argentina would be very high. Second, a prolonged souring of relations would undermine the strategic objective of regional integration: integration as a means of taking forward a national industrial project under new global conditions; of increasing international bargaining power; and of attracting foreign capital and direct foreign investment. Third, MERCOSUR is critical to Brazil's relations with Europe, which continue to rely very heavily on the continued development of the 'region–region'/EU–MERCOSUR ties (although the EU–Mexican agreement launched in 2000 suggests that one should not overdo this point).

Fourth, MERCOSUR provides the political and economic framework for Brazil's broader policy in South America. In October 1993 President Franco proposed that MERCOSUR be expanded into a South American Free Trade Area. In 1996 association agreements were signed with Chile and Bolivia. And at the Summit of South American leaders in Brazil in late August 2000 plans were announced for early negotiations between MERCOSUR and the Andean Community.

Finally, and most importantly, MERCOSUR is central to Brazilian relations with the United States. MERCOSUR was in part a response both to NAFTA and the growing regionalisation of the global economy. The idea of MERCOSUR as a counter-weight, as a negotiating instrument with the United States, has never been far beneath the surface. Brazil, then, has a powerful self-interest in managing the economic and political problems that arise within the grouping, even when these involve concessions to the weaker members.

Overall, the balance of Brazilian interests has certainly provided a strong incentive to resolve tensions. Thus, in addition to intensive efforts to negotiate specific deals, the Brazilian position on institutions has shifted significantly and Brazil has come to see the need for a degree of macroeconomic co-ordination. But it would be wrong to suggest that this pattern of power-political interest makes the management of frictions within MERCOSUR easy. Indeed, while MERCOSUR is central to Brazil's broader foreign policy vision, it is important not to exaggerate the importance of the regional power base in Brazilian foreign policy. On some issues it is clear that the region is not a source of support (as with Brazil's campaign for a seat on the UN Security Council). And it is worth noting that, on economic issues beyond the Free Trade Area of the Americas, Brazil has not been able to make common cause with Argentina and it is noticeable that economic coalitions, especially within the World Trade Organisation (WTO), have become ever more issue- and sector-specific. Outside Europe it has been very hard to maintain regional coalitions within the WTO or other economic fora.

Conclusions

At the time of writing, this analysis of the politics of MERCOSUR points towards its durability, despite the undoubted strains, tensions and conflicts since early 1999. Adversely affected interest groups have clearly been vociferous and have successfully brought economic problems into the political domain. But, in general, they have not been able to dislodge conceptions of interest within the Brazilian and Argentine state that stress the need to continue to manage their relations within the framework of MERCOSUR. Institutions have not developed as institutionalists might have expected and as integrationists might have hoped. Yet they have provided political channels through which conflicts and frictions have been tackled and negotiated. And as constructivists would point out, MERCOSUR does represent a different kind of political space to that which existed in the late 1980s and still more in the 1970s — although older images of mutual distrust have not entirely disappeared.

And yet, even if the overall balance of political interests point towards the containment of conflict, there are very serious dangers. The management of any particular source of friction could very easily get out of hand, given a further serious external economic shock to the region or worsening domestic political weakness, especially in Argentina. Indeed in the short term, the greatest danger is of a power vacuum in Argentina and the inability of the government to develop a consistent policy towards the region. Less dramatic, but just as damaging in the long run, is the potential impact of case-by-case negotiations on the structure of the integration project. Why? First, because successful integration needs a project and a rationale and perhaps a sense of direction. Damage limitation built around an imperfect customs union and weak institutions does not look like a politically saleable, let alone a coherent, regional project. Second, the undoubted need for pragmatism and flexibility in times of stress and the proliferation of case-by-case bargains undermines the formal character of MERCOSUR which, to be sustainable over the longer term, needs to be based on clear and authoritative rules and institutional processes and a generalised expectation that they will be followed. Flexibility and the search for pragmatic solutions in the short term may be achieved at the cost of creating further problems in the future.

CHAPTER 9

US Policy towards Western Hemisphere Integration

Riordan Roett

The election of Governor George W. Bush as president of the United States opened the question of whether or not the new administration would pursue one of the boldest foreign policy initiatives of President Clinton (1993–2001). While both presidential candidates in 2000 supported free trade during the campaign, the future of the Free Trade Area of the Americas (FTAA) is uncertain. Domestic political opposition by labour unions and environmental groups remains strong. The vision promulgated at the Miami Summit of the Americas in 1994 of a trade agreement by 2005 may be difficult to achieve in the short term given the politics of trade in the USA.

The opposition in Congress to granting the president 'fast track' negotiating authority (now known as Trade Promotion Authority), deemed necessary for any successful trade round, remains a key stumbling block. Congressional reluctance, in turn, represents the realities of a series of trends and events since 1994 that were unexpected and probably unavoidable. The first was the emergence of a 'Blue–Green' coalition of organised labour and environmental groups that coalesced during the debate over the North American Free Trade Agreement (NAFTA) in 1993 and quickly consolidated in opposition to NAFTA — and any free trade initiative —following its implementation.

The second was the growing uncertainty in the hemisphere about the probability of implementing the FTAA given the unwillingness of the US Congress to give the president 'fast track' negotiating authority. As part of the shifting attitude in the region, there was nervousness about the position of both presidential candidates — George W. Bush and Al Gore — with regard to further free trade undertakings after the 2000 presidential election. Gore was deeply in debt to organised labour in the American Federation of Labor–Congress of Industrial Organizations (AFL–CIO) because of financial and political support. It was difficult to imagine that the vice president, if elected, would be able to abandon his labour supporters and favour a fast track agreement that lacked labour and environmental safeguards. In a different twist of fate, Bush, if elected, would be unable to free himself from those in his party favourable to free trade (and fast track), but unalterably opposed to linking any agreement to those safeguards. With the United States election now decided, the George W. Bush White House will need to devise a strategy, given the narrow party divisions in the Congress, to attract enough votes for a compromise position on Trade Promotion Authority.

That uncertainty was coupled with a series of perceptual changes within the region about the concept of the FTAA, particularly on the part of Brazil. It also mirrored a resurgence of interest on the part of the European Union in Latin America, which offered, to some in the hemisphere, a reasonable alternative to greater reliance on — or subservience to — the trade and investment interests of the USA.

Finally, the issue of globalisation intersected with these trends and exploded in Seattle at the meeting of the World Trade Organisation (WTO) in November 1999, at the Spring meeting in Washington, DC, of the World Bank and the International Monetary Fund (IMF) in April 2000, and in Prague in October 2000 at the annual meeting of the Fund and the Bank. The situation was further polarised by the intense debate that took place in May 2000 about granting China permanent normal trading privileges. For the Blue–Green Coalition, China represents the embodiment of all their frustrations. To give an authoritarian state with no respect for workers' rights or for the environment permanent trading privileges with the USA was unthinkable. In the end, the final vote favoured China and was strongly supported by the administration and the US business community, but the coalition promised to continue the campaign in 2001.

Free trade is viewed as a tool of international capitalism. Without safeguards for workers and for the environment, free trade is seen as little more than a mechanism for the wealthy to exploit the poor. In this context, trade policy is deemed to be exploitative and inimical with the needs and aspirations of the developing countries. Contrary to the old bipartisan position on trade a decade or two ago, trade policy has come to be seen by some as the worst and most malevolent manifestation of globalisation.

The interplay and overlapping of these trends has redefined the debate in the USA about the efficacy of free trade in general, and about the FTAA specifically. The George W. Bush White House will need to tread carefully to build a new consensus for the FTAA and to outline a new congressional strategy if progress is to be made early in the new administration.

1. The Emergence of the 'Blue–Green' Coalition

It is difficult, today, to remember that since the enactment of the Reciprocal Trade Agreements Act of 1934, the USA has favoured a policy of freer trade as a means of opening the global economy to greater competition. And in the view of most — if not all — participants, this trend was positive and inclusive. Multilateralism was symbolised by the General Agreement on Tariffs and Trade (GATT) and the various 'rounds' of trade negotiations that followed, culminating in the Uruguay Round negotiations in the 1980s and early 1990s. The executive-led trade rounds were facilitated by the almost automatic willingness of the US Congress to grant the president 'fast track' negotiating authority. The sixty-year effort to liberalise world trade culminated on 1 January 1995 with the creation of the WTO.

While the trajectory of trade negotiations favoured free trade, there were always economic and social forces seeking to 'capture' trade policy as a way of mitigating what they saw as the threat from foreign imports. Succeeding administrations, of both political parties, constructed a strategy that shifted responsibility for trade policy from Congress — far more vulnerable to domestic pressures for protection — to the White House. In 1974, as part of the Trade Act of that year, Congress granted the president fast track authority — an up-or-down vote on trade legislation submitted by the White House within 90 days. That authority would be extended routinely for the next 20 years.

Both ends of Pennsylvania Avenue collaborated to maintain the broad legislative-executive consensus on free trade. Congressional committees and the White House trade office (USTR) worked together to balance the interests of industries negatively impacted by imports with those of export-oriented manufacturers, who were typically seen as trade winners.

But, as I.M. Destler has pointed out, this enormously successful system incorporated one major tactical concession to protectionist thinking — it retained the tacit presumption that exports were 'good' and imports 'bad'.[1] The understanding that legitimated the system was that the US would strongly urge its trade partners to grant 'concessions' to its exports, which benefited producers, while downplaying the benefits to import users, who were poorly organised and thus politically weaker. Congress's role in this process was to use new trade legislation to tighten antidumping and other import-regulating laws. Through the decades, White House and congressional leaders became adept at managing this system by playing producer interests against one another and responding to pressures to restrict imports with militant efforts to expand exports.

By being able to limit the agenda to trade barriers at home and overseas, thereby excluding more divisive broader questions of social policy, the process remained bipartisan. While the Democratic left and the Republican right generally opposed trade liberalisation, the leadership of both parties favoured expanded trade. A pragmatic pro-trade

---

[1] Destler and Balint (1999), p. 7.

majority evolved over time and held fast during shifts in control of either branch of government from one party to the other.[2]

A shift in mood began in the 1990s as trade was slowly linked to important national social concerns. It was less and less possible to avoid placing US commercial interests in a broader societal — and political — framework. The enforcement of labour and environmental standards by US trading partners gained salience. And the impact that the rapidly evolving global trade regime might have on the capacity of the USA to strengthen or maintain pro-labour and pro-environmental measures at home drew more attention.

The period was dominated by the debate over Japan Inc., the rise of the Asian Tigers, the yen/dollar ratio, rising US deficits — all of which raised questions about the competitiveness of the US economy. A mood of pessimism dominated the country and a rash of books and articles bemoaned the end of the US era and the appearance of competing and new global economic leaders.

The critical juncture in shifting the terms of the debate was the negotiations over NAFTA. Labour opposed granting President George Bush (1988–92) authority to negotiate a trade deal with Mexico (and Canada), but the administration won the support of swing votes in Congress with a promise to support environmental and labour standards. During the 1992 presidential campaign, candidate Bill Clinton endorsed those goals for the NAFTA negotiations. With labour and environmental side agreements in-hand, President Clinton then won approval in the House of Representatives for the NAFTA legislation on 17 November 1993. Environmental groups generally supported the president; labour was strongly opposed.[3]

While the battle for NAFTA was won, many now think the war for freer trade was lost. The bitter NAFTA debate united a new and often disparate coalition of activist organisations, including grassroots environmental groups, third party and right-wing political organisations, and the AFL–CIO. Following the 1994 implementation of NAFTA, the USTR prepared for the next step in trade liberalisation. To win back the Democratic Party constituents who had opposed NAFTA, USTR suggested that the pending Uruguay Round implementing legislation include the extension of fast track authority, as had been usual in the past; and in mid-1994, the USTR suggested it should include labour and environmental standards.

The US business community, which had strongly supported NAFTA, reacted negatively. Business moved across the House aisle and joined with the anti-standards Republican caucus (the Republican Party would capture control of the House in the November 1994 congressional

---

[2] Destler (1995).

[3] For a detailed analysis of the rise of the activist coalition, see Mayer (1998), Chapter 7.

election). Sensing defeat, the White House dropped the request for fast track extension from the Uruguay Round implementing bill with the intent of re-introducing the request at a later date. The Round legislation was approved on 1 December 1994.

In the late 1980s, free trade still appeared to be potentially feasible. In addition to initiating the NAFTA negotiations, the Bush administration had developed a broader vision of hemispheric integration. The Enterprise for the Americas Initiative (EAI) was announced in June 1990. The EAI comprised a multilateral fund within the Inter-American Development Bank to spur private investment; some bilateral debt relief tied to continued economic reform; and 'free trade' agreements with the ultimate goal of a hemispheric free trade system. The EAI was closely associated with the Bush proposal to create a North American Free Trade Agreement with Mexico. In response to a personal request from President Patricio Aylwin of Chile, the White House also announced that Chile was next in line for a free trade agreement. Preoccupied with the NAFTA negotiations, little substantive progress was made on the EAI before the presidential campaign of 1992. As opposition to NAFTA increased, particularly in labour circles, the administration's tolerance for further trade initiatives diminished.

With the inauguration of the Clinton Administration in January 1993, the campaign to win congressional approval for NAFTA, during the vote that was to take place in November 1993, continued. Immediately after the vote, the White House announced that the vice-president would travel to Mexico and deliver a major speech on US–Latin American relations. The decision was made in the White House to include a proposal for a heads of state summit at a date to be determined. To announce a summit was consonant with President Clinton's frequent statements in 1992 and 1993 that he was committed to freer trade in the Western Hemisphere. Another undertaking that fitted the pattern of presidential free trade thinking was his support for NAFTA parity for the small countries of the Caribbean.

Between the vice-president's announcement in Mexico City in November 1993 and the Miami Summit of the Americas in December 1994 there was a good deal of resistance within elements of the administration to include hemispheric trade integration as the centrepiece of the Summit. The president did not make that decision until a month before the meeting. The FTAA process began in Miami. In the euphoria of the moment, the prime minister of Canada stated that the three amigos would soon be four — it was expected that Chile would quickly be admitted into full NAFTA membership as a sign of the hemisphere-wide support for integration. The expectation was that the administration, following its re-election, would gain fast track approval from Congress.

But the White House kept postponing the request for fast track extension for a number of reasons. The Mexican peso devaluation in December 1994 and the ensuing 'tequila effect' in Latin America soured many in Congress on Mexico and NAFTA and, by extension, the region. It was clear that the new and conservative Republican majority in the House had no interest in bailing out Mexico and little enthusiasm for initiatives that detracted from their domestic agenda.

In the run-up to the 1996 presidential election, the White House did not want to antagonise organised labour — now a major funder of Democratic candidates and of the president. Raising the fast track issue would rekindle the bitter debate of 1993. And by 1995–96, there was increasing criticism from elements in the Blue and Green Coalition that the administration was not serious about the side agreements on labour and environment.

Following his re-election in late 1996, Clinton vacillated. The White House could not decide whether it was worth the fight to build a new trade coalition that would inevitably alienate either business or labour/environment groups. Nothing happened for most of 1997. But as the White House remained undecided, the Asian financial crisis occurred in mid-1997 and an outcry arose against 'emerging markets', 'crony capitalism', and related evils in what was now viewed as a dangerously globalised world economy. For social activists, the crisis in Asia, in which millions were plunged into poverty, was proof positive of their position. The emerging story of the destruction of the Indonesian forests by commercial capitalist development energised the environmental groups. Those fears were confirmed for the growing forces of opposition to freer trade with the Russian default in the summer of 1998 and then the devaluation of the Brazilian real in January 1999.

As this conflict scenario began to unfold, the opponents of NAFTA — and therefore those in favour of labour and environmental standards as protection against globalisation — gathered their forces.[4] A collection of progressive (some would also say aggressive) think tanks and environmental groups — Economic Policy Institute, the Institute for Policy Studies, the International Labour Rights Fund, Public Citizen's Global Trade Watch, the Sierra Club and the US Business and Industrial Council Educational Foundation — published a report entitled *The Failed Experiment: NAFTA at Three Years*. The Report was unrelenting in its criticism of NAFTA:

> more than three years of experience with NAFTA have proven
> that unregulated trade between the US, Canada, and Mexico
> weakens environmental, health, and public safety standards and

---

[4] Rodrik (1997).

threatens public well-being in all three countries... The most serious threat to US workers comes not from foreign competition but from NAFTA itself.[5]

When the White House, in September 1997, finally sent Congress a proposal to renew fast track authority, the Senate appeared receptive. But the House was vehemently opposed, notwithstanding the backing of the trade policy committees and the Republican majority leadership in both chambers. Labour made a vote on the proposal a 'litmus test' for Democrats. Clinton was able to win the backing of about 21 per cent of House Democrats and the president asked the speaker of the House to withdraw the legislation rather than see it defeated in a floor vote. A year later, in September 1998, the speaker re-introduced the legislation and it was defeated 243–180, with just 29 of the 200 House Democrats (14.5 per cent) voting with the president. Bipartisan support for liberal trade was dead. The old coalition was broken and probably it could not be fixed in the near term. The Clinton White House thus abandoned hope of securing fast track, and negotiations on the FTAA continued in a formalistic way but with little political momentum. The George W. Bush administration (2001–) will be confronted with similar realities. While the candidate spoke very positively about the need for free trade negotiations during the 2000 campaign, the balance of forces has changed little.

2. Organised Labour Moves Front and Centre against Free Trade

Organised labour in the USA — and primarily the AFL–CIO Confederation — has long been identified with the Democratic Party. After a period of retrenchment in the 1980s, the confederation emerged in the early 1990s as a powerful lobby and a well-funded organisation on which Democratic candidates came to rely for money and campaign troops. After the Reagan years, in which big business enthusiastically supported Republican candidates, the Democrats began to level the playing field in the 1990s.

Obviously, there are many 'interests' in the dynamic US labour movement. Some unions benefit from trade (longshoremen, teamsters, machinists, for example); others are viewed as trade losers (in the apparel industry, for example). Government employees, one of the largest unions, have little stake one way or the other in trade policy. But the issue that brought labour together in the 1990s was the growing perception that trade *hurts* workers. The slogan that 'trade costs jobs' is a powerful rallying cry with the rank-and-file union members. They have seen industries exposed to foreign competition close plants or

---

[5] See Economic Policy Institute et al. (1997), p. 20.

severely downsize. And while the data indicate that there have been job losses but there has also been job creation, labour argues that the new jobs created are lower paid.

Labour has focused recently on the growing US trade deficits, arguing that the deficits are a clear sign of deindustrialisation — shifting jobs away from US industries that produced traded goods. Closely associated is the argument that trade suppresses wages in particular industries. A third argument is that trade undercuts labour standards. Producers operating outside US law exploit workers with impunity. Exploitation of labour — low wages, long hours and unsafe working conditions — gives goods produced in these conditions unfair competitive advantage in world markets as costs of production are reduced.

From the perspective of organised labour, as business internationalises, the mobility of capital increasingly puts US workers in more direct labour-market competition with their foreign counterparts, and that is inherently unfair to workers worldwide. Thus, the combined impact of these factors — real and imagined — has created a psychosis in the labour movement against the further liberalisation of trade without safeguards that are transparent and enforceable.

NAFTA provided the crucible for organised labour to stand up and be counted. The 'jobs lost' to Mexico became a rallying cry. Even though government studies, and those of independent study organisations, demonstrated that the impact on labour was generally difficult to discern, and only modestly negative when discernible, labour remained unconvinced.[6] But as labour resistance grew, so did the resolve of conservative and business interests to oppose safeguards. The great majority of US trade partners, particularly Third World countries that saw the attempt to bring in labour standards as disguised protectionism, reinforced their stand.

From the viewpoint of US labour, the situation will never improve. A report in 2000 that Fortune Brands Inc. was moving much of its manufacturing capacity to Nogales, Mexico confirmed that pessimism. Cheap labour was one of the motives, the company said. And, of course, US jobs were lost:

> Union members are unhappy with Fortune's move to Nogales. Master Lock's [one of the firms that relocated] Milwaukee work force has been reduced from 1,160 to 350 employees in just over a year, with those left reduced to producing parts for assembly in Mexico.

Does the US labour movement tend to focus more on Latin America

---

[6] US International Trade Commission (1997).

than on the situation of their counterparts in Asia, for example? Probably so. Proximity is one reason. The US labour movement has stronger ties with their Mexican counterparts than with any comparable country in Asia. The Americas loom larger in terms of trade and job creation than do the Asian countries. It is probably inevitable that the Latin American context will remain pivotal for the activities of the US labour movement.

As the debate grew more heated, the leadership of the AFL–CIO saw that it was a potent argument in membership campaigns — and, for the first time in decades, the ranks of the confederation expanded quickly. Democrats in Congress watched the expansion of the organised labour electorate in their home districts with awe and concern. When John Sweeney, elected president of the AFL–CIO in 1996, identified globalisation as the enemy of the American working class, a line in the sand was drawn. Seattle (1999) and Washington, DC (2000) were the culmination of a decade long evolutionary process. Labour took its stand at its biennial convention in Los Angeles in October 1999. By an overwhelming margin, the AFL–CIO approved a resolution demanding changes to NAFTA and fundamental reforms to the global trading system. The director of public policy for the labour confederation stated that 'unless globalisation works for working people, it is not working'.[7]

3. The Environmentalists Mobilise

There was nothing 'inevitable' about the formation of the 'Blue–Green' Coalition. US environmental groups — the greens — were domestically oriented and very successful in forwarding their agenda in the 1970s and 1980s. The broad array of groups lobbied and won approval for the Clean Air Act, the Clean Water Act, the Resource Conservation and Recovery Act, the Toxic Substances Control Act, the Endangered Species Act and a host of related legislation. Not until the negotiations over NAFTA did the environmental community go international.

Underlying the broad concerns of the environmental coalition is a strong belief that market failures provide perverse economic incentives that promote and encourage practices that lead to unacceptable environmental degradation. The coalition is strongly convinced that international economic competition drives down regulatory standards. And it is widely perceived that multilateral trade institutions consistently favour economic over environmental — and social — issues.

Continued, unrestrained economic growth and ever expanding resource use must have a negative outcome for the world environment. Prices in the market deliberately fail to reflect the full costs of pollution, resource depletion, and ecological degradation. International trade

---

[7] Suzman (1999).

regimes embodied in the WTO subvert hard-won environmental laws in progressive states and encourage the regulatory race to the bottom among developing nations competing for direct investment. For the environmental community, international trade is inextricably linked to global economic growth. The rapid expansion of globalisation has very high social and environmental costs and we may already have passed the point where marginal benefits exceed marginal costs.

Governments and the multilateral agencies they create are in collusion. Economic growth at any cost is their mantra. NAFTA emerged to test all of these assumptions. While some moderate groups accepted the US government assurances that environmental safeguards would be included and respected, more radical groups remained sceptical. When the accord was implemented in 1994 the coalition began to evaluate whether or not the promises were kept. The North American Development Bank and the Border Environment Cooperation Commission, which were established in the NAFTA implementing legislation, were supposed to provide subsidised funding for cleaning up environmental damage caused by industrialisation along the border with Mexico. But these institutions have remained under-funded and are viewed as bureaucratically inept. Also, the North American Commission on Environmental Cooperation (CEC), established to implement and monitor compliance with NAFTA's environmental side agreements, has not led to strengthened Mexican enforcement of its existing environmental regulations.

The broad coalition of environmental groups quickly saw organised labour as a well-funded and savvy political actor that could serve as a valuable ally in pursuing complementary interests. While not well co-ordinated, there is a general understanding within the Blue–Green Coalition that trade expansion, globalisation, and the WTO are common threats. Both groups enthusiastically greeted the publication in 1999 of the Public Citizen Global Trade Watch 'Report Card' on NAFTA, which stated that

> NAFTA's proponents promised the pact would create new benefits and gains... The promised benefits — 200,000 new US jobs from NAFTA per year, higher wages in Mexico and a growing US trade surplus with Mexico, environmental clean-up and improved health along the border — have to a one failed to materialise... After five years, NAFTA fails to pass the most conservative test of all: a simple do-no-harm test. Under NAFTA, conditions have not improved; they have deteriorated in many areas. As a result... the only fair grade for NAFTA is a failing one — hard data and real-life examples tell the story.[8]

---

[8] Public Citizen Global Trade Watch (1998), p. 2.

The combined forces of labour and the environmental groups came together in the demonstrations in Seattle, Washington, DC, and Prague. Neither policy-makers in the multilateral institutions nor in the US government appear fully to understand the depth of public backing for the coalition. The foreign policy and trade leadership in the Bush White House will need to carefully evaluate the strength of the Blue–Green Coalition and identify an appropriate strategy to either win them over or neutralise them politically to justify congressional support for fast track legislation.

4. Changing Attitudes in the Hemisphere about the FTAA

For the Latin American countries, Miami and 1994 are history. With the failure, first, to extend NAFTA to include Chile, and, second, with the resurgence of the Brazilian economy and the slow consolidation of MERCOSUR, the major states in the region have begun to reassess their trade and integration strategies. While the FTAA remains within the realm of the possible, it is no longer the major thrust of efforts to better co-ordinate regional integration and trade arrangements.

It became clear very quickly that the election of a conservative Republican majority in the US House of Representatives in November 1994, combined with the impact of the Mexican peso devaluation, in December, changed the terms of the debate almost immediately after the launch in Miami of the FTAA. As years passed, and the Clinton administration procrastinated on seeking fast track authority, a number of developments occurred in the region.

Chile, exasperated, has successfully negotiated bilateral trade agreements with Canada and Mexico. It has recently announced new trade discussions with the European Union. And, in a dramatic initiative, Chile decided in December 2000 to negotiate a free trade agreement with the United States.[9] The administration of President Ricardo Lagos in Chile remains interested in pursuing an FTAA agreement as well.

Former Brazilian Foreign Minister Luiz Felipe Lampreia stated the Brazilian position when he commented that Brazil wants to avoid over-reliance on the FTAA: 'we want to avoid any distortion, we must not take just one route'.[10] President Fernando Henrique Cardoso, responding to the debacle in Seattle in 1999, stated that

> after what happened in Seattle and in the light of the dim prospects of the FTAA, and as a result of the US domestic situation, there will be elections there and some important US

---

[9] Phillips (2000) p. 12.
[10] 'Accord with European Union Avoids FTAA as Only Option to Mercosur', *Gazeta Mercantil Invest News*, 24 June 1999.

sectors have stated their positions clearly — there will be no hope for hemisphere-wide negotiations to get under way in the next two years. Consequently, this will have greater impetus to MERCOSUR negotiations, to the relaunching of MERCOSUR.[11]

And during a visit to Brazil by the president of Uruguay, Cardoso commented:

it is necessary that the axis of development be planned on a regional scale. The use of natural resources, energy ties, and transport should be done with a South American perspective.[12]

The president also called for a continent-wide free trade zone — in his words, a 'little Maastricht'.[13]

It is well known that the USA and Brazil have approached regional integration from very different perspectives. In the planning phase for the 1994 Miami Summit, Brazil was viewed by the US government as an obstreperous partner.[14] But the attitude of Brazil for some years has been to refuse automatically to accept US leadership in hemispheric affairs. The Brazilian position, after the inauguration of the Real Plan in mid-1994, was to recommit itself to the consolidation of the Common Market of the South, MERCOSUR. The USA, prior to Miami, gave little weight to Brazil's pretensions or to the probable success of MERCOSUR. With the immediate devaluation of the Mexican peso, and the concomitant vitality of the Brazilian economy in 1995, Brazil's position took on additional weight and validity. The two countries, while designated as the co-chairs for the final negotiating session in 2003–4, have constantly diverged on tactics as well as strategy.

President Fernando de la Rúa of Argentina, who has called for a strengthening of the common market, has endorsed President Cardoso's support for MERCOSUR. Indeed, his first foreign trip following his election in October 1999 was to Brasilia to meet with President Cardoso and to indicate his interest in strengthening MERCOSUR. After a series of bilateral consultations in early 2000, President Cardoso announced in March — during a state visit of President Hugo Banzer of Bolivia — that a meeting of the heads of state of South America would be scheduled for later in that year. Reflecting official thinking in Brasilia and elsewhere in the region, Brazilian Ambassador to the USA Rubens Barbosa has stated

---

[11] 'Presidents End Mercosur Summit in Montevideo with News Conference,' *Todo Noticias TV,* Buenos Aires, 8 Dec. 1999.

[12] 'Brazil Wants "Little Maastricht",' *Gazeta Mercantil* (International Weekly Edition), 6 March 2000, p. 20.

[13] *Ibid.*

[14] Feinberg (1998).

that:

> it is improbable that, in an election year, we will see any significant
> progress in plans to create a regional common market as Clinton
> promised in the Summit of the Americas. There has emerged a
> great intellectual debate here [in Brazil] about the national
> interest and the strategic interest of the USA. Integration is a
> question of national interest and has nothing to do with security.[15]

The Brasilia Summit, which brought together the heads of state of South
America, strongly endorsed regional and hemispheric trade integration.
A second summit is scheduled to be held in the next year or two to
review the progress made to date in achieving the goals set out in the
final communiqué in Brasilia.

The interest in strengthening MERCOSUR follows a difficult period
from 1999 to 2000. The precipitate Brazilian devaluation of January
1999 created a painful adjustment process for its partners, given the
importance of the Brazilian market for exports from the other members
and associate members. Argentina's financial problems in 2000–01 have
raised questions about that country's enthusiasm, going forward, for a
deepening of the common market concept. And the announcement by
Chile of its decision to postpone full membership in MERCOSUR and to
negotiate a free trade agreement with the United States raises further,
short-term issues regarding the development of MERCOSUR.

But there have been positive signs in MERCOSUR. After a year of
squabbling over trade issues and subsidies, the Argentine and Brazilian
governments reached a landmark agreement in March 2000 on
automobile production that will regulate bilateral trade until 2006. The
deal is especially important for Argentina, since it exports 35 to 40 per
cent of its automotive production to Brazil.[16]

With the new rules, Brazil initially gives up its competitive edge by
accepting limits on exports to Argentina, based on imports. And in a
surprise announcement in early April 2000, Brazil's ambassador to
MERCOSUR stated conversations would begin on the creation of mutual
limitations on subsidies. The discussions are especially intended to curb
regional subsidies that have recently attracted Argentine companies to
Brazil. The issue had become a major political question in Buenos Aires,
with threats of retaliation against Brazil being discussed. While the
agreement does not resolve many of the outstanding issues that need to
be resolved about 'widening' or 'deepening' MERCOSUR, the
automobile deal is very significant, and may prove to be a turning point

---

[15] Raymont, 'Mercosul Pode Se Ampliar Este Ano,' *Jornal do Brasil*, 20 March 2000, p. 7.
[16] 'New Auto Accord with Argentina', *Gazeta Mercantil* (International Weekly Edition),
3 April 2000, p. 20.

in Brazil's willingness to compromise on questions of importance with its associates in the alliance.

Aware of the need to remain committed to the consolidation of MERCOSUR, the presidents met in Florianopolis, Brazil in December 2000. Gathering a day before the summit opened, the finance ministers and central bank governors agreed on a gradual convergence of some macroeconomic targets such as inflation, national debt, and the containment of public sector debt. Annual inflation for the bloc was fixed to a maximum annual five per cent for 2002 to 2005, falling to four per cent in 2006 and then to three per cent .

President Ricardo Lagos of Chile attended the summit in Florianopolis and tried to soothe the feelings of the five other leaders of the bloc over his country's bid to negotiate a bilateral trade agreement with the USA. While declaring loyalty to MERCOSUR, the chief executives of Argentina and Uruguay indicated that they see nothing wrong with Chile's strategy.

With a new determination to advance MERCOSUR, the member-states will need to clarify their approach to trade negotiations in the hemisphere now that the United States election has resulted in a Bush presidency. And the ongoing conflicts between Argentina and Brazil will need to be addressed. In the absence of full membership for Chile, the differences of opinion between Argentina and Brazil may be further exacerbated or it may be an opportunity for a reevaluation of the role of each of the two countries in the regional trading bloc.

5. Latin America Plays the European Card

There has been a resurgence of interest in expanding trade and investment relations with the European Union (EU). This is driven, in part, by a concerted effort of the EU to expand its economic ties with the region. And it is part of the emerging strategy in the hemisphere to keep all of its options open in terms of integration and strategic alliances. This growing debate should not be interpreted as being 'anti-USA'. It is not. But it is a realisation, on the part of the region, that the US trade policy is now driven by a perverse array of coalitions that are suspicious of trade integration schemes with developing countries, since they have a negative impact on workers in the USA and overseas. Inevitably, environmental concerns surface in the debate.

Europe's links to the region are obvious — history, culture and language. Until 1939, European countries were important economic and financial interlocutors with Latin America. Europe's presence receded after 1945 but began to return in the 1970s and 1980s. In 1990, the 'Declaration of Rome' made an explicit commitment to the promotion of integration in Latin America. An Interregional Framework Cooperation Agreement was signed in 1995 with the goal to increase and diversify trade relations. The first meeting of the MERCOSUR–EU Business Forum (MEBF) was held in Rio de Janeiro in February 1999. A meeting of the heads of state and government from MERCOSUR and Chile and from the European Union took place in June 1999. The joint communiqué pledged both groups to further the integration process in all fields of co-operation — political, economic and cultural.[17] The first of three meetings in 2000 of the EU–MERCOSUR Biregional Negotiations Committee was held in Buenos Aires in April. Similar meetings began with the Chilean government in April 2000. Other meetings took place in Brussels in May and in Brazil in November.

On a more concrete level, the European Commission (EC) approved in 2000 a EU–Mexico free trade agreement.[18] It covers industrial tariffs, agricultural goods, and preferential agreements in services, public procurement, investment, competition rules and intellectual property. Under the agreement — hailed in Brussels as the most comprehensive free trade agreement ever finalised — Mexico will phase out import tariffs on all EU industrial goods by 2007, while the EU will extend duty-free access to Mexican industrial products by 2003. Industrial goods account for about 93 per cent of the estimated US$11.3 billion in annual EU–Mexico trade.

After the USA, the EU is Mexico's second largest trading partner, accounting for about nine per cent of goods imported into Mexico and three per cent of exports. Mexico hopes the accord will help diversify its export market, now overwhelmingly dependent on the USA. The EU hopes the deal will greatly increase the competitiveness of EU products in Mexico and give the bloc greater access to the Canadian and US markets.

While the treaty represents Europe's first tariff free entry in the hemisphere, it is not Mexico's burgeoning consumer market that interests car producers and others so much as the gateway it provides into the rest of the hemisphere. Not only is Mexico the third partner in NAFTA, making it the only country outside of Israel to have preferential access to the world's two largest trading blocs, but it also has similar accords with most Latin American countries.

Gazeta Mercantil, reporting on the planning for the April 2000 negotiations between the EU and MERCOSUR, stated that

The EU sees MERCOSUR as the best region for future trade and investment. After observing the consequences of NAFTA... Brussels hopes to maintain the EU as the dominant investor in

---

[17] IDB (1999) p. 89.
[18] 'Brussels Backs Deal With Mexico to Drop Industrial Tariffs', *Financial Times*, 19 Jan. 2000.

Latin America (50 per cent of the total, compared to 32 per cent for the US) and thwart the US FTAA initiative.[19]

The stumbling block, of course, is the Common Agricultural Policy (CAP) of the EU, but the EU foreign trade commissioner commented during a recent visit to Brazil that 'the protection of European agriculture is going to wane in the future, but the rhythm of that change will only come about through a multilateral solution'.[20]

The EU has become an increasingly aggressive investor in the region, led by Spain. That trend will continue and will be spurred even further by the EU–Mexico free trade agreement. The trade issue remains the principal point of contention between the countries of Latin America and Europe. But the search for other options corresponds with the growing sense in the hemisphere that the FTAA, as originally conceived in 1994, is malingering.

6. The Road to Seattle and Washington, DC, 1999–2000

Should the industrial countries — and especially the USA — have anticipated the failure of the WTO meeting in Seattle in November 1999 and the vociferous protest against the semi-annual meeting of the Bank and the Fund in Washington, DC, in April 2000? As the Clinton administration worked to consolidate public support for its trade agenda for Seattle prior to the actual meeting, it appeared to have the upper hand. Corporate and union leaders signed a joint letter on 25 October 1999 that called for a working group to be established within the WTO to study core labour standards and trade. It was the first time both sides had been able to agree on common language. But it was quickly obvious that the consensus was fragile. While the letter made no mention of using trade sanctions against countries with poor labour standards, the AFL–CIO's trade policy director stated clearly that *that* is exactly the goal of the AFL–CIO: 'what we want is the ability to use trade rules to protect worker rights'.[21] A spokesperson for the militant Teamsters commented that 'we in no way agree that the administration's trade policies are good for working men and women. The Teamsters will play a very active role in demonstrations in Seattle.'[22] It was also clear from press reports that many developing countries have fought linking trade and labour and saw the establishment of a working group as the beginning of a move to do just that.

---

[19] 'EU and MERCOSUR Approximate', *Gazeta Mercantil* (International Weekly Edition), 20 March 2000, p. 20.

[20] *Ibid.*

[21] Helene Cooper, 'Corporate, Labor Leaders Both Trumpet Backing for Clinton's Trade-Talk Plan', *Wall Street Journal*, 1 Nov. 1999.

[22] *Ibid.*

A short time before the 25 October letter was released to the press, the AFL–CIO held its biennial convention in Los Angeles.[23] While endorsing Vice President Gore for the Democratic nomination for the presidency — with the critical exception of the Teamsters, the biggest private sector union — the leadership of the confederation was clear in its message regarding Seattle. For the first time, the union organisation held a special session on the negative effects of globalisation. The delegates in Los Angeles declared their commitment to reforming the WTO, and gathered strong support for plans to join environmentalists and consumer groups in a major protest at the start of the trade talks.

Parallel to the AFL–CIO convention, representatives of eight different environmental organisations that had long quarrelled with one another met to co-ordinate their efforts. The new coalition represented groups ranging from the moderate World Wildlife Fund and the National Wildlife Federation to the more liberal Friends of the Earth and the Sierra Club. The coalition stated, 'WTO ministers and the US administration should take heed of the voices being raised, both inside and outside the ministerial proceedings, for legitimate environmental reform'.[24] After a bitter fallout in 1993–94 over NAFTA, the various groups were suspicious of each other. But in 1997, some of the groups joined forces again to oppose fast track authority for the president, saying it lacked environmental assurances. Shared opposition to WTO rules they considered environmentally destructive spurred further collaboration.

As the Seattle meeting opened, it became clear that the street demonstrators from labour and the environment encountered their strongest critics in the representatives of the poorest countries. These delegates abhor the very idea of linking trade liberalisation to environmental standards or to improved labour standards. The situation within the WTO was further polarised when President Clinton, apparently without the knowledge of his White House staff, was quoted in the *Seattle Post-Intelligencer* as saying that 'ultimately, I would favour a system in which sanctions would come for violating a provision of a trade agreement'.[25] This placed the US president in the camp of the protestors. The developing world argued strenuously in Seattle that raising environmental and labour standards and wages in their countries would take away their ability to attract investment and foreign dollars. The diplomats contended that they must compete with cheap labour that, they say, will eventually lead to faster-growing economies and that

---

[23] Burkins, 'Labor to Keep Fighting Clinton on Trade', *Wall Street Journal*, 12 Oct. 1999.

[24] Jim Carlton, 'Environmentalists Present a United Front', *Wall Street Journal*, 2 Dec. 1999.

[25] Steven Greenlowe and Jim Kahn, 'US Effort to Add Labor Standards to Agenda Fails', *The New York Times*, 3 Dec. 1999.

will eventually lead to better labour standards.

Seattle was a personal disaster for the Clinton White House. In his January 2000 State of the Union address, the president had called for a new round of trade talks to go along with the WTO meeting as part of his post-impeachment agenda. But the violence in Seattle, and the anger of the developing countries' representatives over the aggressive defence by the president of the position of the labour and environmental groups, resulted in a public relations fiasco for the White House and an extraordinary setback for further trade talks.

The developing countries' delegates refused to even seek a compromise with the USA. Rather than ending in a stalemate, the meeting actually saw a mobilisation of Third World countries against the protestors — and by extension, the president. India, Brazil and Egypt took the lead to block the creation of a panel that might result in trade sanctions over labour rights. Many ministers from developing countries argued that such sanctions could be disguised protectionist measures that would be used to ban imports from developing countries.

Finally, USTR Charlene Barshefsky wearily announced from the podium that the WTO would take an indefinite 'timeout and find a creative means to finish this job'.[26] Nothing was accomplished at the meeting beyond reaffirming commitments made in 1994 to begin talks on trade in agriculture and services. Ever there, Europe refused to set any deadlines for concluding agricultural talks, a key US demand, nor was any deadline set for liberalising services trade.

Euphoric with the lack of results, the organisers of the Seattle demonstrations targeted the administration's plan to achieve WTO membership for China. To do so successfully required the US Congress to agree to approve normal and permanent trading status for the government in Beijing. As the demonstrators left Seattle, their battle cry was 'China, we're coming atcha'.[27] The second target for 2000, they declared, would be the semi-annual meeting of the World Bank and the IMF in Washington, DC.

It was clear that the White House allowed the meeting to collapse for domestic political reasons. If the administration had left Seattle with a deal that the protestors rejected, it would have reduced support for Mr Gore from two of his traditional backers: labour and environmentalists. On the other hand, the Clinton administration heightened the concern of the developing countries that Washington will attempt to use the WTO for domestic political purposes with disregard for the impact on the poorer states.

---

[26] H. Cooper, R. Davis, and G. Hill, 'WTO's Failure in Bid to Launch Trade Talks Emboldens Protestors', *Wall Street Journal*, 6 Dec. 1999, p. 1.
[27] *Ibid.*

7. China, the WTO and the Politics of Trade

As the fall-out from Seattle and the World Bank–IMF demonstrations continued in April, the administration sent legislation to Congress to grant China permanent normal trade relations (PNTR). A vote in favour would end the 20-year old ritual of annually reviewing China's trade status, putting Beijing on the same footing as most other US trade partners. If approved, the legislation would enable US companies to take full advantage of the market-opening US–China trade agreement negotiated in 1999 as part of China's planned entry into the WTO.

The Blue–Green Coalition immediately moved to oppose the legislation. The *New York Times* stated: 'The American labour movement is mounting its biggest lobbying campaign ever on trade matters in seeking to defeat the Clinton administration's drive to normalise commerce with China.'[28] The arguments on both sides were well known. Administration officials and business executives asserted that the bill would help the US economy and workers by increasing exports to China. In the bill, Congress would approve the administration's agreement with China calling on it to lower tariffs and many trade barriers. And the White House argued strongly that a 'no' vote by Congress would not preclude China's membership of the WTO, and as a full member China would be able to exclude the USA from benefits it extends to other countries in the organisation. The Blue–Green coalition asserted that the deal would not bring about increased exports but an exodus of US factories to China using low-wage Chinese labour to produce for the US market. Once again, the coalition used the example of NAFTA — that is, US jobs exported to Mexico.

At first, it was uncertain whether the administration had the votes in the House of Representatives to approve the legislation. Then, unexpect-edly, both houses approved legislation to promote commerce with Africa and the Caribbean. The approved legislation will lower tariffs and quotas on products from sub-Saharan Africa, the Caribbean and Central America. The legislation received broad bipartisan support for a number of reasons. Some legislators saw it as a way of compensating the Caribbean countries for trade diversion to Mexico after the approval of NAFTA. As always in Congress, the law helped special groups; the measure offers breaks for Israeli nylon woven into Caribbean-made garments and men's suits made with Canadian wool. In a concession to textile manufacturers, the agreement initially caps the volume of duty-free goods at 1.4 per cent of all textile imports. That cap grows to 3.5 per cent over eight years.

While the approval of the Africa, Caribbean and Latin American

---

[28] 'US Labor Leaders Push Hard to Kill China Trade Bill', *The New York Times*, 14 May 2000, p. 1.

trade accord broke the log jam over trade legislation, it was uncertain whether or not it would help the administration secure approval of PNTR for China. The Blue–Green Coalition had opposed the legislation, but not vociferously. The countries were small; there were humanitarian and human rights groups who supported the measure in order to raise living standards in the poorer countries; and the more powerful labour unions were not affected.

The final weeks of the debate about PNTR were highly emotional. Until a few days before the final vote on 24 May, it was not clear that the pro-China lobby had the votes to approve the pending legislation. One issue that helped swing votes in favour was the successful conclusion of talks between China and the European Union on the terms of China's entry into the WTO. It was one of the final steps clearing the way for China's entry into the trade organisation. Supporters of PNTR in Congress pointed out that with the EU negotiations concluded, the USA was the last large trading nation without a full agreement with Beijing.

The final vote was a triumph for the White House. By a surprisingly wide margin, 237 to 197, the Congress voted in favour of PNTR. A larger-than-expected Republican majority delivered President Clinton's last remaining legislative priority: three out of four Republicans voted in favour; two out of three Democrats voted against. While the administration accomplished its goal, it did not necessarily indicate renewed bipartisan support for fast track or for further free trade legislation. Comparing the votes for PNTR with the battle for NAFTA in 1993, the president got 102 out of 258 Democrats to vote for the accord — or 39 per cent . For PNTR, he persuaded far fewer Democrats; 73 out of 211 voting on the bill — or 35 per cent. Ironically, it was the House Republicans who saved the legislation, voting overwhelmingly for PNTR, 164 to 57.

In the end, the president's success had little to do with the bill's economic merits: 'He won over the undecided using a bit of Lyndon Johnson-style vote-buying — one congressman got a zip code for a small town, and two others got a natural gas pipeline near El Paso — and a large dose of Richard Nixon's geostrategy.'[29] And Samuel Berger, the National Security Advisor at the White House, commented 'this was never a fight about the nature of the problem in China. It was a fight about the nature of the solution... It's about whether we best deal with China in a punitive way or by a combination of promoting internal change and external validation of that change.'[30]

---

[29] D. Sanger, 'Rounding out a Clear Clinton Legacy', *The New York Times*, 25 May 2000, p. 1.
[30] *Ibid.*

8. The Implications for the FTAA

Was the successful passage of the PNTR a harbinger for the future of fast track and the FTAA? There are certainly arguments to be made in support of that position. The impasse over trade legislation has apparently been broken with the two victories a few weeks apart. But one must be cautious in reading too much into the trade votes. The first, on Africa and the Caribbean, was highly bipartisan and driven by humanitarian as much as economic concerns. The PNTR vote was a geopolitical and strategic vote. China, for better or worse, is viewed by many in the foreign policy establishment as the most important challenge for US foreign policy in the twenty-first century. 'Getting it right' with China is seen as critical to US leadership and security. That argument has not been made for the Americas — nor will it be made by the next US administration.

The expectation is that the Blue–Green Coalition, badly defeated in the PNTR vote, will turn once again to other free trade initiatives that are more closely linked to home. And the FTAA is an obvious target. While supporters of FTAA will argue that the same bipartisan coalition that backed China should do so for the FTAA, scepticism remains. The debate now returns to the playing field of the coalition. NAFTA will again emerge as the benchmark for support on further free trade initiatives. Congressional districts in which jobs have been lost to Mexico will be targeted. Latin America does not have the same geostrategic importance for the foreign policy establishment as does China. And, perhaps most importantly, PNTR did not require fast track authority. It was a stand-alone law.

This is an important caveat with regard to NAFTA: while labour and environmental groups will continue to criticise the agreement, NAFTA will inexorably deepen and prosper. The private sectors in the three countries remain deeply committed to the concept of an integrated North America. A wide range of non-governmental actors are involved in building bridges across the region. And with the election of Vicente Fox as the next president of Mexico (2000–) the opportunity for further deepening through governmental initiative is highly probable. Both candidates in the presidential race in the USA were strongly supportive of NAFTA as well. Therefore, it is important to differentiate between the hostility of the Blue–Green Coalition and the strong support for NAFTA from groups and institutions that view it as a success.

With the successful conclusion of the debate on PNTR, the FTAA will now become the central trade issue in US politics. While it is not impossible for the next US president to find a means of restoring the traditional bipartisan coalition in favour of free trade, the China vote will not help him do so.

It may be that the recently negotiated free trade arrangement with

Jordan (and one underway with Singapore), which include environmental and labour standards to be enforced by the Jordanian government, will prove to be a suitable compromise. And the Jordan accord will be used as a general framework for the Chile–US negotiations. However, the issue of hemispheric integration is much more salient to the Blue–Green Coalition than security-driven arrangements with small countries like Jordan or Singapore or with a small economy such as that of Chile. We can expect a renewal of the great debate about regional trade integration with the arrival of a new Congress and new president in Washington, DC.

PART 4:
EXTERNAL LINKS

CHAPTER 10

MERCOSUR and the Rest of the World

Ann Bartholomew

The Treaty of Asunción in 1991 established the MERCOSUR trade bloc between Argentina, Brazil, Uruguay and Paraguay. During the transition phase, until 1995, a programme of trade liberalisation was carried out between member countries which led to rapid progress in terms of freeing intra-bloc trade, and establishing a common external tariff (CET). As a result, by the end of the transition period the majority of intra-MERCOSUR trade was duty-free and the volume of trade flows between the member countries had experienced a substantial increase. Nonetheless, prior to MERCOSUR's formation, the majority of trade was with the rest of the world (RoW) and these rapid increases in intra-MERCOSUR trade have led to doubts regarding the degree to which this represents trade creation or trade diversion and the effects that this has had on trade patterns with countries outside the trading bloc.[1]

In fact, the formation of a regional trading bloc can have a variety of effects on trade with non-members as well as members. The theory of economic integration predicts that the formation of a regional trading bloc would be expected to result in increased trade flows between member countries, due to the reduction in intra-bloc trade barriers.[2] This process has occurred within MERCOSUR, with intra-MERCOSUR exports rising from US$3.6bn in 1990 to US$20.4bn in 1998 (Centro de Economía Internacional (CEI) 1999) and falling to US$15.3bn in 1999 due to the Asian crisis and Brazil's devaluation.[3] Nonetheless, at the same time, exports to extra-regional partners have increased from US$42.3bn in 1990 to US$60.4bn in 1998, falling to US$58.9bn in 1999.

Although some of this increase in total trade could be accounted for by the intra-regional trade liberalisation programme, it is unlikely it would fully explain this by itself. In addition, the MERCOSUR countries experienced economic growth during this period, which may account for part of the increase in both intra and extra-regional trade, while

---

[1] Yeats (1996); Tigre et al. (1999); and Hasenclever et al. (1999).

[2] This results in relative price changes as the decrease in tariffs translates into a fall in price of partner country commodities. As a consequence, tariff reductions have the effect of increasing market size and make possible increased production due to the opportunities for reaping economies of scale (El-Agraa, 1994).

[3] Preliminary figures for 2000 suggest that intra-MERCOSUR trade has recovered significantly. See Table A.3 in the Statistical Appendix.

trade creation or trade diversion could also be responsible.[4] Alternatively, external trade augmentation may have taken place due to a general lowering of external trade barriers by all four countries, which would encourage trade with third countries.[5] Lastly, extended trade suppression can result if tariff barriers are higher between member countries than before the formation of MERCOSUR. However, this is unlikely to have happened in the case of MERCOSUR as average tariff levels have fallen.[6] Therefore, a variety of different scenarios may result from the formation of a regional trading bloc.

The new wave of regionalism in the 1980s and 1990s, of which MERCOSUR is a part, professes to be more open, leading not to closed regional groupings but to trade links and alliances with third countries. As a result, it would be expected that a process of trade creation and trade augmentation should take place, leading to the possibility that the formation of a regional grouping could lead to welfare benefits for both member countries and third parties. MERCOSUR itself has objectives in line with those of 'open regionalism', with the intention to use regional integration as a complement to unilateral trade liberalisation and as a result aid in the reinsertion of the member countries back into the global economy.[7] Indeed, prior to the formation of MERCOSUR, considerable trade liberalisation had been carried out unilaterally by member countries and further trade liberalisation was expected to provide additional exposure to foreign competition on a regional basis, which — when completed — would allow domestic producers to be able to compete on international markets. This fits with open regionalism as defined by ECLAC (1994) which has two elements: the first is a process of unilateral trade liberalisation, deregulation and stabilisation that creates more economic dependence between countries, while the second is preferential agreements which enhance this process of economic integration.

Open regionalism involves co-operation with countries outside the trade bloc and MERCOSUR has admitted as associate members Bolivia and Chile. Also, MERCOSUR is currently in trade negotiations with the European Union, the Andean Community and the rest of the Americas

---

[4] Trade creation is the replacement of expensive domestic production by cheaper imports from a partner and trade diversion is the replacement of initial cheaper imports from the outside world by expensive imports from a partner country (Viner, 1950).

[5] External trade augmentation or suppression occurs through the process of implementing a common external tariff. If tariffs are lower than previously, trade augmentation will occur, resulting in increases in trade. If tariff barriers are higher than previously, then trade suppression results in a decrease in trade.

[6] In 1989 Argentina's average tariff was 39 per cent and in 1988 Brazil's average tariff was 51 per cent (ECLAC, 1994). The average common external tariff as of 1999 was 15per cent.

[7] Fuentes (1994); and Manzetti (1994).

for a Free Trade Area of the Americas (FTAA).

MERCOSUR would appear, therefore, to be operating in the spirit of open regionalism. In order to evaluate this in practice, this chapter will examine changes in intra-MERCOSUR trade flows to determine how and why the volume and commodity composition of trade flows have altered since the beginning of the integration process and how this compares with changes in trade flows to external trading partners. This will give some indication as to whether trade flows are being distorted by MERCOSUR. Relations with the European Union (EU) and the North American Free Trade Agreement (NAFTA) are examined, as they have historically been MERCOSUR's main trading partners, while changes in the trading patterns of Argentina and Brazil are analysed as they represent the largest trading partners within MERCOSUR.

Relations with the Rest of the World (RoW) will also be examined through analysing levels of protectionism in MERCOSUR, particularly the common external tariff (CET) and its exceptions, and also by assessing trade agreements that have been negotiated between MERCOSUR countries and third parties. In conclusion, this chapter will then attempt to examine how regional integration in MERCOSUR has affected trade relations with the RoW and to what extent MERCOSUR represents an example of open regionalism.

1. Trade and the MERCOSUR

Table 10.1 illustrates the level of trade increases since the formation of the MERCOSUR trade bloc in 1991, with data shown for each year from 1990 until 1999. It must be noted when considering these figures that trade in 1998 and 1999 was lower than in 1997. This was due to the combined effects of falling commodity prices, a slowdown in private capital flows in the last half of 1998 and weak demand in export markets in Asia and Latin America as a result of the Asian crisis and Brazil's currency devaluation. Nonetheless, not only has intra-MERCOSUR trade increased, but also extra-MERCOSUR trade has risen at the same time. Intra-MERCOSUR exports increased from US$4.13bn in 1990 to US$20.43bn in 1998, although they fell substantially to US$15.3bn in 1999. This represents an average increase of 52 per cent annually between 1990 and 1998. The exception is 1999 when a large decline was experienced for the reasons outlined above. By contrast, extra-MERCOSUR exports rose from US$42.31bn in 1989 to US$60.46bn in 1998, an average increase of only 5.5 per cent annually. Furthermore, in 1998 a similar trend to that of intra-MERCOSUR exports was experienced and extra-MERCOSUR exports fell to US$58.9bn, although the decrease in extra-MERCOSUR exports was less than that of intra-MERCOSUR exports. Therefore, intra-MERCOSUR exports have grown at a significantly faster rate than exports to non-members throughout this time period, although they declined at a greater rate in 1999. In addition, it is worth noting that the value of extra-MERCOSUR exports is still substantially greater than that of intra-MERCOSUR exports.

Imports demonstrate a similar trend, with imports between MERCOSUR members rising from US$4.2bn in 1990 to US$20.9bn in 1998. Imports from non-members increased from US$25.1bn in 1990 to US$74.6bn in 1998. This represents an average increase of 52 per cent annually for intra-MERCOSUR imports and 25 per cent annually for extra-MERCOSUR imports. Both intra- and extra-MERCOSUR imports fell sharply in 1999. Again, extra-MERCOSUR imports are greater in total than intra-MERCOSUR imports.

Table 10.1: Exports and Imports of MERCOSUR: 1990–99
(Billions of dollars)

	1990	1991	1992	1993	1994	1995	1996	1997	1998	1999
Exports Intra-MERCOSUR	4.13	5.10	7.21	10.07	12.05	14.44	17.03	20.70	20.43	15.30
Exports Extra-MERCOSUR	42.31	40.81	43.27	43.98	50.08	56.05	57.91	62.61	60.46	58.90
Total Exports	46.44	45.91	50.48	54.05	62.13	70.49	74.94	83.31	80.89	74.30
Imports Intra-MERCOSUR	4.24	5.25	7.41	9.23	12.03	14.13	17.16	20.69	20.96	16.00
Imports Extra-MERCOSUR	25.06	29.02	33.24	39.20	50.69	65.73	66.28	78.08	74.60	64.00
Total Imports	29.30	34.27	40.65	48.43	62.72	79.86	83.44	98.77	95.56	80.00

Source: Centro de Economía Internacional (1999).

These figures indicate that although trade has risen between both MERCOSUR members and non-members during this time period, trade between members has been growing at a much faster rate than with non-members. Nonetheless, in terms of total trade, MERCOSUR still has a greater volume of trade with the RoW and, as trade has been increasing, this indicates that a CET has not discouraged extra-bloc trade. In fact, a trade augmentation effect may well have resulted, due to the fact that external trade barriers fell during the 1990s as well as internal barriers. This was a result of MERCOSUR countries implementing unilateral trade liberalisation programmes as well as regional liberalisation.

Geographical Changes in Argentine Trade Flows: 1989–99

Since 1989, Argentina has experienced a rapid growth in both total exports and total imports. Total exports have increased by an average of

30 per cent per year between 1989 and 1998 and total imports by an average of 83 per cent during the same time period, showing that growth in imports has clearly outpaced the growth in exports. This is due to the large increase in extra-MERCOSUR imports by Argentina that has not been matched by a correspondingly large increase in Argentine exports to extra-MERCOSUR destinations.

Table 10.2 disaggregates these figures to show differences in rates of export growth between Argentina, its MERCOSUR partners and its major non-MERCOSUR partners. Clearly, the rate of export growth between Argentina and the rest of MERCOSUR between 1989 and 1997 exceeded that to the United States and the European Union. Argentine exports to MERCOSUR rose by an average of 66 per cent a year, to the United States 17 per cent and to the European Union 18 per cent per year. Nevertheless, Argentina's total exports to the rest of the world were almost double those to MERCOSUR in 1998. This indicates that Argentina has remained relatively open to trade with the rest of the world and since 1997 Argentina has experienced an increase in exports to the USA and the EU, while exports have declined to MERCOSUR. During this period (1997–99), intra-MERCOSUR exports fell by 25.8 per cent and extra-MERCOSUR exports by 3 per cent, suggesting that the RoW is still a very important market for Argentina.

Trends in Argentine imports are shown in Table 10.3. Again, imports from MERCOSUR partners increased substantially between 1989 and 1998. Imports from Brazil rose by an average of 109 per cent per year, Paraguay 79 per cent and Uruguay 59 per cent. Furthermore, imports from the USA and the EU have also increased rapidly, with imports growing at a rate of 68.4 per cent a year from the USA between 1989 and 1998 and 76 per cent for imports from the European Union. This indicates that the lowering of tariff barriers internally within MERCOSUR has not significantly inhibited or diverted aggregate imports from countries outside the trade bloc. Both the USA and the EU have been able to take advantage of the general trade liberalisation process. In addition, the general increase in economic growth in Argentina has probably increased domestic demand for imports, and as a result both the USA and the EU have been able to increase their exports significantly. Finally, since 1997, both intra — and extra — MERCOSUR imports have experienced similar declines of 17 per cent and 16.1 per cent, respectively.

Although intra-MERCOSUR trade has grown at a more rapid rate than extra-MERCOSUR trade, the latter is still substantially greater in value terms and has continued to grow in the 1990s, suggesting that a trade augmentation effect may have been experienced in imports. At the same time, Argentina's main external trading partners have been particularly important export markets since 1997, while Argentina's

MERCOSUR trade partners have experienced economic difficulties due to the Asian crisis and Brazil's devaluation.

Table 10.2: Argentine Exports: 1989–99
(Millions of dollars)

Destination	1989	1990	1991	1992	1993	1994	1995	1996	1997	1998	1999
Brazil	1,124	1,423	1,489	1,671	2,814	3,655	5,484	6,615	8,060	7,829	5,720
Paraguay	96	147	178	272	358	499	631	583	619	604	540
Uruguay	208	263	311	384	512	650	654	718	812	828	783
Total Intra-MERCOSUR	1,428	1,833	1,978	2,237	3,684	4,804	6,769	7,916	9,491	9,261	7,043
Bolivia	65	66	115	161	178	192	254	291	457	411	310
Chile	350	462	488	581	592	999	1,475	1,765	1,914	1,697	1,854
United States	1,186	1,699	1,244	134	1,279	1,737	1,804	1,945	2,176	2,057	2,613
European Union	2,518	3,799	4,001	3,784	3,675	3,922	4,466	4,560	3,979	4,586	4,722
Total Extra-MERCOSUR	9,436	10,520	10,001	9,908	9,434	11,035	14,193	15,844	16,773	16,595	16,274
Total Exports	10,864	12,353	11,979	12,235	13,118	15,839	20,962	23,760	26,264	25,856	23,317

Source: Centro de Economía Internacional (1999).

Table10.3: Argentine Imports: 1989–99
(Millions of dollars)

Origin	1989	1990	1991	1992	1993	1994	1995	1996	1997	1998	1999
Brazil	721	715	1,532	3,367	3,664	4,325	4,175	5,326	6,900	7,095	5,600
Paraguay	49	40	40	62	67	63	140	182	320	350	305
Uruguay	99	79	166	247	297	395	279	293	371	522	388
Total Intra-MERCOSUR	869	834	1,738	3,676	4,028	4,783	4,594	5,801	7,591	7,967	6,293
Bolivia	233	236	247	136	106	133	135	136	136	115	40
Chile	111	95	236	395	473	541	514	559	685	710	638
United States	892	820	1,498	2,511	3,124	4,373	4,207	4,719	6,056	6,104	4,946
European Union	1,143	1,124	2,006	3,548	4,287	6,527	6,025	6.902	8,318	8,691	7,124
Total Extra-MERCOSUR	3,331	3,243	6,537	11,195	12,755	16,806	15,528	17,927	22,937	23,470	19,244
Total Imports	4,200	4,077	8,275	14,871	16,783	21,589	20,122	23,728	30,528	31,437	25,537

Source: Centro de Economía Internacional (1999).

Geographical Changes in Brazilian Trade Flows: 1989–99

Brazil has experienced a stronger reorientation of its export trade towards its MERCOSUR partners than Argentina. Table 10.4 below shows that exports to Argentina have risen on average by 95 per cent per year between 1989 and 1998, while exports to Paraguay increased by 38.6 per cent on average per year. Exports to Uruguay have seen a smaller rise of an average 26.3 per cent per year. In contrast, exports to Brazil's external trading partners have risen by a much smaller 4.8 per cent per year during this time period. However, similar to Argentina, between 1997 and 1999, intra-MERCOSUR exports declined by a greater degree than extra-MERCOSUR exports. In fact, Brazilian exports to the USA rose substantially during this period.

Table 10.4: Brazilian Exports: 1989–99
(Millions of dollars)

Destination	1989	1990	1991	1992	1993	1994	1995	1996	1997	1998	1999
Argentina	710	645	1,476	3,040	3,659	4,136	4,041	5,170	6,767	6,747	5,364
Paraguay	323	380	496	543	961	1,054	1,301	1,325	1,406	1,249	744
Uruguay	334	295	337	514	776	732	812	811	870	881	670
Total intra-MERCOSUR	1,367	1,320	2,309	4,097	5,396	5,922	6,154	7,306	9,043	8,877	6,778
Bolivia	229	182	256	333	431	470	530	532	719	670	-
Chile	693	484	677	922	1,100	999	1,210	1,055	1,196	1,031	896
United States	8,047	7,717	6,363	7,059	8,023	8,951	8,798	9,312	9,407	9,754	13,736
European Union	9,954	9,925	10,153	10,868	10,190	12,202	12,912	12,836	14,513	14,744	10,849
Total Extra-MERCOSUR	33,016	30,093	29,313	31,879	33,201	37,637	40,353	40,441	43,943	42,242	41,233
Total Exports	34,383	31,413	31,622	35,976	38,597	43,559	46,507	47,747	52,986	51,119	48,011

Source: Centro de Economía Internacional (1999).

The geographical pattern of imports is shown in Table 10.5. Imports from Argentina rose by 61.9 per cent on average per year between 1989 and 1998. From Paraguay imports rose by an annual average of 4.7 per cent from 1989 to 1997 (due to the Asian crisis and the Brazilian devaluation the level of imports fell significantly between 1997 and 1999)[8] and Uruguay 7.4 per cent. As a total, imports from the rest of the world have risen by an annual average of 27 per cent, but imports from NAFTA and the EU have shown increases of 32.2 per cent and 42.5 per cent, respectively. Again, similar to Argentina, this suggests that NAFTA and the EU have been able to take advantage of the lowering of external trade barriers in MERCOSUR. From 1997 to 1999, total intra-MERCOSUR imports fell by 30.1 per cent, but extra-MERCOSUR imports fell by only 17.2 per cent, indicating that external trading partners are still important markets for Brazil.

---

[8] The Asian financial crisis, which occurred in mid-1997, led to a slowdown in the rate of trade growth not only in Asia but also in the trade performance of all regions.

Table 10.5: Brazilian Imports: 1989–99
(Millions of dollars)

Origin	1989	1990	1991	1992	1993	1994	1995	1996	1997	1998	1999
Argentina	1,297	1,515	1,747	1,833	2,809	3,830	5,570	6,784	8,210	8,028	5,813
Paraguay	360	335	224	191	275	374	531	551	531	349	260
Uruguay	600	594	446	350	440	701	700	931	980	1,048	647
Total Intra-MERCOSUR	2,257	2,444	2,417	2,374	3,524	4,905	6,801	8,266	9,721	9,425	6720
Bolivia	27	34	22	16	19	23	28	61	27	23	-
Chile	549	485	494	478	436	592	1,094	918	995	806	715
United States	4,187	4,432	4,974	4,618	5,163	6,787	10,513	11,829	14,343	13,488	11,871
European Union	3,893	4,602	5,053	4,512	5,543	8,792	13,754	14,088	16,335	16,562	14,989
Total Extra-MERCOSUR	17,772	20,016	20,560	19,972	24,188	31,093	46,756	45,020	51,637	48,034	42,498
Total Imports	20,029	22,460	22,977	22,346	27,712	35,998	53,557	53,286	61,358	57,459	49,218

Source: Centro de Economía Internacional (1999).

Not only has the volume of MERCOSUR trade risen, but at the same time the commodity composition has also altered. These changes will be examined in the next section for Argentina and Brazil, to see if differences have arisen in the pattern of the commodity composition of trade flows between their trade with MERCOSUR and non-MERCOSUR trade partners.

2. The Commodity Composition of Trade

Argentina

Table 10.6 examines Argentine exports to its main trade partners, but disaggregates the data at the one digit Standard International Trade Classification (SITC) level in order to assess in which products increases in trade have occurred and whether similar changes in the commodity composition of trade have occurred with external trade partners. If this is not the case, then it may suggest that a process of trade diversion is occurring.

All Argentine exports to MERCOSUR between 1989 and 1998 have experienced high rates of growth, although some have achieved significantly faster rates of growth than others. The largest increase was in machines and transport equipment, which experienced an average yearly increase of 157.1 per cent. The second largest category was minerals and fuels, with an average growth in exports of 86.4 per cent per year. The third fastest growing export category was raw materials with an average annual increase of 62.3 per cent. This compares to the fastest growing Argentine exports to the RoW which were in miscellaneous manufactured goods with an increase of 367.7 per cent per annum, basic manufactured goods that increased by 48.7 per cent per annum and minerals and fuels with a 45.5 per cent increase per annum. Thus, apart from minerals and fuels, the commodities in which Argentina has seen rapid increases in exports to the RoW are not those that have experienced rapid increases to MERCOSUR.

Table 10.6: Geographic Destination of Argentine Exports at the 1 Digit SITC Level: 1989–98
(by percentage)

SITC	MERCOSUR			NAFTA		EU		RoW	
	1989	1998	1998*	1989	1998	1989	1998	1988	1998
0. Food & Live Animals	39.4	28.3	31.5	26.8	23.5	56.8	59.6	45.0	27.3
1. Beverages & Tobacco	0.2	1.0	0.5	1.3	2.2	1.5	2.1	1.0	0.7
2. Raw Materials	3.2	3.0	6.7	2.3	6.4	12.9	19.1	3.4	6.3
3. Mineral Fuels	5.7	7.3	2.3	11.8	15.0	1.4	0.3	3.3	9.9
4. Animal, Vegetable Oil	3.5	2.4	5.3	4.9	2.0	4.2	3.8	10.4	20.0
5. Chemicals	6.1	9.2	15.0	8.2	10.0	7.1	2.8	6.4	7.5
6. Basic Manufactured Goods	19.8	9.0	17.8	30.0	24.0	12.4	8.1	22.5	16.7
7. Machines & Transport Equipment	15.7	36.4	15.3	5.8	11.3	1.8	3.2	5.2	6.8
8. Miscellaneous Manufactured Goods	4.1	3.4	5.6	8.4	5.5	1.2	1.0	2.7	2.8
9. Non-Classified Goods	2.3	0.0	0.0	0.0	0.1	0.1	0.0	0.1	2.0
Total	100.0	100.0	100.0	100.0	100.0	100.0	100.0	100.0	100.0

* MERCOSUR without managed trade.
Source: Calculated from United Nations COMTRADE Statistics.

Nonetheless, even if Argentina has experienced rapid increases in exports in these commodities, it may be that they still compose only a small percentage of trade; therefore it is useful to examine how the overall commodity composition of trade has altered. Table 10.6 indicates that these increases in Argentine exports have led to changes in the commodity composition of exports to MERCOSUR. In 1989, machines and transport equipment comprised 15.7 per cent of exports; by 1998 it was 36.4 per cent. As a result, basic manufactured goods and food and live animals saw their percentage of export trade fall during this time period. In addition, minerals and fuels experienced an increase in the percentage share of exports from 5.7 per cent to 7.3 per cent, whereas raw materials, which had experienced a rapid increase in exports, saw a marginal decrease in their share. Therefore, an increase in the share of machinery and transport equipment appears to be the most significant change in the Argentine export pattern to MERCOSUR.

However, machines and transport equipment and minerals and fuels are both subject to managed trade agreements between Argentina and Brazil and, as a result, increases in trade are not only the result of tariff reductions due to the regional integration process, but have arisen also from political decisions. For instance, exports of machinery and transport equipment from Argentina were primarily composed of exports of passenger vehicles and lorries to Brazil. This category increased rapidly between 1989 and 1998. In 1989 exports were zero, by 1998 they were US$2.5bn. This was a result of duty-free quotas established under Protocol 21, which regulated bilateral trade in automobiles between Argentina and Brazil during the 1991–94 transition period and was extended further until the end of 2005. In addition, crude petroleum was not being exported to Brazil in 1989, although by 1998 US$523.8m was exported. This stemmed from a strategic decision by Brazil to switch their supply of petroleum imports to Argentina in response to balance of payment problems that Argentina was experiencing. This is a political impact of the formation of MERCOSUR and the majority of trade was between state-owned companies. It is interesting that the Argentine and Brazilian governments' response to trade liberalisation has been to re-regulate trade when the consequences have not been beneficial to them.

Therefore, when comparing changes in the commodity composition of trade flows between Argentina and MERCOSUR and Argentina and the RoW, it is worth examining these trends both with and without the managed trade component to assess to what degree these managed trade agreements have distorted trade patterns.[9] It is notable that, once managed trade has been removed, the commodity composition of MERCOSUR exports in 1998 resembles more closely that of 1989. For instance, machines and transport equipment now represent 15.3 per cent of total Argentine exports to MERCOSUR, the same as in 1989. Minerals and fuels, when adjusted for managed trade, now have a smaller share to that of 1989. Although managed trade also exists in

---

[9] In this study, managed trade is taken to be SITC categories 040 to 047 for cereals, 33 for petroleum products and 78 for automobiles.

cereals, this seems not to have made a difference as the share of food and live animals has fallen from 39.4 per cent in 1989 to 31.5 per cent in 1998. Those commodity categories that have seen their share of export trade increase include chemicals with a shift from 6.1 per cent of exports in 1989 to 15.0 per cent in 1998. The other categories have only experienced very marginal increases. Interestingly, it is now difficult to find much of a 'MERCOSUR' effect as such on Argentine exports.

When changes in the commodity composition of Argentina's exports to MERCOSUR are compared to those with external trading partners, some interesting results occur (see Table 10.6). Argentine exports to NAFTA show a similar change in the commodity composition of trade to that of Argentine exports to MERCOSUR with managed trade included. A decrease by percentage share in basic manufactured goods and an increase in machinery and transport equipment and mineral fuels has occurred. This may well be due to US multinational companies' involvement in these sectors. Their trade has increased as a result of managed trade agreements and, as a result intra-firm trade may well have been created.

In contrast, the commodity composition of exports to the EU has changed very little, with the only notable change being an increase in the share of raw materials and a decrease in the share of chemicals and basic manufactured goods. For the RoW as a whole the share of food and live animals has halved, whereas increases have been experienced with the share of animal and vegetable oil doubling and the share of mineral fuels tripling. Therefore, Argentine exports to the RoW and to the EU are still mainly in primary goods and indeed the share of basic manufactured goods has halved, whereas exports of animal and vegetable oil have doubled.

Imports from Argentina's MERCOSUR partners at the one digit SITC level are shown in Table 10.7. Argentine imports from MERCOSUR displayed a different commodity pattern from exports. The fastest growing import from MERCOSUR was miscellaneous manufactured products, with an average growth rate annually of 225.9 per cent. The second highest growing import from MERCOSUR was machines and transport equipment with an average rate of growth of 197.7 per cent annually. Third were basic manufactured products at 106.7 per cent on average per year between 1989 and 1998. Argentine imports from the RoW increased fastest in the same three commodities: miscellaneous manufactured goods, which increased by 136.9 per cent on average per annum, machines and transport equipment, which rose by an average of 103.2 per cent a year, and basic manufactured goods with a 75.8 per cent increase.

Table 10.7: Geographic Origin of Argentine Imports by Commodity Composition at the 1 Digit SITC Level: 1989-98
(by percentage)

	MERCOSUR			NAFTA		EU		RoW	
	1989	1998	1998*	1989	1998	1989	1989	1989	1998
0. Food & Live Animals	8.2	7.1	9.6	0.9	1.8	0.5	2.0	2.1	2.8
1. Beverages & Tobacco	0.4	0.2	0.3	0.0	0.1	0.2	0.6	0.1	0.4
2. Raw Materials	22.6	5.9	7.9	6.9	3.1	2.3	0.8	7.7	1.9
3. Mineral Fuels	0.6	2.9	3.6	5.5	1.2	2.2	0.8	11.2	2.4
4. Animal, Vegetable Oil	0.3	0.3	0.3	0.1	0.3	0.1	0.2	0.1	0.3
5. Chemicals	26.2	12.3	16.6	34.7	21.5	28.9	17.6	26.2	17.2
6. Basic Manufactured Goods	18.2	21.3	28.7	8.0	7.9	15.0	13.7	11.8	12.7
7. Machine & Transport Equipment	20.6	44.5	25.5	35.8	55.0	45.0	55.0	35.2	51.6
8. Miscellaneous Manufactured Goods	2.2	5.5	7.5	7.8	9.0	5.3	9.3	5.3	10.3
9. Non-classified goods	0.7	0.0	0.0	0.3	0.0	0.5	0.0	0.3	0.4
Total	100.0	100.0	100.0	100.0	100.0	100.0	100.0	100.0	100.0

* MERCOSUR without managed trade.
Source: Computed from United Nations COMTRADE Statistics.

In terms of the total volume of Argentine imports from MERCOSUR, chemicals made up the largest percentage of trade at 26.2 per cent in 1989, which by 1998 had been superseded by machines and transport equipment and basic manufactured goods with 44.5 per cent and 21.3 per cent respectively. Taking out the managed trade component for machinery and transport equipment, the share of Argentine imports of machinery and transport equipment from MERCOSUR still rose from 20.6 per cent in 1989 to 25.5 per cent in 1998. The largest increase, however, is in basic manufactured goods which now accounts for 28.7 per cent of trade. Raw materials decreased from 22.6 per cent of imports in 1989 to 5.9 per cent in 1998. Chemicals also decreased from 26.2 per cent of imports in 1989 to 16.6 per cent in 1998.

Argentina's pattern of imports with the rest of the world and its major trading partners experienced exactly the same trends as shown in Table 10.7. The main shifts are that imports from the NAFTA, the EU and the RoW have decreased in chemicals and raw materials and increased in machines and transport equipment and miscellaneous goods. This suggests that, even though managed trade exists in the machinery and transport sector and external tariffs are still high, external trade partners have still been able to increase their exports of machines and transport goods to Argentina.[10] This again could well be due to the activities of transnational automobile manufactures who have established themselves in Argentina and engage in intra-firm trade. The only significant difference is that basic manufactured goods have experienced a very large increase in percentage share from MERCOSUR once managed trade is taken out. This is not a trend experienced by external trade partners.

These results are interesting as they demonstrate that the shifts that Argentina has experienced in terms of its commodity composition are not unique to its MERCOSUR trading partners. The general shifts that have occurred in Argentine import patterns are not a unique MERCOSUR effect apart from imports of basic manufactured goods, which suggests that Argentina's pattern of imports to external partners has changed in line with that of MERCOSUR. Nonetheless, the pattern of Argentine exports to MERCOSUR is similar to the pattern with NAFTA, but differs for the EU and the RoW, suggesting in this instance that managed trade is distorting export patterns, resulting in a different structure from some MERCOSUR and non-MERCOSUR trade partners.

Brazil

The commodity composition of Brazilian exports is examined at the 1 digit SITC level in Table 10.8. The largest increases in exports to MERCOSUR are in miscellaneous manufactured goods and exports of machinery and transport equipment, which both rose on average by 98 per cent per annum between 1989 and 1998. The third fastest growing sector in terms of exports was basic manufactured goods with a growth rate of 58 per cent.[11] Similarly, the fastest growing Brazilian export to the RoW was miscellaneous manufactured goods, while the other fastest growing exports were beverages at 21.3 per cent and food and live animals at 17.8 per cent.

In terms of the total volume of Brazilian exports in 1989, the largest

---

[10] Under the new automotive regime which was agreed at the beginning of 2000, the external tariff for automobiles imported from third countries will be 35 per cent.

[11] Discrepancies occur between the Argentine figures and Brazilian figures as data are taken from different sources. This accounts for food and live animals being the third fastest growing commodity exported to Argentina from Brazil, but not when Argentine import figures are used.

sector exported by Brazil to MERCOSUR was machinery and transport equipment, followed by basic manufactures and then chemicals. By 1998, with managed trade included the commodity composition was still broadly the same, although machinery and transport equipment had almost doubled its share to 43.7 per cent. Again, once this managed trade is removed, the commodity composition of Brazil's exports is very similar to 1989, apart from a fall in raw materials and a small increase in manufactured goods.

Table 10.8: Geographic Destination of Brazil's Exports by Commodity Composition at the 1 Digit SITC Level: 1989–98
(by percentage)

	MERCOSUR			NAFTA		EU		RoW	
	1989	1998	1998*	1989	1998	1989	1998	1989	1998
0. Food & Live Animals	11.2	7.1	9.2	13.3	11.6	31.7	29.4	16.5	23.0
1. Beverages & Tobacco	0.7	4.1	5.4	1.1	1.2	2.3	4.2	1.8	3.0
2. Raw Materials	11.9	4.1	5.3	0.0	7.8	23.9	26.1	13.5	17.9
3. Fuels & Lubricants	3.8	0.3	0.1	7.1	2.0	0.2	0.2	1.1	0.7
4. Animal & Vegetable Oil	0.4	0.3	0.3	0.4	0.3	0.7	0.5	2.8	2.2
5. Chemicals	19.8	12.7	16.5	9.6	4.2	4.9	4.1	6.2	5.1
6. Manufactured Goods	22.1	21.8	28.3	20.2	23.0	19.8	17.1	32.9	19.5
7. Machinery & Transport Equipment	26.3	43.7	27.1	32.1	34.0	12.8	14.5	21.0	20.6
8. Miscellaneous Manufactured Goods	3.5	5.8	7.6	16.2	12.5	3.6	3.4	2.1	5.6
9. Non-classified Goods	0.3	0.0	0.2	0.0	3.4	0.1	0.5	2.1	2.4
Total	100.0	100.0	100.0	100.0	100.0	100.0	100.0	100.0	100.0

* MERCOSUR without managed trade.
Source: Calculated from United Nations COMTRADE Statistics.

The commodity composition of Brazilian exports to the USA has not changed substantially since 1989. The only changes of note have been a fall in the share of mineral fuels from 7.1 per cent of total exports to two per cent in 1989 and a fall from 9.6 per cent to 4.2 per cent in chemicals.

Miscellaneous manufactured goods have also fallen from 16.2 per cent to 12.5 per cent of Brazilian exports, possibly due to a redirection of these exports to MERCOSUR.

Similarly, the commodity composition of Brazilian exports to the EU has shown even less changes between 1989 and 1998. In terms of exports to the RoW, the share of exports of food and live animals has increased from 13.5 per cent of total Brazilian exports to the RoW in 1989 to 17.9 per cent in 1998 and 16.5 to 23 per cent for raw materials. This may be due to a redirection of exports of basic manufactured goods to MERCOSUR by Brazil.

As a consequence, the major change in the commodity composition of Brazilian exports is the large rise in machinery and transport equipment exported to MERCOSUR. This is not, however, reflected in trade patterns with external trade partners as this is due to the managed trade agreements discussed previously. Once this is removed, then Brazilian export patterns have changed little since 1989 for both MERCOSUR and non-MERCOSUR partners alike. Thus, it is managed trade agreements between Argentina and Brazil that are changing trade patterns between Brazil and its external trading partners. However, once managed trade is excluded, then there is some evidence that Brazilian exports of miscellaneous manufactured and basic manufactured goods to the NAFTA and the RoW may have been diverted to MERCOSUR. This would appear to be an effect of intra-regional trade liberalisation.

Table 10.9 shows Brazil's imports from its MERCOSUR trading partners. The largest increases in Brazil's imports from MERCOSUR were concentrated in machinery and transport equipment with an average increase in imports of 188.5 per cent per year between 1989 and 1998. The second largest increase was in minerals and fuels with average growth rates of 180 per cent per year during this period. In contrast, Brazilian imports from the RoW experienced their greatest increases in miscellaneous manufactured goods with an 87.6 per cent increase per year, then basic manufactured goods with an increase of 40.2 per cent per year and finally an average annual rise of 28.4 per cent for machinery and transport equipment.

In terms of the share of Brazilian imports, food and live animals were overwhelmingly the largest commodity group imported by volume from MERCOSUR in 1989 with 39 per cent. By 1998, the largest sector was still food and live animals, although machinery and transport equipment now had a 33.3 per cent share — an increase from 8.1 per cent in 1989. Again, the increase in machinery and transport equipment was due to significant increases in a few products which were in effect 'managed'. Fuels and mineral imports also grew due to the increase in imported crude petroleum from Argentina.

Table 10.9: Geographic Origin of Brazilian Imports by Commodity Composition at the 1 Digit SITC Level: 1989–98
(by percentage)

	MERCOSUR			NAFTA		EU		RoW	
	1989	1998	1998*	1989	1998	1989	1998	1989	1998
0. Food & Live Animals	39.0	34.0	39.4	3.3	3.3	8.9	2.6	4.7	4.5
1. Beverages & Tobacco	0.2	0.2	0.4	0.0	0.2	0.9	1.0	0.2	0.2
2. Raw Materials	13.9	4.3	8.4	9.5	2.6	3.1	1.0	6.9	5.3
3. Fuels & Lubricants	2.0	7.7	0.6	9.2	4.5	3.3	1.8	29.2	24.7
4. Animal & Vegetable Oil	2.8	2.7	5.5	0.7	0.1	10.8	0.4	0.4	0.4
5. Chemicals	11.8	6.9	13.4	22.8	20.9	27.5	19.4	16.0	14.3
6. Manufactured Goods	18.6	7.8	14.7	9.3	9.4	9.9	12.4	9.1	13.2
7. Machinery & Transport Equipment	8.1	33.3	12.3	37.5	51.7	39.7	55.0	27.4	28.2
8. Miscellaneous Manufactured Goods	3.6	3.1	5.3	7.6	7.4	5.9	6.4	6.1	19.2
9. Non-Classified Goods	0.0	0.0	0.0	0.0	0.0	0.0	0.0	0.0	0.0
Total	100.0	100.0	100.0	100.0	100.0	100.0	100.0	100.0	100.0

* MERCOSUR without managed trade.
Source: Calculated from United Nations COMTRADE Statistics.

Imports from the RoW have not altered in the same manner as imports from MERCOSUR in terms of the commodity composition, either with or without managed trade. A large rise in the share of miscellaneous manufactured goods has resulted and a smaller increase in basic manufactured goods. Imports of miscellaneous manufactured goods only rose slightly from MERCOSUR and those of basic manufactured goods fell. Imports from NAFTA increased from 37.5 per cent of imports to 51.7 per cent in machinery and transport equipment, probably — as noted in the section on Argentina above — due to the activities of multinational companies and the intra-firm trade generated by them. The share of minerals and fuels has decreased from 9.2 to 4.5 per cent of total imports, but apart from those two changes little change in import patterns has occurred with NAFTA. Similarly, imports of machinery and transport equipment from the EU have risen substantially with their share of imports rising from 39.7 per cent in 1989 to 55 per cent in 1998, probably for the same reason. Therefore, the pattern of imports for the EU and the NAFTA are nearer that of Brazil's trade with MERCOSUR including managed trade.

This is significant as Argentina's main changes in the commodity composition of trade were in imports and this change was then reflected in similar changes in imports from external trade partners. The only exception was basic manufactured goods in which imports rose rapidly from MERCOSUR but not from other trading partners. For Brazil, imports have altered in the same manner for MERCOSUR, the EU and for NAFTA, but not for the RoW. In exports, external trade partners have not displayed the same trends as Brazil's trade with MERCOSUR. Thus, it seems that managed trade agreements have changed export patterns between Argentina and Brazil, particularly in the automobile sector, a trend which has not been reflected in exports to third countries. Furthermore, Argentina appears to have less divergence in patterns of commodity trade with its trading partners than Brazil during this period.

3. MERCOSUR and Trade Policy for the Rest of the World

Although tariff barriers have fallen rapidly during MERCOSUR's existence, MERCOSUR has been termed an imperfect customs union. Protectionism still exists in some sectors and, despite the elimination of most tariff barriers, non-tariff barriers still remain. This obviously has an impact on external trading partners. This section, therefore, examines MERCOSUR's trade policy and evaluates the effect that it has had on third parties.

Levels of protectionism reduced sharply in MERCOSUR countries during the late 1980s and 1990s due to the implementation of unilateral tariff reduction programmes. The simple average most favoured nation (MFN) tariff for MERCOSUR fell from 41 per cent in 1986 to 12 per cent by 1996 (IDB, 1999) and since January 1995 a common external tariff (CET) has been implemented with a tariff structure ranging from zero to 20 per cent (with only automobiles outside this range). Furthermore, Ethier (1998) has noted that additional preferential tariff reductions agreed by MERCOSUR are smaller than the MFN tariff reductions and, as a result, there has been a substantial reduction in the average level of protectionism to external countries as well as within MERCOSUR. As the analysis of trade patterns has shown, this has appeared to have resulted in a process of trade augmentation, whereby third countries have been able to take advantage of average tariff reductions and have increased their levels of exports to MERCOSUR, thus expanding trade. It should also be noted that increases in economic growth are also likely to have encouraged trade. This suggests that MERCOSUR is likely to be less trade diversionary than other regional integration schemes, as a low CET should not discourage imports, even if the least cost producer is outside the bloc.

Despite this, the CET is still to date incomplete in terms of its implementation and some sectors have remained highly protected from competition from the outside world. As a result, each MERCOSUR country is able to levy its own tariff on these products. Convergence to a common level of 14 per cent has been agreed in principle for capital goods. For computers and related software and telecommunications equipment a 16 per cent external tariff must be implemented by 2006.

As discussed previously, the automobile sector has been an area where it has proved difficult to reach an agreement on a common trade policy and automobiles have been dealt with under a separate managed trade regime. This was granted during the 1991–94 transition period and then amended in 1996 when Brazil felt trade in automobiles was becoming unbalanced in Argentina's favour. This agreement allowed for tariff free imports of vehicles on the understanding that imports matched exports. It was envisaged that this agreement would be transitional and an agreement for a new automotive regime was expected to come into force on 1 January 2000. However, this was postponed due a lack of agreement.

In the event, the transition period towards free trade was extended until 31 December 2005. In the interim period, a MERCOSUR Automotive Policy was agreed with a CET of 35 per cent for automobiles from third countries and the elimination of all quotas.[12] In addition, Argentina will converge with Brazil on external tariffs for trucks and buses by the sixth year of the agreement, which in practice means an increase of Argentine tariffs to 35 per cent. In the case of tractors, convergence from 19 per cent for Brazil to the Argentine level of 14 per cent will be achieved by the sixth year. Furthermore, a system has been introduced to phase out the compensation system which operated under the previous managed trade system.

Clearly, this new transitional regime represents an increase in the general level of protectionism and the CET of 35 per cent on automobiles that will remain after 2005 is well above the average tariff level. Nonetheless, although high tariffs have been levied on the automobile sector, as the analysis above has shown, both the NAFTA and the EU have managed to increase their trade flows in this sector.

Sugar has been another area where little progress has been achieved in establishing either a common external trade policy or free trade. Argentina levies a 23 per cent tariff for intra-MERCOSUR imports and 39 per cent for extra-MERCOSUR partners, which also rises with a specific tax calculated on the basis of international sugar prices.[13] Intra-bloc free trade has been difficult to negotiate as Argentine producers

---

[12] INTAL (2000a).
[13] INTAL (1999).

argue that government policies for sugar/alcohol production give a cost advantage to Brazilian producers. Despite the signing in December 1998 by Argentina and Brazil of an agreement to lower Argentine sugar tariffs, negotiations towards a common internal and external sugar policy appear to be stalled.

In addition to some sectors not being included within the CET, the average CET itself was raised, further increasing the level of external protection. In 1997, the MERCOSUR Council approved Argentina's proposal to raise the CET 'temporarily' by three percentage points from 12 to 15 per cent. This was an Argentine response to instructions from the World Trade Organisation to abolish its statistical surcharge of three per cent on imports. Thus, the increase in the CET meant that Argentina's external tariff remained the same and for the other MERCOSUR countries it increased (Paraguay and Uruguay were opposed to the measure and only applied it selectively). This had a negative consequence for external trade partners who saw levels of protectionism against their exports increase. The three percentage point increase was finally phased out at the beginning of 2001.

Although MERCOSUR has been generally successful in reducing tariff barriers, non-tariff barriers (NTBs) still remain and indeed new NTBs have been introduced which have affected members and non-members alike. Brazil introduced a system of prior import licensing in 1998 and also a new system of customs valuation.[14] Argentina in 1999 adopted new import control mechanisms and new import quotas for textile and clothing products and anti-dumping duties on imports of steel laminates from all countries. In these instances, both countries have been non-discriminating in terms of applying import restrictions on MERCOSUR members and non-members alike.

4. MERCOSUR and Trade Agreements with the RoW

In line with the principle of open regionalism, MERCOSUR has been willing to admit new associate members while at the same time negotiating preferential trade agreements with third parties.[15] Chile gained associate membership in 1996 that resulted in the establishment of a MERCOSUR–Chile free trade area, with a commitment to remove tariffs on all goods over a ten-year period, except for a small number of commodities where duties will remain for 15 to 18 years. The agreement includes rules of origin, transport, investment services, intellectual

---

[14] This led to a dispute within MERCOSUR which went to the dispute settlement system, where it was judged to be incompatible with customs union rules (see Chapter 4).

[15] ECLAC (1994) states that one of the requirements of open regionalism is to 'apply moderate levels of protection against third party competitors and favour the use of common external tariffs' and 'the new entry of new members should be facilitated', particularly 'important natural trading partners'.

property and investment. Bolivia also gained associate membership in 1997 and a MERCOSUR–Bolivia free trade area came into existence which again will lead to the elimination of tariffs on all goods. Concluding these agreements with these two countries was important to MERCOSUR due to their geographical proximity and high levels of trade already established with Chile and were part of the 4 + 1 principle under which MERCOSUR has negotiated preferential trade agreements.

Additionally, MERCOSUR has looked to sign preferential trade agreements with other trade blocs. An inter-regional Framework Co-operation Agreement was signed between the EU and MERCOSUR in December 1995. This was designed to initiate a process of increased economic co-operation, enhance political dialogue and prepare the way for future trade liberalisation between the two areas. Negotiations began at the end of 1999 and were widened in 2001 to include tariff reductions and conditions of access for goods and services, although no date has been set for the conclusion of the talks. Despite internal pressure within the EU, particularly from France who wished to see a delay of the talks due to worries over the effect on the Common Agricultural Policy, all sectors will be included.[16] Both sides expect to gain from a preferential trade agreement. MERCOSUR would like to see better market access for agricultural products, whereas the EU would like to see a lowering of tariff barriers for industrial imports and perceives the main business opportunities to be in the service sector. In addition, the EU is keen to counter the influence of the USA in Latin America and in particular the FTAA initiative. A European Commission study estimates that benefits from free trade and a substantial lowering of tariff barriers in agriculture would amount to approximately US$6bn for the EU and US$5bn for MERCOSUR.[17]

MERCOSUR also signed a Framework Agreement on Trade and Investments with the Central American Common Market. The main objective of the agreement is a co-operation programme to promote trade, investment and the transfer of technology. A similar agreement of co-operation was signed between MERCOSUR and Canada in June 1998, with the aim of expanding trade and investment and to strengthen economic relations. These agreements did not allow for a programme of tariff reductions, as this would occur within the framework of the FTAA negotiations.

MERCOSUR has usually negotiated as a bloc, but difficulties in renegotiating old trade agreements between MERCOSUR members and the rest of Latin America has led to a break with the 4 + 1 principle. This has resulted in perforation of the CET. In 1997, negotiations began with Mexico when bilateral accords expired. Mexico favoured the formation

---

[16] Bulmer-Thomas (2000).
[17] IDB (1999).

of a free trade agreement, whereas MERCOSUR wanted to multi-lateralise the bilateral preferences as MERCOSUR did not want to include electronic goods and the automotive sector or agricultural and agro-industrial goods.[18] Due to these issues remaining unresolved, Argentina, Paraguay and Uruguay re-established tariff preferences with Mexico under the original complementarity agreement which was to be extended until the end of 2001.[19] Furthermore, this resulted in Mexico extending tariff preferences to them as compensation for preferences given by Mexico to other NAFTA members. Brazil did not renew its agreement as the government felt that there was not enough reciprocity offered under the complementarity agreement. This further undermined the CET.

Similarly, although a Framework Agreement was signed between MERCOSUR and the Andean Community in April 1998, negotiations ran into problems as the Andean countries were not prepared to allow significant preferential treatment for some agricultural and related products, whereas MERCOSUR wanted the agreement to cover the entire tariff schedule. This resulted in an inability to reach a free trade agreement by the deadline of 31 March 1999. Due to this, Brazil separately negotiated a temporary tariff preference agreement with the Andean Community. Although it is not a FTA it allowed for up to 100 per cent reductions on import tariffs for 2,700 selected products. At the South American presidential summit in 2000 Brazil persuaded its MERCOSUR partners to restart talks with the Andean Community with a view to create a South American Free Trade Area (SAFTA). However, this objective remains a distant dream.

The conclusion of the agreements discussed above indicates that MERCOSUR is actively pursuing a policy of widening the integration process both within and outside Latin America. This appears to fit very much into a strategy of open regionalism apart from in a few sectors, notably automobiles where a deliberate policy has been put in place to keep markets closed. Furthermore, these trade agreements with external trading partners reduce the likelihood of trade diversion, as having to purchase imports from higher cost producers outside the bloc is then less likely and thus the welfare benefits are greater. The main problem is perforation of the CET, rendering the customs unions ever more imperfect and increasingly reducing MERCOSUR to little more than a FTA.

---

[18] *Ibid.*

[19] The most common type of ALADI accord is the 'Economic Complementarity Agreement where trade in goods is either liberalised for some goods only or for all. Therefore many of these agreements are in fact free trade agreements' (INTAL periodic notes).

Conclusions

This chapter has shown that since its formation MERCOSUR has remained relatively open to third countries. Despite rapid increases in intra-regional trade, the volume of external trade is still large and in particular a large rise in imports from outside MERCOSUR has been experienced. This suggests that a trade augmentation effect has resulted with third countries taking advantage of unilateral trade liberalisation and a return to economic growth in the region resulting in an expansion of trade.

Nonetheless, in certain sectors protectionist tendencies have emerged and managed trade agreements between Argentina and Brazil have altered trade flows in automobiles and fuels, leading to an increase in trade between the two countries. In automobiles, exports to MERCOSUR face high rates of protection and will continue to do so even after a CET is introduced in 2006. Interestingly, in some instances, both NAFTA and the EU have adapted to this and experienced similar increases in their trade flows in these commodities, probably due to the activities of MNCs in these sectors. If this managed trade is excluded from the figures then the commodity composition of Argentine trade with both the RoW and MERCOSUR has changed very little since its formation. However, Brazil has appeared to have experienced some shift in export patterns with a redirection of some exports of manufactured products from the RoW to MERCOSUR. Thus, the intra-MERCOSUR trade liberalisation programme appears to have had little effect on the commodity composition of trade flows and as such has not had a great effect on trade with third parties. It is the managed trade agreements designed to control internal trade that have had the most influence on the commodity composition of trade in both intra and extra-MERCOSUR trade.

Therefore, it would appear that generally MERCOSUR is operating in the spirit of open regionalism, as trade with the RoW has increased substantially albeit not at the same rate as intra-MERCOSUR trade. Even in sectors where managed trade agreements have distorted trade, similar changes in the pattern of imports have been observed in trade with the NAFTA and EU in some instances, particularly in trade with Argentina. Thus, trade expansion appears to be occurring with external trade partners, probably due to the fact that average tariff levels have decreased for external trade partners as well as for MERCOSUR members.

The introduction of new trade barriers or increases in them in recent years is of concern, as this means average levels of protection have risen. In addition, the non-inclusion of some sectors in the CET disadvantages external trade partners, particularly in the case of automobiles where the CET will be significantly higher than for other commodities. Finally, the negotiation of trade agreements with other countries and regions also indicates a willingness to liberalise trade arrangements with trading partners other than MERCOSUR. Therefore, overall, the trade policy of MERCOSUR suggests an approach to regional integration that fits into the framework of open regionalism.

CHAPTER 11

Central America: Towards Open Regionalism or Towards an Opening without Regionalism?

Pablo Rodas-Martini[1]

Open regionalism is understood to be a process of regional integration that contributes to a successful insertion into the world economy, that is to say, a process which goes hand in hand with multilateral liberalisation. The question which arises in relation to Central American intra-regional trade today is whether the Central American Common Market (CACM), which has throughout its long history suffered a series of ups and downs, is framed within this paradigm of open regionalism, or whether, on the other hand, it is being overtaken by globalisation and thus becoming an opening without regionalism.

This chapter combines a microeconomic (Section 1) and a macro-economic perceptive (Section 2) in order to try to answer the above question. For the former, a survey was made of 45 Guatemalan industrial companies, many of which exported to Central America.[2] Although the sample is small, it does allow us to separate out intra- and extra-regional commerce, from the business point of view. I used trade statistics from SIECA (the CACM Secretariat) and the UN Economic Commission for Latin America and the Caribbean (the TradeCAN software) for the purpose of estimating the indicators needed to measure tendencies in intra- and extra-regional trade. The chapter concludes with some final considerations.

1. A Microeconomic Perspective

The results of the survey are clear. A microeconomic vision of regional integration transmits a positive and optimistic message: the market should be Central America and not only Guatemala. Existing barriers to intra-regional commerce may be bothersome, but not impossible obstacles for Guatemalan companies to overcome. Changes in recent years may not have done irreparable damage to the integration of the area; on the contrary, they may even have provided incentives. The future looks more optimistic than the present: the FTA with Mexico will not do irreparable damage to sales in Guatemala or to exports from

---

[1] The author wishes to thank Paola Gabriela Enriquez for her assistance in obtaining the interviews.
[2] The questionnaire and the names, industrial classification and products of the companies can be found in www.asies.org.gt

Central America. [3] In brief, the trade opening of the area in the last decade and a half should not have affected regional integration.

To these optimistic expressions must be added two elements of scepticism. First, the companies interviewed are by definition companies that have survived regional integration — successful companies, with the exclusion of companies that could not meet the challenges; the latter simply can no longer be interviewed. Second (and more important), the choice of companies interviewed was not random. They were taken from the directories of AGEXPRONT (the association responsible for promoting agricultural exports) and the Chamber of Industry of Guatemala and tended to be companies that had an export department, that is, the sample was biased towards such companies. Perhaps a different result might have been obtained if the selection of companies had been made on the basis of the telephone directory.

Table 11.1: Basic Profile of Companies Interviewed

1. How long have you been in business?			
More than 40 years	Between 11 and 40 years	Between 5 and 10 years	Less than 5 years
17.8%	66.7%	13.3%	2.2%

2. How many permanent workers do you have?		
More than 100 workers	Between 31 and 100 workers	Between 5 and 30 workers
73.3%	20%	6.7%

3. What products do you manufacture?		
Goods for final consumption	Intermediate goods or raw materials used by other companies	Both
57.8%	35.6%	6.7%

4. Regarding your principal product, what share of the Guatemalan market to you have?				
More than 90 %	Between 66% & 90%	Between 33% & 65%	Between 10% & 32%	Less than 10%
4.7%	23.3%	34.9%	30.2%	7%

Table 11.1 provides basic information on the companies interviewed. The results can be summarised as follows:

- Most of the companies interviewed are relatively mature. Many of them may have risen out of the process of import substitution carried out at regional level by the Central American countries.

---

[3] Guatemala, together with El Salvador and Honduras, signed a free trade agreement with Mexico in 2000.

- The companies are large in terms of workers employed (according to the pattern of employment in Central America).
- Most of the companies produce goods for final consumption, although an appreciable number manufacture intermediate products or raw materials, for other companies.
- Their markets in Guatemala range from quasi-monopolistic to very competitive, with companies mostly having a market share ranging from ten per cent to 90 per cent.
- The companies interviewed tend to be established companies, with knowledge of the national and Central American markets, and which have survived the trade opening of the area.

The companies depend strongly on inputs and raw materials imported from outside the Central American area, followed by a dependence on local inputs and raw material (see Appendix 1 to this chapter). Most of the companies interviewed export to other Central American countries. Most of the companies consider that exporting to Central America is as difficult as exporting outside the area. A further considerable number of companies think that it is simpler to export to Central America. However, there are companies (the minority) who think that it is simpler to export to the rest of the world.

The companies tend to export the same products that they sell in Guatemala. However, an appreciable number of companies export a smaller range of their products (their most successful products). More than 60 per cent of companies interviewed said that their sales to Central America in recent years have grown faster than their sales in Guatemala; only 16 per cent indicated the opposite. This result could be due to macroeconomic reasons (e.g. improvement in the growth of the GDP of neighbouring countries), commercial reasons (e.g. reduction of customs duties) or microeconomic reasons (e.g. part of the company's growth strategy). The reasons given by those companies for which the opposite was true are in general more subjective and would explain the conservatism of some companies that prefer to stay in known markets rather than venture into new markets (see Appendix 1).

It is evident that the companies interviewed are leaders in exports to Central America, as this represents almost 30 per cent of their total production. The companies mention a number of obstacles to exporting to Central America. There are still bureaucratic restrictions in both Guatemala and the importing countries, and there are transport and security problems. The companies interviewed have taken many measures to increase their exports to Central America. These improvements could be classified as technological, training, logistical and promotional.

The sales are mainly in US dollars. This means that sales to Central

America are not yet carried out in local currency. Most of the exports are transported overland, which is not surprising given the relatively short distance between countries, but which in turn reflects the need for a road infrastructure in perfect conditions. There is practically no movement of trade by sea. Most of the companies reported that it is the same exporting to one country or another. However, 30 per cent said that they perceive differences from one market to another.

Companies from other Central American countries are not seen as strong competitors in the Guatemalan market. Some 50 per cent said that most of the competition comes from other national companies, close to 30 per cent said that it came from companies outside the region, and seven per cent said that they have practically no competition. This changes when it comes to evaluating competition in the markets of other Central American countries. In this case, it is considered that the greatest competition comes from extra-regional companies or from companies in those same Central American countries.

The companies interviewed believe that their exports to Central America will grow more rapidly (or at least at the same pace) than sales in Guatemala. Less than ten per cent believe that the opposite will occur (see Appendix 2 to this chapter). This is due to a perception that there is a need to consolidate in new markets and that there is an opportunity to expand in such markets. Many of the companies already could be responding to their own strategies for the regionalisation of sales more than to a local strategy which sees exports as simply as an outlet for excess production.

Most of the company representatives interviewed believe that the FTA with Mexico will only affect some of their sales or will not affect them at all. Close to 20 per cent believe that it will affect them significantly. This is combined with the perception of the majority (more than 60 per cent) that the FTA will make it possible to start (or increase) exports to Mexico. In this case, however, there is an appreciable number of companies (close to 40 per cent) that believe that they will not enter the Mexican market.

It is claimed that both the government and private sector entities (in particular, AGEXPRONT) are taking concrete measures to increase exports to Central America. (This of course does not mean that there are no further actions to be taken.) No less than 100 per cent of the companies interviewed (and which answered the last question) expressed optimism in regard to their companies' future exports to Central America.

2. A Macroeconomic Perspective

Regional integration was seriously affected by the political and economic difficulties of the last two decades. The return to democracy and subsequent economic recovery in the 1990s contributed to improving intra-regional trade (see Tables A.4 and A.5 in Statistical Appendix), despite the fact that, in parallel, there has been a strong reduction of customs duties vis-à-vis the rest of the world.

Table 11.2: Intra-Regional Trade (as % of Total Trade)

	1970	1975	1980	1985	1990	1995	1996	1997	1998	1999	2000
Costa Rica	21	19	20	12	8	10	9	9	12	7	8
El Salvador	30	25	31	19	21	24	26	17	28	29	30
Guatemala	29	20	21	13	15	16	16	18	19	18	19
Honduras	19	11	11	6	7	15	15	14	17	17	17
Nicaragua	25	23	28	6	13	21	21	21	26	30	27
CACM	24	20	22	12	13	16	16	16	18	16	17

Source: On the basis of SIECA statistics.

The improvement in intra-regional trade, however, is modest. Intra-regional trade as a share of total trade has not reached the levels of the 1970s (see Table 11.2), and the situation is even less favourable if one takes into account the omission of two very dynamic but not integrationist phenomena: *maquila* (which do not appear in SIECA's trade statistics) and the exports of INTEL (a recent phenomenon).[4] One should also add that Costa Rica tends to diverge from the rest of the area: intra-regional trade represents a smaller and smaller share of total trade (see Table 11.2).

The new Central American integration of the twenty-first century will be modest (as a percentage of total trade) but stable for a considerable number of producers. Although they must still face the acid test of the FTA with Mexico and a possible Free Trade Area of the Americas by 2005, it could be said that an appreciable segment of Central American companies has already found a niche in the regional market and not just in the domestic market.

Despite the modest value of intra-regional trade, the Central American countries maintain relatively strong trade links among themselves. If there were a 'neutral' relation, the trade concentration index would have a value of one.[5] However, it reaches much greater values (see Table 11.3). Geographical proximity, in other words, appears

---

[4] The INTEL factory in Costa Rica has been responsible for a large increase in exports to the rest of the world in the last few years.
[5] The percentage participation of intra-regional trade would be equal to the total trade of Central America in world trade.

to be an important determining factor of the trade pattern for the Central American countries.

Table 11.3: Trade Concentration

	1980	1985	1990	1995	1996	1997
Trade concentration index	83	51	80	75	75	75

Source: Author's calculations based on SIECA and WTO.

There is also a big difference in the degree of concentration (i.e. the share of the main export in total exports) when comparing trade with the rest of Central America and trade with the rest of the world. Exports to industrialised countries[6] show a greater concentration than exports towards developing America[7] as evidenced by the comparison of maximum values and standard deviations (Table 11.4).[8]

Table 11.4: Degree of Concentration of Central American Exports

	1986	1988	19990	1992	1994	1995	1996
Exports to Industrialised Countries							
Max.[1]	42.2%	31.7%	25.9%	23.6%	19.7%	19.8%	20.1%
SD	3.16	2.71	2.34	2.05	2.00	1.99	2.00
Exports to Developing America							
Max.[1]	12.4%	11.7%	10.8%	9.9%	8.8%	8.3%	8.3%
SD	1.04	1.03	0.98	0.95	0.93	0.91	0.91

[1] Percentage participation of principal export product to this market.
Source: Author's calculations on the basis of TradeCAN.

Exports, however, directed at industrialised countries and those which go to developing America show appreciable stability over time (Tables 11.5a and 11.5b). The matrices of correlation of the Spearman rankings present relatively high values in both cases. It is noteworthy, however, that the correlations tend to be slightly higher in more recent years (e.g.

---

[6] Taken as a proxy for exports to the rest of the world.
[7] These exports had to be used as a proxy for intra-Central American exports, as the TradeCAN software does not include this breakdown.
[8] It is obvious that the proxies used are not the most fortunate for approximating exports to the rest of the world and exports to Central America. This location places in the wrong group exports towards non-Central American Latin American countries. Of the total exported to Latin America, these non-Central American exports represent close to 45 per cent for Costa Rica, 12 per cent for El Salvador, 29 per cent for Guatemala, 19 per cent for Honduras, 20 per cent for Nicaragua and 30 per cent for Central America as a whole.

1994–96 or 1992–94 in relation to 1988–90 or 1986–88), which suggests a certain consolidation of the export sectors both towards industrialised countries and developing America.

Table 11.5(a): Matrix of Correlations for Exports from Central America to Industrialised Countries

	1986	1988	1990	1992	1994	1995	1996
1986	1.000	0.923	0.861	0.840	0.797	0.794	0.783
1988		1.000	0.937	0.888	0.858	0.856	0.842
1990			1.000	0.936	0.897	0.887	0.879
1992				1.000	0.930	0.897	0.891
1994					1.000	0.972	0.957
1995						1.000	0.991
1996							1.000

Source: Author's calculations on the basis of TradeCAN.

Table 11.5(b): Matrix of Correlations for Exports from Central America to Developing America

	1986	1998	1990	1992	1994	1995	1996
1986	1.000	0.963	0.924	0.919	0.901	0.875	0.863
1988		1.000	0.965	0.944	0.925	0.904	0.895
1990			1.000	0.973	0.938	0.916	0.907
1992				1.000	0.966	0.943	0.932
1994					1.000	0.989	0.978
1995						1.000	0.996
1996							1.000

Source: Author's calculations on the basis of TradeCAN.

The average tariff has fallen appreciably in each Central American country. Its value is under eight per cent in four countries, and only reaches 11 per cent in the case of Nicaragua (see Table 11.6). Costa Rica has a less stable tariff structure (the standard deviation is almost double that of the other countries), with a maximum tariff of 253 per cent. Both Costa Rica and Guatemala have close to 50 per cent of their tariff schedules at 0 per cent tariff. The data in Table 11.6, however, are limited to recording nominal tariffs, without taking into account the value imported under each schedule. If the tariff is re-estimated by taking the imported value in each schedule, the following approximate results are obtained: there is a fall in the average tariffs of Costa Rica (-33.5 per cent), El Salvador (-11 per cent) and Guatemala (-25 per cent) and an increase in those of Honduras (11.4 per cent) and Nicaragua (15.2 per cent).

Table 11.6: Tariff Situation in Central America, 2000

	# Tariff[1]	Min.	Max.	Avg.	SD	Mode	% min.[2]	% max.[2]
Costa Rica	7769	0%	253%	7.2%	13.8	0%	48.5%	0.1%
El Salvador	5885	0%	40%	5.6%	7.9	0%	2.6%	0.1%
Guatemala	5953	0%	28%	7.6%	8.7	0%	46.1%	0.4%
Honduras	5913	0%	70%	7.8%	8.0	1%	0.2%	0.1%
Nicaragua	6232	0%	195%	10.9%	7.5	5%	1.9%	0.0%

[1] Number of tariff schedules.
[2] Refers to the percentage of customs schedules which have minimum (maximum) tariffs.
Source: http://www.iadb.org.

3. Conclusions

Regional integration in Central America has not led to trade diversion — there has been a continuing reduction of customs duties in relation to the rest of the world — nor has it diverted attention from globalisation — subjects such as the FTA with Mexico, parity with NAFTA or FTAA have acquired as much if not more importance than the integration of the five countries.

While other integration schemes discuss the convenience of deepening versus broadening, in Central America there has been no great advance in either direction. Trade relations with Panama, Belize or the Dominican Republic continue at very low levels, and nor have the five countries been able to remove many non-tariff barriers, which a deeper integration requires.[9]

CACM is destined, in the medium term, to be absorbed by other more powerful trade schemes: NAFTA or the FTAA. The signing of the FTA with Mexico is merely a mechanism which complicates regional integration and comes prior to the adherence of Central America to full NAFTA parity or the entry of the five countries into the FTAA.[10] Central

---

[9] Bulmer-Thomas (1998).
[10] Moreover, it must be stressed that the Central American countries have erred in regard to equating being 'successful with globalisation' with the desire to sign bilateral FTAs with any country showing interest in so doing (e.g. Mexico, Dominican Republic or Chile), when what was in order was a more selective agenda with each potential partner (e.g.

American integration will certainly continue, but it will no longer rest on trade but rather on other regional processes in other dimensions: e.g. infrastructure, environment, tourism and finance. There will always be the question as to whether the inevitable destiny of all integration schemes of small countries is to be absorbed by larger schemes and expand by non-trade means, or whether the destiny sought by the Central American countries themselves is due to lack of political interest or the insistence on creating obstacles to integration.

However, both a micro and a macro vision of the integration allows us to predict that intra-trade flows will not disappear. Although these flows may not have the importance that trade with industrialised countries has, they do represent an appreciable segment of total trade (see Table 11.2). The trade opening, which has sought to take the countries from an import substitution scheme to another of export promotion, has not led to the death of all the companies which were born under the protection of the former scheme. A considerable number of these have managed to survive the change in the rules of the game. They continue exporting to Central America, they have a regional — not just domestic — vision of their production.

There are, therefore, companies which can properly be called 'Central American'. They have survived the political and economic disadjustments of years gone by and the trade opening of more recent times, and they will surely cope with the FTA with Mexico or future tariff reductions, just as they are taking advantage of the geographic proximity between countries. However, these firms do not manage — except in exceptional cases — to use the Central American market as a springboard for exporting to the rest of the world; if they do so, it is marginal. In other words, import substitution reached at regional level has not allowed for moving on to exports of manufactured products to the rest of the world (again with the exception of *maquila* products). intra-Central American trade does not, by any means, alter the trade pattern with the North, which is still firmly based on the Heckscher-Ohlin theorem (see Chapter 3).

Central American integration, therefore, cannot be catalogued as open regionalism, as this would give it an excessively positive look, which it definitely does not have. Nor is it failed regionalism or an opening without regionalism, because, although modest, there is a trade flow among the countries. What exists is a dwarf regionalism. This is neither open or closed regionalism, but it is a pattern that is found quite frequently in small countries that continue to do most of their trade with the North.

---

seeking agro-industrial joint ventures with Chile, foreign investment — *maquila* — with South Korea, joint lobbying in the USA and Canada with the Dominican Republic).

Appendix 1: Trade Relations with Central America

1. Approximately what percentage of inputs and raw materials used in your company come from?		
Guatemala	Other CA countries	Rest of the world
32.0%	3.3%	64.7%

2. Does your company export or does it sell only on the Guatemalan market?

Exports	Only in Guatemala
93.3%	6.7%

3. Why have you stopped exporting or why have you never exported to Central America?

Some of the reasons given:
- Demand in Central America is very low in relation to demand from the United States and other markets.
- The company is too small.
- Freight costs are too high.
- The Central American market is not suitable for the company's product.

4. If you export to Central America and the rest of the world, would you say that the former in relation to the latter is?

Easier	The same	More difficult
37.9%	44.8%	17.2%

5. If you export only to some countries in Central America and not to all, why do you not export to the other Central American countries?

Some of the reasons given:
- There is no market in other countries.
- Producers in that country supply the market.
- There is too much competition in the country not covered (in particular, the case of Costa Rica).
- Costa Rica is a closed market with excessive formalities.
- Costa Rica has very high tariffs and the non-tariff barriers are numerous.
- Transport costs differ.
- It is not the company's decision; exports are made through a representative.
- The company is new in exporting to Central America.
- The company is at present working to the maximum of its installed capacity.

6. **What products do you export to Central America?**	
The same as those sold in Guatemala	A smaller number
73.7%	26.3%

7. In the last ten years, approximately, your sales to Central America in relation to your sales in Guatemala have?

Grown less	Grown at the same pace	Grown more
15.8%	23.7%	60.5%

8. To what do you attribute this result?

Some of the reasons given by those who said **less**:
- Consequence of Hurricane Mitch (1998).
- The company prefers the Guatemalan market.
- Demand in Guatemala has grown more.
- The company is better organised and has better control of the Guatemalan market.
- Competition is very strong in other countries.

Some of the reasons given by those who said **the same**:
- The company has increased its installed capacity.
- The markets are similar.
- The company pays attention to both markets.

Some of the reasons given by those who said **more**:
- Demand has been greater in Central America.
- The economic situation in Central America has improved.
- The markets have opened.
- Central America is a new market for the company.
- Greater competition in those markets has increased the company's efficiency.
- In the other countries competition is weaker.
- There has been an economic crisis in Guatemala.
- It has been the product of a marketing strategy by the company.
- They have sales representatives in the area.
- The company has entered into strategic alliances.
- It has been possible to sell direct (without intermediaries)
- The company has increased its production capacity.
- Prices are better in other countries.

9. Of your company's total production, approximately what percentage is represented by?		
Domestic sales	Exports to Central America	Exports to the rest of the world
53.4%	30.1%	16.5%

10. Mention some of the main difficulties your company encounters when exporting to Central America

- Customs problems.
- Theft.
- Legal differences and other requirements (for example, health requirements).
- Limitations to licences by the Bank of Guatemala.
- Local problems in other countries (such as strikes).
- Lack of daily air transport (or excessively expensive).
- Condition of the roads.
- Requirement for special bills of import by some countries.
- High tariffs.
- Unexpected changes in customer demand.
- Lack of professionalism by transport companies.

11. Mention some of the measures that your company has taken and that have allowed it to continue exporting to Central America

- Product quality has been improved and variety has been expanded.
- Costs have been reduced in order to keep prices competitive.
- New machinery and software have been acquired in order to increase productivity.
- Personalised attention is given to customers: better forms of payment, follow-up of the product until it reaches the customer.
- Continuous process of product improvement, for which changes in style are taken into account.
- Co-ordination with distributors has been improved.
- There are direct representatives in each country.
- Customs formalities are anticipated, communications with customs authorities have been improved, and advice has been received from AGEXPRONT.
- Advertising has been increased.
- There is participation in public tenders.
- Delivery times have been minimised.

- Skills of personnel have been improved.
- There has been patience, accepting the fact that in the early years of exporting there is a tendency to lose.
- Regional strategies are defined: creation of export department, strategic alliances.
- Sales are adjusted to local differences in each market.
- Security has been provided to lorries and trailers, and shipments are better programmed to avoid theft.
- The product is insured.

12. In what currency do you sell to Central America?

- Mainly in dollars; just in a few cases in quetzals (local currency).

13. How do you transport your exports to Central America?

Overland	By sea	By air	A combination of these
84.2%	0%	2.6%	13.2%

14. Do you think that it is the same exporting to one Central American country as it is to another, or do you believe that there are appreciable differences between these markets?

The same	There are differences
71.1%	28.9%

15. Who are your principal competitors in Guatemala?

National companies	Others from Central America	Companies from outside the area	Combination of the former	Have no competition
50%	11.9%	28.6%	2.4%	7.1%

16. And in the case of your exports to Central America, who are your main competitors?

Guatemalan Companies	Others from Central America	Companies from outside the area	Combination of the former	Have no competition
13.9%	30.6%	36.1%	13.9%	5.6%

Appendix 2: Outlook for the Future

1. How do you believe that exports to Central America will respond in the next three to five years in relation to your sales in Guatemala?		
Less rapidly	At the same pace	More rapidly
7.9%	39.5%	52.6%

1(a)For what reason?

More rapidly:
- There are market niches in Central America.
- The national market is already satisfied and competition is more intense.
- The national market is small.
- The quality of products in other Central American countries is inferior.
- The opening of markets in Central America is beneficial.

At the same pace:
- Similar growth is expected in the different markets.
- There are market niches in each country.
- The company's policy is regionalised.

Less rapidly:
- The national market is growing faster.
- Demand in Central America has decreased.

2. And what do you think the impact of the Free Trade Agreement with Mexico will be on the exports that your company makes to Central America?		
Will affect them greatly	Will affect them somewhat	Will not affect them
18.4%	44.7%	36.8%

3. And do you think that as result of the Agreement your company will begin to export (or increase its exports) to Mexico?	
Yes	No
61.5%	38.5%

3(a) For what reason?

Yes:
- Because there is a market in Mexico.
- Their products have already been well received in Mexico and with the FTA they will be more.
- Mexico has neglected its southern region.
- The Mexican market will stop being protectionist.

No:
- They are part of a multinational company which already has a subsidiary in Mexico (or they are part of a Mexican company).
- Mexican companies are more productive: better technology, lower costs.
- They have already defined their market.
- Competition in Mexico is very strong (for example, the privately-owned company is very small).

4. Can you mention some strategy or measure being taken by the government or the private sector to increase Guatemalan sales to Central America?

Government:
- Free trade treaties and bilateral agreements (for example, towards a customs union with El Salvador).
- Speeding up of export formalities in customs.
- The creation of the Tax Administration Superintendency (SAT) has strengthened the operation of customs and reduced corruption.
- Has eliminated tariff barriers.
- Has improved the infrastructure.

Private sector:
- AGEXPRONT promotes products and provides advice.
- AGEXPRONT provides information on demand in other countries.
- AGEXPRONT arranged for speeding up export formalities and an extension of hours of attention to customers.
- It has a programme for support of cargo transport.
- Encourages technification and improves the quality of products.

5. In brief, what are your company's exporting expectations for Central America?

Optimistic	Indifferent	Pessimistic
100%	0%	0%

CHAPTER 12

Open Regionalism: CARICOM Integration and Trade Links

Helen McBain[1]

Economic integration succeeded the failed attempt at political federation of the British Caribbean territories in the 1960s. The attempt at forging unity was intended to overcome the constraints of small size on economic and political viability. It began with the establishment in 1968 of the Caribbean Free Trade Area (CARIFTA) and developed into the Caribbean Common Market and Community (CARICOM) in 1973. The integration scheme reinforced at the regional level the inward-oriented import-substitution industrialisation (ISI) model of development that was being pursued by individual countries. It also enlarged the market for import-substitution manufactures. Because countries in the region remained dependent on export earnings from primary commodities to sustain ISI, declining terms of trade as well as production and foreign exchange crises in the 1970s made the ISI strategy unsustainable in the 1980s.

Under structural adjustment loan programmes, with or without the support of the international financial institutions, Caribbean countries embarked on economic reforms that were aimed at shifting from an inward-oriented ISI model toward an outward and export-oriented model of development. Liberalisation of trade was a key component of the programme. However, the change in economic development strategy did not adversely affect the pursuit of integration. In fact Caribbean governments at a CARICOM Summit in 1989 agreed to deepen as well as widen the integration grouping. And it is this two-pronged approach to development — trade preferences among countries in a regional grouping along with the lowering of barriers erected against third countries — that is termed 'open regionalism'. It is compatible with, and is indeed expected to facilitate global openness and at least function as a safeguard against protectionist challenges to that openness.[2]

The first section of this chapter looks at three aspects of open

[1] The author gratefully acknowledges constructive comments and suggestions from Norman Girvan on an earlier version of this chapter as well as research assistance provided by Philip Castillo.
[2] For the origin of the concept of 'open regionalism' and its application to Latin America and the Caribbean, see ECLAC (1994).

regionalism: the deepening of the integration grouping; the expansion in terms of bilateral free-trade agreements; and the opening up to the world economy. The next two sections evaluate the region's trade performance and competitiveness under open regionalism. This is followed by the conclusions.

1. Implementing Open Regionalism

The objectives of CARICOM in 1973 were to: co-ordinate and regulate the economic and trade relations among member countries; integrate their economies; and strengthen their bargaining position vis-à-vis other countries. There was limited achievement with regard to the first two objectives given the different ideological paths to development taken by countries during the 1970s. The socialist orientation adopted by Guyana, Jamaica and Grenada put severe pressure on the regional movement between the latter half of the 1970s and the early years of the 1980s. The trade provisions of CARICOM were never fully implemented. Moreover, Jamaica and Guyana imposed restrictions on intra-regional trade during balance-of-payments crises during the late 1970s.

A true free-trade area only became effective in the 1990s after CARICOM governments decided in 1989 to deepen regional integration by creating a CARICOM single market and economy. The latter sought to achieve: free intra-regional movement of goods originating within CARICOM countries; free movement of services, capital and labour; greater harmonisation of laws and regulations governing trade, intellectual property, competition policy, corporate taxation, dumping and subsidisation. Nine protocols amending the original Treaty of Chaguaramas were prepared to realise these objectives.

Protocol I restructures the organs, institutions and procedures of CARICOM. It allows for majority rather that unanimous voting in some areas as well as a quicker pace of integration for some countries in the community. Protocol II allows for movement of persons providing services or establishing businesses as well as liberalisation of restrictions on providing services. Protocol III is concerned with legislative measures, infrastructure and macroeconomic policies to enhance international competitiveness. Protocol IV consolidates trade policies regarding the common external tariff (CET), free movement of goods, etc. Protocol V deals with agriculture — diversification, sustainable and globally competitive agricultural production. Protocol VI deals with common transport policies — air and maritime transport services. Protocol VII gives privileges to less developed countries to adjust to the greater competition in the single market and economy. Protocol VIII and Protocol IX deal with dispute settlement and competition policy, respectively. Although the agreement was approved in 1999 to set up a

Caribbean Court of Justice to interpret the treaty and rule on trade disputes, implementation has been delayed by the controversy surrounding its establishment and the intention to replace the Privy Council in Great Britain as the final appellate body. As can be seen from Table 12.1, most countries have signed the first seven protocols. The legal framework of the single market and economy was therefore largely completed by the end of 2000, but it will be some time before it becomes fully operational.

Table 12.1: Status of the Protocols Amending the CARICOM Treaty

Protocol		Status
I	Organs, Institutions and Procedures	Signed and Ratified by all States
II	Right of Establishment, Provision of Services and Movement of Capital	Signed and Ratified by 13 States
III	Industrial Policy	Signed and Provisional Application Approved by 11 States
IV	Commercial Policy	Signed and Provisional Application Approved by 10 States
V	Agricultural Policy	Signed and Provisional Application Approved by 11 States
VI	Transport Policy	Signed and Provisional Application Approved by 11 States
VII	Disadvantaged Countries, Regions and Sectors	Signed and Provisional Application Approved by 11 States
VIII	Dispute Settlement	Signed in 2000
IX	Competition Rules	Signed in 2000

Source: Caribbean Community Secretariat (CARICOM), http://www.CARICOM.org.

CARICOM governments have embarked not only on deepening integration among member countries, but also widening the grouping and expanding trade relations with other countries in the Western Hemisphere. Suriname and Haiti became full members in 1995 and in 1999 respectively.[3] In 1992 CARICOM negotiated a one-way preferential trade agreement with Venezuela under which specific products from the region gain duty-free or duty-reduced access to the Venezuelan

---

[3] Although the Bahamas joined CARICOM in 1983, it is not a member of the Common Market.

market. A trade, economic and technical cooperation agreement was signed in 1994 with Colombia. This agreement is an asymmetrical reciprocal agreement under which exports from the region gain preferential access to the Colombian market for a period of four years, after which the arrangement becomes reciprocal, but only in relation to the more developed countries in the region (Barbados, Guyana, Jamaica and Trinidad & Tobago). From 1999, these countries must provide duty-free or duty-reduced access to specific products from Colombia, and Colombia in turn has to provide similar access to different products from the region. A framework for a more comprehensive free-trade agreement was signed between CARICOM and the Dominican Republic in 1998. It provides for elimination of duties on all but sensitive products. However, negotiations for a reciprocal trade agreement were only recently concluded on account of failure to agree on the extent of exceptions to duty-free treatment.

The CARICOM treaty of 1973 provided for the achievement of a common external tariff (CET) by 1983. This was not realised because of the economic problems in the late 1970s. The CET structure was simplified in 1991 and a schedule devised for its phased reduction (Table 12.2). The reductions are in relation to tariffs on manufactures. Agricultural products are still subject to a maximum tariff of 40 per cent.

Table 12.2: Schedule of CET Reform

1992	1993–94	1995–96	1997	1998
5–45	5–30/35	5–25/30	5–20/25	5–20

Source: CARICOM: Common External Tariff of the Caribbean Common Market,1993.

The majority of countries have reduced the maximum rate to 25 per cent. Only Barbados, Jamaica, Trinidad & Tobago and St Vincent & the Grenadines have implemented the final phase or maximum tariff of 20 per cent; however, these countries accounted for the bulk (83 per cent) of extra-regional imports in 1997.[4]

The CARICOM regime provides for all goods of common market origin to be free of customs tariffs, tariff quotas and quantitative restrictions. All existing barriers to such goods were to have been removed by the end of 1996. However, it was found that some member countries still had licensing requirements on a number of CARICOM products.[5] In addition to the CET, there are extra-CET tariffs as well as

---

[4] WTO (2000).
[5] *Ibid.*

Table 12.3: Extra-CET Tariffs in CARICOM Countries

Country	Stamp Duty	Customs Surcharge	Customs Service Charge*	FX [a] Trans. Tax +
Antigua	None	None	5% on dutiable goods	1%
Bahamas	2–10% on all imports	None	None	None
Barbados	20% — extra-regional imports 10% — regional imports	35% until 2000	None	1%
Belize	14%	None	None	None
Dominica	None	15% on motor vehicles, motor cycles, apples, grapes and pears	1% on dutiable goods	1.25%
Grenada	None	None	5% except on imports by government, flour mill, telephone company and enclave manufacturers	None
Guyana	None	None	None	None
Jamaica	25–56% on alcoholic beverages and tobacco; aggregate duty of 65–90% on agricultural imports	None	None	None
St Kitts	2%	None	3%	None
St Lucia	None	None	1% on imports by enclave industries; 4% on all other imports	None
St Vincent	None	None	2.5%	1%
Trinidad & Tobago	5–45% on agricultural imports; 60% on unrefined sugar; and 75% on refined sugar	None	None	None

(a) FX = Foreign Exchange
*This is a charge applied by the Bureau of Standards
+This tax is levied on the foreign exchange transaction associated with the import
Note: Suriname imposes a statistical tax of 0.5 per cent and a consent tax of 1.5 per cent on all imports.
Source: Unpublished data, Association of Caribbean States.

licenses, quotas and outright bans against products from non-CARICOM countries. Barbados, Jamaica, Trinidad & Tobago and to a lesser extent Bahamas and St Kitts-Nevis impose stamp duties in addition to the CET. Jamaica and Trinidad & Tobago apply the highest duties to agricultural imports. Barbados, on the other hand, has a higher rate for non-CARICOM countries and a lower one for regional partners (Table 12.3). Only Barbados and Dominica still impose custom surcharges. The Barbadian charges were as high as 75 per cent before 1999, but have since been reduced to 35 per cent and are due to be eliminated. Only the Organisation of Eastern Caribbean States (OECS) countries impose a customs service charge (or standards tax) and a tax on the foreign exchange transaction associated with the importation. These charges are really intended to compensate these countries for loss of revenue due to reduction in the CET.

The extra-CET charges reinforce and extend the protection of regional products against imports, especially of agricultural products. They also provide a level of protection for producers in some countries against both regional and extra-regional imports. Non-tariff barriers such as import licensing give preference to regional imports in the food, beverage and consumer goods categories (Table 12.4). The more developed CARICOM countries (MDCs) are the main beneficiaries of the regional preferences since it is the OECS countries, as well as Belize and Suriname, that still employ extensive licensing systems against extra-regional imports.

2. Trends in Trade Performance

Intra-regional trade grew significantly after CARIFTA came into effect in 1968. More specifically, intra-regional exports grew by 2.7 per cent between 1960 and 1968 and by 20.2 per cent between 1968 and 1973, when the free-trade area evolved into CARICOM. Growth was more modest between 1974 and 1980 when the annual rate of increase averaged 13.6 per cent. Growth of intra-regional exports declined by over eight per cent between 1980 and 1986. This was due largely to the balance-of-payments problems of Jamaica and Guyana and the abolition of the regional payments system that had facilitated intra-regional trade. Liberalisation of payments and some non-tariff trade barriers provided the impetus for resumption of growth of intra-regional trade after 1986. Intra-regional exports grew rapidly during 1992–95, averaging 24 per cent per year; this coincided with the reduction in the region's common external tariff.

Table 12.4: Non-Tariff Measures in CARICOM Countries

Country	Import Licence	Import Quota	Prohibition
Antigua	Most goods from non-CARICOM countries		
Barbados	A number of food items and consumer goods such as soap, T-shirts and motor vehicles from non-CARICOM countries	Annual global quotas on apples, sugar, canned fruits and pet food, refined rice, peanuts and chewing gum	Phytosanitary
Belize	Several items such as food, beverages, fuel, fertiliser, lumber and furniture from non-CARICOM sources		Certain non-CARICOM goods such as jams, jellies, rice, flour, pasta, beans and matches
Dominica	Non-CARICOM imports of food, beverages, industrial gases, solar water heaters and paints		
Grenada	Non-CARICOM imports of food, beverages, furniture and water heaters		
Guyana	Meat, peanuts, pharmaceuticals		
Jamaica	Milk, cream, plants, motor vehicles*		
St Kitts	Non-CARICOM imports of fish, meat, vegetables, beverages, television, fertiliser, some furniture and agricultural machinery		
St Lucia	Non-CARICOM imports of food, beverages and furniture		
St Vincent	Non-CARICOM imports of food, some rum, mattresses and bed linen; non-OECS and Belize imports of aerated beverages, beer, fats, pasta, curry spice, toilet paper, furniture, solar water heaters	Annual global quotas set on dead poultry, bird eggs and egg yolk	
Suriname	All imports	Items such as powdered milk, potatoes, peanuts, clothing, furniture	Wide range of foods
Trinidad & Tobago	All imports* of oils and fats; non-CARICOM imports of livestock, fish, some motor vehicles, ships and boats, tobacco, cigarettes, paper, pesticides	Livestock for specific period	

*License used only for monitoring these imports.

Source: Unpublished data, Association of Caribbean States.

Despite the growth in intra-regional trade, intra-regional imports remain a relatively small proportion of total imports. As a share of total imports the average was five per cent during the 1960s, seven per cent during the 1970s, eight per cent during the 1980s and nine per cent in the 1990s. The major importers from the regional market have been the more developed countries (MDCs), but the less developed countries (LDCs) significantly increased these imports from the region from the late 1980s. The major exporters have been Barbados, Dominica, Grenada, St Vincent, St Lucia, especially during the 1980s, and Trinidad & Tobago since the 1990s. However, it is the MDCs — Barbados, Guyana, Jamaica and Trinidad — that have largely determined the pattern of intra-regional trade since they constitute the largest markets in the region.

A comparison of the export performance of Barbados, Jamaica and Trinidad & Tobago (Table 12.5) reveals that regional exports from Barbados are a more significant portion of that country's total exports (30 per cent in 1995) than regional exports from Jamaica (four per cent in 1995) and from Trinidad & Tobago (23 per cent in 1995). Trinidad & Tobago and St Lucia are the leading regional markets for exports from Barbados. Almost all the CARICOM countries are leading regional markets for Trinidad & Tobago's exports. Barbados is the only leading regional market for the main exports from Jamaica. Barbados and Trinidad & Tobago have become leading exporters within the region whereas Jamaica has not been taking advantage of the regional market, in particular that of Trinidad & Tobago.[6]

Table 12.5: Intra-Regional Exports of Selected CARICOM Countries as Percentage of Total Exports

	1980	1983	1986	1989	1992	1995
Barbados	18	16	10	26	28	30
Jamaica	5	13	7	6	5	4
Trinidad	7	8	8	14	12	23

Source: CARICOM Trade Report, 1996.

The most significant goods traded within the region are mineral fuels and related products, food, manufactures, and chemicals and related products. The OECS countries and Belize export mainly food and some manufactures, whereas Dominica exports an equally significant amount

---

[6] In a trade simulation exercise using data for 1995–96, it was found that Jamaica's export potential to Trinidad & Tobago far exceeded its current level of exports. International Trade Centre, http://www.intracen.org.

of food and chemical products. Jamaica's exports are dominated by raw materials, which represent over half of total exports. Food and manufactures are the other significant categories. Mineral fuels dominate Trinidad's exports, but that dominance has declined over the years from 79 per cent in 1985 to 46 per cent in 1997. On the other hand, chemicals, manufactures and food have been increasing in importance since the late 1980s. Manufactures are the main category of exports from Barbados. Food, beverages and chemicals have become significant export categories since the late 1980s.

Figure 12.1: CARICOM Export of Manufactures 1980s   **Figure 12.2: CARICOM Export of Manufactures 1990s**

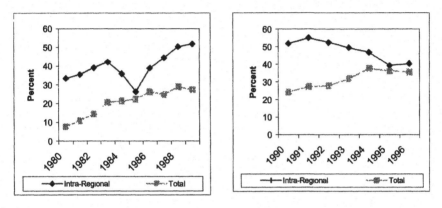

The share of manufactures in intra-regional exports is greater than the share of manufactures in total exports and at first increased significantly after 1985 (Figure 12.1). For example, export of manufactures within the region grew from 26 per cent in 1985 to 55 per cent in 1991 whereas total export of manufactures grew only from 22 per cent in 1985 to 27 per cent in 1991. However, the former declined to 39 per cent whereas the latter increased to 36 per cent in 1995. The experience of Latin American integration groups is that the share of manufactures in intra-regional exports grew faster than the share of manufactures in total exports from 1990 to 1996.[7] Yet CARICOM's share of manufactures in intra-regional exports declined steadily after 1990 whereas its share of manufactures in total exports increased. The trend is towards convergence of the share of manufactures in intra-regional and total exports (Figure 12.2). This suggests export diversion to the rest of the world of manufactures that had previously been oriented towards domestic and regional markets.

---

[7] IDB (1999).

Figure 12.3: CARICOM Exports 1970s

Figure 12.4: CARICOM Exports 1980s

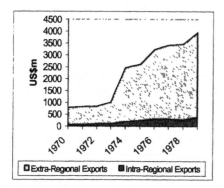

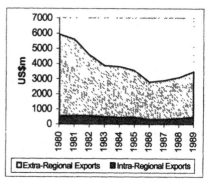

Figure 12.5: CARICOM Exports 1990s

Figure 12.6: World Exports and CARICOM Extra-Regional Exports 1970s

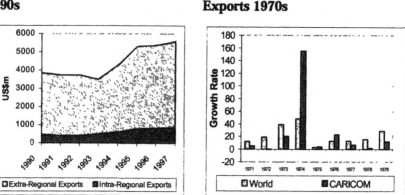

Within the region, the less developed countries (LDCs) have a significant trade deficit with the MDCs. The former have in fact sustained the significant growth in intra-regional imports from the late 1980s whereas the latter have been the sole contributors to the significant expansion in intra-regional exports over the same period. The result has therefore been a deterioration of the LDC trade deficit since the late 1980s. Among the MDCs, however, it is only Trinidad that has experienced a positive balance on its intra-regional trade. Its trade surplus increased significantly from 1993 at the same time as Jamaica's deficit on intra-regional trade deteriorated.

Despite the significant growth in intra-regional trade, the bulk of CARICOM trade consists of exports to the rest of the world. Extra-regional exports increased significantly during the 1970s — especially after 1973 due largely to exports of minerals and fuel (Figure 12.3) although they declined from the early 1980s to 1986 (Figure 12.4).

Extra-regional exports again grew rapidly after 1993 (Figure 12.5). However, significant growth of extra-regional exports has occurred in spurts rather than consistently over the years (Figures 12.6, 12.7 and 12.8). The major destination for CARICOM exports is the USA followed by the European Union (EU). Extra-regional imports also grew significantly during the 1990s. Most of the increase in imports came from the USA, which is the major source of imports for the region with the EU being the second major source.

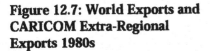

Figure 12.7: World Exports and CARICOM Extra-Regional Exports 1980s

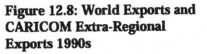

Figure 12.8: World Exports and CARICOM Extra-Regional Exports 1990s

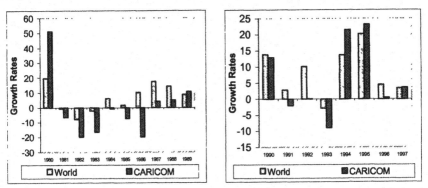

The region's principal extra-regional exports are refined petroleum products, bauxite and alumina, crude petroleum oils, inorganic chemical elements, apparel and clothing accessories, sugar, iron and steel, bananas, methanol and urea, edible products and paper. Petroleum and other mineral oils, motorcars and other transport vehicles, clothing, paper, medicaments, telecommunications and data-processing equipment, inorganic chemical elements and machinery and equipment constitute its main imports.

Raw materials dominate exports to Canada whereas mineral fuels dominate exports to the USA. Exports of manufactures and chemicals to the USA have increased from the mid-1980s. At the same time CARICOM countries have been importing more mineral fuels and chemicals from the USA. The composition of imports from Canada has remained more or less the same. CARICOM has enjoyed a positive trade balance with Canada since 1993 due to the region's significant increase in exports. On the other hand, the region has had a negative trade balance with the USA since 1986 due to the growth in imports but no corresponding growth in exports.

The European Union exports mainly machinery and transport equipment to CARICOM countries and in turn imports mainly food and raw materials. Latin America has become a significant trade partner during the 1990s partly on account of the trade agreements between CARICOM and Venezuela and CARICOM and Colombia. Trinidad & Tobago is the only significant exporter to Latin America. Its major markets in that region are Colombia, Dominican Republic, Guatemala, Honduras, Mexico and Venezuela. And its major sources of imports are Colombia and Venezuela. Jamaica is a significant importer from Latin America, in particular Brazil, Mexico, Panama and Venezuela. Mineral fuel is the dominant category of imports from that region although manufactures, raw materials and machinery and transport equipment have also become significant. CARICOM has a deteriorating trade imbalance with the Latin American countries. For example, Trinidad & Tobago's trade deficit with Venezuela increased from US$51.1 million in 1990 to US$158.6 million in 1998; and the deficit with Colombia increased from US$11.6 million to US$163 million over the same period.

Figure 12.9: CARICOM Balance of Trade 1980s

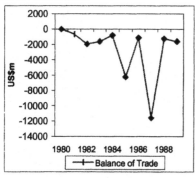

Figure 12.10: CARICOM Balance of Trade 1990s

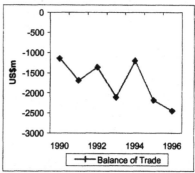

Figure 12.11: CARICOM Services Balance 1990s

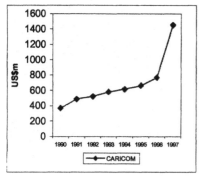

Figure 12.12: CARICOM Transfers 1990s

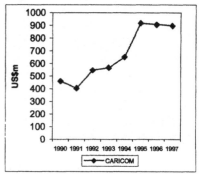

CARICOM's trade with Japan has not grown in significance since the 1980s. Japan is a major supplier of machinery and transport equipment whereas exports by CARICOM consist mainly of food and some manufactures. Export of chemicals ceased to be important after 1987 and raw materials after 1990. The region has a significant trade deficit with Japan on account of increasing imports of motor vehicles facilitated by import liberalisation policies.

Open regionalism has had a more dynamic impact on intra-regional than on extra-regional exports. Average annual growth of intra-regional exports was eight per cent between 1990 and 1997 whereas average annual growth of extra-regional exports was three per cent over the same period. On the other hand, extra-regional imports have grown at about the same rate (eight per cent) as intra-regional imports.[8] The result has been a significant increase in the region's trade deficit since the 1980s (Figures 12.9 and 12.10).

A somewhat different picture emerges when the total output structure of the economy is taken into account. Services are the largest sector in every economy with the exception of Guyana (see Table 12.6). And its contribution to total output has been growing. Whereas the balance on visible trade has been increasingly negative during the 1990s, CARICOM's services balance has been increasingly positive (Figure 12.11). Most of the latter are in relation to tourism and to a lesser extent offshore financial services. The region appears to be more competitive in the export of services than in the export of goods. The positive services balance along with increasing levels of income transfers (Figure 12.12) contribute toward offsetting the trade deficit.

3. Competitiveness and Open Regionalism

The relatively slow growth of extra-regional exports and the deteriorating trade balance of CARICOM during the 1990s raise the issue of competitiveness which is a central objective of open regionalism. The preferences inherent in regional integration along with the opening up of regional economies to the world economy are intended to enhance competitiveness of industries and sectors within national economies; that is, to facilitate acquisition, maintenance and expansion of market share in the world economy.

Fresh food, processed food and clothing are principal exports for most CARICOM countries. The main source of foreign exchange earnings in the goods-producing sectors of Guyana, Belize and Jamaica and most of the OECS countries are primary products. Trinidad & Tobago's main source of earnings is fuel, whereas Barbados and Dominica have more diversified sources of earnings.

---

[8] World Trade Organisation based on data from CARICOM Secretariat.

Table 12.6: Sector Shares (%) of GDP for CARICOM Countries (1996–97)

Country	Agriculture		Mining		Manufacturing		Services	
	1996	1997	1996	1997	1996	1997	1996	1997
Antigua & Barbuda	3.8	4.1	1.7	1.7	2.2	2.2	88.2	87.9
Barbados	6.2	4.9	0.6	0.6	6.1	6.3	82.6	83.1
Belize	17.1	15.6	0.6	0.6	13.7	13.8	62.8	64.4
Dominica	20.8	20.5	0.9	0.9	7.3	6.3	70.6	71.2
Grenada	8.8	8.3	0.5	0.5	6.8	6.5	81.7	82.5
Guyana	38.9	35.8	18.9	17.5	10.3	11.5	27.3	30.2
Jamaica	8.3	8.0	5.9	5.6	16.7	16.3	77.1	77.3
Montserrat	5.0	1.1	1.0	1.3	6.0	3.7	86.2	84.0
St Kitts & Nevis	5.2	5.1	0.3	0.3	10.3	10.1	79.8	80.1
St Lucia	9.0	8.0	0.4	0.5	6.8	6.5	85.3	87.2
St Vincent/ Grenadines	12.7	10.4	0.3	0.3	8.4	8.1	74.7	75.9
Trinidad & Tobago	1.8	1.6	13.7	12.5	17.7	18.6	56.4	55.8
Average	11.5	10.3	3.7	3.5	9.3	9.2	72.7	73.3

Source: World Trade Organisation based on data from CARICOM.

All CARICOM countries have comparative advantage in fresh and/or processed foods. Only Barbados, Trinidad and Dominica have comparative advantage in chemical products and only Guyana has comparative advantage in wood products. The combination of products in which countries have comparative advantage is ranked in descending order of revealed comparative advantage (RCA) values[9] (see Table 12.7):

- Barbados — processed food, electronic components and basic manufactures;
- Guyana — processed food, minerals, wood products and fresh food;
- Jamaica — minerals, clothing, fresh food and processed food;
- Trinidad & Tobago — minerals, chemicals, basic manufacturing and processed food;
- Belize — processed food, fresh food and clothing;
- Antigua — processed food, fresh food, electronic components;
- Dominica — chemicals, minerals and fresh food;

---

[9] The RCA index is calculated as the ratio of net exports (net imports) to total trade for each product group.

Table 12.7: Revealed Comparative Advantage (RCA) Indices for CARICOM Countries

Principal Sectors	Barbados	Guyana	Jamaica	Trinidad & Tobago	Belize	Antigua	Dominica	Grenada	St Lucia	St Kitts	St Vincent
Fresh Food	-9	34	18	-11	102	5	1	120	134	-13	121
Processed Food	69	158	9	8	181	20	-39	-21	-26	123	66
Chemicals	5	-48	-34	61	-56	0	95	-21	-23	-21	-10
Wood Products	-5	34	-21	-6	-10	-2	-14	-10	-2	-19	-9
Minerals	-15	81	181	144	-58	-5	22	-25	-21	-16	-52
Textiles	-4	-8	-10	-8	-6	0	-63	-5	1	-3	-2
Clothing	-1	2	35	1	31	-1	-15	1	9	-2	5
Basic Manufacturing	8	-49	-29	12	-45	0	-43	-28	-28	-33	-12
Miscellaneous Manufacturing	-2	-20	-24	-14	-32	-3	-18	-27	-17	-17	-2
Electronic Components	19	-10	-16	-15	-22	2	-10	62	2	17	-8
Non-electrical Machinery	-21	-92	-34	-115	-45	-2	0	-17	-17	5	-31
Transport Equipment	-27	-57	-51	-35	-27	-10	-35	-12	-18	-13	-103
Consumer Electronics	-13	-23	-21	-20	-10	-4	15	-14	6	-8	38

Source: International Trade Centre 2000, http://www.intracen.org.

- Grenada — fresh food, electronic components and clothing;
- St Lucia — fresh food, clothing, consumer electronics, electronic components and textiles;
- St Kitts — processed food, electronic components and non-electrical machinery;
- St Vincent — fresh food, processed food, consumer electronics and clothing.

In Table 12.8 a comparison is made of the competitiveness of Barbados, Jamaica and Trinidad & Tobago at the product level. Jamaica is the most competitive in exports of beer, perfumery and cosmetics and furniture and furniture parts. Trinidad is the most competitive in chocolate confectionery, aerated beverages and animal feed. And Barbados is the most competitive in the export of pigments, paints and varnishes, medicaments, paper products and textile articles. Jamaica's competitiveness in chocolate confectionery, aerated beverages, paper and paperboard and furniture declined between 1994 and 1996 partly on account of the macroeconomic imbalances experienced during the 1980s and 1990s, the adjustment measures employed to address them and the low/negative growth in the economy that resulted. Trinidad and Barbados also experienced a decline in competitiveness in a number of the major product groups over the same period.

Table 12.8: Revealed Comparative Advantage (RCA) Indices for Selected Products of Jamaica, Trinidad & Tobago and Barbados (1994–96)*

Product Group	Jamaica	Trinidad & Tobago	Barbados
Coffee	282	43	—
Chocolate Confectionery	91	183	—
Animal Feed	18	499	40
Aerated Beverages	8	193	63
Beer	416	228	363
Pigments, Paints & Varnishes	34	62	501
Medicaments	124	117	545
Perfumery & Cosmetics	228	102	—
Paper & Paperboard	10	160	264
Textile Products	—	84	654
Furniture & Parts	208	115	—

* The RCA indices were calculated for these three countries in relation to the countries in the CARICOM integration group.
Source: Calculated from CARICOM's Trade, UN International Statistics Yearbook and data from http://www.intracen.org.

Despite competitiveness in a number of products, Caribbean countries tend to have overall weak manufacturing competitiveness. This was determined in an exercise that measured manufacturing sector competitiveness in the Caribbean between 1986 and 1996.[10] The index for Barbados was -0.626, which means that the trade deficit in manufactures averaged nearly 63 per cent of total trade in manufactures for that period. Trinidad & Tobago was less uncompetitive with an index of -0.331. By contrast, the index for Hong Kong was 0.094 showing a trade surplus of 9 per cent in manufactured trade.

Table 12.9: Position of Leading CARICOM Exports in World Markets (percentage)

Country	Winners[a] in Growth Markets	Losers[b] in Growth Markets	Winners[c] in Declining Markets	Losers[s] in Declining Markets
Barbados	60	26	13	—
Guyana	16	27	50	5
Jamaica	47	31	5	15
Trinidad	52	13	19	13
Antigua	70	20	10	—
Belize	25	6	37	31
Dominica	42	28	28	—
Grenada	54	30	—	15
St Kitts	66	16	16	—
St Lucia	64	28	—	7
St Vincent	46	15	23	15

[a] Dynamic products that are internationally competitive.
[b] Growth in supply failing to meet growth in international demand.
[c] World market not growing in line with national supply.
[d] Fall in national supply in world markets that are growing slowly or declining.
Source: Same as for Table 12.7.

Competitiveness can also be determined by the position of leading exports in international markets (Table 12.9). More than half of the major exports of Barbados, Trinidad, Antigua, St Lucia, St Kitts and St Vincent are internationally competitive. Jamaica and Grenada have failed to maintain the share in world markets. For Guyana, Belize and the OECS countries except Antigua, Dominica and St Kitts, the

---

[10] CEPAL (1999).

percentage of internationally uncompetitive major exports is between 30 and 37.

The exports of CARICOM countries tend to be based on one or a small number of primary products: bananas in the Windward Islands; nutmegs in Grenada; raw sugar in St. Kitts; aluminium ores and oxides in Jamaica and Guyana; sugar in Barbados; and petroleum oils and fuels in Trinidad & Tobago. The last named and most of Jamaica's exports are losing their share in the world market. Guyana's exports are highly concentrated around three products — gold, raw sugar and aluminium ores — with gold experiencing erosion in its world market share. Most of the leading exports of Antigua, Barbados, St Kitts and Trinidad are dynamic exports, that is, they have been increasing market share in growing world markets. Jamaica and Grenada have the most losers in growth markets, that is, leading exports that are losing market share in expanding world markets. Most of the leading exports from Belize are concentrated in declining or slow-growing world markets.

Table 12.10: Percentage Share in Exports of Specific Product Groups (1994–98)

Country	Primary Products	Natural Resource Intensive	Labour Intensive	Technology Intensive	Human Capital Intensive
Barbados	37	-	21	26	13
Guyana	64	29	3	3	-
Jamaica	65	-	28	3	1
Trinidad & Tobago	25	3	3	23	14
Belize	86	-	9	2	1
Antigua	30	7	37	17	6
Dominica	57	3	3	17	16
Grenada	60	0	4	29	5
St Lucia	75	-	11	6	8
St Kitts	30	-	4	49	1
St Vincent	61	-	19	14	5

Source: Same as for Table 12.7.

Examination of the export structure throws light on a country's position in world markets as well as the competitiveness of its exports (Table 12.10). The more dynamic exporters, namely Barbados and Trinidad & Tobago, have significant amounts of exports that are skill- and technology-intensive. Antigua's exports tend to be mainly labour- and technology-intensive whereas St Kitts' dynamic exports are essentially technology-intensive exports. Countries that lose or fail to expand market share, notably Guyana and Belize, are those that rely on resource-based and natural resource-intensive export products. Skill- and technology-intensive structures support the growth of dynamic exports. Most of the OECS countries have technology-intensive exports, but these tend to be based on assembly operations such as electrical switches and other instruments. These are low-technology operations using relatively cheap labour. Export-growth dynamism depends on more technologically advanced export structures, although export growth can be maintained by upgrading existing products.[11]

4. Conclusions

Trade liberalisation as a feature of open regionalism has significantly increased intra-CARICOM trade since the late 1980s. The free trade area for trade in goods only became fully effective in the 1990s; less than one per cent of intra-regional trade is still subject to non-tariff barriers in some member states.[12] Trade liberalisation has also led to a significant increase of extra-regional imports; imports increased by 78 per cent from 1990–98. But its effect on the increase of extra-regional exports was less significant — 24 per cent over the same period. Trade performance was also very skewed. Trinidad & Tobago was by far the largest exporter in the region.

Whereas intra-regional trade liberalisation facilitated increased intra-regional exports, it is the significant protection that still existed in the form of other statutory taxes that facilitated growth in intra-regional trade after the lowering of the CET. Elimination of these barriers could reduce the level of intra-regional trade. In that event, CARICOM members would need to pursue production integration and hence the model of open regionalism — production integration and lower intra-regional trade — that is applicable to countries in East and South-East Asia.

Open regionalism is largely about developing competitiveness. The leading exports of CARICOM countries enter the markets of developed countries under preferential schemes. Cessation of preferences will show how competitive these goods are. Few countries in the region have dynamic exports, that is, exports growing in expanding world markets. This is due largely to existing export structures that are skewed towards resource-based and natural resource-intensive exports. Countries need to increase the skill and technological intensity of exports and to upgrade existing products where feasible in order to enhance their

---

[11] Lall (1999).
[12] World Trade Organisation based on CARICOM data.

competitiveness.

Finally, for most CARICOM countries trade in services is more important than trade in goods. The region has an increasingly positive balance in the former and an increasingly negative balance in the latter. Tourism is the most significant component of export services. However, data on trade in services are highly aggregated, thus constraining analysis of export trends. The CARICOM Treaty does not make provision for preferential access to the regional market by service providers. Amendments to the Treaty provide for the right of establishment, provision of services and movement of capital and service providers within CARICOM. The free movement of skilled persons is already a reality in some countries in the region. There is also significant cross-border investment in services, mainly in the tourism and financial sectors. The region tends to be more competitive in service exports. Enhancement of that competitiveness would compensate for lack of competitiveness in visible trade.

Statistical Appendix

Table A.1: Trade Agreements in the Americas in the 1990s

AGREEMENT	DATE
Caribbean Community (CARICOM)[1]	1989
Chile–Mexico[2]	1991
Central American Common Market (CACM)[3]	1990
CARICOM–Venezuela	1992
Chile–Venezuela	1993
North American Free Trade Agreement (NAFTA)[4]	1992
Colombia–Chile	1993
Southern Cone Common Market (MERCOSUR)	1991
Costa Rica–Mexico	1994
Group of Three (G-3)	1994
Bolivia–Mexico	1994
Chile–Ecuador	1994
Andean Community[5]	1988
Chile–MERCOSUR	1996
Canada–Chile	1996
Bolivia–Mexico	1996
Mexico–Nicaragua	1997
CACM–Dominican Republic[6]	1998
CARICOM–Dominican Republic[6]	1998
CACM–Chile	1999
Mexico–European Union	2000
Mexico–Israel	2000
Mexico–Northern Triangle (El Salvador, Guatemala, Honduras)	2000

SELECTED AGREEMENTS UNDER DISCUSSION

Regional — Free Trade Area of the Americas; Canada–Costa Rica; Mexico–Panama; CACM–Panama; Northern Triangle–Andean Community; Chile–USA.

Extra-Regional — MERCOSUR–European Union; Chile–European Union; Chile–South Korea; APEC, Mexico–Japan.

Source: Integration, Trade and Hemispheric Issues Division of the Integration and Regional Programs Department, IDB.

---

[1] CARICOM began its reform processes in 1989 (Declaration of Grand Anse) and agreed to launch a harmonised CET in 1990.

[2] The two countries substantially revised and upgraded this accord in an agreement that entered into force on 1 August 1999.

[3] The presidents agreed to reactivate the CACM in 1990 (Montelimar Summit) and opted to definitively pursue a customs union in 1993 (Protocol of Guatemala).

[4] Proceeded by a free trade area between the USA and Canada in 1987.

[5] In 1988, the presidents agreed (in the Protocol of Quito) to amend the founding Charter of the Andean Group and alter the existing tariff reduction programme. In 1996, the leaders officially agreed to change the Group's name to the Andean Community and reform certain existing institutional structures (Declaration of Trujillo).

[6] Awaiting sufficient legislative approval.

Table A.2: LAIA Intra-Regional Exports, 1990–98 (in US$ millions and percentages)

Subregion / Country	1990	1991	1992	1993	1994	1995	1996	1997	1998
In millions of dollars									
Intra-CAN	1,265	1,768	2,214	2,889	3,759	4,859	4,702	5,634	5,442
Intra-MERCOSUR	4,127	5,103	7,216	10,028	12,049	14,453	17,042	20,585	20,027
CAN–MERCOSUR	2,306	2,909	3,149	3,436	3,976	5,925	4,789	5,952	5,436
CAN–Chile	776	967	1,000	996	1,272	1,727	1,787	1,895	1,855
CAN–Mexico	629	718	951	1,085	1,507	1,723	1,822	2,524	2,148
MERCOSUR–Chile	1,649	2,030	2,589	2,902	3,434	4,537	4,659	5,099	4,494
MERCOSUR–Mexico	1,270	1,449	2,049	2,026	2,098	1,926	2,607	2,618	2,590
Chile–Mexico	148	171	242	324	463	662	902	1,340	1,239
LAIA	12,169	15,114	19,411	23,689	28,557	35,812	38,311	45,647	43,231
In percentages									
Intra-CAN	10.4	11.7	11.4	12.2	13.2	13.6	12.3	12.3	12.6
Intra-MERCOSUR	33.9	33.8	37.2	42.3	42.2	40.4	44.5	45.1	46.3
CAN–MERCOSUR	18.9	19.2	16.2	14.5	13.9	16.5	12.5	13.0	12.6
CAN–Chile	6.4	6.4	5.2	4.2	4.5	4.8	4.7	4.2	4.3
CAN–Mexico	5.2	4.7	4.9	4.6	5.3	4.8	4.8	5.5	5.0
MERCOSUR–Chile	13.5	13.4	13.3	12.3	12.0	12.7	12.2	11.2	10.4
MERCOSUR–Mexico	10.4	9.6	10.6	8.6	7.3	5.4	6.8	5.7	6.0
Chile–Mexico	1.2	1.1	1.2	1.4	1.6	1.8	2.4	2.9	2.9
LAIA	100.0	100.0	100.0	100.0	100.0	100.0	100.0	100.0	100.0

Note: CAN = Andean Community.
LAIA's membership is Argentina, Bolivia, Brazil, Chile, Colombia, Ecuador, Mexico, Paraguay, Peru, Uruguay and Venezuela. Cuba joined in 2000.
Source: INTAL Newsletter, no. 46, May 2000.

Table A.3: LAIA Intra-Regional Exports, 1999–2000 (in US$ millions FOB and percentages)

| ROUTE | US$ millions | | % of LAIA Total | | % Growth |
	1999	2000	1999	2000	2000–1999
Intra-CAN	3,974	5,370	11.4	12.2	35.1
Intra-MERCOSUR	15,164	18,048	43.6	40.9	19.0
CAN–MERCOSUR	4,499	5,822	12.9	13.2	29.4
CAN–Chile	1,771	2,210	5.1	5.0	24.8
MERCOSUR–Chile	4,365	5,933	12.5	13.4	35.9
CAN–Mexico	1,686	1,991	4.8	4.5	18.1
MERCOSUR–Mexico	2,117	3,328	6.1	7.5	57.2
Chile–Mexico	999	1,196	2.9	2.7	19.7
Cuba–Rest of LAIA (1)	218	284	0.6	0.6	30.3
LAIA	34,792	44,181	100.0	100.0	27.0

Notes: CAN= Andean Community. Data for 2000 are estimates based on partial information for this period.
(1)   Includes LAIA exports to Cuba but not Cuban exports to LAIA.
Source: INTAL Newsletter, no. 41, May 2000.

Table A.4: CACM Intra-Regional Trade (US$'000), 1990-98

SOURCE	Costa Rica	El Salvador	Guatemala	Honduras	Nicaragua	Panama	Exports to Central America	Total Exports
1990								
Costa Rica		35,868	52,287	18,317	28,127	48,211	182,810	1,361,371
El Salvador	48,300		101,676	17,620	9,150	8,971	185,717	582,243
Guatemala	73,716	144,197		38,006	32,277	27,613	315,809	1,162,970
Honduras	2,037	9,731	10,648		1,715	2,109	26,240	554,612
Nicaragua	16,668	9,519	12,486	8,873		1,531	49,077	272,844
Panama	29,202	3,500	3,370	3,547	1,507		41,126	321,946
1992								
Costa Rica		55,480	75,163	43,215	74,465	58,077	306,400	1,782,858
El Salvador	59,863		136,592	33,389	33,866	12,041	275,751	596,650
Guatemala	89,612	182,544		61,050	62,169	26,447	421,822	1,295,291
Honduras	4,134	23,267	11,922		8,860	2,191	50,374	740,312
Nicaragua	17,173	13,650	5,294	5,540		2,109	43,766	236,493
Panama	30,905	9,686	7,594	5,053	3,119		56,357	480,912
1994								
Costa Rica		72,264	102,621	43,432	67,534	65,632	351,483	2,242,724
El Salvador	71,911		177,387	56,078	36,493	12,024	353,893	817,774
Guatemala	97,623	228,979		87,036	61,355	32,679	507,672	1,502,556
Honduras	21,500	43,500	34,700		40,200	3,599	143,499	965,499
Nicaragua	25,504	37,114	8,708	12,575		4,532	88,433	351,108
Panama	37,961	13,006	11,572	9,047	4,591		76,177	532,538
1996								
Costa Rica		100,559	134,301	71,037	105,267	92,083	503,247	3,410,177
El Salvador	93,277		210,655	97,470	53,667	24,533	479,602	1,024,268
Guatemala	99,787	258,045		140,238	79,911	46,327	624,308	2,030,734
Honduras	27,200	59,100	56,100		64,000	12,794	219,194	1,320,799
Nicaragua	13,339	58,098	10,160	19,594		4,517	105,708	660,183
Panama	37,946	9,422	14,957	9,922	4,339		76,586	566,408
1998								
Costa Rica		112,860	173,090	91,130	143,390	123,080	520,460	5,515,880
El Salvador	110,319		282,534	148,753	74,966	24,280	640,852	1,257,070
Guatemala	119,986	320,055		215,913	92,592	67,363	815,909	2,581,675
Honduras	29,900	65,000	61,600		70,400	5,655	232,555	1,532,900
Nicaragua	25,490	57,646	16,449	22,911		1,325	123,821	552,824
Panama	46,408	11,340	18,014	22,233	13,021		111,016	705,458

Source: Website of SIECA www.sieca.org.gt

Table A.5: CACM Intra-Regional and Total Exports (US$'000), 1998–2000

	EXPORTS			IMPORTS		
	CACM	Rest of World	Total	CACM	Rest of World	Total
CENTRAL AMERICA						
1998 (P)	2,634,308	7,882,702	10,517,010	2,263,902	15,415,621	17,679,523
1999 (P)	2,289,779	8,885,838	11,175,617	2,374,867	15,674,792	18,049,659
2000 (E)	2,537,101	9,258,862	11,795,963	2,626,108	16,696,924	19,323,032
GUATEMALA						
1998 (P)	748,547	1,833,129	2,581,676	607,931	4,042,917	4,650,848
1999 (P)	789,916	1,668,300	2,458,216	484,620	4,069,717	4,554,337
2000 (E)	769,144	1,854,238	2,623,382	618,699	4,227,270	4,845,969
EL SALVADOR						
1998 (P)	616,572	640,498	1,257,070	599,238	2,510,499	3,109,737
1999 (P)	627,245	536,914	1,164,159	637,555	2,492,309	3,129,864
2000 (E)	731,300	615,800	1,347,100	765,400	2,932,200	3,697,600
HONDURAS						
1998 (P)	184,776	789,378	974,154	421,165	2,149,415	2,570,580
1999 (P)	150,929	610,084	761,013	432,706	2,221,604	2,654,310
2000 (E)	251,800	1,076,466	1,328,226	464,000	2,422,987	2,886,987
NICARAGUA						
1998 (P)	122,495	430,329	552,824	418,156	1,115,937	1,534,093
1999 (P)	145,061	364,087	509,148	519,222	1,203,845	1,723,067
2000 (E)	157,631	455,227	612,858	492,224	1,327,245	1,819,469
COSTA RICA						
1998 (P)	961,918	4,189,369	5,151,287	317,412	5,596,853	5,914,265
1999 (P)	576,628	5,706,453	6,283,081	300,764	5,687,616	5,988,380
2000 (E)	627,226	5,257,151	5,884,377	285,785	5,787,222	6,073,007

P = Provisional
E = Estimate
Source: Website of SIECA, www.sieca.org.gt

Table A.6: NAFTA Intra-Regional Trade, 1994–99 (US$ millions)

	1994	1995	1996	1997	1998	1999
MEXICAN EXPORTS						
To US	51,943	66,475	80,673	94,531	103,306	120,393
To Canada	1,470	1,979	2,170	2,157	1,521	2,391
Total	60,882	79,541	96,000	110,431	117,494	136,391
NAFTA %	87.7	86.1	86.3	87.6	89.2	90.0
MEXICAN IMPORTS						
From US	57,009	53,995	67,629	82,182	93,252	105,267
From Canada	1,600	1,374	1,744	1,968	2,292	2,949
Total	79,346	72,452	89,971	109,808	125,190	141,975
NAFTA %	73.9	76.4	77.1	76.6	76.3	76.2

Source: IMF, Direction of Trade Statistics, Washington, DC, 2000.

Table A.7: Value and Distribution of CARICOM's Imports by Principal Sources: 1990–99

(EC$'000)

	1990		1991		1992		1993		1994		1995		1996		1997		1998		1999	
	VALUE	%	VALUE	%	VALUE	%	VALUE	%	VALUE	%	VALUE	%	VALUE	%	VALUE	%	VALUE	%	VALUE	%
CARICOM TOTAL IMPORTS	13,675,982	100.0	14,062,350	100.0	13,776,218	100.0	15,359,360	100.0	15,358,451	100.0	19,573,989	100.0	18,759,276	100.0	22,752,310	100.0	21,746,997	100.0	14,104,946	100.0
Caribbean Community & Common Market	1,258,555	9.2	1,215,679	8.6	1,271,356	9.2	1,416,353	9.2	1,613,340	10.5	1,927,959	9.8	1,822,654	9.7	2,092,679	9.2	2,065,332	9.5	2,042,135	14.5
Caribbean Common Market	1,257,546	9.2	1,214,673	8.6	1,270,192	9.2	1,409,951	9.2	1,604,046	10.4	1,912,455	9.8	1,819,032	9.7	2,078,718	9.1	2,057,897	9.5	2,035,862	14.4
The Bahamas	1,009	0.0	1,006	0.0	1,164	0.0	6,402	0.0	9,294	0.1	15,504	0.1	3,622	0.0	13,961	0.1	7,435	0.0	6,273	0.0
Other Caribbean Countries	477,162	3.5	555,456	3.5	482,942	3.5	522,872	3.4	478,499	3.1	467,914	2.4	476,573	2.5	571,044	2.5	331,310	1.5	337,140	2.4
Canada	736,394	5.4	652,875	4.6	593,714	4.6	629,567	4.1	669,302	4.4	721,736	3.7	630,581	3.4	669,012	2.9	719,655	3.3	472,943	3.4
USA	5,636,111	41.2	5,823,069	41.4	6,225,733	45.2	6,678,818	43.5	7,227,083	47.1	8,331,823	42.6	8,330,248	44.4	10,859,415	47.7	10,045,060	46.2	6,376,363	45.2
Latin American Integration Association	1,536,794	11.2	1,568,489	11.1	1,404,755	10.2	1,617,260	10.5	1,128,790	7.3	1,770,571	9.0	2,290,691	12.2	2,240,622	9.8	2,259,294	10.4	871,109	6.2
Central American Common Market	93,473	0.7	85,838	0.6	99,002	0.7	104,237	0.7	118,712	0.8	123,857	0.6	152,452	0.8	176,590	0.8	204,821	0.9	197,765	1.4
European Union	2,115,518	15.5	2,281,075	16.2	1,948,353	14.1	2,193,185	14.3	1,996,885	13.0	2,970,599	15.2	2,641,928	14.1	3,181,302	14.0	2,981,044	13.7	1,560,250	11.1
UK	1,172,682	8.6	1,187,126	8.4	1,095,155	7.9	1,154,918	7.5	1,132,838	7.4	1,179,463	6.0	1,098,899	5.9	1,225,558	5.4	1,199,250	5.5	781,400	5.5
Rest of EU	942,836	6.9	1,093,949	7.8	853,198	6.2	1,038,267	6.8	864,047	5.6	1,791,097	9.2	1,543,029	8.2	1,955,744	8.6	1,781,794	8.2	778,850	5.5
European Free Trade Association	235,812	1.7	177,749	1.3	208,904	1.5	198,145	1.3	240,764	1.6	179,309	0.9	149,300	0.8	160,917	0.7	165,932	0.8	118,782	0.8
Selected Asian Countries	1,051,527	7.7	1,294,678	9.2	1,157,120	8.4	1,489,064	9.7	1,346,568	8.8	1,636,520	8.4	1,535,945	8.2	1,916,597	8.4	2,090,884	9.6	1,368,167	9.7
Japan	625,458	4.6	844,887	6.0	686,406	5.0	879,957	5.7	748,817	4.9	935,614	4.8	904,788	4.8	1,194,016	5.2	1,239,908	5.7	866,941	6.1
Rest of Selected Asian Countries	426,069	3.1	449,791	3.2	470,714	3.4	609,107	4.0	597,751	3.9	700,906	3.6	631,157	3.4	722,581	3.2	850,766	3.9	501,226	3.6
Rest of the World	534,636	3.9	427,442	3.9	386,339	3.0	509,859	2.8	538,508	3.5	1,443,741	7.4	727,904	3.9	884,132	3.9	883,755	4.1	760,292	5.4

Note: EC$ - Eastern Caribbean dollar (EC$2.70 = US$1).

Table A.8: Intra-Hemispheric Exports by Destination in 1999 – Preliminary Estimates[1] (US$ millions)

REGIONS	MERCOSUR	MERCOSUR + Chile + Bolivia	CAN	G-3	LAIA	CACM	Latin America	CARICOM	NAFTA	Hemisphere	World Total
MERCOSUR	13,924	16,903	2,438	2,203	19,698	354	20,372	169	14,483	34,003	69,939
Andean Community (CAN)	1,165	2,116	3,559	2,822	6,173	1,087	8,429	1,507	19,487	28,983	40,648
Group of Three (G-3)[3]	1,365	2,109	3,601	2,763	6,100	2,067	9,870	1,619	131,963	143,486	159,414
LAIA	17,072	21,489	7,871	6,609	30,555	2,596	35,141	1,844	153,832	188,041	252,964
CACM	11	44	72	277	364	2,226	2,920	81	5,841	8,275	10,951
Latin America[2]	17,084	21,536	7,962	6,915	30,958	4,934	38,144	1,952	160,004	196,798	264,625
NAFTA	19,972	23,716	12,896	91,183	117,928	9,816	134,877	4,289	546,602	603,431	1,017,025
Hemisphere Total	36,427	44,288	19,935	97,469	147,112	13,604	169,578	6,074	590,532	680,688	1,152,528

Notes:

(1) Projections based on data available on 30 September 19992.

(2) Includes the members of LAIA, the Central America Common Market (CACM) and Panama.

(3) G-3 = Colombia, Mexico and Venezuela.

Source: IDB, Statistics and Quantitative Analysis Unit.

Bibliography

Abbott, F.M. (2000) 'NAFTA and the Legalisation of World Politics: A Case Study', *International Organisation*, vol. 54, no. 3, (Summer), pp. 519–47.

Abbott, K.W. et al. (2000) 'The Concept of Legalisation', *International Organisation*, vol. 54, no. 3, (Summer), pp. 401–19.

Adams, Laurel A. (1998) 'Southern Multinationals', *Review of International Economics*, August.

Anderson, K. and Norheim, N. (1993) 'History, Geography and Regional Economic Integration', in K. Anderson and R. Blackhurst (eds.) (1993) *Regional Integration and the Global Trading System* (New York: St Martin's Press).

Arbix, Glauco Antônio Truzzi (1995) 'Uma aposta no futuro: Os três primeiros anos da câmara setorial da indústria automobilística e a emergência do meso-corporatismo no Brasil', PhD diss., Universidade de São Paulo.

Avery, William and Friman, H. Richard (1999) 'Who Got What and Why: Constructing North American Free Trade', in Kenneth Thomas and Mary Ann Tétreault (eds.) *Racing to Regionalize* (Boulder, CO: Lynne Rienner).

Balassa, B. (1961) *The Theory of Economic Integration* (Illinois: George Allen and Unwin).

Balassa, B. (1977) 'Revealed Comparative Advantage Revisited: An Analysis of Relative Export Shares of the Industrial Countries, 1953–1971', *The Manchester School of Economic and Social Studies*, vol. 4, pp. 327–44.

Baldwin, David (ed.) (1993) *Neo-Realism and Neo-Liberalism: The Contemporary Debate* (New York: Columbia University Press).

Baldwin, R. (1993) 'A Domino Theory of Regionalism', Working Paper no. 4465 (Cambridge, MA: NBER).

Banco de México (1999) *Informe Anual 1999* [http://www.banxico.org.mex].

Bartholomew, A. (2000) 'MERCOSUR: An Analysis of Regional Integration Between Argentina and Brazil in the 1990s', PhD thesis, Institute of Latin American Studies, University of London.

Baumann, R. (1992) 'An Appraisal of Recent Intra-Industry Trade for Latin America', *CEPAL Review*, no. 48.

Baumann, R. (1998) 'Nota sobre as relações intra-setoriais no comércio externo brasileiro: 1980–96' (Brasilia: CEPAL, LC/BRS/DT.017).

Bayoumi, T., Eichengreen, B. and Taylor, M.P. (eds.) (1996) *Modern Perspectives on the Gold Standard* (Cambridge: Cambridge

University Press).

Behar, J. (1991) 'Economic Integration and Intra-Industry Trade: The Case of the Argentine–Brazilian Free Trade Agreement', *Journal of Common Market Studies*, vol. 29, no. 4, pp. 527–52.

Berg, A. and Borensztein, E. (2000) 'Full-Dollarization: The Pros and Cons', *IMF Working Paper* WP/00/50 (Washington, DC: International Monetary Fund).

Bergsten, C.F. (1997) 'Open Regionalism', *World Economy*, vol. 20, no. 5, pp. 545–65.

Bhagwati, J. (1991) *The World Trading System at Risk* (Princeton: Princeton University Press and Harvester Wheatsheaf).

Bhagwati, J. (1993) 'Regionalism and Multilateralism: An Overview', in Jaime De Melo and Arvind Panagariya (eds.) *New Dimensions in Regional Integration* (Cambridge: Cambridge University Press and World Bank).

Birle, Peter (1997) *Los empresarios y la democracia en Argentina* (Buenos Aires: Belgrano).

Blomström, Magnus and Kokko, Ari (1997) *Regional Integration and Foreign Direct Investment*, World Bank Policy Research Working Paper no. 1750 (Washington, DC: World Bank).

Boldorini, M.C. and Zalduendo, S. (1995) 'La estructura jurídico-institucional del MERCOSUR después del Protocolo de Ouro Preto', *Boletín Informativo Techint*, no. 283, July–September.

Bollin, Christina (1999) *Centro América: Situación y perspectivas del proceso de integración a finales de los 90* (Guatemala: INCEP).

Borner, Silvio, Brunetti, Aymo and Weder, Beatrice (1995) *Political Credibility and Economic Development* (New York: St Martin's Press).

Bouzas, R. (1998) 'Strategic Issues and Market Access Negotiations in the Americas: A Perspective From MERCOSUR', Buenos Aires, Universidad de San Andrés, Documento de Trabajo, no. 15, October.

Bouzas, R. (1999) 'Las perspectivas del MERCOSUR: desafíos, escenarios y alternativas para la próxima década', in J. Campbell (ed.) *MERCOSUR. Entre la realidad y la utopía* (Buenos Aires: CEI-Editorial Nuevohacer).

Bouzas, R. and Ros, J. (1994) 'The North South Variety of Economic Integration', in R. Bouzas and J. Ros (eds.) *Economic Integration in the Western Hemisphere* (South Bend: University of Notre Dame Press).

Buitelaar, R. (1993) 'Dynamic Gains from Intra-Regional Trade in Latin America', in Richard Belous and Jonathan Lemco (comps.) *NAFTA as a Model of Development: The Benefits and Costs of Merging High and Low Wage Areas* (Washington, DC: National Planning Association).

Buitelaar, R. and Padilla, R. (1996) 'El comercio intraindustria de Mexico con sus principales socios comerciales', *Estudios Económicos*, vol. 11, no. 1.

Buiter, W.H. (1999) 'The EMU and the NAMU: What is the Case for North American Monetary Union?', CEPR Discussion Paper Series, no. 2181.

Bulmer-Thomas, Victor (1994) *The Economic History of Latin America since Independence* (Cambridge: Cambridge University Press).

Bulmer-Thomas, Victor (ed.) (1997) *The Political Economy of Central America since 1920* (Cambridge: Cambridge University Press).

Bulmer-Thomas, Victor (ed.) (1998) *Centroamérica en reestructuración* (Sede Costa Rica: Facultad Latinoamericana de Ciencias Sociales).

Bulmer-Thomas, Victor (1998a) 'The Central American Common Market: From Closed to Open Regionalism', *World Development*, vol. 26, no. 2, pp. 313–22.

Bulmer-Thomas, Victor (1998b) *Reflexiones sobre la integración centroamericana* (Tegucigalpa: Banco Centroamericano de Integración Económica).

Bulmer-Thomas, Victor (2000) 'The European Union and MERCOSUR', *Journal of Interamerican Studies and World Affairs*, vol. 42, no. 1, (Spring), pp. 1–22.

Bulmer-Thomas, V., Craske, N. and Serrano, M. (1994) *Mexico and the North American Free Trade Agreement: Who Will Benefit?* (London: Macmillan).

Bulmer-Thomas, V. and Page, S. (1999) 'Trade Relations in the Americas: MERCOSUR, the Free Trade Area of the Americas and the European Union', in V. Bulmer-Thomas and J. Dunkerley (eds.) *The United States and Latin America: The New Agenda* (Boston and London: David Rockefeller Center for Latin American Studies and Institute of Latin American Studies).

Burki, Javed and Perry, G. (1998) *Beyond the Washington Consensus: Institutions Matter* (Washington, DC: World Bank).

Burkins, G. (1999) 'Labor to Keep Fighting Clinton on Trade', *Wall Street Journal*, 12 October.

Burrell, Jennifer and Cason, Jeffrey (2000) 'Turning the Tables: State and Society in South America's Economic Integration', unpubl. ms.

Calvo, Ernesto (2000) 'Disconcerted Industrialists: The Politics of Trade Reform in Latin America', dissertation draft, Northwestern University.

Calvo, G. and Vegh, C.A. (1992) 'Currency Substitution in Developing Countries', *IMF Working Papers WP/92/40*, http://vegh.sscnet.ucla.edu/calvo-vegh-rae.pdf.

Cameron, J. and Campbell, K. (eds.) (1998) *Dispute Resolution in the World Trade Organisation* (London: Cameron May).

Caprio, Gerard Jr., Dooley, Michael, Leipziger, Danny and Walsh, Carl

(1996) 'The Lender of Last Resort Function Under a Currency Board: The Case of Argentina', *Open Economies Review*, vol. 7, pp. 617–42, July.

Cason, Jeffrey (2000) 'Democracy Looks South: Mercosul and the Politics of Brazilian Trade Strategy', in Peter Kingstone and Timothy Power (eds.) *Democratic Brazil* (Pittsburgh: University of Pittsburgh Press).

Cason, Jeffrey (2000a) 'On the Road to Southern Cone Economic Integration', *Journal of Interamerican Studies and World Affairs*, vol. 42, no. 1, (Spring), pp. 23–42.

Centro de Economía Internacional (1999) *Panorama del MERCOSUR*, vol. 2, March.

CEPAL (1993) *Directorio sobre inversión extranjera en América Latina y el Caribe 1993: marco legal e información estadística* (Santiago: CEPAL).

CEPAL (1994) *Open Regionalism in Latin America and the Caribbean* (Santiago: CEPAL).

CEPAL (1997) *Centroamérica: evolución de la integración económica durante 1996* (Mexico City: CEPAL).

CEPAL (1999) *Foreign Investment in Latin America and the Caribbean* (Chile: United Nations and CEPAL).

CEPAL/BID (n.d) *La integración centroamericana y la institucionalidad regional* (Washington: Interamerican Development Bank and CEPAL).

CEPAL (2000) *La inversión extranjera en América Latina y el Caribe. Informe 1999* (Santiago: CEPAL).

Chudnovsky, Daniel (ed.) (1996) *Los límites de la apertura* (Buenos Aires: Alianza Editorial/CENIT).

Cohen, B. (1993) 'Beyond EMU: The Problem of Sustainability', *Economics and Politics*, vol. 5, pp. 187–202.

Confederação Nacional da Indústria (1994) *Abertura Comercial & Estratégia Tecnológica*, 4th survey, Rio de Janeiro.

Confederação Nacional da Indústria (1995) *Abertura Comercial & Estratégia Tecnológica*, 5th survey, Rio de Janeiro.

Cooper, H. (1999) 'Corporate, Labor Leaders Both Trumpet Backing for Clinton's Trade-Talk Plan', *Wall Street Journal*, 1 November.

Cooper, H., Davis, R. and Hill, G. (1999) 'WTO's Failure in Bid to Launch Trade Talks Emboldens Protestors', *Wall Street Journal*, 6 December, p. 1.

Cooper, R.N. (1982) 'The Gold Standard: Historical Facts and Future Prospects' *Brookings Papers on Economic Activity*, no. 1, pp. 1–45.

Córdoba, J. (1996) 'Rules of Origin in Free-Trade Agreements: The NAFTA Case' (mimeo).

Costa Vaz, A. (1999) 'A integração no MERCOSUR: novos ators e o desafio da participação política e social', in Y. Chaloult and P.R. de

Almeida (eds.) *MERCOSUR, NAFTA e ALCA. A dimensão social* (São Paulo: Editora LTR), pp. 69–94.

CPC. 'Cuenta de Actividades', Various years.

Cusack, David (1972) 'The Politics of Chilean Private Enterprise under Christian Democracy', PhD diss., University of Denver.

da Motta Veiga, P. (1999) 'Brazil in MERCOSUR: Reciprocal Influences', in R. Roett (ed.) *MERCOSUR. Regional Integration, World Markets* (Boulder, CO: Lynne Rienner).

Danthine, J-P., Giavezzi, F. and von Thadden, E-L (2000) 'European Financial Markets after EMU: A First Assessment', *CEPR Discussion Paper 2413* (London: Centre for Economic Policy Research).

De Grauwe, P. (1992) *The Economics of Monetary Integration* (Oxford: Oxford University Press).

de la Balze, Felipe A.M. (ed.) (1995) *Argentina y Brasil enfrentando el siglo XXI* (Buenos Aires: Consejo Argentino para las Relaciones Internacionales).

de la Balze, Felipe (2000) 'El destino del MERCOSUR: entre la unión aduanera y la "integración imperfecta"', in Felipe de la Balze (ed.) *El futuro del MERCOSUR. Entre la retórica y el realismo* (Buenos Aires: CARI), pp. 18–24.

Destler, I.M. (1995) *American Trade Politics*, 3rd ed. (Washington, DC: Institute for International Economics; New York: Twentieth Century Fund).

Destler, I.M. and Balint, P.J. (1999) *The New Politics of American Trade: Trade, Labor, and the Environment* (Washington, DC: Institute for International Economics) Policy Analyses in International Economics, no. 58.

Detken, C. and Hartmann, P. (2000) 'The Euro and International Capital Markets', *CEPR Discussion Paper 2461* (London: Centre for Economic Policy Research).

Devlin, R. and Ffrench-Davis, R. (1999) 'Towards an Evaluation of Regional Integration in Latin America in the 1990s', *The World Economy*, vol. 22, no. 2, March 1999.

Devlin, R., Estevadeordal, A. and Katona, A. (2001) 'The Old vs. the New Regionalism in the Americas', forthcoming INTAL/ITD Working Paper, IDB, Washington DC.

Díaz-Fuentes, D. (1999) 'Latin America during the Interwar Period: The Rise and Fall of the Gold Standard in Argentina, Brazil and Mexico', pp. 442–69 in J.H. Coatsworth and A.M. Taylor (eds.) *Latin America and the World Economy since 1800* (Cambridge. MA: Harvard University Press).

Dick, T.J.O., Floyd, J.E. and Pope, D. (1996) 'Balance of Payments Adjustment under the Gold Standard: Canada and Australia

Compared', in T. Bayoumi et al. (eds.) *Modern Perspectives on the Gold Standard* (Cambridge: Cambridge University Press).

Dornbusch, R. et al. (1989) *Meeting World Challenges: United States Manufacturing in the 1990s* (Rochester, NY: Eastman Kodak Company) (pamphlet).

Duran, Roberto (1996) 'Democracy and Regional Multilateralism in Chile', in Gordon Mace and Jean-Philippe Thérien (eds.) *Foreign Policy and Regionalism in the Americas* (Boulder: Lynne Rienner).

EC (1990) *One Europe, One Money* (Brussels: European Commission).

Echavarría, J. (1998) 'Trade Flows in the Andean Countries: Unilateral Liberalisation or Regional Preferences?', in World Bank, *Trade Towards Open Regionalism* (Washington, DC).

ECLAC (1994) *Open Regionalism in Latin America and the Caribbean* (Santiago).

Economic Policy Institute, Institute for Policy Studies, International Labor Rights Fund, Public Citizen's Global Trade Watch, Sierra Club and US Business & Industrial Council Educational Foundation (1997) *The Failed Experiment: NAFTA at Three Years* (Washington, DC).

Eichengreen, B. (1992) *Golden Fetters: The Gold Standard and the Great Depression 1919–39* (New York: Oxford University Press).

Eichengreen, B. (1994) 'History of the International Monetary System: Implications for Research in International Macroeconomics and Finance', in J. van der Ploeg (1994) *Handbook of International Macroeconomics* (Oxford: Blackwell).

El-Agraa, A.M. (1994) *The Economics of the European Union*, fourth edition (London: Harvester Wheatsheaf).

El-Agraa, A. and Nicholls, S. (1997) 'The Caribbean Community and Common Market' in A. El-Agraa (ed.) *Economic Integration Worldwide* (London: Macmillan).

Estevadeordal, A. (1999) 'Negotiating Preferential Market Access: The Case of NAFTA', INTAL-Integration Trade and Hemispheric Issues Division Working Paper, no. 3 (Washington, DC: IDB).

Estevadeordal, A, Goto, J and Saez, R. (2000.) 'The New Regionalism in the Americas: The Case of MERCOSUR', Working Paper, no. 5 (Buenos Aires: BID-INTAL).

Ethier, W.J. (1998) 'The New Regionalism', *The Economic Journal*, vol. 108, July, pp. 1149–61.

Evans, Peter B. (1995) *Embedded Autonomy: States and Industrial Transformation* (Princeton: Princeton University Press).

Farlie Renoso, Allan (1997) 'The Andean Community Case', in Paul De Maret, Jean François Bellis, and González García Jiménez (eds.) *Regionalism and Multilateralism after the Uruguay Round* (Brussels: European InterUniversity Press).

Fawcett, Louise and Hurrell, Andrew (eds.) (1995) *Regionalism in World Politics* (Oxford: Oxford University Press).

Federal Reserve Board (1994) http://www.federalreserve.gov/fomc/transcripts/.

Federal Reserve Bank of Dallas (1999) [http://www.dallasfed.org/].

Feinberg, R.E. (1998) *Summitry of the Americas: A Progress Report* (Washington, DC: Institute for International Economics).

Ferguson, N. (1998) *The World's Banker* (London: Weidenfeld and Nicholson).

FitzGerald, E.V.K. (1983) 'Mexico–United States Economic Relations and the World Cycle: A European View', pp. 349–68 in C.W. Reynolds and C. Tello (eds.) *US–Mexico Relations: Economic and Social Aspects* (Stanford, CA: Stanford University Press).

FitzGerald, E.V.K. (1999) 'Trade, Investment and the NAFTA: The Economics of Neighbourhood', in V. Bulmer-Thomas and J. Dunkerley (eds.) *The United States and Latin America: The New Agenda* (Boston and London; David Rockefeller Center for Latin American Studies and Institute of Latin American Studies) pp. 99–122.

FitzGerald, E.V.K. (2000) 'Short-Term Capital Flows, the Real Economy and Income Distribution in Developing Countries', in S. Griffith-Jones, M. Montes and A. Nasution (eds.) *Managing Capital Flows in Developing Countries* (Oxford: Oxford University Press).

FitzGerald, E.V.K. (2000a) 'Capital Surges, Investment Instability and Income Distribution after Financial Liberalisation', in W. Mahmud (ed.) *Adjustment and Beyond: The Reform Experience in South Asia* (Basingstoke: Macmillan in association with the International Economic Association).

FitzGerald, E.V.K. (2000b) 'External Money: Lessons of Experience in the Use of an Exogenous Currency for Dollarisation in the Americas' [paper presented at the conference 'Dollarization in the Western Hemisphere' organised by the North-South Institute in collaboration with the Canadian Centre for Policy Alternatives, Ottawa, 4–5 October 2000. Available on http://www.nis-ins.org.ca].

FitzGerald, E.V.K. and Grabbe, H. (1997) 'Integración financiera: la experiencia europea y sus lecciones para América Latina', *Integración & Comercio*, vol. 1, no. 2, pp. 85–124.

Freund, C. and McLaren, J. (1999) 'On the Dynamics of Trade Diversion: Evidence from Four Trade Blocks', (Federal Reserve Board, Washington, DC [mimeo]).

Fuentes, J.A. (1994) 'Open Regionalism and Economic Integration', *CEPAL Review*, August, no. 53.

Fundación Invertir Argentina (1996) *Invertir*, June.

Garay, L.J. and Estevadeordal, A. (1996) 'Protection, Preferential Tariff

Elimination and Rules of Origin in the Americas', *Integration and Trade*.

Garay, L.J. and Quintero, L.F. (1999) 'Characterization and Structure of the Rules of Origin of the G-3, NAFTA and ALADI: Their Relevance to the Case of Colombia' (mimeo).

Gereffi, G. and Martinez, A. (1999) 'The Blue Jeans Boom in Tarreon', Department of Technology (Durham, NC: Duke University Press).

Giacalone, Rita (1999) *Los empresarios frente al Grupo de Los Tres* (Caracas: Nueva Sociedad).

Gil-Díaz, F. and Carstens, A. (1996) 'One Year of Solitude: Some Pilgrim's Tales about Mexico's 1994–5 Crisis', *American Economic Review*, 86, no. 2, May.

Giordano, Paolo and Santiso, Javier (1999) 'La course aux Amériques: les stratégies des investisseurs européens en Argentine et au Bresil', *Les Etudes de CERI*, no. 52.

Giovannini, A. and Tutelboom, B. (1994) 'Currency Substitution', in F. van der Ploeg (ed.) *Handbook of International Macroeconomics* (Oxford: Blackwell).

Gomes, Eduardo (1998) 'After Import-Substitution: Brazil's Export-Oriented Growth and the Politics of the Industrial Enterpreneurs', PhD diss., University of Chicago.

González, F. (1999) 'MERCOSUR: incompatibilidad de sus instituticiones con la necesidad de perfeccionar la unión aduanera. Propuesta de cambio', *Integración y Comercio*, año 3, no. 9, septiembre–diciembre.

Goodin, R. (1997) 'Institutions and their Design', in R. Goodin (ed.) *The Theory of Institutional Design* (Cambridge: Cambridge University Press).

Graham, Edward M. and Wada, Erika (2000) 'Domestic Reform, Trade and Investment Liberalisation, Financial Crisis, and Foreign Direct Investment into Mexico', *The World Economy*, vol. 23, no. 6.

Granados, J. (1999) 'La integración comercial centroamericana: Un marco integrativo y cursos de acción pública', Integration, Trade and Hemispheric Issues Division, IDB, Washington, DC. (mimeo).

Greenaway, D. and Milner, C. (1983) 'On the Measurement of Intra-Industry Trade', *Economic Journal*, vol. 93.

Grieco, J. (1997) 'Systemic Sources of Variation in Regional Institutionalisation in Western Europe, East Asia and the Americas', in E. Mansfield and H. Milner (eds.) *The Political Economy of Regionalism* (New York: Columbia University Press).

Griffith-Jones, S. (2000) 'The Mexican Peso Crisis' in S. Griffith-Jones, M. Montes and A. Nasution (eds.) (2000) *Managing Capital Flows in Developing Countries* (Oxford: Oxford University Press).

Griffith-Jones, S., Montes, M. and Nasution, A. (eds.) (2000) *Managing Capital Flows in Developing Countries* (Oxford: Oxford University Press).

Gruben, W.C. and Welch, J. (1994) 'Is NAFTA More than a Free Trade Agreement? A View from the United States', in V. Bulmer-Thomas, N. Craske and M. Serrano (eds.) *Mexico and the North American Free Trade Agreement: Who Will Benefit?* (London: Macmillan), pp. 177–202.

Guidotti, P.E. and Rodriguez, C.A. (1992) 'Dollarization in Latin America: Gresham's Law in Reverse' *IMF Staff Papers*, no. 39, pp. 518–44.

Hadjimichael, M.T. and Galy, M. (1997) 'The CFA Franc Zone and the EMU', IMF Working Paper WP/97/156.

Hall, Kenneth and Benn, Denis (eds.) (2000) *Contending with Destiny* (Kingston: Ian Randle Publishers).

Hallwood, C.P and MacDonald, R. (1994) *International Money and Finance* (Oxford: Blackwell).

Hasenclever, L. et al. (1999) 'Impacto del MERCOSUR sobre la dinámica del sector petroquímico', in *Impacto Sectorial de la Integración en el MERCOSUR* (Buenos Aires: INTAL).

Hasenclever, L., Lopez, A and Clement de Oliveira, J. (1999) 'The Impact of MERCOSUR on the Development of the Petrochemical Sector, *Integration and Trade*, vol. 3, nos. 7/8, January–August, Inter-American Development Bank, Integration and Regional Programs Department, INTAL.

Hathaway, Oona (1998) 'Positive Feedback: The Impact of Trade Liberalisation on Industry Demands for Protection', *International Organization*, vol. 52, no. 3, (Summer), pp. 575–613.

Havrylyshyn, O. and Civan, E. (1983) 'Intra-industry Trade and the Stage of Development: a Regression Analysis of Industrial and Developing Countries', in P. Tharakan (ed.) *Intra-industry Trade* (Amsterdam: North-Holland).

Heymann, D. (1999) 'Interdependencias y políticas macroeconómicas: reflexiones sobre el MERCOSUR', in J. Campbell (ed.) MERCOSUR. *Entre la realidad y la utopía* (Buenos Aires: CEI-Editorial Nuevohacer).

Hix, S. (1999) *The Political System of Europe* (Basingstoke: Macmillan).

Hufbauer G., Schott, J. and Clark, D. (1994) *Western Hemisphere Economic Integration* (Washington, DC: Institute for International Economics).

Hufty, Marc (1996) 'Argentina', in Gordon Mace and Jean-Philippe Thérien (eds.) *Foreign Policy and Regionalism in the Americas* (Boulder: Lynne Rienner).

Hurrell, A. (1995) 'Regionalism in the Americas', in L. Fawcett and A. Hurrell (eds.) *Regionalism in World Politics* (Oxford: Oxford University Press), pp. 258–9.

Hurrell, A. (1998) 'An Emerging Security Community in South America?' in Emanuel Adler and Michael Barnett (eds.) *Security Communities* (Cambridge: Cambridge University Press).

Hurrell A. and Menon, A. (1996) 'Politics like any Other? Comparative

Politics, International Relations and the Study of the EC', *West European Politics*, vol.19, 2 April.

IMF (2000) *World Economic Outlook* (Washington, DC: International Monetary Fund).

IMF Direction of Trade Statistics Yearbook, Washington, DC, 1988–98.

INTAL (1996) *MERCOSUR Report* (Buenos Aires).

INTAL (1997) *MERCOSUR Report January–June 1997*, no. 4, Inter-American Development Bank, Integration and Regional Programs Department, Buenos Aires.

INTAL (1998) *MERCOSUR Report January–June 1998*, no. 4, Inter-American Development Bank, Integration and Regional Programs Department, Buenos Aires.

INTAL (1999) *MERCOSUR Report 1998–1999*, no. 5, Inter-American Development Bank, Integration and Regional Programs Department, Buenos Aires.

INTAL (1999a) *Impacto sectorial de la integración en MERCOSUR* (Buenos Aires: INTAL/IDB).

INTAL (2000) MERCOSUR Report, no. 6 (Buenos Aries: INTAL/IDB).

INTAL (2000a) 'Argentina and Brazil Agree on Automotive Policy Guidelines', *Integration and Regional Programs Department Monthly Newsletter*, no. 44, March (Inter-American Development Bank).

Inter-American Development Bank (IDB) (1984) *Economic and Social Progress in Latin America: Economic Integration*, 1984 Report (Washington, DC: Inter-American Development Bank).

Inter-American Development Bank (IDB) (1992) *Economic and Social Progress in Latin America*, 1992 Report (Washington, DC: IDB).

Inter-American Development Bank (IDB) (1996) *Report: MERCOSUR 1* (Buenos Aires: INTAL/IDB).

Inter-American Development Bank (IDB) (1997) *INTAL Monthly Newsletter*, March (Buenos Aires: INTAL/IDB).

Inter-American Development Bank (IDB) (1997a) *Report: MERCOSUR 3* (Buenos Aires: INTAL/IDB).

Inter-American Development Bank (IDB) (1999) 'Integration and Trade in the Americas', Periodic Note, Division of Integration, Trade and Hemispheric Issues, October.

Inter-American Development Bank (IDB) (1999a) 'Integration and Trade in the Americas', Periodic Note, Division of Integration, Trade and Hemispheric Issues, February.

Inter-American Development Bank and Institute for European-Latin American Relations (IDB/IRELA) (1996) *Foreign Direct Investment in Latin America in the 1990s* (Madrid: IRELA).

Inter-American Development Bank and Institute for European-Latin American Relations (IDB/IRELA) (1998) *Foreign Direct Investment in Latin America:*

Perspectives of the Major Investors (Madrid: IRELA).

IRELA (2000) 'La inversión directa europea en América Latina: Los réditos de la apertura y la privatización' (Madrid: IRELA).

Jardel, S. (1998) 'Las instituciones del MERCOSUR', 2° Congreso de Economía, Consejo Profesional de Ciencias Económicas de la Capital Federal (mimeo).

Jenkins, Barbara (1999) 'Assessing the 'New' Integration: The MERCOSUR Trade Agreement', In Kenneth Thomas and Mary Ann Tétreault (eds.) *Racing to Regionalize* (Boulder: Lynne Rienner).

Kaufman, Robert, Bazdresch, Carlos, and Heredia, Blanca (1994) 'Mexico: Radical Reform in a Dominant Party System', in Stephan Haggard and Steven Webb (eds.) *Voting for Reform* (New York: Oxford University Press).

Keohane, R. (1993) 'Institutionalist Theory and the Realist Challenge after the Cold War', in David Baldwin (ed.) *Neo-Realism and Neo-Liberalism* (New York: Columbia University Press), p. 274.

Keohane, R. and Hoffmann, S. (eds.) (1990) *The New European Community* (Boulder: Lynne Rienner).

Khaler, M. (1995) *International Institutions and the Political Economy of Integration* (Washington, DC: The Brookings Institution).

Kingstone, Peter (1994) 'Shaping Business Interests: The Politics of Neo-Liberalism in Brazil, 1985–92', PhD diss., University of California, Berkeley.

Kingstone, Peter (1998) 'Corporatism, Neoliberalism, and the Failed Revolt of Big Business: Lessons from the Case of IEDI', *Journal of Interamerican Studies and World Affairs*, vol. 40, no. 4, (Winter).

Kingstone, Peter (1999) *Crafting Coalitions for Reform* (University Park: Penn State University Press).

Krugman, P. (1990) 'The Move Toward Free Trade Zones', in P. King (ed.) *International Economics and International Economic Policy* (New York: McGraw-Hill).

Krugman, P. (1993) 'Regionalism and Multilateralism: Analytical Notes' in Jaime De Melo and Arvind Panagariya (eds.) *New Dimensions in Regional Integration* (Cambridge: Cambridge University Press and World Bank).

Lall, S. (1999) 'India's Manufactured Exports: Comparative Structure and Prospects', *World Development*, vol. 27, no. 10, pp. 1769–86.

Lavagna, Roberto (1998) 'Opening of a Medium-Size Economy', in Harry Costin and Hector Vanolli (eds.) *Economic Reform in Latin America* (Fort Worth, TX: Dryden Press).

Lipsey, Richard G. and Meller, Patricio (eds.) (1996) *NAFTA y MERCOSUR* (Santiago: CIEPLAN/Dolmen).

Lizano, E. (1982) 'Disparidades nacionales e integración económica', *Integración Latinoamericana*, no. 69, INTAL, June.

Lucángeli, Jorge (1995) 'Hacia una nueva relación en la construcción de un espacio competitivo común' (Brasilia: Embajada Argentina en Brasil).

Lucángeli, Jorge (1996) 'Reflexiones sobre la necesidad de profundizar el proceso de integración del MERCOSUR' (Buenos Aires: Centro de Economía Internacional).

Luján Olivera, Noemí (2000) 'La participación de las organizaciones empresariales en las negociaciones del MERCOSUR', paper presented at the 50th Congress of Americanists, Warsaw, July.

Lustig, Nora (1992, repr. 1998) *Mexico, the Remaking of an Economy* (Washington, DC: The Brookings Institution).

McKinnon, Ronald I. (1963) 'Optimum Currency Areas', *American Economic Review*, vol. 53, pp. 717–25.

McKinnon, Ronald I. (1982) 'Currency Substitution and Instability in the World Standard', *American Economic Review*, vol. 72, pp. 320–33.

Mace, Gordon and Thérien, Jean-Philippe (eds.) (1996) *Foreign Policy and Regionalism in the Americas* (Boulder: Lynne Rienner).

Mansfield, E. and Milner, H. (1997) 'The Political Economy of Regionalism: An Overview', in E. Mansfield and H. Milner (eds.) *The Political Economy of Regionalism* (New York: Columbia University Press).

Mansfield, E. and Milner, H. (1999) 'The New Wave of Regionalism', *International Organisation*, vol. 53, no. 3, pp. 602–08.

Manzetti, Luigi (1990) 'Argentine–Brazilian Economic Integration', *Latin American Research Review*, vol. 25, pp. 109–40.

Manzetti, Luigi (1994) 'The Political Economy of MERCOSUR', *Journal of Interamerican Studies and World Affairs*, (Winter 1993–94), vol. 35, no. 4. pp. 101–41.

Marchand, M. and Boas M. (1999) 'The Political Economy of New Regionalisms', *Third World Quarterly*, vol. 20, no 5, pp. 897–911.

Martínez, Leonardo and Schneider, Ben Ross (2000) 'Gatekeepers of Influence: The State, Mexican Agroindustry, and NAFTA', paper.

Mattli, W. (1999) *The Logic of Regional Integration. Europe and Beyond* (Cambridge: Cambridge University Press).

Mayer, F.W. (1998) *Interpreting NAFTA: The Science and Art of Political Analysis* (New York: Columbia University Press).

Mazey, S. and Richardson, J. (1996) 'The Logic of Organisation: Interest Groups', in J. Richardson (ed.) *European Union. Power and Policymaking* (London: Routledge).

Mellor, Patricio and Donoso, Rodrigo (1998) *La industria chilena y MERCOSUR* (Santiago: Dolmen).

Mercado de Valores. Data on investment in Mexico, April 1994.

Michaely, R. (1996) *Trade Preferential Agreements in Latin America: An Ex-ante Assessment*, Policy Research Working Paper 1583 (Washington, DC: The World Bank).

Mills, G., Burton, C., Lewis, Oneil, J. and Sorhaindo, C. (1990) *Report on a Comprehensive Review of the Programmes, Institutions and Organisations of the Caribbean* (Georgetown : CARICOM).

Milor, Vedat, Biddle, Jesse, Ortega, Juan and Stone, Andrew (1999) 'Consultative Mechanisms in Mexico' (Washington DC: World Bank).

Moravcsik, Andrew (1998) *The Choice for Europe. Social Purpose and State Power from Messina to Maastricht* (Ithaca, NY: Cornell University Press).

Muller, Geraldo (1995) 'The Kaleidoscope of Competitiveness', Cepal *Review*, vol. 56.

Mundell, R.A. (1961) 'A Theory of Optimal Currency Areas', *American Economic Review*, vol. 51, pp. 657–65.

Nagarajan, N. (1998) 'La evidencia sobre el desvío de comercio en el MERCOSUR', *Integración y Comercio*, no. 2 (Buenos Aires: INTAL/BID).

Neto, Raúl de Gouvea and Bannister, Geoffrey (1997) 'Trading Blocks: Incubators for Emerging Multinationals?' unpublished paper (Albuquerque: University of New Mexico).

Nicholls, S. (1996) 'Economic Integration in the Caribbean Community (CARICOM): from Federation to the Single Market', PhD thesis, Queen Mary and Westfield College, University of London.

Nicholls, S., Birchwood, A., Colthrust, P. and Boodoo, E. (2000) 'The State of and Prospects for the Deepening and Widening of Caribbean Integration', *World Economy*, vol. 23, issue 9, pp. 1161–94.

Nofal, B. and Wilkinson, J. (1999) 'La producción y el comercio de productos lácteos en el MERCOSUR', in *Impacto Sectorial de la Integración en el MERCOSUR* (INTAL, Buenos Aires).

Nordström, H. and Vaughan, S. (1999) 'Trade and Environment', World Trade Organisation Special Studies, no. 4, Geneva.

North, D. (1990) *Institutions, Institutional Change and Economic Performance* (New York: Cambridge University Press).

North, D. (1994) 'Economic Performance through Time' *American Economic Review*, vol. 84, no. 3, pp. 359–68.

OAS (1996) *Special and Differential Treatment in International Trade.* (Washington, DC).

OAS (1996a) Organisation of American Studies Compendium, http://www.sice.oas.org./cp061096/english/toc.stm.

Ocampo J. and Esguerra, P. (1994) 'The Andean Group and Latin American Integration', in Roberto Bouzas and Jaime Ros (eds.) *Economic Integration in the Western Hemisphere* (Notre Dame, IN: University of Notre Dame Press).

Ohmae, K. (1995) *The End of the Nation State: The Rise of Regional Economies* (New York: Free Press Paperbacks).

Oman, C. (1998) 'The Policy Challenges of Globalization and Regionalisation', in Jan Joost (ed.) *Regional Integration and Multilateral Cooperation in the Global Economy* (The Hague: FONDAD).

Orego Vicuña, F. (1977) 'Los presupuestos jurídicos de un proceso de integración económica efectivo', *Derecho de la Integración*, no. 24, INTAL, March.

Ortíz, G. (1983) 'Dollarization in Mexico: Causes and Consequences' *Journal of Money, Credit and Banking*, vol. 15, pp. 174–85.

Ostiguy, Pierre (1990) *Los capitanes de la industria: grandes empresarios, política y economía en la Argentina de los años 80* (Buenos Aires: Legasa).

Page, Sheila (1995) 'The Relationship between Regionalism and the Multilateral Trading System', paper prepared for UNCTAD.

Page, Sheila (1998) 'South-North Investment by Developing Countries in the EC: A Sign of the Emergence of New Investors', in Bert G. Hickman, and Lawrence Klein (eds.) *Link Proceedings 1991–1992* (Singapore: World Scientific Publishing).

Page, Sheila (2000) *Regionalism among Developing Countries* (Basingstoke: Macmillan).

Parra, Antonio R. (1993) 'A Comparison of the NAFTA Investment Chapter with Other International Investment Instruments', paper presented at training programme for Mexican NAFTA panellists, Mexico City, December.

Pastor, Manual and Wise, Carol (1994) 'The Origins and Sustainability of Mexico's Free Trade Policy', *International Organization*, vol. 48, no. 3, pp. 477–84.

Peña, Félix (1999) 'Contribución al análisis de la experiencia institucional del MERCOSUR', Informe para IRELA (mimeo).

Peña, Félix (1999a) 'Broadening and Deepening', in Riordan Roett (ed.) *MERCOSUR* (Boulder: Lynne Rienner).

Pfeifer, Alberto and de Oliveira, Amâncio Jorge (2000) 'Third Generation Private Sector: The Latin American Business Council (CEAL) and its Role in Promoting Regional Integration in Latin America', paper presented at the meetings of the International Political Science Association, August.

Phillips, M.M. (2000) 'US, Chile Put a Priority on Talks for a Labor-Friendly Trade Pact', *Wall Street Journal*, 30 November, p. 12.

Pierson, P. (2000) 'The Limits of Design: Explaining Institutional Origins and Change', *Governance*, vol. 13, no. 4, pp. 475–99.

Public Citizen Global Trade Watch (1998) *School of Real-Life Results, Report Card*, December, p. 2.

Puga, Cristina (1994) 'Las organizaciones empresariales en la negociación del Tratado de Libre Comercio', in Ricardo Tirado (ed.)

Los empresarios ante la globalización (Mexico: UNAM).

Ramírez-Rojas, C.L. (1985) 'Currency Substitution in Argentina, Mexico and Uruguay' *IMF Staff Papers*, no. 32, pp. 629–67.

Raymont, H. (2000) 'Mercosul Pode Se Ampliar Este Ano', *Jornal do Brasil*, 20 March, p. 7.

Rehren, Alfredo (1995) 'Empresarios, transición y consolidación democrática en Chile', *Revista de Ciencia Política*, vol. 27, nos. 1–2, pp. 5–61.

Reich S. (2000) 'The Four Faces of Institutionalism: Public Policy and and a Pluralistic Perspective', *Governance*, vol. 13, no. 4, pp. 501–22.

Robinson, S. and Thierfelder, K. (1999) 'Trade Liberalisation and Regional Integration. The Search for Large Numbers', Trade and Macroeconomics Division Discussion Paper Series. no. 34, International Food Policy Research Institute.

Rodas-Martini, P. (1996) 'The Hecksher-Ohlin Theorem and Intra-industry Trade: An Empirical Application to Newly Industrialising Countries', PhD thesis, Queen Mary and Westfield College, University of London.

Rodas-Martini, P. (1998) 'Intra-Industry Trade and Revealed Comparative Advantage in the Central American Common Market', *World Development*, vol. 26, no. 2, pp. 337–44.

Rodríguez, F. and Rodrik, D. (1999) 'Trade Policy and Economic Growth: A Skeptic's Guide to Cross-National Evidence', NBER Working Paper, no. W7081, April (mimeo).

Rodríguez-Mendoza, Miguel (1998) 'The Andean Group's Integration Strategy', in Harry Costin and Hector Vanolli (eds.) *Economic Reform in Latin America* (Fort Worth, TX: Dryden Press).

Rodrik, D. (1997) *Has Globalization Gone Too Far?* (Washington, DC: Institute for International Economics).

Rodrik, D. (1999) *Making Openness Work: The New Global Economy and the Developing Countries* (Washington, DC: The Overseas Development Council).

Roett, Riordan (ed.) (1999) *MERCOSUR* (Boulder: Lynne Rienner).

Roy, A. (1999) *The Third World in the Age of Globalisation: Requiem or New Agenda?* (New York: Zed Books).

Sandholtz, W. and Stone Sweet, A. (eds.) (1998) *European Integration and Supranational Governance* (Oxford: Oxford University Press).

Sanger, D.E. (2000) 'Rounding Out a Clear Clinton Legacy', *The New York Times*, 25 May , p. 1.

Schenk, C.R. (1994) *Britain and the Sterling Area: from Devaluation to Convertibility in the 1950s* (London: Routledge).

Schneider, Ben Ross (1991) 'Brazil under Collor: Anatomy of a Crisis', *World Policy Journal*, vol. 8, no. 2, (Spring), pp. 321–47.

Schneider, Ben Ross (1997) 'Big Business and the Politics of Economic

Reform: Confidence and Concertation in Brazil and Mexico', in Sylvia Maxfield and Ben Ross Schneider (eds.) *Business and the State in Developing Countries* (Ithaca, NY: Cornell University Press).

Schneider, Ben Ross (1997–98) 'Organized Business Politics in Democratic Brazil', *Journal of Interamerican Studies and World Affairs*, vol. 39, no. 4, (Winter).

Schneider, Ben Ross (2000) 'States and Collective Action: The Politics of Organizing Business in Latin America', draft paper.

Schneider, Ben Ross (forthcoming 2002) 'Why is Mexican Business so Organized?' *Latin American Research Review*, vol. 37, no. 1.

Schneider, Ben Ross and Maxfield, Sylvia (1997) 'Business, the State, and Economic Performance in Developing Countries', in Sylvia Maxfield and Ben Ross Schneider (eds.) *Business and the State in Developing Countries* (Ithaca, NY: Cornell University Press).

Schvarzer, Jorge (1991) *Empresarios del pasado: La Unión Industrial Argentina* (Buenos Aires: CISEA).

Serra, J. et al. (1996) *Reflections on Regionalism* (Washington, DC: Carnegie Endowment for Peace).

Shadlen, Kenneth (2000) 'Neoliberalism, Corporatism, and Small Business Political Activism in Contemporary Mexico', *Latin American Research Review*, vol. 35, no. 2, pp. 73–106.

Silva, Eduardo (1996) *The State and Capital in Chile: Business Elites, Technocrats, and Market Economics* (Boulder: Westview)

Silva, Patricio (1995) 'Empresarios, neoliberalismo y transición democrática en Chile', *Revista Mexicana de Sociología*, vol. 57, no. 4 (octubre–diciembre), pp. 3–25.

Silva, Veronica (2000) 'Política comercial y la relación público-privado en Chile durante los años noventa', in Oscar Muñoz (ed.) *El estado y el sector privado* (Santiago: Dolmen)

Snidal, D. (1985) 'Coordination Versus Prisoners' Dilemma: Implications for International Cooperation and Regimes', *American Political Science Review*, vol. 79, December.

Soares de Lima, Maria Regina (1996) 'Brazil's Response to the "New Regionalism"', in Gordon Mace and Jean-Philippe Thérien (eds.) *Foreign Policy and Regionalism in the Americas* (Boulder: Lynne Rienner).

Solingen, E. (1998) *Regional Orders at Century's Dawn* (Princeton: Princeton University Press), pp. 119–64.

Soloaga, I. and Winters, A.L. (1999) 'Regionalism in the Nineties: What Effect on Trade?' (mimeo).

SRA (1999) *Anales* (Buenos Aires).

Srinivasan T. and Bhagwati, J. (1999) 'Outward-Orientation and Development: Are Revisionists Right?' Columbia University (mimeo).

Stone Sweet, A. (1994) 'What is a Supranational Constitution?' *Review of Politics* 56, pp. 441–74.

Stone Sweet, A. (1999) 'Judicialization and the Construction of Goverance', *Comparative Politics*, vol. 32, no. 2, April.

Story, Dale (1982) 'Trade Politics in the Third World: A Case Study of the Mexican GATT Decision', *International Organization*, vol. 36, no. 4, (Autumn), pp. 767–94.

Sugden, R. (1989) 'Spontaneous Order', *Journal of Economic Perspectives*, vol. 3.

Summers L. (1991) 'Regionalism and the World Trading System', Symposium sponsored by the Federal Reserve Bank of Kansas City on Policy Implications of Trade and Currency Zones.

Suzman, M. (1999) 'American Labour Takes its Stand Against Freer Trade', *Financial Times*, 13 October.

Tavares de Araujo Jr., José and Tineo, Luis (1997) *The Harmonization of Competition Policies among MERCOSUR Countries* (Santiago: Organization of American States Trade Unit).

Tavlas, G.S. (1997) 'The International Use of the US Dollar: An Optimal Currency Area Perspective' *World Economy*, vol. 20, no. 6, pp. 709–47.

Thacker, Strom (1999) 'NAFTA Coalitions and the Political Viability of Neoliberalism in Mexico', *Journal of Interamerican Studies and World Affairs*, vol. 41, no. 2.

Thacker, Strom (2000) *Big Business, the State, and Free Trade: Constructing Coalitions in Mexico* (New York: Cambridge University Press).

Thomas L.R. (1985) 'Portfolio Theory and Currency Substitution' *Journal of Money, Credit and Banking*, vol. 17, pp. 347–57.

Thorp, R. (ed.) (1984) *Latin America in the 1930s: The Role of the Periphery in the World Crisis* (London: Macmillan).

Thorp, R. (1998) *Progress, Poverty and Exclusion: An Economic History of Latin America in the 20th Century* (Washington, DC: IDB).

Tigre, P.B., Laplane, M, Lugones, G. and Porta, F. (1999) 'Technological Change and Modernisation in the MERCOSUR Automotive Industry', *Integration and Trade*, vol. 3, nos. 7/8, January–August, Inter-American Development Bank, Integration and Regional Programs Department, INTAL.

Toral, P. (2001) 'Globalizing Capital: Who Invests in Latin America Now... and Why?' paper delivered at 2001 International Studies Association Annual Convention.

Townsend, E. (1988) *Nación de repúblicas: proyecto latinoamericano de Bolívar. Tópicos: ciencias políticas-estudio histórico y geográfico* (Caracas: Ministerio de Relaciones Exteriores).

Trigueros, I. (1994) 'The Mexican Financial System and NAFTA' pp. 43–57 in V. Bulmer-Thomas, N. Craske and M. Serrano (1994)

Mexico and the North American Free Trade Agreement: Who Will Benefit? (London: Macmillan).

Tybout, J. (2000) 'Manufacturing Firms in Developing Countries: How Well Do They Do, and Why?' *Journal of Economic Literature*, vol. XXXVIII, no. 1.

UNCTAD (1989 and 1995) Comtrade Trade Statistics; Argentina and Brazil (Geneva: UNCTAD).

UNCTAD (1994) *World Investment Directory, Latin America and the Caribbean* (Geneva: UNCTAD).

UNCTAD (1997) *World Investment Report 1996* (Geneva: UNCTAD).

UNCTAD (1999) *World Investment Report 1999* (Geneva: UNCTAD).

US International Trade Commission (1997) *The Impact of the North American Free Trade Agreement on the US Economy and Industries: A Three-Year Review*, USITC Publication 3045 (Washington, DC).

US Treasury (2000) *Treasury Bulletin*, June 2000 [http://www.fms.treas.gov/bulletin].

Van Beek, F., Rosales, J., Zermeño, M., Randall, R. and Shepherd, J. (2000) 'The Eastern Caribbean Currency Union: Institutions, Preferences and Policy Issues', IMF Occasional Paper 195, Washington, DC.

van der Ploeg, J. (1994) *Handbook of International Macroeconomics* (Oxford: Blackwell).

Vandenbeele, A. (2000) 'Currency Substitution in Theory and Practice: The Case of Mexico', M phil. Diss., Oxford University.

Veiga, Pedro da Motta (1999) 'Brazil in MERCOSUR', in Riordan Roett (ed.) *MERCOSUR* (Boulder: Lynne Rienner).

Vigevani, T. (1998) *MERCOSUR. Impactos para Trabalhadores e Sindicatos* (São Paulo: LTR Editora).

Viner, J. (1950) *The Customs Union Issue* (New York: Carnegie Endowment for International Peace).

Wallace, H. (2000) 'The Institutional Setting. Five Variations on a Theme', in H. Wallace and W. Wallace (2000) *Policy-Making in the European Union* (Oxford: Oxford University Press).

Walt, Stephen (1987) *The Origins of Alliances* (Ithaca, NY: Cornell University Press).

Waltz, K. (1993) 'The Emerging Structure of International Politics', *International Security*, vol. 18, no. 2, (Autumn).

Wei, S.J., and Frankel, J. (1995) 'Open Regionalism in a World of Continental Trade Blocs', *NBER Working Paper 5272*.

Wendt, Alexander (1992) 'Anarchy is what States Make of it', *International Organization*, vol. 46, pp. 391–425.

Wendt, Alexander (1999) *Social Theory of International Politics*

(Cambridge: CUP).

Weyland, Kurt (1996) *Democracy without Equity: Failures of Reform in Brazil* (Pittsburgh: University of Pittsburgh Press).

Weyland, Kurt (1997) '"Growth with Equity" in Chile's New Democracy?' *Latin American Research Review*, vol. 32, no. 1, pp. 37–68.

Weyland, Kurt (1998) 'The Fragmentation of Business in Brazil', in Francisco Durand and Eduardo Silva (eds.) *Organized Business, Economic Change, and Democracy in Latin America* (Miami: North-South Centre Press).

Wise, Carol (1999) 'Latin American Trade Strategy at Century's End', *Business and Politics*, vol. 1, no. 2, August, pp. 117–54.

World Bank (1997) *World Development Report: The State in a Changing World* (Washington, DC: World Bank).

World Bank (1999) 'Trade Blocs and Beyond: Political Dreams and Practical Decisions', Policy Research Report (draft).

World Bank (2000) *World Development Indicators* CD-Rom.

World Trade Organisation (WTO) (1995) *Regionalism and the World Trading System* (Geneva).

World Trade Organisation (WTO) (2000) *Caribbean Community and Common Market*, April.

Wrobel, Paul S. (1998) 'The European Union Direct Investment in Mercosul: Current State and Prospects for the Future', paper presented at Forum Euro-Latinoamericano, Lisbon, May.

Wyatt-Walter, A. (1995) 'Globalization, Corporate Identity and Technology Policy', *Journal of European Public Policy*, vol. 2, pp.12–24.

Yarbrough, B. and Yarbrough, R. (1997) 'Dispute Settlement in International Trade: Regionalism and Procedural Coordination', in E. Mansfield and H. Milner *The Political Economy of Regionalism* (New York: Columbia University Press).

Yeats, A. (1996) 'Does MERCOSUR's Trade Performance Justify Concerns about the Effects of Regional Trade Arrangements?' (World Bank, Washington, DC: International Trade Division).

Zuckerman, Leo (1990) 'Inflation Stabilisation in Mexico: The Economic Solidarity Pact', MSc thesis, Oxford University.

Lightning Source UK Ltd.
Milton Keynes UK
UKOW04f0057080118
315717UK00002B/23/P